Rethinking Visual Anthropology

Rethinking Visual Anthropology

Edited by
Marcus Banks and Howard Morphy

Yale University Press
New Haven and London

Copyright © 1997 by Yale University

First published in paperback 1999

Set in Garamond Simoncini by SX Composing DTP, Rayleigh, Essex
Printed and bound in Great Britain by Redwood Books, Wiltshire

Library of Congress Cataloging-in-Publication Data

Rethinking visual anthropology/edited by Marcus Banks and Howard Morphy.
  Includes bibliographical references and index.
  ISBN 0–300–06691–0 (hbk.)
  ISBN 0–300–07854–4 (pbk.)
  1. Visual anthropology. I. Banks, Marcus. II. Morphy, Howard.
  GN347.R45 1997   96–35202
  301—dc20   CIP

10 9 8 7 6 5 4 3 2

A catalogue record for this book is available from the British Library.

Contents

Illustration credits

All images are copyright and, unless otherwise acknowledged, belong to the author of the essay in which they appear.

1.1 Howard Morphy; **1.2** Françoise Dussart; **1.3** National Film and Television Archive, copyright Cambridge University Museum of Archaeology and Anthropology; **1.4** Pitt Rivers Museum, Oxford; **1.5** Pitt Rivers Museum, Oxford, photo: Baldwin Spencer; **1.6** New York Academy of Sciences/Catherine Bateson; **1.7** Napoleon Chagnon/Patsy Asch; **1.8** Marcus Banks; **1.9** Howard Morphy; **1.10** Oxford University Press; **1.11** Kim MacKenzie; **1.12** Hitachi Ltd, copyright © 1994, 1996, all rights reserved; **1.13** Lowe-Howard Spink; **1.14** Unichrome (Bath) Ltd; **3.1** Nu Color-Vue Productions Pty Ltd; **3.2**, **3.3**, **3.4** and **3.5a** and **b** Elizabeth Williams; **3.6a** and **b** Jorma Puranen; **3.7** Claudette Holmes; **4.1**, **4.2** and **4.3** Alan Ereira, with thanks to S.C. Bennett; **4.4a** and **b** Dennis O'Rourke; **4.5**, **4.6** and **4.7** Robert Boonzajer Flaes, with thanks to S.C. Bennett; **4.8**, **4.9**, **4.10**, **4.11** and **4.12** Christine Lloyd Fitt/Yoshi Tezuka, with thanks to S.C Bennett; **5.3** and **5.4** with thanks to Isolde Standish; **7.3** Stanley Haynes; **7.4** IRCAM, with thanks to Xavier Rodet and Pierre Cointe; **7.5** IRCAM; **7.6** IRCAM, with thanks to Xavier Rodet; **7.7** IRCAM, with thanks to Andrew Gerzso; **9.4** photo: A. Kurzweil; **12.3** Tully House, Co. Kildare; **13.1** private collection, Napier, New Zealand, photo: Mark Adams; **13.2** private collection, Wellington, New Zealand, photo: Geoffrey Short; **13.3** Ian Scott, photo: Geoffrey Short; **13.4** Auckland City Art Gallery; **13.5** and **13.6** John Pule; **13.7** Australian Museum, Sydney; **13.8** Gow Family Collection, Auckland; **14.1** photo: W.N. Downey; **14.2** Cambridge University Museum of Archaeology and Anthropology; **14.3** Department of Library Services, American Museum of Natural History, neg. no. 33002, photo: J. Kirsher; **14.4b** photo: J. Audema; **14.5a** State Library of South Australia; **14.5b** State Library of South Australia, photo: Richard; **14.7** National Film and Television Archive, copyright Cambridge University Museum of Archaeology and Anthropology; **14.8** Centro de Trabalho Indigenista, Brazil ('Video in the Villages' project), photo: Vincent Carelli; **14.10** National Film and Television Archive, with thanks to Françoise Foucault; **14.11** New York Academy of Sciences/Catherine Bateson.

List of contributors

Marcus Banks is Lecturer in Social Anthropology at the University of Oxford

Debbora Battaglia is Professor of Anthropology at Mount Holyoke College, Massachusetts

Georgina Born is Lecturer in the Department of Media and Communications at Goldsmiths College, University of London

Françoise Dussart is Assistant Professor of Anthropology at the University of Connecticut

Elizabeth Edwards is Archives Curator at the Pitt Rivers Museum, University of Oxford

Gillian Gillison is Professor of Anthropology at the University of Toronto

Anna Grimshaw is Lecturer in Visual Anthropology at the Granada Centre for Visual Anthropology, University of Manchester

Joy Hendry is Professor of Social Anthropology at Oxford Brookes University

Felicia Hughes-Freeland is Lecturer in Social Anthropology at the University of Wales Swansea

Peter Loizos is Reader in Anthropology at the London School of Economics and Political Science, University of London

David MacDougall is a filmmaker and Queen Elizabeth II Fellow and Convener of the Program in Visual Research at the Centre for Cross-Cultural Research at the Australian National University, Canberra

D.P. Martinez is Lecturer in Anthropology with reference to Japan at the School of Oriental and African Studies, University of London

Howard Morphy is Professor of Social Anthropology at University College London, University of London and Honorary Curator of the Pitt Rivers Museum, Oxford

Nicholas Thomas is Professor and Senior Research Fellow in Anthropology and Director of the Centre for Cross-Cultural Research at the Australian National University, Canberra

Acknowledgements

Several of the papers in this volume were first presented at an associate section meeting of the ASA IV Decennial Conference, 'The Uses of Knowledge: global and local relations', held in Oxford during July 1993. We are grateful to the conference convenor, Marilyn Strathern, and the local co-ordinator, Wendy James, for inviting us to organise a session on visual representation and visual knowledge.

Since then many people have helped us bring this volume into being. In particular, we would like to thank Ian Dunlop, Frances Morphy and all the contributors for reading our introduction and for their constructive comments. We also wish to thank Patsy Asch, Gillian Crowther, Françoise Dussart, Elizabeth Edwards, Malcolm Osman, Gwil Owen and Alison Petch for their practical help with the illustrations for the introduction, and Catherine Bateson, Hitachi Ltd, Kim MacKenzie, the New York Academy of Sciences, Oxford University Press, Unichrome Ltd, and Giles Walker of Lowe Howard Spink for providing a number of the illustrations.

More generally we are grateful to a number of friends and colleagues who provided advice, help and support along the way, particularly Frances Morphy and Barrie Thomas. Robert Baldock at Yale University Press was encouraging from the outset, and Candida Brazil coped cheerfully with an increasingly complicated manuscript. Finally, our home institutions at the time of preparing the book – the Institute of Social and Cultural Anthropology and the Pitt Rivers Museum – provided invaluable assistance and resources.

1

Introduction: rethinking visual anthropology

Howard Morphy and Marcus Banks

By most of the usual criteria, visual anthropology has become an established subdiscipline of sociocultural anthropology. It has its own section of the American Anthropological Association, it has two established journals, there are regular conference sessions and symposia on visual anthropology and an increasing number of students are being taught or are conducting research within the field. However, visual anthropology has suffered as much as any other branch of anthropology from what in other contexts is one of the great virtues of the discipline: the breadth of its agenda and the reluctance to leave any aspect of the study of humans outside its orbit. The interdisciplinary nature of anthropology means that there is a constant tension between centripetal and centrifugal forces. This is manifest in a continual budding-off process resulting in a plethora of subdisciplines which can always pose a threat to the coherence of the centre. Historically anthropology has been riven by debates as to whether what someone else does is really anthropology. Yet if the centre is an uncomfortable place to be, it is precisely this reference back to the centre, to some more general concept of the discipline, that gives coherence to anthropology: it is this that makes social anthropology different from sociology and biological anthropology, different from human genetics or human physiology. Visual anthropology is itself an example of such tendencies – it is a relatively recent offshoot from the main body and, like other sub-branches, it also has suffered at times from an identity crisis.

Visual anthropology is broad both in the substantive topics which it investigates and through the fact that it lies at the interface between anthropology and its audiences; it is as much concerned with the presentation and consumption of anthropological knowledge as with the production of that knowledge. At the most general level there is a duality of focus: on the one hand visual anthropology concerns the use of visual material in anthropological research (well exemplified by the essays in Hockings 1975) and on the other it is the study of visual systems and visible culture (well exemplified by the essays in Taylor 1994) – it both produces visual texts and consumes them.[1] These interests are not necessarily opposed. It could be argued that visual anthropology is concerned with the whole process of anthropology from the recording of data, through its analysis to the dissemination of the results of research. Anthropology as a discipline is itself a representational process, engaged in an activity of cultural translation or interpretation. It involves the representation of one culture or segment of society to an anthropological audience which itself includes people with different cultural backgrounds who operate on varying premises. An understanding of the nature of representational processes across cultures is thus integral to the overall objectives of anthropology. Visual anthropology has indeed been part of the discourse over objectivity and has been involved in anthropological metadiscourse which takes account of the positioned nature of actors and interpreters.

Some of the more recent developments in anthropological theory can be seen to reflect an increased sensitivity to the variety of human representational systems, with increased attention being directed towards the body, house forms, art and material culture, and more generally to the objectification of social and cultural process in cultural form and performance. At times such insights have been associated with particular theoretical positions: a rhetoric against the concept of culture, a critique of semiotics, and the use of linguistic analogies in anthropology. It has been possible at times to discern a kind of reverse Saussureanism, as if the discovery of the diversity and complexity of particular human representational processes and the role of agency invalidates the more general concept of the existence of structured communicative and representational processes in the reproduction of human sociocultural systems. Certainly anthropology itself is embedded in representational processes that may reflect political interests and which are an integral part of a particular system of knowledge, affecting what is known and how it is interpreted and understood by others. One agenda of visual anthropology is to analyse the properties of visual systems, to determine the properties of visual systems and the conditions of their interpretation and to relate the particular systems to the complexities of the social and political processes of which they are a part. A second agenda is to analyse the visual means of disseminating anthropological knowledge itself. As reflexivity becomes a central component of anthropological method then visual anthropology with its history of reflexivity, with its element of reportage and its potential to monitor action and process has become an increasingly central field (see Ruby 1980).

In this book we wish to push back the boundaries of inclusivity of visual anthropology, and in some cases our readers may feel that we have pushed the boundaries too far. However, boundaries are almost by definition somewhat problematic, especially if the objective is to reintegrate a subdiscipline within a wider whole. The visual is such an important

Figure 1.1 Frances Morphy showing photographs taken at Narakarani, Northern Territory, Australia in 1872, by the Adelaide photographer and steamship captain Henry Sweet, to a group of Ngalakan women. The photographs show the workers' camp near Roper Bar on the northern section of the Overland Telegraph and the wreck of the *Young Australian* in the Roper River. Edna Nyuluk who is showing the photographs to some of her grandchildren was born in the 1890s and could recall seeing the remains of the camp and the ship in her childhood. The photographs are being used as part of a discourse over history and provided evidence in the Roper Bar land claim.

component of human cultural, cognitive and perceptual processes, that it can be relevant to all areas of anthropology. Whether a particular paper belongs to the core of the subject must depend in part on subtle factors such as the way the author conceives of their work, the literature to which they refer, and the discourse of which they are a part. The nature of anthropological disciplines is that many contributions can be included within a variety of different subdisciplinary frames, indeed the logic of a holistic anthropology makes such a potential inevitable. Cross-fertilisation is achieved in part through multiple inclusion. Adam Kendon's work on Warlpiri sign language, for example, is equally relevant to linguistic anthropology and the anthropology of ritual and, across the disciplinary boundary, to sociolinguistics and ethology (see for example Kendon 1988). Yet, although every work on (Warlpiri) sign language is going to have some relevance to visual anthropology, not every work on sign language is going to be readily accepted as visual anthropology. Kendon's work is visual anthropology because he is an anthropologist who has used visual media extensively in his research, because he has a background in ethology and ekistics in which the visual dimension of non-verbal behaviour figures prominently, and because he has been part of the discourse of the subject as it has developed.

3

Figure 1.2 Judy Nampijinpa Granites tells a story at the Yuendumu school, Central Australia. She is demonstrating the sign for goanna.

In this book we engage on the boundaries with many other subdisciplines: with the anthropology of art (Banks, Thomas and Dussart); with the study of landscape (Hendry); with the anthropology of ritual (Battaglia, Gillison); with the anthropology of media and communication (Born, Martinez and Hughes-Freeland); with the history of anthropology (Grimshaw) and, across the disciplinary boundaries themselves, we engage with art practice and production (Born, Edwards, Loizos and MacDougall). But in stretching the boundaries our intention has been always redirected back towards the centre; towards the relevance of the papers to an understanding of the place of the visual in human culture (see MacDougall, chapter 14).

Film, photography, and the history of visual anthropology

Reappraising the work of Kroeber, Ira Jacknis notes: 'In many minds the term visual anthropology conjures up a specialised study involving film and video. Actually its scope is much broader, including the production and analysis of still photos, the study of art and material culture, and the investigation of gesture, facial expression and spatial aspects of behaviour and interaction. In fact many anthropologists have been doing visual anthropology without realizing it' (1994: 33).

The current volume has a dual agenda: to rethink the place of visual anthropology in the discipline as a whole, and to rethink the subdiscipline itself. In particular we aim to disentangle the relationship between visual anthropology, film and photography. Visual anthropology has had an uncomfortable (or perhaps too comfortable!) relationship with photography and ethnographic film. Recently ethnographic film has tended to dominate the subdiscipline, not so much internally as in the perceptions of other anthropologists about the focus of the project. Visual anthropology can be viewed as an easy subject to incorporate in anthropology teaching – one simply develops an ethnographic film programme. At an even more basic level, one simply screens an ethnographic film as a way of providing an easily digestible chunk of ethnography. The ethnographic film programme approach can all too easily lead students away from anthropology into film production for its own sake. The film screening approach encourages a view of visual anthropology as an optional extra, as an entertaining introduction to the real business in hand. At very worst, ethnographic films are babysitting devices for busy teachers.

We seek to deflect the centre of the discipline away from ethnographic film and photography, allowing them to be re-incorporated in a more positive way and in a way that is more cognizant of the broader anthropological project. There are very good reasons why film has come to occupy such a central position in recent years. The long neglect by anthropologists of visual recording media as a methodological tool was so extraordinary that the initial agenda of visual anthropology became the filling of this lacuna. The emphasis was on the way film could be used in anthropological research (see in particular the essays by Richard Sorenson and Alison Jablonko, Asen Balikci, Stephanie Krebs, Alan Lomax, and J.H. Prost in Hockings 1975). Film is also the area of visual anthropology which engages most readily with a broader audience: it seems to provide anthropology with a space to advertise its public strengths and liberal values (an assumption that has recently been challenged by Wilton Martinez 1990). The use of film as a research tool for use in anthropological fieldwork and later analysis has been greatly facilitated in recent years by the development of cheap, lightweight video technology. Finally, the sheer 'sexiness' of film and video, and their association with the glamorous worlds of cinema and television cannot be altogether discounted (Banks 1990).

If film is to be more than a method in anthropology, more than a medium of public relations, more than the stepping-stone to a career in the media, the focus must be on the contribution that film can make to anthropology as a theoretical discipline, as David MacDougall emphasises in his chapter. As soon as this perspective is adopted film takes its place with other visual phenomena. Visual anthropology as we define it becomes the anthropology of visual systems or, more broadly, visible cultural forms. In adopting this definition we are not changing the agenda of the subject but making explicit what has always been the case. The book includes precisely the range of topics that were covered in the 5 issues of Larry Gross's and Jay Ruby's pioneering journal *Studies in Visual Communication* (originally founded in 1974 by Sol Worth) which set the framework for the subdiscipline. We argue that by specifying the role of film in anthropology in theoretical as well as methodological terms its relevance to anthropology as a whole is likely to be enhanced, even if it occupies a smaller space within the subdiscipline.

Certainly film and photography form an important part of visual anthropology both in its contemporary practice and its historical origins. Visual anthropologists include a coalition of people who find film relevant to their work in anthropology (in contrast to the general neglect of film by other anthropologists) and who have in common an interest in film as a recording medium. Anthropologists of art, dance, material culture, ethology, and non-verbal communication have characteristically used film and photography as tools in their research. Historically the use of film in research is an important theme of visual anthropology. Historically, too, film (and increasingly video) have been used in allied projects to anthropology – in proxemics and choreometrics, for example (see essays by Prost and Lomax in Hockings 1995), and more recently as a development within conversation analysis (see Goodwin 1981; Heath 1986).[2]

In the late nineteenth century photography was for a while an essential part of general anthropological method. Anthropologists such as Haddon, and Spencer and Gillen seized on each new recording technique – photography, wax cylinder recording, the movie camera – as if it offered the key to future research by providing a means of bringing back data to the laboratory (see Anna Grimshaw, chapter 2). Reading the letters written from Gillen in Central Australia to his co-researcher Spencer in Melbourne, it is impossible not to feel their excitement at the success of new recording technologies and the prospect of better ones to come. It is clear that anthropology was embedded at the time in the paradigm of a descriptive science in which the essence was the recording of new facts and their interpretation by evolutionary theory.

Figure 1.3 Frame from A.C. Haddon's 1898 Torres Strait footage: 'Murray Island: Islanders Dancing in Dari Headdress'.

The conventional view has been that the photographic methods of early anthropologists were constrained by the theoretical paradigms that they adhered to and by the power relations of nineteenth-century colonialism. Certainly there is much evidence to support the view that in particular cases images were constructed to fit a particular scientific paradigm or interpretative agenda: the anatomical portraits inspired by Huxley's biological anthropology that simultaneously objectify the powerlessness and subject status of the people captured by the camera, and provide biometric information (Edwards 1988, 1990); the photographs by E.H. Man arranged to illustrate pages out of *Notes and Queries*, that fitted in with the culture trait concept (Edwards 1992); and the romantic images of Curtis, Kerry or Lindt that were designed to record the last images of a dying race killed through contact with a higher civilisation (Lyman 1982).

Figure 1.4 Studio photograph of Clarence River Aborigines by J.W. Lindt, early 1870s.

However, these ideologically constructed images represent only part of the story since from early on many pioneer ethnographers were motivated by the desire to document what they observed. Nineteenth-century anthropologists can be accused of having a naïvely realist perspective on film and photography, and of failing to see the constructed nature of their imagery and the cultural biases of their own ways of seeing. But that very naïvety may have had virtues in retrospect (even though in most cases, photography was viewed as an enhanced presentational method and not merely as a medium of transcription; see, for example, Chris Pinney on Seligman [Pinney 1990: 279–82]). While

7

assuming that photography was an objective recording practice they took photographs that fundamentally contradicted the theoretical propositions that they endorsed and revealed a world of far greater complexity than their evolutionary framework allowed. Their photographs purport to exemplify evolutionary perspectives, but simultaneously reveal a fascination with the cultural richness of living societies (an ambiguity of intent recognised in modern theoretical perspectives on photography such as those developed by Sontag 1978 and Barthes 1993).

For example, while Spencer and Gillen always adhered to a framework that positioned Australian Aborigines in evolutionary terms, their published data, in particular the data on Aboriginal ritual and social organisation, was from the beginning interpreted by others to show the complexity and richness of Aboriginal society (Morphy 1988). Spencer and Gillen were motivated to take photographs not by their evolutionary paradigm but by the documentary ethos of participant observation. Spencer and Gillen's excitement was over the potential of the camera to record what they had seen and felt otherwise inadequate to convey (see Cantrill and Cantrill 1982). They focused on recording ritual events and, to a lesser extent, daily life; they used the camera because they could see no other way of recording what occurred. Despite the constraints of an immobile camera and the need for long exposure times, and granted the artificiality of ceremonial performances organised in daylight hours so

Figure 1.5 Aranda boy, Alice Springs Station, Central Australia, 1901.

that the photographs could be taken at all, the surprising thing about their photographs is how natural and unconstructed they appear. They break with the earlier paradigms of biometrical photography and romantic reconstruction, and fit well within the later tradition represented by those such as Malinowski and Jenness.

Anna Grimshaw shows in chapter 2 that in British anthropology this lack of engagement between photography and film as recording techniques and theory construction continued through the transition from evolutionary theory to functionalism; Malinowski was an active photographer in the mould of Spencer whereas there is little record of Radcliffe-Brown's photographic achievements. However, in neither case did photography play a significant role in analysis. In Malinowski's case photographs were used extensively as illustrations, whereas in Radcliffe-Brown's they are entirely absent after *The Andaman Islanders.* The documentary excitement that is evident in the work of Haddon's 1898 Torres Strait expedition and in the work of Spencer and Gillen was absorbed, almost deadened, by the intellectual movement that succeeded them (see also Pinney 1992b).

In the post-evolutionist era photography and film, as tools for the anthropological method, suffered the same fate as did art and material culture as subjects of anthropological research. Tarred by the evolutionists' brush they were left out of the fieldwork revolution that became associated with structural-functionalism. With hindsight there appears no rational reason for the association of new recording technologies with the discredited theoretical perspective, especially if, as we have argued, photography was potentially a liberating influence which undermined the evolutionary paradigm. Flaherty's achievements in *Nanook of the North* (1922) provide an interesting contrast to the situation within 'professional' anthropology. It can be argued that Flaherty used functionalist and cultural relativist premises in his films, emphasising the ingenuity of Inuit technology, the ways in which their life was adapted to the environment and the uniqueness and relative autonomy of their cultural system.

Film, photography and sound recording should have been ideal complements to participant observation. Yet ironically in British anthropology the camera only occasionally provided company in the field and it was hardly incorporated into field methodology at all. As MacDougall argues (this volume), this was reflected in the decline in the use of photography even as illustrative material in ethnographic monographs. The shift of focus to social organisation, the importance of the genealogical method, the emphasis on oral tradition, may all have been contributory factors in the neglect of new recording technology, since researchers in these areas may have found the notebook an adequate tool. The neglect of art, material culture, and ritual form, all areas where the camera comes into its own (and all inherently visual forms of interest to evolutionary anthropologists), may have been complementary factors. Certainly photography became associated with earlier phases of anthropology and with the study of art and material culture.

Photography continued to find a place in ethnographic museums and continued to be part of the methodology of museum anthropology, but ironically this was precisely the area of anthropology that missed out on the fieldwork revolution. Photography, a medium that is designed to capture the actuality of an event and to establish the presence of the anthropologist, became associated with anthropology at a distance.[3]

In American anthropology similar developments occurred, though anthropology maintained its breadth much more than it did in Britain. Indeed in America, 'anthropology at a distance' can be seen in the case of Ruth Benedict and others to have involved a highly innovative use of photographs as cultural information. It was in America that visual anthropology began to take shape as a separate subdiscipline around the time of the Second World War. Margaret Mead, a student of Benedict's, in her own work and in particular in her collaboration in Bali with Gregory Bateson (1936–37), made a strong case for the use of technologies of recording in the field. Mead and Bateson both had strong roots in the tradition of Western science and their use of film and photography can be seen as following directly on from the observational science model of anthropology espoused by those such as Spencer, Haddon and to an extent Boas (Jacknis 1989). For Mead the value of film lay in part in the fact that it was infinitely re-analysable by others. Despite its selectivity and biases it could not but reveal more than it concealed of the events that it recorded: 'Photographs taken by one observer can be subjected to continual re-analysis by others' (cited in Scherer 1990: 134). And, we might add with reference to Hughes-Freeland's paper, to conflicting analysis and re-analysis.

In *Balinese Character* (1942) Bateson and Mead combined the methodological with the theoretical by arguing that it was only through photography that certain aspects of the reality of Balinese culture could be revealed and communicated cross-culturally (see Wood 1989). Bateson and Mead (1942: xii) wrote that 'we are attempting a new method of stating the intangible relationship among different types of culturally standardised behaviour by placing side by side mutually relevant photographs. Pieces of behaviour spatially and contextually separated may all be relevant to a single discussion, the same emotional thread may run through them.'

It is interesting to see the foreshadowing of more recent concepts such as Bourdieu's 'habitus' with its emphasis on embodiment, affect, and on the role of dispositions and habitual behaviour in the reproduction of social systems. The assumption behind Bateson and Mead's study was that the Balinese represented a way of being that was reflected in the visible world that they created through their behaviour in a lived environment, and that aspects of that world could be sensed through

10

Figure 1.6 Three images to illustrate 'the body as a tube' from *Balinese Character* (Plate 31, Figures 6–8). In this sequence the child's play of running a ball inside his jumper is said by Bateson and Mead to be 'perfectly consonant with the Balinese cultural emphases which classify eating with defecation, and defecation with birth'.

photography in a way that it was impossible to convey through the written word alone (MacDougall's theoretical writings can be seen in many respects as attempts to take that agenda forward [e.g. MacDougall 1975 and 1992]). There was also a strong element of reflexivity built into the method that they developed, since they contextualised their more subjective statements by associating them in their documentation with photographs and other recordings which helped locate their thoughts in time and place. In effect they provided the evidence for the deconstruction of their representations of Balinese society. Unfortunately, perhaps because they generated so much data, they never completed the analyses that would have convincingly demonstrated the theoretical power of the method they were advocating (see also Hagaman 1995). Perhaps as MacDougall argues (this volume) there was a fundamental difference in Mead's and Bateson's conceptions of what photography could contribute to anthropology: Bateson used the mediums of photography and film as a means of exploration, through which process an understanding of Balinese culture might develop, and Mead used them in a more positivistic sense as a means of recording data for subsequent analysis.[4]

In the short term what should have been an inspiring step in the use of visual methods in anthropology instead confirmed their more conservative colleagues in their negative attitudes to the use of photography in research. Mead's long-term influence on American visual anthropology, however, should not be underestimated and can be seen in the development of ethnographic film as an exploratory as well as a documentary medium, in the works of practitioners such as Timothy Asch (especially in his pioneering and innovative Yanomami films and also in his later collaborative work in Bali – see Connor et al. 1986).

11

Moheseiwa's younger brother again comes to his aid. This time carrying a machete. He arrives just as Kebowa manages to rest the ax from Moheseiwa.

[At a later stage of the fight] Kebowa sees that his back is turned and rushes him from behind. He strikes a powerful overhead blow with his ax the dud side forward, hitting Moheseiwa's younger brother severely in the middle of the back.

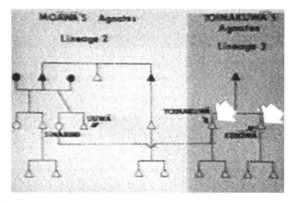

When Yoinakuwa and his younger brother [Kebowa] escalated the conflict to an ax fight, the situation worsened. Members of lineage number 2 were now being forced to divide their loyalties.

Figure 1.7 Tim Asch always stressed the importance of the anthropological relevance of a still or moving image over other aspects, such as image quality or aesthetic composition. While the latter are desirable they should not be overriding factors in determining the selection of an image. Asch's 1975 film *The Ax Fight*, made in collaboration with the anthropologist Napoleon Chagnon, contains a number of innovations which facilitate interpretation by the viewer and add to the information contained in the film. The sequence of the fight is shown three times with additional information being added through subtitles, kinship diagrams, commentary and the use of arrows to highlight key actors and events. The stills selected above show how the arrows are used and they are captioned with the text of the accompanying commentary. As well as the final commentary the film also contains interpretations made at the time by the anthropologist, which subsequently had to be revised. This adds a reflexive dimension to the film which reveals filmmaking in anthropology to be part of an interpretative process in which understanding of an event develops over time.

Bateson and Mead failed to move from using photography as a means of recording a world that was the product of a particular way of being and which involved a distinctive way of seeing, feeling and relating to the world, to an analysis that convincingly demonstrated how that world was seen, felt and understood by the Balinese. They failed to achieve the move from visual anthropology as a mode of representation by the anthropologist to visual anthropology as a study of people's own visual worlds, including the role of representations within cultural process. Their insight was that the latter would be better achieved by using a full range of representational systems – sound, film, objects themselves, as well as writing – but they failed to carry the project through. In chapter 6 Hughes-Freeland demonstrates how, in a sense, the project has been taken up in contemporary Bali by the Indonesian state. As she convincingly shows, even on this one small island regional identities and experience can easily subvert any attempt to represent 'the Balinese'.

Visual anthropology: method or theory?

The separation of method from theory is never straightforward and this is particularly so in a discipline that at times defines itself in terms of its methods: fieldwork and participant observation. A methodological tool cannot in practice be theoretically neutral since it should always be chosen with reference to the objectives of the research and in the light of the knowledge of the biases and assumptions which underlie it and its history. Part of the postmodern critique of anthropology has been that its methodology has been based on the double illusion of the neutral observer and the observable social phenomenon. In order to counter such criticism, method in anthropology has to be recognised as inherently theoretical in its implications and it is today a requirement to make explicit these theoretical underpinnings. Nonetheless, it is possible and perhaps even essential to make a pragmatic distinction between theory and method that separates out the aims of the research and the interpretative framework or paradigm used in the analysis of data, from the ways in which the data are obtained.

In anthropology the separation of data collection from analysis and interpretation has a particular significance, since traditionally there has been a bias towards collection of data as a separate exercise in advance of the development of a particular problematic, even though overarching theoretical paradigms have exerted their influence. The idea of ethnography originally presupposed the existence of a relatively unknown reality that was to be recorded and subsequently analysed, the problematic emerging through the research process (the Colliers' 1986 visual methodological work is a good example of this approach). 'You *13* won't know what you will find until you get there' is still an informal dictum of field research, and one that infuriates equally the advocates of methodological formalism and the radical critics of the ethnographic method. In reality what is discovered reflects what is sought and the accumulation of anthropological knowledge has led to the development of more structured and problem-oriented fieldwork projects. But the holism of anthropology still requires of its practitioners a broad-brush approach, and neutrality in data collection, if acknowledged to be impossible in absolute terms, is nonetheless a desirable reference point.

In methodological terms visual anthropology is concerned with the recording of visual or visible phenomena, with obtaining visual data. The dangers of defining the subject in this way is that on the one hand it is liable to become too broad and lack coherence, and on the other hand it is liable to deflect attention from other properties and qualities of the media involved – sound, for example, in the case of film. As method, visual anthropology is in the first instance a flag, a reminder that much that is observable, much that can be learned about a culture can be recorded most effectively and comprehensively through film, photography or by drawing. This view is linked to the inductive comprehensive tendency in anthropology. The justification is not that the total recording of everything is possible, but rather that in neglecting visual data we may be reflecting a Western bias (the elevation of the intellectual over the experiential or phenomenological)[5] or neglecting the importance of visual phenomena across cultures. Increasingly film and photography are not simply means of recording data by and for the anthropologist, but data in themselves – in the form of television, cinema, tourist promotional literature and art (see in particular the chapters by Hughes-Freeland, Martinez, Loizos and Edwards) – and, of increasing prominence in recent years, in the form of so-called 'indigenous media' (see Ginsburg 1991; Michaels 1986, 1991; Turner 1992). The position defended here does not require that visual methods be used in all contexts but that they should be used where appropriate, with the rider that appropriateness will not always be obvious in advance.

The two main bodies of data in visual anthropology – visual recordings and material products of culture – have different ontological statuses. By the use of film, photography, drawing and so on, the anthropologist is able to make a permanent record of events and objects observed, to retain them for subsequent analysis, or use them in the further elicitation of information. Thus one major advantage of visual recording methods is that they enable the ethnographer to scan and record for later inspection and re-analysis. Visual recording methods have properties such that they are able to record more information than memory alone, or notebook and pencil, and that certain of them are indexically related to the reality they encode.[6] The indexical properties of photography, film and video ally them to sound recording, which often occurs simultaneously with mechanical visual recording, and can only be separated from visual anthropology on an arbitrary basis. Indeed Mead and Bateson's Balinese project was really an exercise in material data gathering. As well as using photography and film, they made sound recordings, collected objects, and commissioned a large set of indigenous paintings. We do not mean to imply that visual or sound recordings are in any sense 'transparent'. The anthropologist must still perform an interpretative task when faced with such data, even if recorded by other anthropologists, and especially so when the recordings were made by anthropologists distant in time or space from the observing anthropologist, as is the case with Mead and Bateson's material today.

However, sound and vision may and perhaps should still be kept separate on theoretical grounds, as Gillian Gillison makes clear in chapter 8. Similarly, Georgina Born's analysis of computer music shows the complex nature of the interrelationship between different representational systems and the role that pragmatic factors have in production and performance. She shows the practical difficulties of integrating visual, technological and sound systems in the production of computer music at IRCAM, the computer music centre in Paris. To an extent Born is concerned with the genesis of new media, computer media, which share some of the characteristics of visual systems (particularly in relation to art and aesthetics) and oral/linguistic systems but which are conceptualised as neither. At IRCAM some understanding of computer programming instructions is a prerequisite for the production and composition of musical sound. She analyses the problematic status of the visual codes and texts that are produced to communicate the computer programs, and shows how they necessitate recourse to oral communication. Clearly the oral tradition requires the continual presence of the translator yet this in some respects contradicts the ideology of the use of computer technology which is based on computers being the most advanced form of communication system, one that obviates human intervention and one apparently free of human social and cultural bias. Computer music in effect becomes dependent on an oral tradition for its users, in a way analogous to the oral exegesis on which anthropologists of art have often relied in their attempts to 'decode' paintings and other images in the field.

The materiality of the visual

Although in some cases the anthropologists may be recording visible phenomena of long duration – a rock engraving, a village site, a house form, or a wooden sculpture – on other occasions they are making a permanent record of temporary phenomena – a pristine sand sculpture or body painting, a sequence of dance movement or even a fleeting glance. *15*

Figure 1.8 Worshippers at a Jain temple in Dhrangadhra, Gujarat, India in 1983. As James Laidlaw (personal communication) notes, the Jains consider the worshippers to be as much a part of the adornment and decoration of a temple as the more permanent paintings, carvings and other ritual objects.

In such cases, something that is quite different from what is experienced in the 'real' world may be created by freezing an image for contemplation.

In the case of material culture, the forms under analysis are the direct product of members of the culture, and are visible forms transported from one context to another. In the new context they are transformed because the conditions in which they are viewed are different. They are separated from the world of action in which they were meaningful and placed in a world in which they will be interrogated and interpreted from a multiplicity of different perspectives, as Françoise Dussart demonstrates in her chapter.

There are both methodological and theoretical reasons why it can be argued that these two types of data – visual recordings and material culture – have much in common. The methodological justification is that both are permanent records that are produced in their different ways by the behaviour of members of the respective cultures. Material culture is the direct product of intentional action, and film and sound recording is indexically linked to that which it records. Interestingly Ucko justifies the study of material culture objects in exactly the same terms that Mead justifies the use of visual recording methods: 'the essential quality of material culture objects is that reanalysis is possible at all times' (1970: 29).[7] In both cases the data allow more to be seen or analysed than was possible at the time 'of collection', and in both cases the data can be used in later dialogue with the producers. Nor is this a process confined to the anthropologist alone; Chris Pinney has very ably demonstrated the importance of the materiality of Indian visual forms, where the transformations of form and the crossing of media boundaries have local significance and interpretation (Pinney 1992a).

The theoretical justification for including material products of culture and recordings of visible culture within the same discourse is arguably the main subject of this book. Visual anthropology is the exploration of the visual in the process of cultural and social reproduction. On the one hand this involves the dematerialisation of artefacts by recasting them as concepts embedded in systems of knowledge and action. It also involves the reverse: the fixing, through film and photography, of the ongoing flow of everyday action in a more concrete form. Thus visual anthropology explores whether in some senses it is possible to capture in such a way the position of the informed actor socialised into observable behaviour patterns, and sharing the presuppositions of the participants. Morphy has argued (1994b) that action in the context of unfamiliar cultures can take on an extemporary quality since to the observer everything is new and it is all too easy to underestimate the extent to which behaviour is structured, routinised, and integrated in conceptual and cognitive processes. Ritual presents a special case where behaviour is consciously

Figure 1.9 The yellow ochre dance, Trial Bay, 1976. According to Australian Aboriginal ideology dance forms are passed on from the ancestral past where they were performed for the first time by Dreamtime beings to commemorate their creative actions. The dances are restored in a contemporary context to perform a particular ritual event, in this case opening the shade where a child's body lies for burial (Dunlop 1979).

17

stored in a repeatable form, abstracted as a particular kind of performance from the more individualistically directed flow of everyday life.
But in the case of both ritual and everyday behaviour, filmic and photographic records may give access to a dimension of reality that is otherwise unrecoverable.

Coming from a more phenomenological perspective Banks (1994b)
has pointed out the reverse danger: the structuring of ethnographic film,
especially those films produced for television, can impose a false fixity
and narrative coherence on the fluidity of quotidian social interaction.

As well as having the potential to reveal and evoke the experience of
the habitual or routinised nature of much social behaviour from an emic
perspective, film can also in other contexts shift the emphasis away from
the concrete nature of material forms towards properties that emerge in
context, or to processual aspects of their production that may be more
salient than the final form that is produced. The Western concept of art
objects and the Western tendency to appropriate ritual products as permanently preserved objects may give them a false concreteness (see also
Witherspoon on Navaho sand paintings [1977]). Film, by recording the
production of the object or the ritual in which the object appears, may
be recording the object closer to the ways in which it is conceived by the
actors. It also may facilitate the analysis of the variable relations between
object and process, between materiality and sociality.

The oppositions that we have highlighted between object and process,
and between something being visibly present or visibly absent, may in
themselves be profoundly misleading as in their different ways both

PLATE IV

Figure 1.10 'Movement in
wedding dance'; plate IV from
Evans-Pritchard's *Nuer
Religion*. As Brenda Farnell
points out: '[t]his photograph
raises an important
anthropological question:
where is the movement?'
(emphasis in original) (1994:
929)

Movement in wedding dance

Born's and Battaglia's chapters suggest. To Born the written inscriptions that are thought to be integral to computer software programs give a false indication of the nature of the process of which they are a part. She generalises her argument to refer to the tendency of visual inscriptions in Western scientific practice to be a sign of the autonomy or even reality of the thing to which they refer: 'inscriptions – visual/textual translations and extensions of scientific practice – play an essential role in separating the scientific from the social so as to establish the autonomy of the scientific object' (p. 142). However, Born argues that it is the very materiality of the graphic representations of software that resists such a separation, and hence the separation of object from process. Battaglia's chapter is concerned in some respects with the false concreteness of what is present and visible, and with the fact that the absence of something (its invisibility) can be as crucial to processes of interpretation as the presence of something. To Battaglia 'ambiguation' occurs at the borders conjoining the domains of the stated and the unstated. The absence of an object or representation conventionally associated with a particular context or performance, in Battaglia's example the absence of a polished stone axe, problematises the event: 'the detachability and deliberate slippage of authority from the face of social action gives expression to the authority's hidden life of negotiation' (p. 211).

Battaglia's invisible foregrounding is the reciprocal of Born's inscription. It is productive to relate Born's discussion of graphic representation or inscription and the role that it has in creating an illusion of autonomy and certainty in Western science, with the complementary role that Battaglia gives to invisible foregrounding (and to absence of inscriptions) in Trobriand practice. Invisible foregrounding creates the space for negotiation, which Born argues is the reality of scientific practice. In Western science the space for negotiation is masked by a particular kind of presence, the visible portable inscriptions; in the Trobriand case it is revealed by a particular kind of absence. Born notes that Michael Fischer, in his recent book on computing in anthropology (1994), concludes by being unable to recommend or name specific software packages and invites readers instead to negotiate directly or indirectly with him. This she interprets as reflecting the reality of the social and negotiated nature of computing in practice, necessitated both by the absence of effective graphic representations, and by the instability and rapid evolution of the technologies.[8]

Born and Battaglia are using concepts which can be applied cross-culturally to show the different significance of inscription and invisible foregrounding in different cultural and historical contexts. Kim McKenzie's film *Waiting for Harry* (1980) provides a multiply reflexive example of the significance of absence both from the perspective of the Aboriginal participants in the ritual, and the filmmaker's construction of the event. The film is of an Aboriginal mortuary ritual in Central Arnhem Land in which the bones of deceased relatives are being 'reburied in a hollow log coffin'. The film gives a prominent role to the anthropologist Les Hiatt who has worked with the Gidjingali over many years and who provides a partial explanation for the presence of the cameras. Harry is one of the senior right-holders in the bones and in the ritual, although the prime mover behind the ritual is a close friend and long-time collaborator of Hiatt. The two main themes of the film, apart from the ritual, are the absence of Harry and the relationship of the anthropologist to the community. Harry's absence from the preparation of the mortuary ritual reflects the negotiated nature of the ritual and the lack of consensus. The fact that the filmmaker takes this up as a theme can partly be explained in relation to conventions of European drama. Harry's absence creates a sense of suspense, a space for uncertainty. However, Harry's absence also problematises the place of the anthropologist in the proceedings, partly because it emphasises Hiatt's relationship with those who are present and partly because it makes him an agent as well as an observer of the proceedings. Hiatt is called upon as a broker and is asked to negotiate with Harry and perhaps even to bring him to the ceremony. It is possible that Hiatt the anthropologist will bring about the presence of Harry, yet the viewer is able to think that below the surface it is precisely the presence of Hiatt that has been responsible for Harry's absence in the first place – Hiatt's presence has somehow problematised the ritual by becoming a factor in the performance. Aboriginal ritual is shown to be more negotiable than the audience might have thought, and simulta-

Figure 1.11 Men sitting in the shade at Kopanga on the Blyth River in Central Arnhem Land, 1975, while they wait for Harry.

neously the audience is made aware of the possible effect of the anthropologist. The foregrounding of Harry through his invisibility creates precisely 'that destabilising of relations in space and time' that Battaglia suggests occurs in her Trobriand Island example. Visual anthropology must be concerned with problematising the visual in relation to cultural process in addition to understanding the nature of visual representations and the way in which seeing and what is seen are part of people's conceptual worlds.

This perspective brings us back to Bateson and Mead and to the idea that visual worlds reflect different ways of seeing. Theory in visual anthropology revolves around the issues of visual culture, the structuring of the visible world and how visual phenomena are incorporated within cultural process and influence the trajectory of socio-cultural systems. It is in this respect that visual anthropology must include equally the anthropology of art, of material culture, and of ritual form. Visual understanding, what we see and how we interpret it, is an important part of the way we exist as humans in the world and the ultimate justification for the discipline of visual anthropology must lie in this direction: it is the study of the properties of visual systems; of how things are seen and how what is seen is understood.

Visual systems and ways of seeing

We use the term 'visual systems' to convey a very general concept: the processes that result in humans producing visible objects, reflexively constructing their visual environment and communicating by visual means. There are visual dimensions to most human actions, from speech to the manufacture of artefacts. We incorporate our capacity to see into virtually every aspect of our lives. Thus the focus of visual anthropology includes both the properties of the anthropologist's own representational systems (for example, the way meaning is constructed in film and how it is interpreted by an audience: see Morphy 1994b and Banks 1996 for our own views on this) and the properties of those visual systems studied by anthropologists in the field (see Morphy 1991 and Banks chapter 11 in this volume for our views on this, and Ginsburg 1994 and O'Hanlon 1993 for relevant discussion on both of these issues). The 'field' must include the visual cultures of the West and not assume that the visual practice of anthropologists is coincident with any one of them. Indeed, increasingly studies must take into account the interrelationship between anthropological and indigenous practice without collapsing the one into the other. In addition, some visual anthropologists have diverted their energies into a variety of collaborative projects (Turner's work [1992] with the Kayapo being the most cited example – see also Banks 1995), and into examining the reception of visual mass media, notably television (see, for example, Abu-Lughod 1995, Das 1995).

Most of the contributors to this volume hold to a position that vision is to some extent socially and/or culturally constructed, and that there is a relationship between how people learn to use visual systems and how the world is seen by them. In the contemporary West, visual systems in art, communication, and scientific research affect the way individuals are socialised into the world in innumerable ways. From the Renaissance onwards, artists developed techniques of illusion such as perspective, and subsequently, with the onset of modernism, fragmented images into their component parts and created an aesthetic of formal effects. In doing so they have, at different times, organised and reorganised the way in which Europeans have been conditioned to the world through art. In chapter 2 Grimshaw contrasts the visual world associated with the Renaissance view with the vision that developed in association with Cubism. She sees a relationship between them and two different anthropological conceptualisations of the world, two 'ways of seeing in anthropology': respectively the integrated distancing functionalism of Malinowski and the more reflexive and deconstructive perspective of Rivers.

During the twentieth century changing technology has altered and expanded the possibilities for seeing the world and has created familiar images of previously invisible objects. The technology of film and photography, as well as its conceptualisation, has become very different from what it was in the days of the pioneers of visual anthropology, Spencer and Haddon or even Mead and Bateson. The previously hidden worlds of sub-atomic particles and galactic clusters have been made visible through photography and computer rendering. The consequences of this have been multiple. Martinez argues in chapter 5 that on the one hand modern technology, through its association with the paradigm of observational science, may have reinforced the authority of visual representation in Western systems of knowledge; Hughes-Freeland talks of the respect for authoritative others that may mute or conceal criticism. On the other hand that new technology, by opening up the possibilities for going inside (in Grimshaw's terms), by creating unusual juxtapositions and framings and by revealing the potentiality of photography and electronic media to construct surprising images, has stimulated a reflexive and interrogative perspective in photography that has, as Edwards shows in chapter 3, challenged the dominant paradigm of realism and questioned the very authority of visual imagery as evidence.

It has been an elementary lesson of the anthropology of aesthetics that the bases of representational systems vary cross-culturally both in terms of what is selected out for representation and how those features are represented or encoded (Coote 1992; Morphy 1994a). One of the objectives of visual anthropology must be to reveal these different 'ways of seeing'

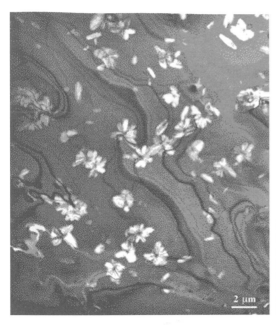

Figure 1.12 'Cherry Blossoms in a Clear Stream.' An electron-micrograph of a partially crystallised form of silicon accumulated on amorphous silicon dioxide (SiO_2) on a silicon monocrystal and published on the World Wide Web by Hitachi Ltd.

within and between societies and to show how they influence action in the world and people's conceptualisations of the world. Visual representational systems are part of more general cultural processes. They can affect the unseen and the unseeable through the creation of particular concepts of spiritual existence, as Banks shows for the Jains in chapter 11; equally they can create emotional states and feelings of identity and separation, as Gillison shows for Gimi initiation in chapter 8.

Banks focuses on Jain representations of the body and the embodiment of religious goals, ideals and actions. He shows how the Jain concept of the soul as an empty form, a shape without substance, is reflected in Jain art by empty shapes outlining the body, by the unstated, subdued and non-individualistic character of Jain sculpture, and by the abstemious and purgative character of fasting and meditation. He shows clearly the potential cross-over between seeing and feeling – how the visible world is constructed to create feelings of fullness and emptiness, adhesion and freedom, colour and blandness that make up the experience of the Jain concept of the soul. Soul and body are to be understood as interdependent concepts, and the complex relationship between them, in which the soul must ultimately extricate itself from the body's presence, is manifest in the Jains' experience of their visual system. As such, visual systems are not simply 'out there', not merely cultural afterthoughts that redundantly repeat messages the diligent anthropologist can retrieve elsewhere. As most of the contributors to the volume demonstrate, visual systems are implicated in most if not all areas of human activity through active engagement, not passive contemplation.   *23*

In South Asian Hinduism and Jainism, the act of beholding a revered object, image or person (*darshan*), is an act of religious force and value.

As this example shows, the very value of vision itself can vary cross-culturally. Martinez shows how visual representations of knowledge have less authority to the Japanese television audience than the words of an acknowledged expert or person (usually a man) of knowledge. She shows how this produces kinds of documentary film in Japan that are very different from those produced in the West. She argues that in contemporary Western documentaries the voice of authority is subordinated to the visual image or at least allowed a minor authenticating role, for the truth is revealed by the camera. What is seen is believed, and to be believed it almost has to be seen. Indeed this statement could be generalised to characterise the whole way in which the culture of television has developed in the West. The emotions felt at death need to be confirmed by the tears in the eyes of the mourner, as if nothing is real unless it is captured on film. Though against this it can be argued that the style of television documentary, with its overemphasis on a scripted story, can be seen as a way of subordinating the visual to oral text as the primary means of communication. Hughes-Freeland also argues for the cultural specificity of documentary film styles. In her analysis of the practice of viewing television in Bali she concludes that 'the Balinese bring specific ideas of order and meaning to narrative sequences' (p. 122) which to an outsider may appear incoherent or internally contradictory.

Gillison is concerned to explore the question of what it means for something to be seen. Her chapter is really about the phenomenology of seeing among the Gimi – not so much what is seen but how seeing something is felt. She draws an analogy between the experience of bonding between the mother and child, and the bond created between the initiate and the flute revealed in the context of male initiation. The male child is encompassed in the mother's gaze and Gillison shows how in the cultural logic of the Gimi that gaze is valued as something that both unites the child with the mother and separates him from the father. The mother is denied sight of the sacred flutes, though she hears their sound, just as she is separated from her son. The denial of looking evokes the pain of separation from the child. Gillison draws attention to a phenomenon that has not been sufficiently explored across cultures: the nature of shared experience of 'being there' which among the Gimi is structured to reproduce particular kinds of relationships between men and women, who both share and are denied part of the other.

Visual anthropology and global discourse

The transportability of visual images, the very reason why Mead and Bateson saw photography as such an important methodological tool for anthropology, is precisely the property that makes them accessible to a wider Western audience, as Elizabeth Edwards shows in her chapter. Visual images provide the most readily accessible representations of other cultures. Moreover, at first sight they require little interpretation – they present a direct record of 'what is there'. As Edwards argues, however, photographs operate at such a general level, partly because they contain at the same time so much and so little information, that given the appropriate caption they can be used to mean any number of different things. It is always possible for the photographs to be appropriated and interpreted according to Western presuppositions, with no reference to the significance of their content in their indigenous context. In this way images of the Other become in reality images of the West: as Martinez shows, the images of Japan on British television reflect and support British images of Japanese society which are related to the construction of Britain's own image by politicians and the media (a point also made by Dussart with respect to the Warlpiri). The process is similar to the one to which the material culture of non-Western societies is subjected. When material culture is removed from its context of production it is often recreated anew as a Western art object, with a meaning and a value that bears little relation to its use in an indigenous cultural context, beyond the fact of the very existence of that context granting the value of authenticity. The object becomes associated with an aesthetic, a way of seeing, that belongs to a quite different cultural tradition (Vogel 1988; Price 1989).

The relationship between anthropological and non-anthropological uses of visual images is an important issue for visual anthropology (see

Figure 1.13 Mud Men (Eastern Highlands, Papua New Guinea), featured in advertising poster for the Vauxhall Frontera

Ginsburg 1994; Turner 1992). Analyses of the similarities and differences between ethnographic films and exoticising documentaries, between anthropological and tourist board uses of photography, should make us aware of the extent to which visual images enter global discourse and should enable us to specify what an anthropological perspective is, and what is distinctive about the nature of its representational processes (see Ruby 1975 and MacDougall, chapter 14 in this volume). This is why the study of our own visual systems has to be integral to the agenda of visual anthropology.

Edwards and Grimshaw, writing respectively on photography and film, are concerned with the boundaries between anthropological and non-anthropological discourse, and in particular with the uses of images in anthropology and in art. Both show how photography may be part of the process of creating the relationship between self and other in the context of anthropology, art, and global political relations, whether that self concerns the individual's discrete 'inner' identity (a particularly modern, Euro-American notion), their identity as a member of the early twentieth-century bourgeoisie, or their identity as a member of a nation-state. Edwards and Grimshaw are concerned with the non-use of film and photography in anthropology for much of the twentieth century in contrast to its use in other contexts. As we have suggested earlier, anthropology rejected photography as an investigative tool partly because it was used by evolutionary theorists; those who continued to use photographs did so in a largely unreflective way. Photography got left behind by developments in anthropological theory: it was not part of the development of structural functionalism and it played no role in the postwar critique of functionalism. Ironically this has resulted in a situation which allows Edwards to argue that in theoretical terms modern anthropology is more in harmony with modern innovative art photography than with the realist ethnographic images that characterise anthropological writings and which are still to be found in postcards and tourist brochures. In looking at tourist images of the late twentieth century Edwards argues that there is still a tendency to represent indigenous peoples as romantic savages, unchanging people in unchanging lands. They present a view of the Other that has long been challenged by anthropologists, yet which has not been reflected in the anthropological use of photographs. Rather the use of photographs, from Malinowski on, as exotic illustrative material fits well with the tourism paradigm.

In anthropological film, as Grimshaw states, the challenge to the realist paradigm came quite early on. Indeed ethnographic filmmakers such as Rouch were at the forefront of reflexive anthropology. Perhaps because of the complex constructed nature of film and because of the existence of alternative paradigms in the cinema from early on, some visual anthropologists in the postwar years have been concerned to demonstrate the constructed nature of film. They have emphasised the

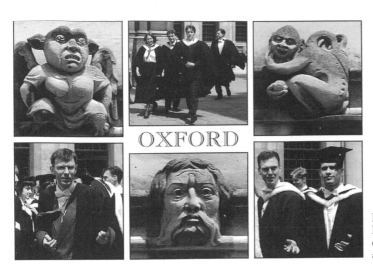

Figure 1.14
Exoticising the
other: 'Gargoyles
and Graduates'.

presence of the filmmaker, the observer effect, and the techniques of editing. They have been concerned with releasing the potential of film to go beyond the constraints of a written genre by developing what MacDougall has termed 'participatory cinema' (MacDougall 1975) and by using indigenous voices as an important part of their texts. None of this negates the indexical character of film, the fact that (before the advent of computer manipulation at least!) it does record something of what is happening in front of the camera. But by drawing attention to the selective nature of the filming process, and the possibilities opened up by editing and the flexibility and range of the camera lens, ethnographic filmmakers have shown that film may be used in different ways according to the communicative intention of the filmmaker.

Loizos demonstrates this potential using a technique analogous to Rouch's dialogic style of filmmaking. He engages in a dialogue with a set of films that are structured on very different bases but which have in common the theme of a journey. The theme is an appropriate one since it is locatable both in the concept of linear time associated with the realist tradition – the idea of anthropology as cross-cultural exploration – and in the postmodernist idea of the individual venture. Loizos draws attention to the relationship between the practice of film construction and meaning creation in film, and to the necessity for creative choice. It was an important point, first made explicitly perhaps by MacDougall (1975) but evident in the filmmaking of Rouch, that if film is to make its proper contribution to anthropology it has to do so by using its own properties, creating a system of meaning parallel to that of written ethnographies.

Edwards shows that anthropological photography has on the whole been less innovative than film. However, she argues that some developments in art photography have followed an anthropological paradigm and photography has moved to a point where anthropologists should be able to use it again as a productive resource. It has become culturally aware just as anthropology has become sensitive to the positioned nature of the anthropologist as author and the role of anthropology in global discourse.

If we take a positive view we could argue that one hundred years of anthropology has had an effect on the world outside. Anthropologists at the beginning of this century first rejected the evolutionist paradigm and replaced it with the message of cultural relativism. Subsequently they have recognised that cultural diversity exists in the context of complex global economic and political relations (see essays in Miller 1995), in which anthropologists are equally the subjects of their own research. Thus their subjectivity influences the nature of that research. Rather than concluding that this results in an anthropology that is inherently subjective, we would argue that anthropologists can now achieve a kind of objectivity, by being both outside and inside themselves, by adopting a reflexive attitude to their practice.

Edwards discusses how a tourist postcard labelled 'Australian Aborigines' which shows a set of people engaged in stereotypical activities – hunting, playing the didgeridoo and so on – perpetuates an image of culture that was rejected by early twentieth-century anthropologists. That rejection has influenced twentieth-century artists to look at other cultures with an anthropological rather than an evolutionary eye. But because anthropologists have remained separate from developments in photographic practice, because many of them still view photography as essentially realist, there is always a danger of them remaining associated in their own and their critics' eyes with a genre that they were in the forefront of rejecting.

The movement of visual images and their reincorporation into new contexts is part of many global economic and cultural processes. In her analysis of Japanese gardens in England and English gardens in Japan, Joy Hendry shows in her chapter that we are dealing with representations of representations. The Japanese gardens in England eventually become unrecognisable to the Japanese themselves, containing as they do plants that won't grow in Japan, and structured through concepts that are alien to the Japanese. Hendry demonstrates that visual forms are subject to change, as well as to changing interpretations. In the process of actual and semantic transformation the original visual form can generate non-visual counterparts and associations, such that the sensible properties of Japanese gardens may be transposed to apparently unrelated areas such as personal and domestic hygiene.

The consequences of such transformations through cross-cultural representational processes depend on the nature of the discourse involved and the aims of the respective parties. Françoise Dussart shows in chapter 9 how European-made films designed ostensibly to show the indigenous context of Warlpiri art, produce an account of a cultural arte-fact that is unrecognisable to the Warlpiri. Ironically, however, such films fit perfectly with the agenda of the artists. In releasing their paint-ings to outsiders Warlpiri are concerned that they will lose control of their system of knowledge with its connection to the ownership of land and ritual and its empowerment of knowledgeable individuals. The Europeans do not possess the body of knowledge which would enable them to decode Warlpiri art. They do not see the paintings as the Warlpiri do, and the European documentary film enables the artists to realise that they need worry no more. Interestingly this example reveals how, in the context of interaction with Europeans, aspects of the struc-ture of the indigenous system must be seen in a new light because the anticipated consequences of previous models do not eventuate. Until recently anthropologists have probably placed too much emphasis on the role of secrecy *per se* in Australian systems of knowledge. It seems that the maintenance of control over interpretation and the revelation of meaning is more important than control over access to particular forms (see also Morphy 1991, though see Michaels 1988 for an alternative per-spective).

The Warlpiri are increasingly part of the world of global art discourse (see e.g. Myers 1991), influencing it and being influenced by it. They are active participants playing a role in setting their own agenda and influ-encing the production of other artists. In contemporary Australia they are part of postmodernism, they interact with other artists from different traditions; they are able to step inside and outside themselves (as Grimshaw in chapter 2 argues anthropologists must themselves do). Nicholas Thomas, in chapter 13, takes up this theme in the context of neighbouring New Zealand by focusing on the relationship between Maori and Pakeha (white) themes in New Zealand art. He argues that the themes of identity and the concern with categories are part of a wider political discourse which operates as much outside the visual image as within ('invisibly foregrounded' in Battaglia's terms), and may indeed be denied by the artist. Significantly, the subject of Thomas's ethnography is not the contemporary Maori artists but the Pakeha who are involved in the same discourse. As with contemporary Aboriginal artists such as Gordon Bennett, the Maori artists are explicitly challenging the way that the concept of ethnography has been used to pigeon-hole their art as Other (a view prefigured in the work of earlier Aboriginal artists such as Narritjin Maymuru [Morphy 1991]). Gordon Bennett defines his own practice as an ethnography of European systems of representation (Bennett 1993).

Visual anthropology, because it *requires* reflexivity and the continual monitoring of changes in Western visual practice and conceptual under-standing, is in an excellent position to observe and mediate such cross-cultural interactions. It can provide method, tools and analysis to allow both the space for such global agendas to be exercised and the precision and fixity necessary to highlight local concerns and detail.

Conclusion

The contributors to this volume are all involved in stretching the boundaries of visual anthropology and reflecting back inside anthropology from outside the boundaries of the subject. These essays on film, photography, television, computers, gardens, art objects and ritual objects, provide a small sample of the visual systems that influence the construction of the world. All consider the movement of images from one context to another, between and within societies; their incorporation, conscious or unconscious, in new frames; their transformation across time and space and from medium to medium; and their association with particular purposes and conceptualisations. Visual anthropology exists in part to monitor these journeys and to provide a perspective on the changes of meaning, the mistranslations and intentional distortions, and to relate them to the sociopolitical and cultural processes of which they are a part (indeed, this is a central focus of Loizos's chapter [4]).

People are often unaware how radically different images become as they cross boundaries. Born, in chapter 7 on computer software, shows how even within the same institution and, theoretically, the same cultural system, there are continual misunderstandings and misrepresentations of the attributes of computer media. Ironically the supposed attributes of such systems have been used for decades in information theory and cognitive science (by people who have no ethnographic understanding of their operation) to develop the very sociological and psychological models that are intended to give an understanding of the social behaviour of their operators as actors in the world.

As anthropology moves to interrogate its own visual representations as part of its interpretative process, it is increasingly involved in a discourse about boundaries with other disciplines and other practitioners – artists, documentary filmmakers, photographers and television producers. By moving outside itself anthropology becomes engaged with others while simultaneously engaging others in its own agenda. Through looking at Japanese television documentary, Martinez is able to ask questions both about the nature of anthropology and about what is anthropological data. If anthropology frees itself from rigid disciplinary boundaries, it may be possible for the television documentary to become a form of local anthropology, rather than a slot where anthropological films can be shown. In other words, as anthropology expands its area of relevance then its boundaries will become less defined, and it will become harder to push it into narrow spaces. It is in this context that it is so important to bring indigenous media within 'the discursive space of anthropology' (Ginsburg 1994: 12; also Michaels 1986). It is the task of visual anthropology, having been for so long in essence a deconstructive discipline, to transcend the political nature of representation and to rethink its strategies for engaging with the world.

Notes

1. While this book was in press we were made aware of two recent edited collections that substantially advance work in the study of visual systems and visible culture – Devereaux and Hillman 1995 on film and photography as representational modes, and Marcus and Myers 1995 on the global contexts of indigenous arts.

2. Clearly, an understanding of the history and development of ethnographic film (see Banks 1992; Henley 1985; and Loizos 1980 for British perspectives; see Fuchs 1988 and various essays in Piault 1992 for other national perspectives) and of its practical methodological aspects (see Rollwagon 1988) are also important for locating the place of film within visual anthropology. Equally important is an understanding of the relationship between ethnographic film and the wider documentary film project. Here the work of Eric Barnouw (1983), Bill Nichols (for example, 1991) and Brian Winston (for example, 1988) has been especially helpful in providing non-anthropologists' assessments of the place of ethnographic film in its broader context.

3. By chance, our own institutional base at the University of Oxford provides a concrete example of this contradiction. Whereas photographs from the field became part of the collections in Tylor and Balfour's Pitt Rivers Museum, the photographs on the walls of what was the Institute of Social Anthropology, founded by Radcliffe-Brown, continue to be of members of the anthropological Establishment. As elsewhere in the world, social anthropology became associated with the images of the theorists whereas the ethnographic museum became associated with images of the Other, even though it was the theorists who were busily constructing the image of the Other that later critics would try to attribute to photography and to the ethnographic museum. (The merger, in 1990, of the teaching wing of the Pitt Rivers Museum with the Oxford Institute, resulting in the Institute of Social and Cultural Anthropology, is indicative of the 'rethinking' that motivates this volume.)

4. See also Doug Harper's four-fold typology of scientific, narrative, reflexive and phenomenological visual ethnographic types (Harper 1987); Harper assesses Bateson and Mead's *Balinese Character* as a rare example of the narrative type, where certain sequences of photographs 'appear like segments of a filmed ethnography' (ibid.: 7).

5. There has of course been much argument over the place of vision and the visual in the development of Western culture (see Levin 1983 for an excellent discussion of ocularcentricism) and in the development of anthropology (e.g. Clifford 1988). These debates are concerned in particular with the constructed nature of visual representations through the use of techniques such as perspective and with constrained and constructed visual framings such as are created by the panopticon, which has become a core metaphor of the postmodern critique. Often the reference in anthropology has been to the constructed nature of texts which are perhaps best conceived as metaconcepts independent of particular senses (see Clifford and Marcus 1986). Nonetheless the actual use of visual recording techniques and attention to the visual side of culture was neglected by social anthropology in particular during the first part of this century – participant observation was not as Clifford (1986: 11) implies a visual practice, nor can it be taken to imply a priority of seeing over just 'being there' as part of anthropological method. Perhaps it was not prioritising the visual as such but a particular narrowing down of vision that characterised a certain kind of modernity and which the relatively unmotivated and dense record of film and photography implicitly challenged.

6. Sadly, few anthropologists have yet tried to effect other-cultural representations primarily through artistic representation (but see Michael Carrithers' illustrations for his monograph on forest monks in Sri Lanka [1983], and Gillian Crowther's attempt to present her field ethnography of the Haida, British Columbia, in a strip cartoon format [1990]), while the use of drawings or diagrams in the published work of anthropologists has not, to our knowledge, been addressed.

7. Mead's position has been echoed more recently by Duranti who writes: 'linguistic anthropologists have refined their skills at recording and then transcribing the words (and more recently, with the improvement of video technology, some other actions) of the people whose linguistic practices they want to study. . . . However selective and skewed by an author's specific arguments, the display of what was said by a social actor at a particular time opens the door to potential refutations and interpretative criticisms' (Duranti 1994: 39).

8. Thus, in line with Born's observations, we remain sceptical about some of the claims advanced by advocates of 'multimedia' and other computer-based technologies (for example, Biella 1994; Seaman and Williams 1992) for the ability of these technologies to transform visual anthropology and even anthropology itself (Banks 1994a).

References

Abu-Lughod, Lila (1995) 'The Objects of Soap Opera: Egyptian Television and the Cultural Politics of Modernity'; in *Worlds Apart: Modernity through the Prism of the Local*, ed. Danny Miller, London: Routledge.

Asch, Timothy (1975) *The Ax Fight*, USA: Pennsylvania State University.

Banks, Marcus (1990) 'Experience and Reality in Ethnographic Film', *Visual Sociology Review* 5(2): 30–33.

— (1992) 'La Vie existait-elle avant la télévision?', *Journal des anthropologues* – Special issue on Visual Anthropology, 47–8: 39–47.

— (1994a) 'Interactive Multimedia and Anthropology – a Sceptical View', electronic document published on the University of Oxford RSL W3 server. URL: http://rsl.ox.ac.uk/isca/marcus.banks.01.html

— (1994b) 'Television and Anthropology: An Unhappy Marriage?' *Visual Anthropology* 7(1): 21–45.

— (1995) 'Visual Research Methods'. *Social Research Update* 11

— (1996) 'Constructing the Audience through Ethnography', in *The Construction of the Viewer: Media Ethnography and the Anthropology of Audiences*. Proceedings from NAFA 3, eds Peter I. Crawford and Sigurjon B. Hafsteinsson, Højbjerg, Denmark: Intervention Press.

Barnouw, Erik (1983) *Documentary: A History of the Non-Fiction Film* (rev. edn), Oxford: Oxford University Press.

Barthes, Roland (1993 [1980]) *Camera Lucida: Reflections on Photography*, London: Vintage.

Bateson, Gregory and Margaret Mead (1942) *Balinese Character: A Photographic Analysis*, New York: New York Academy of Sciences.

Bennett, Gordon (1993) 'Aesthetics and Iconography: An Artist's Approach', in *Aratjara: Art of the First Australians*, ed. B. Luhti. Düsseldorf: Kunstsammlung Nordrhein-Westfalen.

Biella, Peter (1994) 'Codifications of Ethnography: Linear and Non-linear', electronic document published on the University of Southern California E-LAB W3 server. URL: http://www.usc.edu/dept/elab/welcome/codifications.html

Cantrill, Arthur and Corinne Cantrill (1982) 'The 1901 Cinematography of Walter Baldwin Spencer', *Cantrill's Film Notes* 37–8: 27–43, 56–8.

Carrithers, Michael (1983) *The Forest Monks of Sri Lanka: An Anthropological and Historical Study*, New Delhi: Oxford University Press.

Clifford, James (1986) 'Introduction', in *Writing Culture,* eds J. Clifford and G. Marcus, Berkeley: University of California Press.
— (1988) *The Predicament of Culture*, Cambridge Mass: Harvard University Press.
Clifford, James and George Marcus (eds) (1986) *Writing Culture*, Berkeley: University of California Press.
Collier, John Jn and Malcolm Collier (1986) *Visual Anthropology: Photography as a Research Method*, Albuquerque: University of New Mexico Press.
Connor, Linda, Patsy Asch and Timothy Asch (1986) *Jero Tapakan: Balinese Healer. An Ethnographic Film Monograph*. Cambridge: Cambridge University Press.
Coote, Jeremy (1992) '"Marvels of Everyday Vision': the Anthropology of Aesthetics and the Cattle-keeping Nilotes', in *Anthropology, Art and Aesthetics*, eds J. Coote and A. Shelton, Oxford: Clarendon Press.
Crowther, Gillian (1990) 'Fieldwork Cartoons', *Cambridge Anthropology* 14(2): 57–68.
Das, Veena (1995) 'On Soap Opera: What Kind of Anthropological Object Is It?', in *Worlds Apart: Modernity Through the Prism of the Local*, ed. Danny Miller, London: Routledge.
Devereaux, Leslie and Roger Hillman (eds) (1995) *Fields of Vision: Essays in Film Studies, Visual Anthropology, and Photography*, Berkeley: University of California Press.
Dunlop, Ian (1979) *Madarrpa Funeral at Gurka'wuy*, Sydney: Film Australia.
Duranti, Alessandro (1994) *From Grammar to Politics: Linguistic Anthropology in a Western Samoan Village*, Berkeley: University of California Press.
Edwards, Elizabeth (1988) 'Representation and Reality: Science and the Visual Image', in *Australia in Oxford*, eds H. Morphy and E. Edwards, Oxford: Pitt Rivers Museum.
— (1990) 'Photographic "Types": the Pursuit of Method', *Visual Anthropology* 3(2–3): 235–58.
— (1992) 'Science Visualized: E.H. Man in the Andaman Islands', in *Anthropology and Photography 1860–1920*, ed. E. Edwards, New Haven/London: Yale University Press in association with The Royal Anthropological Institute, London.
Farnell, Brenda M. (1994) 'Ethno-graphics and the Moving Body', *Man* 29(4): 929–74.
Fischer, Michael (1994) *Applications in Computing for Social Anthropologists*, London: Routledge.
Flaherty, Robert (1922) *Nanook of the North*, USA: Revillon Frères.
Fuchs, Peter (1988) 'Ethnographic Film in Germany: an Introduction', *Visual Anthropology* 1(3): 217–33.
Ginsburg, Faye (1991) 'Indigenous Media: Faustian Contract or Global Village?' *Cultural Anthropology* 6(1): 92–112.
— (1994) 'Culture/Media: A (Mild) Polemic', *Anthropology Today* 10(2): 5–15.
Goodwin, C. (1981) *Conversational Organisation: Interaction between Speakers and Hearers*, New York: Academic Press.
Hagaman, Dianne (1995) 'Connecting Cultures: Balinese Character and the Computer', in *The Cultures of Computing*, ed. S.L. Star, Oxford: Basil Blackwell.
Harper, Douglas (1987) 'The Visual Ethnographic Narrative', *Visual Anthropology* 1(1): 1–20.
Heath, C. (1986) *Body Movement and Speech in Medical Interaction*, Cambridge: Cambridge University Press.
Henley, Paul (1985) 'British Ethnographic Film: Recent Developments', *Anthropology Today* 1(1): 5–17.
Hockings, Paul (ed.) (1975) *Principles of Visual Anthropology*, The Hague: Mouton.
— (ed.) (1995) *Principles of Visual Anthropology* (2nd edn), The Hague: Mouton.
Jacknis, Ira (1989) 'Margaret Mead and Gregory Bateson in Bali: Their Use of Photography and Film', *Cultural Anthropology* 3(2): 160–77.
— (1994) 'Society for Visual Anthropology', *Anthropology Newsletter* 35(4): 33–4.
Kendon, Adam (1988) *Sign Languages of Aboriginal Australia: Cultural, Semiotic and Communicative Perspectives*, Cambridge: Cambridge University Press.
Levin, David Michael (ed.) (1993) *Modernity and the Hegemony of Vision*, Berkeley:

University of California Press.

Loizos, Peter (1980) 'Granada Television's Disappearing World Series: An Appraisal', *American Anthropologist* 82: 573–94.

Lyman, Christopher (1982) *The Vanishing Race and other Illusions: Photographs of Indians by Edward S. Curtis*, New York: Pantheon Books.

MacDougall, David (1975) 'Beyond Observational Cinema', in *Principles of Visual Anthropology*, ed. P. Hockings, The Hague: Mouton.

— (1992) 'Complicities of Style'. In *Film as Ethnography*, eds. P. Crawford and D. Turton, Manchester: Manchester University Press in association with the Granada Centre for Visual Anthropology.

Marcus, George and Fred Myers (eds) (1995) *The Traffic in Culture: Refiguring Art and Anthropology*, Berkeley: University of California Press.

Martinez, Wilton (1990) 'Critical Studies and Visual Anthropology: Aberrant vs. Anticipated Readings of Ethnographic Film', *CVA Review* Spring: 34–47.

McKenzie, Kim (1980) *Waiting for Harry*, Australia: Australian Institute for Aboriginal Studies.

Michaels, Eric (1986) *The Aboriginal Invention of Television in Central Australia, 1982-1986: Report of the Fellowship to Assess the Impact of Television in Remote Aboriginal Communities*, Canberra: Australian Institute of Aboriginal Studies.

— (1988) 'Bad Aboriginal Art', *Art and Text* 28: 59–63.

— (1991) 'Aboriginal Content: Who's Got It – Who Needs It?', *Visual Anthropology* 4(3–4): 277–300.

Miller, Danny (ed.) (1995) *Worlds Apart: Modernity through the Prism of the Local*, London: Routledge.

Morphy, Howard (1988) 'The Original Australians and the Evolution of Anthropology'. In *Australia in Oxford*, eds H. Morphy and E. Edwards, Oxford: Pitt Rivers Museum Monographs.

— (1991) *Ancestral Connections: Art and an Aboriginal System of Knowledge*, Chicago: University of Chicago Press.

— (1994a) 'The Anthropology of Art' in *Companion Encyclopedia of Anthropology: Humanity, Culture and Social Life*, ed. T. Ingold, London: Routledge.

— (1994b) 'The Interpretation of Ritual: Reflections from Film on Anthropological Practice', *Man* (NS) 29(1): 117–46.

Myers, Fred (1991) 'Representing Culture: The Production of Discourse(s) for Aboriginal Acrylic Paintings', *Cultural Anthropology* 6(1): 26–62.

Nichols, Bill (1991) *Representing Reality: Issues and Concepts in Documentary*, Bloomington: Indiana University Press.

O'Hanlon, Michael (1993) *Paradise: Portraying the New Guinea Highlands*, London: British Museum Press.

Piault, Colette (ed.) (1992) *Journal des anthropologues 47–8: Special Issue on Visual Anthropology*.

Pinney, Christopher (1990) 'Classification and Fantasy in the Photographic Construction of Caste and Tribe', *Visual Anthropology* (Special issue): *Picturing Cultures: Historical Photographs in Anthropological Enquiry*, ed. Joanna Scherer 3(2–3): 259–88.

— (1992a) 'Montage, Doubling and the Mouth of God', in *Ethnographic Film Aesthetics and Narrative Traditions: Proceedings from NAFA 2*, eds P.I. Crawford and J.K. Simonsen, Aarhus: Intervention Press.

— (1992b) 'The Parallel Histories of Anthropology and Photography', in *Anthropology and Photography 1860–1920*, ed. E. Edwards, New Haven: Yale University Press in association with The Royal Anthropological Institute, London.

Price, Sally (1989) *Primitive Art in Civilised Places*, Chicago: University of Chicago Press.

Rollwagon, Jack (ed.) (1988) *Anthropological Film-making*, Chur: Harwood Academic Publishers.

Ruby, Jay (1975) 'Is an Ethnographic Film a Filmic Ethnography?' *Studies in the Anthropology of Visual Communication* 2(2): 104–11.

— (1980) 'Exposing Yourself: Reflexivity, Film and Anthropology', *Semiotica* 3, 153–79.

Scherer, Joanna (1990) 'Introduction. Historical Photographs as Anthropological Documents: A Retrospect', *Visual Anthropology* 3(2-3): 131–55.

Seaman, Gary and Homer Williams (1992) 'Hypermedia in Ethnography', in *Film as Ethnography*, eds P. Crawford and D. Turton, Manchester: Manchester University Press in association with the Granada Centre for Visual Anthropology.

Sontag, Susan (1978) *On Photography*, Harmondsworth: Penguin.

Taylor, Lucien (ed.) (1994) *Visualizing Theory: Selected Essays from V.A.R. 1990–1994*, New York: Routledge.

Turner, Terence (1992) 'Defiant Images: The Kayapo Appropriation of Video', *Anthropology Today* 8(6), 5–16.

Ucko, Peter J. (1970) 'Penis Sheaths: A Comparative Study', *Proceedings of the Royal Anthropological Institute of Great Britain and Northern Ireland for 1969*, 27–67.

Vogel, Susan (ed.) (1988) *Art/Artefact: African Art in Anthropology Collections*, New York: Center for African Art.

Winston, Brian (1988 [1978]) 'Documentary: I Think We Are in Trouble', in *New Challenges for Documentary*, ed. A. Rosenthal, Berkeley: University of California Press.

Witherspoon, G. (1977) *Language and Art in the Navaho Universe*, Ann Arbor: University of Michigan Press.

Wood, W. (1989) 'The Visualization of Cultural Process', *SVA Newsletter* 5(1): 29–33.

2

The eye in the door: anthropology, film and the exploration of interior space[1]

Anna Grimshaw

An age of war and revolution

Film critics often write as if Griffith invented techniques as Edison invented the electric light. But the film techniques which Griffith created are the result of the extended interests, awareness, needs and sensibilities of modern men.

Our world of the twentieth century is *panoramic*.

Contemporary society gives man a sense, on a scale hitherto unknown, of connections, of cause and effect, of the conditions from which an event arises, of other events occurring simultaneously. His world is one of constantly increasing multiplicity of relations between himself, immense mechanical constructions and social organization of world-wide scope. It is representation of this that demanded the techniques of *flash-back, cross-cutting* and a camera of extreme mobility.

Along with this panoramic view we are aware today of the depth and complexities of the individual personality, as opened up by Freud and others.

This finds its most plastic representation in the *close-up*.

Modern content demanded a modern technique, not vice versa. What is the content that this technique serves? Ours is an age of war. D.W. Griffith's *Birth of a Nation* portrays the American Civil War, the first great modern war. Ours is an age of revolution. The *Birth of a Nation* is the first great epic of a modern nation in revolutionary crisis.

C.L.R. James: Popular Art and the Cultural Tradition
[1992 (originally 1954)][2]

The questions which James raises in this passage are, I believe, central to any project concerned with 'visualising anthropology'. My intention in this essay is to explore two overlapping and contrasting texts which may be constructed out of the same historical moment. Central to both, however, is a re-contextualisation of anthropology. By this I mean shifting the focus away from questions concerning the project's literary dimensions, 'anthropology as a kind of writing' (Spencer 1989), to consideration of those new features which emerge when anthropology is juxtaposed with developments in the visual arts at the turn of the century.[3]

I began with James because his remarks about D.W. Griffith and cinema are anchored in the same historical moment as the inauguration of modern anthropology. Indeed the symbolic dates which mark the birth of cinema and modern British anthropology are separated by only three years. Lumière's first cinema programme ran in 1895, while Haddon's expedition to the Torres Strait set out in 1898. Such a correspondence in dates invites a closer scrutiny.

In the above passage James situates the question of new forms for a new content at the centre of his understanding of cinema. The cinematic innovations of Griffith, specifically his use of the close-up, flash-back, cross-cutting and a camera of great mobility, are, James argues, his creative response to the new and distinctive characteristics of the age in which he worked. It was an age marked by war and revolution. Fundamental challenges were posed to established practices in all areas of human activity, from aesthetics to social and political structures.

Following James, I will argue that anthropology, like cinema, has to be understood as an expression of this moment. Its distinctive features as a twentieth-century project were moulded by figures such as Boas and Rivers,[4] men who, like Griffith, were struggling to develop new forms capable of giving expression to a new and expanded conception of humanity, one which recognised people everywhere as a growing force in society.

Both projects – anthropology and cinema – may be seen as modern, as distinctively twentieth-century practices which represent a decisive break with existing forms and conventions. But their connection goes beyond the moment of their birth. There is a striking symmetry in the first four decades of their evolution. I propose to explore this symmetry through the juxtaposition of key moments/figures in one tradition with their equivalents in the other.

There are three important pairs. (1) Haddon and Lumière; (2) Malinowski and Flaherty; (3) Radcliffe-Brown and Grierson.

Thus, at one level, my argument will be concerned to expose a remarkable parallel development in anthropology and cinema, a movement which culminates in the establishment of distinct categories: 'scientific ethnography' and 'documentary film' by the 1930s. At this level the two traditions mirror one another. But what is equally striking is that, despite their early combination in the Torres Strait expedition, cinema and anthropology became separate, not integrated practices. This separation is most exaggerated in Britain; and it prompts questions about the kind of anthropology established by Malinowski and taken to be synonymous with the British school. Moreover, it raises important points of comparison with other traditions. How or why have the founders of other national schools, such as Boas and Mead in America and Griaule and Rouch in France, been more able and willing to integrate visual media creatively into their anthropological practice?

These questions form the background to my essay; but I leave them largely unanswered at this time. Instead, I intend to construct an alternative text, in opposition to the symmetrical but separate histories of anthropology and film from the 1890s to the 1930s. This text focuses more narrowly on a brief moment of social disintegration and cultural invention during and immediately after the First World War and the Russian Revolution. It juxtaposes an anthropologist and psychologist, W.H.R. Rivers, with two filmmakers, D.W. Griffith and Dziga Vertov, each of whom reached out for a dialectical synthesis of subject and object which stands in marked contrast to the predominantly objectifying trend of the twentieth-century world. Here too the roots of this moment can be traced to Lumière and to the Torres Strait expedition of which Rivers was in some ways the most notable member.

By focusing on Rivers we can begin to excavate interesting ruptures in the terrain of modern history and to evoke new connections and associations which expose some of the issues lying at the heart of the quest for a genuinely visual anthropology. It means exploring the division between inside and outside which marks the duality of the subject–object pair, the line between interior space and social life, personality and history; or, returning to James's remarks about Griffith, the dialectical relationship between close-up and panorama. This requires us to break with a superficial objectivism which cannot examine its own rationality in the light of the irrational or the unconscious. In short, we will have to dismantle the barriers between social anthropology and psychology, as Rivers did, towards the end of his remarkable life.

The means by which I will attempt to construct this alternative, hidden text are unconventional. For I take as my starting point the work of a contemporary novelist, Pat Barker, and the writings of art critic John Berger (specifically, *Ways of Seeing, The Moment of Cubism* and *Success and Failure of Picasso*). Indeed the title of my paper, *The Eye in the Door*, is taken from Barker's recently published novel, the second volume in her trilogy about the First World War. But why, you might ask, should two novels about the First World War be important in uncovering this other text?[5]

First and foremost, Barker's central character is Rivers. Both of her novels, *Regeneration* (1991) and *The Eye in the Door* (1993) are based on
detailed research into his life and work; but it is through the exercise of

her creative imagination as a novelist that she is able to suggest some new and interesting questions in the early history of modern anthropology. The second part of the trilogy is most evocative; and the reason is immediately obvious from its title: *The Eye in the Door*. For here, by placing Rivers in a more expanded social context than that of *Regeneration*, Barker makes central one of the most prominent features of Rivers' work – vision and perception. But Barker takes this feature as a metaphor, and through an exploration of different processes of visualisation, she establishes a fundamental opposition in her novel between seeing as insight and seeing as surveillance, the mind's eye or the spying eye.

The eye in the door looks inwards – and I will argue that in Rivers' case it looks into the self as a prelude to engaging with the world; while after Malinowski the eye of the anthropologist spies into society, but not into the self. In Malinowski's own case, as we all know, there was a serious rupture between inside and outside, subjectivity and the world. This division, symbolised in the stark contrast between Malinowski's fieldwork diary (Malinowski 1967) and his 'scientific ethnography', marked the beginning of the modern ethnographer's fragmented personality.

By contrast, in recognising their dialectical relationship, I believe that Rivers participated in a modernist moment seen most vividly through the visual arts. He might even, following Berger (Berger 1985), be considered 'cubist' in his approach to humanity, choosing, as he did in the context of war, to synthesise a multifaceted vision of the world and to place himself unambiguously within the picture of it he was struggling to construct. Such a project was arguably taken to its furthest extreme by Dziga Vertov, the 'man with a movie-camera', whose best films were made in the aftermath of the Russian revolution (Michelson 1984; Tomas 1992). If we juxtapose Rivers and his exact contemporary Griffith with Vertov, we will, I believe, reveal unexplored sources of creative inspiration for the project of 'visualising anthropology'.

The essay which follows represents an attempt to match form with content, to set up a series of creative connections which evoke a cinematic rather than literary experience. My argument is assembled through three interconnected parts – thesis (a parallel history of anthropology and cinema in the early decades of this century); antithesis (a subversive text constructed out of a revolutionary moment); and, finally, notes towards a synthesis for our own times. The method is experimental; speculative rather than empirical; and hence my recourse to works of fiction and criticism. My aim is to 'see' anthropology from a number of cross-cutting perspectives: in juxtaposition with cinema and the visual arts; diachronically and synchronically; through the observing eye and the mind's eye. If, as a result, the boundary between subject and object is sometimes blurred, the scope for imaginative connection should be enhanced.

Thesis: symmetries in history

My first attempt to 'visualise' anthropology consists of placing the modern project alongside cinema. As I have already mentioned, I think it is possible to discover remarkable symmetries in their early twentieth-century development, beginning with the close proximity in dates of Lumière's first cinema programme (1895) and British anthropology's first fieldwork-based expedition to the Torres Strait (1898). Their shared context was the tremendous period of change which picked up pace at the end of the nineteenth century and reached a new intensity with the Great War (Bradbury and McFarlane 1976).

There was an increase in the movement of people, goods and ideas. New capitalist expansion was matched by increased imperial rivalry; and the rise of a world market was founded upon an integrated system of production and consumption in which millions of people participated. But this period was also characterised by a shift in a number of key ideas. For example there was a break-up of existing notions of time and space; the eye was displaced from occupying a privileged place at the centre of the world; the principle of perspective in painting was undermined; an increased interest in the irrational or non-rational led to a questioning of evolutionary models of humanity. Above all, the old notion of 'European civilisation', one built on separation, hierarchy and exclusion, was shattered. If, as the Great War was to reveal, barbarism lurked in the breast of so-called civilised men, then perhaps civilisation could be discovered among those people previously considered barbaric.

Modern anthropology and early cinema were a reflection and a part of these fundamental changes. Specifically they embodied a new and expanded conception of humanity. Their content was the lives of people at home and abroad. For, unlike the established intellectual class who were horrified by the growing power and presence of people in world society (Carey 1992), the pioneers in film and anthropology were open to the emergence of this new subject matter. Moreover, they recognised the necessity of developing new forms for exploring the complexity of people's lives. Critical was the notion of going out into the world to discover humanity at first hand.

And this is precisely what Louis Lumière did with his new invention, the cinematographe. In the early 1890s he took his camera out into the streets of Paris, he walked about with it, setting it up in front of any aspect of social life which interested him. Lumière used his camera to get closer to social life, capturing its movement and its detail. At the centre of his early films were people doing everyday things (feeding the baby, workers leaving a factory, playing cards, etc.).

When A.C. Haddon organised his expedition to the Torres Strait islands in 1898 he included a cinematographe among his advanced scientific instruments.[6] Haddon and his team, like Lumière, were committed to going out into the world to see for themselves. This was something new, representing a break with the older practices of armchair anthropology; and it began the process of establishing fieldwork at the heart of the modern project. But what is especially interesting here is that the movie camera was part of that modern project – at least in its inception. Writing in 1900 to the Australian anthropologist, Baldwin Spencer, who was about to undertake fieldwork in the Northern Territories, Haddon exclaimed: 'You really *must* take a kinematographe or a biograph or whatever they call it in your part of the world. It is an indispensable piece of anthropological apparatus.'[7]

Although only a fragment of film remains, there are a number of striking similarities with the early Lumière shorts. For both are marked by a filmmaking style which is about 'showing', rather than 'telling', that is people perform for the camera and there is a direct relationship between the film subjects and the audience.[8] Furthermore, both Lumière and Haddon shoot from a fixed point; their camera is static and immobile, while life is animated around it.

The next point of coincidence between cinema and anthropology is symbolised by the year 1922. It is the year in which Malinowski published *Argonauts of the Western Pacific* and Flaherty released his film, *Nanook of the North*. Both works are, I believe, inspired by remarkably similar visions of the world. Moreover, they celebrate a new method – the importance of living with 'the people' themselves over a considerable period of time.

Argonauts and *Nanook* represent a profound rejection of the notion that European society embodies the pinnacle of civilisation; and yet at the same time both reveal in peoples previously excluded from definitions of civilised humanity the sort of values associated with European bourgeois society. Trobriand man emerges like Nanook as a rational, reasonable, calculating individual, negotiating the division between self-interest and the need for social co-operation.

Both text and film are distinguished by their detail, by their integration of parts into a coherent whole, and by their creation of an ethnographic present outside of history and contemporary society. More profoundly, however, Malinowski and Flaherty share a static vision of the world. It is based on a particular way of seeing which privileges the single eye of the observer. Malinowski elevates the human eye with all its limitations to a privileged place in the acquisition of knowledge, while Flaherty's camera-eye reflects and confirms a certain order in the world based on its appearance.

But it is this illusion of 'showing' the world which marks the work of each as transitional in the creation of specialised practices, scientific ethnography and documentary film. For while each claims to show the world as it is, they are in fact 'telling' us about that world; and it is this incompletely realised movement in their work which provokes the end- 41 less re-examinations of it. We never tire of Malinowski as we do of Radcliffe-Brown, for instance. But what is equally important to recognise in this moment of coincidence, 1922, is the complete separation of Malinowski and Flaherty, of anthropology and cinema. For Flaherty, the amateur, the explorer, the Hollywood-fêted filmmaker, stands for everything which threatens Malinowski's notion of professional authority and scientific expertise (Clifford 1986).

The final pair I wish to juxtapose in this symmetrical history links the groups associated with two key figures, A.R. Radcliffe-Brown and John Grierson. By the 1930s the professional practices of documentary film and scientific ethnography were now radically separate, each with their own rules of method and complementary locus of operation, at home and abroad, in the media and the universities. The two nevertheless share a remarkably similar approach to society. Their vision of society is essentially the functionalist one pioneered by Durkheim (Durkheim 1915). Emphasis is placed on what people do; their individuality is suppressed beneath a neat division of labour which oils the machinery of collective life. In both a 'mission to explain' shades into the reproduction of statist propaganda. Telling has taken over from showing.

This congruence comes out of the joint movement of ethnography and documentary film away from direct engagement with society, as practitioners increasingly sought state support for their professional activities and adapted their projects to the needs of ruling bureaucracy. Although neither the anthropologists nor filmmakers of the interwar period achieved the secure professional recognition that they desired, by 1939 they had established two areas of specialist practice.

I have suggested in this section of my paper that anthropology may be placed alongside cinema as a first step in 'visualising' the project. A shift of anthropology's context from literature to cinema reveals striking symmetries in their histories. Indeed, the moment of their birth seemed to promise integration. But, over the course of four decades from the 1890s to the second outbreak of war, we can trace the gradual clarification which separated scientific ethnography and documentary film from associated areas of practice and from each other. Critical to this process is the emergence of a number of key oppositions – entertainment and education, amateurs and professionals, fiction and fact, showing and telling, subject and object, individual and society.

Anthithesis: a subversive text

Torres Strait, which I linked to Lumière as the point of departure for my previous discussion, remains something of an enigma. For it seemed to promise the integration of cinema and anthropology at the moment of the modern project's birth; and yet by the end of the First World War they have diverged, even though each tradition remains remarkably close to the other in its approach to exploring the world.

I believe that this paradox is important in any project concerned with 'visualising' anthropology in this period, not least because of the participation of W.H.R. Rivers in the Torres Strait expedition. He is one of the most interesting and original figures at the turn of the century, credited as a founder not just of one modern discipline, anthropology, but of psychology too. His work, however, was denigrated and marginalised by his successor, Malinowski. Although a handful of recent historians of the discipline have sought to return him to his rightful place as a modern pioneer in the study of society,[9] Rivers' work remains largely unknown to practitioners and students of anthropology today. But Rivers has to be one of the central characters in any attempt to 'visualise anthropology' – not least because of his lifelong interest in vision and perception.

His work is marked by an extraordinary range and variety. It encompassed physiology and neurology, the psychology of perception, kinship, social organisation, ethnology and world history. In the early part of his career these intellectual areas developed as separate parts of a scientific project; but it is my contention that the pressure of the First World War forced Rivers to synthesise them, launching him, before his premature death, on the path towards a dialectical, reflexive and engaged anthropology.

Thus, by focusing on Rivers in this second section, and taking 'the eye in the door' as a metaphor, I hope to suggest a different sort of text, pieced together from a series of connections and associations which are speculative and open-ended. This alternative history seeks to place Rivers alongside the Hollywood filmmaker D.W. Griffith and the Russian revolutionary filmmaker Dziga Vertov.

As I said at the beginning, my initial sources for such a task may seem unconventional – novels and art criticism; but I believe that they enable us to excavate interesting ruptures in the terrain I have just mapped.

I will start with the novels of Pat Barker.[10] Barker is interested in the work Rivers carried out during the First World War. Her two novels, *Regeneration* and *The Eye in the Door*, are set in 1917 and 1918; and they focus on Rivers' treatment of patients suffering from shell shock (psychological trauma associated with trench warfare).

The first novel is largely confined to Craiglockhart, the military hospital where Rivers worked, and it traces the different relationships Rivers develops with a number of key characters, including the celebrated poet Siegfried Sassoon. Barker's emphasis, through Rivers, is on individual disintegration, the complete breakdown of the human personality under the stress of war. It is manifested in the totalising and dominant quality of a patient's visual life as expressed through dreams, nightmares, memories. Rivers believes that it is his duty to science and society to find methods of treatment which will restore patients and enable them to return to the battlefield. His treatment consists of persuading patients to remember, to confront the visual dimensions of their personality – something which Rivers himself does at certain key moments in the novel.

The title of the novel, *Regeneration*, is taken from the famous experiment that Rivers conducted on his friend, Henry Head. In his rooms at St John's College, Cambridge, Rivers cut the nerves in Head's upper arm; and, over a period of five years, they studied the process of nerve regeneration, the recovery of feeling and sensation. This was characterised by a two-fold process. First the 'protopathic' faculty was restored which had a primitive, totalising quality; later, the 'epicritic' faculty, characterised as rational, discriminating judgement, returned.

This experiment stands as a metaphor for the book. Rivers begins to recognise the contradiction embodied in this experiment, one reproduced at Craiglockhart, between his sense of duty to science and society and his knowledge of the pain and distress caused by his work. Moreover, he increasingly recognises that the protopathic may not necessarily be 'primitive' or irrational; indeed, in the context of war, it is the epicritic (duty, rationality) which is profoundly irrational.

The individual disintegration that Rivers confronts as a doctor gradually comes to stand for the social disintegration precipitated by war. This is the major concern of Barker in the second novel of the trilogy, *The Eye in the Door*. In a much more expanded social context than *Regeneration*, Barker's characters (many of them from the earlier novel) are conscious of the break-up of a certain social order; and the author plays with transgressions across boundaries of class, sexuality and consciousness.

Rivers comes to be opposed to Billy Prior, a former Craiglockhart patient, as in the course of the book he completes the transformation begun in *Regeneration* – from a rather aloof and detached scientist into an engaged social critic. Such a transformation is achieved through Rivers' understanding of the creative integration of the subjective and the objective, protopathic and epicritic, irrational and rational, art/poetry and science. Prior, by contrast, experiences a 'fugue' state, dissociation, a complete Jekyll and Hyde split in his personality.

Again we can see that the Rivers–Head nerve experiment lies behind the book. It reappears at its climax, as Rivers, through reflection on the loss of his own visual powers, explores the nature of the relationship between the protopathic and the epicritic. It is neither coexistence nor an issue of the epicritic replacing the protopathic; but it involves both a partial suppression of the latter and an integration of the two levels.

Central to this second book, as indicated by its title, is the metaphor: 'the eye in the door' – the mind's eye or the eye of surveillance; the eye looking inwards, into the self as the basis for understanding the world or the eye spying into society, suppressing the self and objectifying the world. Prior suffers from an enormous fear of the eye in the door – it is watching him. His problem is his marginality, an interloper who spies and is fearful of looking inwards. In fact Prior's state of dissociation is akin to Malinowski's attempted separation of the objective from the subjective, as reflected in the gap between his professional monographs (notably *Argonauts*) and his posthumously published fieldwork diary (*A Diary in the Strict Sense of the Term*).

Barker's creative exploration of the character of Rivers and the sociopolitical context in which he worked takes its inspiration from his late writing: *Instinct and the Unconscious* (1920) and *Conflict and Dream* (1923). Both books are marked by an extraordinary degree of self-consciousness. Rivers' explorations into the workings of the unconscious draw extensively not only on his encounters with patients, but also on his own experiences. These recollections depend heavily on the process of visualisation. Rivers was keenly aware of his own early loss of this faculty in his waking life, a lack which was heightened by its reappearance in his dreams.

Now what, you might wonder, has all this to do with visualising anthropology?

There is a recurrent motif in both of Barker's novels: Rivers takes off his glasses and sweeps his hand across his eyes. Indeed eyes are everywhere – in the door, unseen yet watching, in the hand, picked up off the battlefield, inside the self. But what Barker draws attention to is Rivers' interest in the area between the conscious and the unconscious, rational and irrational, between subject and object, personality and the world. It is the war which forces Rivers to recognise that there is no intrinsic contradiction between his work in ethnology and psychology. Both indeed are indispensable parts of a single project concerned with exploring the human condition.

Rivers' attempt to integrate these areas, it might be argued, was matched by Griffith's work in cinema. For Griffith's period of greatest achievement – *Birth of a Nation* (1915), *Intolerance* (1916) and *Broken Blossoms* (1919) – coincided with Rivers' late burst of writing. Moreover, he was using the camera to probe into the same areas of the human personality, exposing, through the development of the close-up shot, hidden dimensions of subjectivity. But his revelation of the complex, multi-layered nature of the human personality was always creatively anchored in broader social and historical contexts. Griffith, like Rivers, sought to look inside, using the camera as a sort of mind's eye looking into the self; but the self he uncovered was as fluid as the vast, interconnected, moving world of which it was part. The creative dialectic of personality and history, subject and object, close-up and panorama was expressed in perhaps Griffith's greatest innovation – the movement of the camera. The great American journalist and photographer James Agee recognised the significance of this moment, writing:

As a director Griffith hit the picture business like a tornado. Before he   *45* walked on the set motion pictures had been, in actuality, static. At a respectful distance the camera snapped a series of whole scenes clustered in the groupings of a stage play. Griffith broke up the pose. He rammed his camera into the middle of the action. He took close-ups, cross-cuts, angle shots and dissolves. His camera was alive, picking off shots . . . For the first time the movies had a man who realised that while a theater audience listened a movie audience watched. 'Above all . . . I am trying to make you see,' Griffith said.

(Agee 1963: 397)

But ironically Griffith's shattering of cinema's static pose was achieved in the context of the studio, not in the world. If Lumière took his camera out into society and held it static while life was animated around it, Griffith moved his camera in the static world of the studio. It was Dziga Vertov, the Russian filmmaker, working in the revolutionary climate of the 1920s, who brought the two, the camera and the world, into a creative relationship where the mobility of one was matched by the other.

Vertov's account of his debut in films is unusual.[11] In it he imagines the camera recording all his fleeting shifts of mood as he jumps one and a half storeys from a summer house. It is striking, not just for the emphasis placed on the question of seeing – what the human eye can and cannot see – but for the notion of the camera as a mind's eye as much as a spying eye. The two are, in fact, inseparable. For a brief yet brilliant moment before Stalin's suppression, Vertov experimented with a mobile camera in a mobile world, exploring the shifting relationships between subjective and objective, the camera eye seeing itself at the same time as it sees the world, looking inside as it looks outside.[12]

Although perhaps the connections between Vertov and Rivers may seem tenuous, I believe their projects are remarkably similar. Indeed, by juxtaposing them in this way the work of each takes on new dimensions. Rivers' lifelong fascination with the question of vision was brought to a new intensity by the First World War. In particular his treatment of shell-shock victims forced him to re-examine, through a study of processes of visualisation, not just the mind, but society itself. Vertov too, like Rivers, was fascinated by the eye in the door. In his most original film, *The Man with a Movie Camera* (1929), Vertov's kino-eye probes spaces not normally accessible, breaking down conventional categories of inside and outside, subject and object, ways of seeing and seeing itself. Above all Vertov delights in the camera's own self-consciousness, its reflexivity as an integral part of its discovery of the world.

But the eye in the door sees further than the First World War and the Russian revolution. For beyond the immediate connections I have suggested between Rivers, Griffith and Vertov lies the work of the anthropological filmmaker Jean Rouch. I believe that the set of five films he made in the context of West Africa's anti-colonial revolution, beginning in 1954 with *Les Maîtres Fous* (*The Mad Masters*) and culminating in 1960 with *Chronique d'un Été* (*Chronicle of a Summer*), constitute the creative core of Rouch's work, as he sought to integrate his own complex subjectivity into his anthropological explorations of social life. Rouch drew no line around his own professional self. His eye looks both inwards and outwards. Like Rivers, but unlike Malinowski or Barker's character, Billy Prior, Rouch has no fear of the eye in the door.[13]

Notes towards a synthesis

Although in many important ways we have come to resist Malinowski and his famous declarations, much contemporary debate is about 'anthropology as a kind of writing' (Spencer 1989). Its inspiration owes much to Malinowski's famous boast: 'Rivers is the Rider Haggard of anthropology; I shall be its Conrad.'[14] But I think we have to resist this contextualisation too. For, as I argued at the beginning, 'visualising anthropology' involves a decisive shift of perspective, taking anthropology out of its literary context and placing it instead among the visual arts.

Rivers and Malinowski may still remain the key figures in such a project; but by considering them as 'visual artists', akin to filmmakers or painters rather than writers, we are led to pose some interesting new questions. These questions reach into the core of a 'visual' anthropology. But to suggest that we think of Rivers and Malinowski as filmmakers or painters is not entirely perverse, for each of these pioneers of anthropology's modern history was centrally concerned with the question of seeing. In Rivers' case, vision was at the core of his life's work, inseparable from his preoccupation with the relationship of the primitive to the civilised, the individual to society, the unconscious to the conscious. But, for him, vision was never an easy metaphor for the acquisition of knowledge; rather it was something deeply problematic and worthy of a lifetime's study. Malinowski, through his emphasis upon intensive fieldwork, elevated observation to a central place in anthropological practice; but he never subjected vision to close examination. This fundamental contrast between them is a key to any project concerned with visualising anthropology today.

I have explored a metaphor, the eye in the door – the mind's eye versus the spying eye – in an attempt to cast light on the nature of this difference.[15] Indeed this paper itself expresses these two aspects of seeing. The first part, tracing mirrored or symmetrical histories and featuring Malinowski as the official founder of the modern British school, uses the eye as a form of surveillance; it is a spying eye, detached and objective. Whereas the latter part, taking Rivers as its central figure, draws on the metaphor of the mind's eye, an eye which is introspective and reflexive, aware both of itself and its object, one which inserts the subject into the object. The metaphor thus stands for two kinds of anthropology whose relative standing is still crucial to the discipline's future today.

Barker draws a sharp contrast between the characters of Rivers and Billy Prior in both of her novels. It takes on a new intensity in the second, when Rivers in the course of a dream (for him an unusual experience of visualisation) recognises that his ethnology and psychology are not contradictory interests but indispensable to a unified anthropological project. Prior, however, experiences the opposite, as his personality disintegrates into a pathological dissociated state. He becomes a Jekyll and Hyde character. I think of Malinowski as a Billy Prior figure, an interloper, who endlessly crosses boundaries of identity and community, and belongs nowhere. Like Prior he becomes unable to connect the subjective and objective, inside and outside; and like Prior he is terrified of the eye in the door.

I believe that the crux of the matter lies in two fundamentally different 'ways of seeing' in anthropology (Berger 1972). Both emerged at a critical moment in the evolution of the modern project. But there was nothing modern about Malinowski's vision. Indeed it was extraordinarily archaic. For he was elevating human observation to a central place in the new science of anthropology at a time when the human eye was being widely displaced elsewhere from its privileged position as a source of knowledge (Jay 1993).

I suggest then that we think of Malinowski as a sort of Renaissance painter. His style was based on a careful examination of what was observed; there was emphasis on man's place in the world, on harmony, holism and integration. The great innovation of the Renaissance artists was the development of the principle of perspective, or as Berger writes: '*Man was the eye for which reality had been made visible*: the ideal eye, the eye of the viewing point of Renaissance perspective' (Berger 1985: 172, original emphasis). The eye becomes the centre of the visible world. Just as the world was once laid out for God and later for man, it is now laid out for the ethnographer.

But what I find intriguing in Malinowski's Renaissance project are the flaws in his monographs. For he is not, in fact, able to achieve that stillness, order and symmetry which distinguish the classic Renaissance work of art. Part of the problem stems from his transposition of a Renaissance project into the twentieth century, where it becomes merely an exercise in nostalgia: as Berger says, 'a means of diminishing instead of interpreting reality' (Berger 1985: 160). Moreover, Malinowski's Renaissance style contains unruly traces of all the other elements of art's history since then (notably, mannerism and romanticism), and he can never successfully extinguish these from his work.

In contrast, I believe that Rivers lies close to what Berger calls 'the moment of Cubism' (Berger 1985), a moment of transformation in our understanding and conception of the world which resonated far beyond the visual arts in the years before the First World War. It was expressed

in the Cubist shattering of the ordered perspectival space of the

Renaissance painting; there was no longer any single viewing point situated outside the picture, rather a multiplicity of viewpoints and perspectives emerged through the fluid interaction of space and form. For a brief creative moment, the Cubists found a way of synthesising whole and part, structure and process, object and subject.

Seen in this light, Rivers' scientific project had much in common with Cubism from its inception. It certainly was not a Renaissance project, as his early development of the genealogical method suggests. For, like the Cubists, he distrusted appearances, what Berger calls 'a frontal facing of nature' (Berger, 1985: 176). Rivers, whose anthropology ranged from neural science to world history via psychoanalysis and social organisation, approached an idealised whole through an exploitation of different angles and viewpoints, acknowledging always the partiality of perspectives, the subjective as inseparable from the objective. 'The Renaissance artist imitated nature. The Mannerist and Classic artist reconstructed examples from nature in order to transcend nature. The nineteenth-century artist experienced nature. *The Cubist realised that his awareness was part of nature*' (Berger 1985: 176, my emphasis).

I seem to have travelled a long way from D.W. Griffith and C.L.R. James's interpretation of his cinematic inventions which I cited at the beginning. But we have not, in fact, left that historical moment when the twentieth century was formed. By way of conclusion I want to return to a more explicit recognition of its uniqueness, and to underline its importance for anthropology today.

I have constructed an argument in this paper which has two parts – thesis and antithesis – followed by notes towards a tentative synthesis. Its context is the age of war and revolution to which James refers, that is, the First World War and the Russian revolution. The thesis of the paper took the notion of symmetrical histories, that cinema and modern anthropology share a separate but mirrored evolution in the period from 1890 to 1939. Specifically I argued that they both developed a professional ethos which was anchored in the creation of specialised practices: documentary film and scientific ethnography. Their privileged status as sources of truth and knowledge about the world, as forms of objective realism, was eventually underwritten by the state.

The antithesis I sought to construct, however, took as its starting point the work of Rivers in the context of the First World War. I suggested an alternative history which established new links between Rivers and the filmmakers Griffith and Vertov. What they share is a concern not just with questions of subjectivity (in opposition to the objective realism of the symmetrical history), but a concern with the integration of subject and object, individual and society, close-up and panorama in a moving, dialectical relationship.

Following Berger I have used the mirror as a metaphor for the narrative of my thesis; while the notion of a diagram evokes my argument in   *49* the antithesis. Mirrors reflect external appearances, objective reality; while diagrams are analytically constructed images of the relationship between parts and wholes. But these visual metaphors have deeper resonance, taking us to the heart of modern anthropology. For in exploring them I have opposed a Malinowskian way of seeing with that of Rivers; a Renaissance vision with a Cubist one; an eye which sees but cannot be seen and one which sees and can be seen.[16] As Berger reminds us, the Cubist revolution was not just about seeing the world differently; it also involved a fundamental change in our relationship to the world.

Much of what I have argued in this paper hinges on my contention that there were two fundamentally different responses to the disintegration of a social and political order; and they were expressed in different ways of seeing. One response was a retreat into professional expertise underwritten ultimately by the state; the other was a brief explosion of creative synthesis. Both Malinowski and Rivers stand at this point of fracture. Malinowski was remote from a disintegrating world (literally on a desert island), while Rivers was located at its centre, among shell-shock patients in Craiglockhart where the sense of collapse was palpable. Although Malinowski's work contains both subjective and objective dimensions, individual as well as society, his version of scientific ethnography laid the foundations for the suppression of the former in favour of the latter. It led to the complete separation of the pair in later anthropology. In this way professional anthropology adapted itself to the rise of state bureaucracy between the wars, as individuality became suppressed beneath the oppressive weight of impersonal society. It is the break-up of these state structures which has brought questions of subjectivity back to the fore. Anthropology, as we all know, has been deeply affected by this history.

Although such an interpretation can be made without any reference to a project concerned with 'visualising anthropology', Rivers' exploration of interior space through 'seeing' in dream and memory is highly suggestive. For the importance of his contribution to the task of 'visualising anthropology' lies in this attempts to bridge anthropology and psychology. We return once again to Griffith's cinematic innovation of a mobile camera tracking between close-up and panorama. In much the same way, Rivers (and the moment of Cubism) points to the elements necessary to anthropology's renewal as a project capable of bringing whole and parts once more into creative synthesis. If the door between inside and outside becomes unhinged, the eye has to learn to see both sides at once.

Notes

1. This experiment in visualising anthropology is written in a style which owes something to the techniques of cinema (Marcus 1994). Accordingly, the argument which I pursue is more impressionistic than scholarly; and I have sought to keep notes and references to a minimum.

I am grateful for their comments on earlier drafts to Keith Hart, Nikos Papastergiadis and Nigel Rapport; to the editors of this volume and its anonymous reviewers; and to colleagues at the Universities of Oxford, Manchester, Edinburgh and St Andrews.

2. Reprinted in James 1992: 247, original emphases.
3. A full discussion of the relationship between anthropology and cinema could not rest with the question of vision alone, since there is also the issue of voice, of the dialectic between sight and sound, the visual and the oral. A book in preparation, *The Anthropological Eye*, addresses this larger question.
4. See, for example, Schaffer 1994.
5. Barker's creative interpretation of Rivers' life opens up new possibilities in understanding his significance in twentieth-century intellectual history. As a novelist she has foregrounded his war work and explored the period in his life which is widely acknowledged by others to have been one of remarkable personal transformation, e.g. Slobodin 1978. The third volume of Barker's trilogy, *The Ghost Road*, won the Booker Prize in 1995. Its publication came too late for consideration here.
6. The original footage is now held at the National Film and Television Archive in London. A copy is held in the Rivers Laboratory, Department of Social Anthropology, University of Cambridge. See also Schaffer 1994. The islands lie between Australia and Papua New Guinea.
7. Original emphasis. Quoted by Dunlop 1983. I am grateful to the editors for reminding me that Baldwin Spencer's use of film was far more extensive and innovative than that made by the members of the Torres Strait expedition. See Cantrill 1982.
8. Gunning 1990.
9. For example, Langham 1981, Kuklik 1991, Slobodin 1978 and Urry 1972.
10. I am aware that some readers may find my characterisation of Rivers to be, like Barker's, somewhat idealised, especially in the context of the contrast I draw later between Rivers and Malinowski. My aim in this is to draw attention to the remarkable developments in Rivers' work and personality triggered off by his experience of the war. See also Grimshaw and Hart 1993.
11. See Michelson 1984.
12. Tomas 1992.
13. See *The Anthropological Eye*; Eaton 1979 and Stoller 1992.
14. Malinowski to Brenda Seligman, cited in Firth 1957.
15. I am aware that the contrast drawn here between subjective and objective modes of knowing is polemical. Indeed, their interdependence was established by Kant. My emphasis here is a response to the objectivism of much twentieth-century science, including the scientific ethnography of Malinowski's school. See Grimshaw and Hart (1995) and, for example, Okely 1975.
16. This conception finds echoes in Jackson's call for a new experiential anthropology. He writes: 'Eschewing the supervisory perspective of traditional empiricism (which, as Foucault observes, privileges gaze as an instrument of both knowledge and control), the radical empiricist tries to avoid fixed viewpoints by dispersing authorship, working through all five senses, and reflecting inwardly as well as observing outwardly' (Jackson 1981: 8).

References

Agee, J. (1963) *Agee on Film*, London: Peter Owen.
Barker, P. (1991) *Regeneration,* London: Viking.
—— (1993) *The Eye in the Door*, London: Viking.
—— (1995) *The Ghost Road*, London: Viking.
Bradbury, M. and McFarlane, J. (eds) (1976) *Modernism*, Harmondsworth: Penguin.

Berger, J. (1972) *Ways of Seeing*, Harmondsworth: Penguin.
— (1985) 'The Moment of Cubism', in *The White Bird*, London: Chatto & Windus (original edn 1969, London: Weidenfeld & Nicolson).
— (1992) *Success and Failure of Picasso*, London: Granta Books (original edn 1965, Harmondsworth: Penguin).
Cantrill, A. and C. (1982) 'The 1901 Cinematography of Walter Baldwin Spencer', *Cantrill's Film Notes* 37–8: 27–43, 56–8.
Carey, J. (1992) *The Intellectuals and the Masses*, London: Faber.
Clifford, J. (1986) 'On Ethnographic Authority', in J. Clifford and G. Marcus (eds) *Writing Culture*, California: University of California Press.
Dunlop, I. (1983) 'Ethnographic Film-making in Australia: The First Seventy Years 1889–1968', *Studies in Visual Communication* 9 (1):11–18.
Durkheim, E. (1915) *The Division of Labour in Society*, London: Macmillan.
Eaton, M. (1979) *Anthropology–Reality–Cinema*, London: British Film Institute.
Firth, R. (ed.) (1957) *Man and Culture: Essays in Honour of B. Malinowski*, London: Routledge.
Grimshaw, A. and K. Hart, (1993) *Anthropology and the Crisis of the Intellectuals*, Cambridge: Prickly Pear Press (Pamphlet no.1).
— (1995) 'The Rise and Fall of Scientific Ethnography' in A. Ahmed and C. Shore (eds) *The Future of Anthropology*, London: Athlone.
Gunning, T. (1990) 'The Cinema of Attractions: Early Film, its Spectator and the Avant-Garde', in T. Elaesser (ed.) *Early Cinema: Space, Frame, Narrative*, London: British Film Institute.
Jackson, M. (1981) *Paths Toward a Clearing*, Bloomington: Indiana University Press.
James, C.L.R. (1992) 'Popular Art and the Cultural Tradition', in A. Grimshaw (ed.) *The C.L.R. James Reader*, Oxford: Basil Blackwell.
Jay, M. (1993) *Downcast Eyes*, Berkeley and Los Angeles: University of California Press.
Kuklick, H. (1991) *The Savage Within: the Social History of British Anthropology, 1885–1945*, Cambridge: Cambridge University Press.
Langham, I. (1981) *The Building of British Social Anthropology*, Dordrecht: D. Reidel.
Malinowski, B. (1922) *Argonauts of the Western Pacific*, London: Routledge.
— (1967) *A Diary in the Strict Sense of the Term*, London: Routledge.
Marcus, G. (1994) 'The Modernist Sensibility in Recent Ethnographic Writing and the Cinematic Metaphor of Montage', in L.Taylor (ed.) *Visualising Theory*, London and New York: Routledge.
Michelson, A. (ed.) (1984) *Kino-Eye: The Writings of Dziga Vertov*, London: Pluto Press.
Okely, J. (1975) 'The Self and Scientism', *Journal of the Anthropological Society of Oxford* 6 (3):171–88.
Rivers, W.H.R. (1920) *Instinct and the Unconscious*, Cambridge: Cambridge University Press.
— (1923) *Conflict and Dream*, London: Routledge.
Schaffer, S. (1994) *From Physics to Anthropology – And Back Again*, Cambridge: Prickly Pear Press (Pamphlet no. 3).
Slobodin, R. (1978) *W.H.R. Rivers*, New York: Columbia University Press.
Spencer, J. (1989) 'Anthropology as a Kind of Writing', *Man* (n.s.) 24 (1):145–64.
Stoller, P. (1992) *The Cinematic Griot*, Chicago and London: University of Chicago Press.
Tomas, D. (1992) 'Manufacturing Vision: Kino-Eye, *The Man with A Movie Camera*, and the Perceptual Reconstruction of Social Identity', *Visual Anthropology Review*, 8 (2):27–38.
Urry, J. (1972) '*Notes and Queries on Anthropology* and the Development of Field Methods in British Anthropology, 1870–1920', *Proceedings of the Royal Anthropological Institute*: 45–57.

3

Beyond the Boundary: a consideration of the expressive in photography and anthropology[1]

Elizabeth Edwards

This essay attempts a reconstitution of the usefulness of still photography in anthropology.[2] Visual anthropology has concentrated largely on film, and discussion of, for instance, the political, structural or expressive possibilities of the visual has focused on these dilemmas as they have manifested themselves in film, regardless of who is behind the camera. The consideration of still photography has been centred on how-to manuals of method and analysis working within a largely unmediated realist frame (e.g. Collier and Collier 1986). Historical analyses, especially those concerned with deconstructing the historical sociopolitical relations of photographs, have made important contributions to historical perceptions within anthropology (e.g. Geary 1988; Corbey 1989; Theye 1989; Edwards 1992). Finally, there are a number of antiquarian ruminations, picture-books which have made images accessible but have added little to analysis or historiography (for instance Worswick 1979). But where can modern production in still photography go from here if it is to contribute beyond the level of the visual note-book[3] to which it has been largely relegated and its possibilities for visual interrogation be admitted?

Just as the success of film has often resulted from the informed and intelligent use of the possibilities of the *medium*, I shall argue here that the way to restore photography to a concrete contribution within the discipline is to harness those qualities peculiar to the *medium* of still photography. I shall argue that to achieve this anthropology must look beyond the disciplinary edges and reposition its practice within a wider photographic discourse. The polarisation of visual production should not necessarily be read therefore as oppositional, realist versus expressive, document versus art, but as objectively related and dialectically interdependent phenomena (Jameson 1990: 14). I shall also argue implicitly that this depends in part on the very materiality of the photographic object itself.[4] The argument is consequently an exploration of the interaction of anthropology and still photography on and beyond the disciplinary boundary.[5] As such, photography becomes the site for the articulation of other frames and other forms of expression and consumption. In so doing it establishes a fluidity between the scientific and   53 the popular, realism and expressionism, admitting images which are normally described as ethnographic into a broader photographic currency. Conversely, this fluidity allows the experimental inclusion of a specifically photographic expression, bringing to the fore the full and cogent extension of the medium's qualities. This latter is not a restatement of the modernist position of fetishistic concentration on the medium as message, that photography is ultimately about photography (Grunberg 1990: 6). In this context photography as a medium is not about photography *per se* but about its potential to question, arouse curiosity, tell in different voices or see through different eyes from beyond The Boundary.[6] Furthermore there are components of culture which require a more evocative, multidimensional, even ambiguous expression than the realist documentary paradigm permits (Anderson and Anderson 1989: 99). Through its increasing global strategies photography is capable of articulating its own particular culturally grounded voice within the discipline, one which anthropologists should recognise as capable of different but perhaps equally revealing ways of seeing over their traditional domain.[7] While the results of such enterprises might not necessarily be 'anthropological' in terms of a fully informed and integrated theoretical position, they nonetheless constitute documents of culture or cultural documents whose legitimacy is drawn from the fact that their creators are attempting to communicate values and negotiated realities which are integral to human experience and consciousness.

By its very nature this essay is exploratory and argumentative rather than presenting any clearly defined model. This will only emerge when some of these ideas have been tried out on the ground by anthropologists who are skilled photographers, not merely in the technical sense, but in the sense of the possibilities of photographic seeing and interrogation. In the words of Edward Weston, a photographer whose work is fraught with the tensions between realism and formalism, this involves: 'learning to see his subject matter in terms of the capacity of his tools and processes so that he can instantaneously translate the elements and *values* in a scene before him into the photograph he wants to make (Weston 1980: 173, added emphasis). In which case,

> Photography is basically too honest a medium for recording superficial aspects of a subject. It . . . exposes the contrived, the trivial, the artificial for what they really are . . . looking deeply into the nature of things, and presenting his subject in terms of their basic reality. It enables him to recall the essence of what lies before his lens with such clear insight that the beholder may find the recreated image more real and *comprehensible* than the actual object.
>
> (Weston 1980: 174, added emphasis)

While this statement comes from a more accepting realist position (even though Weston was a strong formalist) than one would argue within a modern photographic discourse, it stands as a valuable statement of belief on the incisive possibilities of photography that I shall argue here. Only through a photographic practice so informed, which presently might appear merely interesting and intriguing from within the discipline, can the *empirical* basis of these possible approaches be strengthened.

I am going to look at three bodies of material as short 'case-studies' which exemplify, in different ways, movement across The Boundary. The first might be construed as 'negative'. It examines the way in which modern tourist fantasy has been sustained by images of ethnographic veracity (of both material culture and social behaviours) which are legitimated through traditional anthropological concepts of culture and authenticity, premised on notions of 'visual truth'. I am using this 'negative movement' out of the discipline into popular culture, not only to highlight the fluidity of the realist image/anthropological document, but, at a more theoretical level, to reveal the ambiguities of the realist paradigm. As entrenched in 'ethnographic photography', it represents one of the cruxes of the documentary dilemma in still photography, that the more specific the image the more general its meaning; the more general, ambiguous, the image the more incisive it can become in its revelatory possibilities. This ambiguous space becomes central to the other two short 'case-studies' which look at the currency of images moving in the opposite direction, from beyond The Boundary into anthropology. They posit totally different ways of expressing culture visually which are seldom allowed to surface. As such they represent an opening of The Boundary, admitting the metaphorical, allegorical and expressive. First I discuss a series of photographs taken by photo-artist Elizabeth Williams working in Northern Sinai, Egypt, which explores the intersecting space between aesthetic expressive and ethnographic documentary in photography. The second of these 'experimental case-studies' constitutes a sampling of a diverse body of photography emanating from contemporary visual arts practice in which photographers are incorporating the very documents of anthropology's history. Their work is not only a direct challenge to anthropology's traditional constitution of the 'other' and the latter's visual encapsulation in the disciplinary archives but a confrontation with the past, in which history and experience are decentred, repositioned and reactivated through an expressive medium. It thus concentrates attention on the interface between anthropology and 'cultural expressive', a more intuitive and subjective rendering. Here the relation between fact and allegory is the site of institutional or disciplinary struggle. The nature of boundaries is such that, in this instance, there is no definite way of separating the factual from allegory, for cultural 'facts' are not necessarily 'true' and allegory 'false' (Asad 1986: 119). As every anthropologist knows, boundaries are dangerous spaces: the consolidation of the disciplinary paradigm depends on the exclusion or relegation to the status of 'art' or 'impression', 'those elements of the changing discipline that call the credentials of the discipline itself into question, those research practices that . . . work on the edge of disorder' (Clifford 1988: 135).[8] In such a context photography perhaps occupies what Winnicott, in psychology, has identified as the 'paradoxical third space' being neither inside in the world of fantasy (expression) nor outside in the world of shared reality. Rather it partakes of both these positions at once (cited in Davis and Wallbridge 1983: 163).

In part I am picking up two gauntlets. On the one hand is that thrown down by Peter Wollen (1982) in relation to the connection between knowledge, art and information and on the other is that argued by Bill Nichols in the context of film (1981). Nichols, drawing on Feyerabend and Kuhn, exhorts the anthropologist to admit the possibilities of alternative strategies to establish a non-antagonistic relation of converse priorities and recognise the occasional need of science for rhetorically induced imperatives and the overturn of 'reason'. Receptiveness to such activities, he argues, may open up 'new possibilities of what comprehending culture might entail' (ibid.: 248). It is precisely this that I would argue for still photography; through strengthening and articulating weaker or alternative positions, the motion or energy of the whole is sustained (Feyerabend 1993:21) thereby reinvigorating still photography's anthropological contribution. Within this frame, Feyerabend argues the desirability of pluralist methodology. To maximise the empirical and didactic content of held views, it becomes essential to introduce other views which he terms 'counter-rules' or 'counter-inductives' which are inconsistent with well-established theories. Furthermore, revelations cannot necessarily be made from within The Boundary. Rather we need an external standard, an alternative set of assumptions constituting an alternative world. In a position that parallels Winnicott's, Feyerabend argues, 'We need a dream world in order to discover the features of the real world we think we inhabit' (ibid.: 22). Further, he argues that formal properties of a practice (such as ethnographic photography) are revealed by contrast, not by the analysis of the thing itself. Knowledge is not a series of self-consistent theories converging towards an ideal view,[9] rather it is an *'ocean of mutually incompatible alternatives'* forcing others into greater articulation (ibid.: 21, original emphasis).[10] For this reason I am drawing a large part of my argument from discourses outside the accepted canons of visual anthropology: from contemporary photographic criticism, the dilemmas of photographic practice and the ambiguous spaces of postmodern documentary practice. The experience of considered and articulate photographic practice represented in these discourses constitutes precisely that set of 'counter-rules' which might enable still photography to constitute an active and individual voice within the discipline, premised on the expressive rather than the realist.

Anthropology is already familiar with these demands. The relationship, for instance, between ethnography and surrealism, where the continuous play of the familiar and strange establishes complementary and related elements in twentieth-century meaning and expression (Clifford 1988: 118–21). Literary awareness – the value of metaphor, figuration and narrative – has become recognised in anthropological writing as active at every level and capable of contributing to the anthropological endeavour (Clifford 1988: 4). Likewise creative texts expressive of culture such as novels, diaries, short stories and autobiography have come from beyond The Boundary to be absorbed into the new canon. In ethnographic writing they constitute the 'counter-inductive' in which, as I am arguing for photography, the two categories of compelling narrative (the expressive) and rigorous analysis (of which photography is the documenting tool) might be complementary rather than mutually exclusive (Behar 1993: 309, 317).[11] Nor are these ideas strange to photography. As early as 1922 Paul Strand was calling for the integration of science and expression, lest they develop independently as 'the destructive tool of materialism' and as 'anemic phantasy' (quoted in Wollen 1982: 181). Consequently what is being proposed here as a 'counter-inductive' is a creative photographic expressive[12] which constitutes and is constituted by a cogent, coherent interrogation, expression and interpretation of the subject and its significances within the full range of the medium's characteristics in which objective and subjective agendas come together.

Perhaps the first step in the production of a 'counter-inductive' for photography is to challenge the entrenched positivist, realist position in which photographic contribution to scientific knowledge depended on the accumulation of visual facts. Film was similarly implicated. What has emerged in these practices over the last twenty years has been the negation of the transparency of the medium. While the authorial voice has become an integral part of the structure of film, for the most part it has yet to permeate still photography as it is used in anthropology. Much consideration of photography has indeed been concentrated on the characteristics of the medium but these have been seen to limit its potential. The stillness of photography lies diametrically opposed to the flow which is the process of life (Sontag 1978: 81). Its spacio-temporal dislocations, its incipient fetishism and associated appropriating qualities (Metz 1990: 156–62), its narrative muteness, its ambiguities, its apparent dependence on text, its dangerous syllogisms, the rawness of its data, its apparent prevailing of surface detail over depth of understanding, its free-floating closures of meaning and its sociopolitical enmeshments have all been seen as embodying a dangerous ambivalence; a visual fracture of the cultural whole which 'threatens the context-seeking anthropologist who yearns for an explanatory "mesh" in which to entrap his intentions' (Pinney 1992b: 28). With the exception of Pinney, who argues strongly and convincingly for the filmic possibilities within the plane of the still photograph and the 'self-presence' of the photograph through the analysis of the lexical spaces of photography and film to reveal similarities rather than polarities, these inherent characteristics of the photographic medium have been couched in negative terms. They have concentrated on the objectifying or fetishising qualities (Sontag 1978; Burgin 1982; Barthes 1984; Metz 1990) of the ambiguity and fluidity of photography's signifiers (Barthes 1984). Further, much analysis has stressed the sociopolitical constructions and signifying properties of the image as an opaque, highly cultured and coded artefact, analogous with language. This position left little room for the subjective response for which Barthes (1984) has argued equally eloquently.

Were such characteristics of the medium to be constituted positively then it would follow that photography could be formulated so as to make deep and crucial visual incisions, which depend precisely on those ambiguities and essentialist metaphors. Photography can communicate about culture, people's lives, experiences and beliefs, not at the level of surface description but as a visual metaphor which bridges that space between the visible and invisible, which communicates not through the realist paradigm but through a lyrical expressiveness. As a consequence, as Kracauer has argued (1960: 22), the expressive (aesthetic) value of photographs 'would in a measure seem to be a function of their explorative powers'.

The use of the medium is linked to aesthetic style. The inevitability of style, while not unproblematic, has long been recognised in anthropology and is, of course, integral to its practices. Margaret Mead viewed aesthetic sensitivity as an added benefit to scientific fidelity (1975: 5). Formalist tendencies of photography do not necessarily conflict with realist interests; on the contrary they may help substantiate and fulfil it (Kracauer 1960: 16). However, one must distinguish here between an expressive approach which, in maintaining the integrity of the subject matter has revelatory potential, and a raw aestheticism, an overtly self-conscious collapse into formalism and *self*-expression. Style in photographic practice within anthropology should explore and communicate, not overwhelm the content in a way that objectifies and fetishises. If expressive visual dialects are to remain relevant within anthropology the transformational qualities of photography should not be over-exploited. Rather, the raw material should be focused upon so as simultaneously to record 'fact' and to make transparent, thus extending our vision in cultural terms beyond the surface by making that vital visual incision which can communicate beyond words. Indeed it is the tension between realism and reduction to regular communicable forms that creates the expressive stimulus (Firth 1992: 31) and should perhaps be seen as the crucial point of entry from beyond The Boundary. Nichols, following Brecht, has argued that realism runs deeper than unmediated verisimilitude. For Brecht realism involved 'discovering the casual complexities of a society/unmasking the prevailing view of things as the view of those who rule it . . . making possible the concrete and making possible the abstraction from it' (quoted in Nichols 1981: 64). In the context of this discussion this form of realism becomes doubly relevant, unmasking not only the structures and metaphors of the things themselves but those of the inscription and performances of their 'realist' representation: a 'counter-inductive' moving from the abstract to possible realities.

Expressive quality is the result of expressive or even poetic intent, the articulation of a subjective response. However, it cannot be constituted as a heightened form of Barthes' *punctum* which is grounded equally in subjective viewer response, although, of course, one does not preclude the other. Although like *punctum*, expressive modes refer to memory and allegory beyond the thing itself, they do not annihilate the medium (Barthes 1984: 42–5). Rather the modes refer to a presence of a kind of 'subtle *beyond*', the *punctum* which takes the viewer outside the frame (ibid.: 56), a bridging indexicality between the visible and the non-visible that is the root of the power of documentary incision, to reveal a thing, real and concrete though not actually visible (Mulvey 1989: 134).

However one can no longer assume that the incision is grounded in the social realist tradition which dominated photographic documentary from the interwar years, and was in part, at least in Britain, constituted through a currency of ideas and practices across The Boundary.[13] The crisis of representation which forced anthropology into its current reflexive position, and in which film played a major part, is paralleled beyond The Boundary in documentary practice. In the last fifteen years or so many perceptive photographers have moved increasingly away from recording surfaces, 'this-is-how-it-was', or even a politically charged 'this-is-how-it-is'. Rather, photographs have been conceived as capable of unravelling the deeper meanings and metaphors of cultural being. In many ways much of the work of this postwar generation, in Britain at least photographers such as Graham Smith, Chris Killip and, later, Owen Logan all photographing as 'insiders', might be described in broad terms as 'anthropological', for such photography is informed by acute observation of the interconnectedness of social and cultural identity. In this work the incisive and expressive nature of the image is judged by its ability to reach out and refer to an articulated cultural wholeness that underpins the fragments (Moore 1981: 195–6; Jeffrey 1992: 351–2). While such photographers might use the dislocating and distorting photographic frame as a meta-comment on the tensions between cultural or social identity and wider alienations of modern existence, others have broadened this ambiguity to explore the complexity of issues and events in order to convey their experience of those events and their confusion over events as much as the events themselves, acutely aware of the abyss between photographic appearances and the 'realities' they portray (Grunberg 1990: 186–7). The viewer no longer has the certainty of understanding 'this-is-how-it-was'. Instead, in works such as Gilles Peress's *Telex: Iran* or some of Susan Meiselas' work in Nicaragua, the viewer has a space and is conscious of the ambiguity of the image which allows access to the *experience* of a situation in all its complexity rather than the pretence of surface understanding. Instead of imposing a single meaning upon the viewer, held by context or caption, such work leaves open the different levels of interpretation: the image itself is a textual analysis (Chopra 1989: 3). As Grunberg has pointed out (1990: 194) this ambiguity, even blankness has its drawbacks; there is a fine line between a photograph of a confusing situation and a confusing photograph. But then I would argue that the documentary strength of such images lies precisely in their expressive understatement of the realist position. The potential of such experimental forms coming in from beyond The Boundary is in the clearly ambiguous structure. The difference between the sign and the referent, the connotating expression and the thing itself is made explicit, whereas the realist tradition has obscured the relationship (Nichols 1981: 43).

Postcards and the commoditisation of lives

It is precisely these apprehensions on the nature of still photography which enable the appropriation of reified representations of culture. Tourist postcards of traditional culture draw strongly on realist assumptions of the unmediated image, the analogue of visual experience. Thus they draw the legitimating structure of their images from precisely the realist, positivist assumptions of a knowable and recordable world which have informed the conventional use of the camera within anthropology.[14] Similarly the production, appropriation and consumption of such photographs within the tourist industry is based on a conception of the marketable product of 'culture' in terms of the 'traditional' or 'authentic'. This in turn has its origin within the disciplinary boundary in the constitution of the anthropological object.

Many of the photographs which are made into postcards present an ethnographic reality which at a purely denotative level might be described as 'real' or 'true': that is, they make some claim to represent and communicate accurately and without mediation, experience or social behaviours which have cultural relevance to the subject. Without such realist reassurance the image would fail to fulfil the fundamental tourist desire for 'authenticity' of experience which is couched firmly in the 'authenticity' of that observed. The content of the photography may appear documentary in quality, often captioned with 'ethnographic' information. This signifies another level of the real, that of objective observed science, a verifiable and indeed quantifiable authenticity. However, despite the strong realist signifiers, consumption of postcard images themselves is on a metaphorical plane, external to the image itself and its referent. For instance a series of high-quality postcards produced in Kenya show Maasai culture in the full lush 'Kodachrome' range. Typical is a photograph by A. Bertrand of a Maasai woman dressed in her beads, head shining with ochre. As a denoted image it is closed: it is 'of' something, ethnographically speaking, but it *means* nothing within the specifics of its content. Its multiple meanings begin emerging from its ethnographic veracity only when it moves beyond The Boundary gathering meanings as it goes, but those meanings are vested in the photograph itself, as signifier and signified collapse into one another. As such its meaning is metaphorical. Images of tourism cannot merely be seen as aberrant readings of ethnographic images because their context and material form dominate. Conversely the tourist industry depends precisely on easy closed readings of images. It is in its interests to control aberrant readings of the 'primitive', therefore the images are highly structured. This does not necessarily argue the transparency of the image, rather, that the images suggest closure in appropriate meanings that best fit the consumers' expectations in relation to the latter's own sense of rightfulness, rejecting those that challenge (Hall 1980). The strategies of realism are used to elicit 'right' or 'truthful' responses, just as is found in the more didactic forms of ethnographic film (Martinez 1992: 136).

The tourist industry bases its relentless placement of images on a concept of culture, long superseded within anthropology itself, as a perennial legacy of habits and understanding accumulated from the past, and constituted within a small-scale, wholly integrated group. This position depends almost entirely on images and the signifying properties of those images are circumscribed by the characteristics of photography itself in the strong tension between content and meaning. The power of these images resides in their creation of fragments which come to stand as wholes, reifying culture in the endless repetition of images. In many ways postcards functioning in this way fulfil Baudrillard's concept of 'simulation' which threatens the difference between true and false in that they mask the absence of a basic reality; that is, in the tourist fantasy of unchanging 'other worlds' of 'primitive' society that stand diametrically opposed to the modern world. Further, when the real is no longer what it used to be (in this instance 'modernisation' corrupts the object of desire), nostalgia assumes its full meaning: *signs* of reality (such as postcards) proliferate, but confer a spurious truth and authenticity (Baudrillard 1988: 170–71).

The function of postcards as both images and objects in this context can be clearly articulated if considered in terms of two influential theories of tourism; first MacCannell's argument (1976) that the tourist quest is a quest for the authentic, a desire which is integral to the structure of modern consciousness, an internal response to differentiation and alienation in modern society. Second is that postulated by Graburn (1978), that tourism is akin to a sacred experience, a form of ritual journey from the ordinary state to a spatially separated non-ordinary for a finite period. It follows that experience gained by contact with the 'Other' during this non-ordinary period constitutes life-enhancing 'spiritual capital' (Cohen 1989: 36; Brunner 1991: 239). In this context the postcard, a fragment of 'sacred reality', assumes the character of a relic, a souvenir from the other side. The postcard thus becomes an icon of tourist experience, a representation of the focus of devotion. The nature of photography enhances this consumption of images. In fragmenting both space and time, the photograph[15] mirrors tourist experience in which fragments are incorporated into a unified experience, one shaped by images.

The desire for what constitutes an authentic experience is informed by internalised concepts of what constitutes 'real' or 'authentic' as applied to any specific culture. This perception is rooted invariably in the past. 'Real' Aboriginals are shown in traditional activities – making boomerangs, playing didgeridoos and doing dot-paintings – authenticity and thus desirability is expressed through a series of markers of differentness yet is instantly recognisable. Cohen has shown (1989), for instance, how 'remote', 'primitive' and 'unspoilt' are used almost universally in material produced by the tourist industry as markers of desirability. These markers are presented in a timeless vacuum which photography sustains for, like the sacred, still photographs stand diametrically opposed to the flow of life. Indeed as both Barthes (1984) and Metz (1990) have argued, the photograph is a silent immobile *rigor mortis* of reality, a symbolic death. Thus for the use of ethnographic realist images within the tourist industry it could be argued that culture becomes dead through the act of photography, represented for tourist consumption by a moment that has vanished, or perhaps never existed in terms of the subject's experience. The image becomes a record of the constructed, inauthentic or pseudo-event fulfilling Baudrillard's model for emerging simulation (1988: 170–72). Clifford's comments (1988: 44) on the salvage paradigm as a 'relentless placement of others in a present becoming past' assumes particular relevance when applied to postcards where culture, or its simulations, is presented as a spectacle to be gazed at rather than as an active engagement with the world. This monolithic and timeless vision is reinforced by the postcard as the dislocation of photography collapses the past and the present into the synchronic: 'there–then' becomes 'here–now' and indeed vice versa (Barthes 1984: 44). This is exemplified by a postcard 'Australian Aborigines' (Figure 3.1)[16] which comprises a grid-like arrangement of images showing Aboriginal people engaged in stereotypical activities of hunting, playing the didgeridoo and making bark paintings. Individual technologies are not identified, rather they are collapsed into generalised cultural markers of alterity. The visual suggestion of the past is reinforced by the embalming nature of the caption

Figure 3.1 'Australian Aborigines'. First published c. 1960, purchased Melbourne, Australia, 1990.

which states 'Ancient traditions and crafts still thrive among modern-day Aborigines.' This is, of course, correct in ethnographic terms, but is couched in terms of a model of culture which positions 'authenticity' as residing in the past, unchanging without internal dynamic.

I have outlined this position of concepts and images moving out of the discipline across The Boundary, not because they are in themselves intellectually coherent in anthropological terms but because they constitute a body of material that draws its legitimation from popular assumptions of the discipline's project. Furthermore, precisely the same style of traditionalist genre images are found illustrating serious works on material culture. This highlights the ambiguity of the realist image, the scope, indeed depth, of its misappropriations and thus the fragility of a discourse where grounded in realism. Further, it constitutes an extreme position in demonstrating the problems which underlie assumptions of realist or document photography: its dislocations, the ambiguity of the relationship between signifier and signified, the ambivalence of its meanings (apparently didactic in appearance but metaphorical in consumption). As such it becomes an extreme example of the position against which this paper is arguing.

Strange Territory

I am now going to consider the positive possibilities of the character of   *63* photography as a medium and suggest their constitution as a 'counter-rule' to the realist visual-notebook. I am going to consider a series of photographs taken by Elizabeth Williams in Northern Sinai in 1993[17] which constitute a joint project with the Pitt Rivers Museum, University of Oxford. The photographs were conceived precisely as a critique of the fixity of imagery of photographs normally described as ethnographic, in that they are conceived as having a high level of verisimilitude. As we have seen, such imagery which crosses The Boundary can be absorbed into fictions diametrically opposed to the anthropological. As such Elizabeth Williams's photographs suggest an alternative, the creation and examination of the intersecting space between the aesthetic expressive and ethnographic documentary in photography, and where 'art' and 'document' should be seen as two rhetorical modes within the overall photographic discourse (Anderson and Anderson 1989: 99).

The project was conceived as a critical dialogue of images and text which used the postcard as the common medium. Images were sent in postcard format by Williams in the field to me, the curator. I responded in text and image, purchasing postcards of stereotypical views of Oxford, dreaming spires, gowned figures and All Souls in the morning mist, which also had some visual or metaphorical comment on the Sinai material. Williams responded visually, and so the dialogue continued.[18] Consequently the notion of the postcard as a cultural object which moves across boundaries is central, representing as it does both the appropriation of the ethnographic into the fantasies of popular consumption and as an object, becoming an archetype of the 'inauthentic' and stereotypical.

The photographs reject the premising and privileging of visual truth, preferring to use the poetics of image and object, metaphor and quotation. The photographs actually draw, rather, on the very nature of photography itself, exploring the balance between form and content, between intellect and intuition. For the role of the photographic expressive is to *intuit* the form for the content, carefully moulding the precise, contained, connate delineations of surface and moment into the fluid narrative which is the defining feature of a photographic work. The realist mode of these images anchors them not only in the physical world, in a culture, but in those very characteristics which are inherently photographic: of fragment, of ambiguous temporal relationships, of an expression of a reality through ephemeral configurations. Their intention is equally poetic or allegorical, but paradoxically – and this is central to my argument – formative or expressive elements do not necessarily conflict with the realist tendency. On the contrary, they may help to substantiate and fulfil it (Kracauer 1960: 16; Badger 1992: 91), commenting on profound issues relevant to the experience of people represented.

A case in point is Williams's series of four sets of images of a deserted Bedouin camp (Figures 3.2 and 3.3). These were produced as fold-out

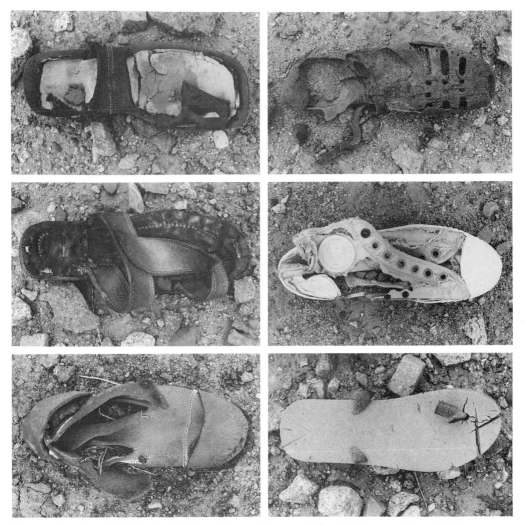

Figure 3.2 (read vertically) Elizabeth Williams, 'Strange Territory: Deserted Bedu camp – Shoes', 1993.

postcards[19] thus forming a narrative through the juxtaposition of images and choice of subject matter.

Despite their surface similarities to late Abstract Expressionism[20] especially Rauchenberg, they remain true to photographic integrity in using the interplay of the realist and expressive to communicate about culture and to allude to wider issues (in this instance the Arab–Israeli War [1967] and changing uses of land). Edited like ethnographic text, linear narrative becomes a metaphor for social change, the realism of the recorded material culture has a didactic quality but assumes a symbolic quality as through all this the desert remains inviolate, consuming and overpowering the material records of human encounter with it. *65*

Figure 3.3 (read vertically) Elizabeth Williams, 'Strange Territory: Deserted Bedu camp – Cloth', 1993.

Photographs such as these are questioning, positing issues, rather than proclaiming 'this-is-how-it-is'. The metaphors signified by the material culture and its relation with the desert – the multiple frames, the rhythm of repetition, the possibilities of abstraction – communicate an incisive truth about the relationship of the Bedouin with their desert and their *experience* of it in the late twentieth century.

A series of thirteen photographs of tourist transactions in a market uses the telling power of minute circumstantiality in another way. The photographs are consciously framed as fragments (Figure 3.4). The hands of the parties to the transaction (of selling/buying jewellery) fill the frame; fingering jewellery, offering and passing money. It is not clear how many people are involved or which objects precisely are for sale, for the links between proffered object and worn object are continuous.

All these relationships are left ambiguous.[21] The focus is entirely on the nature of the commodity transaction. The images are captioned through fragments of text (taken from Edwards 1996) which are not tautological: they constitute a different voice but still one standing for the confusion of the encounter. The denoted image is thus intentionally confusing. The characteristics of the medium are used to present quotations of the specific encounter as a wider metaphor of the ambivalence of tourist relationships. These metaphors counter precisely the clearly articulated cultural 'truths' of the postcard. Thus the expressive use of the fragment within the medium, where the fragment is used self-consciously to play on its signifying role, articulating a set of correspondences which preclude the notion of completeness. The fragments refer rather to contents outside the frame, to history or memory or cultural experience. Such recognition of expressive quality may be merely tacit, but the point of visual incision comes when this becomes consciously articulated in response to the photograph (Kracauer 1960:19; Berger and Mohr 1982: 122; Jeffrey 1992: 352).[22]

Yet on another level the fragmenting nature of the photographs – the framed fragment, teased out, removed and caressed through the interplay of colour, texture and form – relate very directly to anthropological practice. Participant observation in anthropology has stressed the minutiae, not out of a desire for wholeness *per se* but of the realisation that what looks insignificant to one way of thinking and perceiving may be singularly significant to another. It is this concept which is central to any

Figure 3.4 Elizabeth Williams, 'Strange Territory: Bedu market', 1993. Detail, one image from installation.

extension of photographic practice within anthropology which reaches beyond a realist paradigm. Williams's series entitled 'Domestic Surveillance' comprises a series of photographs taken from a fixed location overlooking boundary space, the opening and shutting of a door between the street and the courtyard and house. The construction of this set becomes an allegory of ethnographic writing for, like anthropology, it constructs a generality from specific instances of significance. Although the series appears as an integrated narrative of a day, close reading of the images betrays the series' construction. While its mode is realist, the narrative constitutes a 'serious fiction' as a poetic examination of spatial relations. In its Foucauldian reference, the series title forces the viewer to place him/herself consciously in relation to the photograph, hinting at the appropriating nature of such fictions.

Clearly this is a subjective space, and a dangerous one at that, where the blending of stylistic conventions allows for greater efficiency in packaging common values (Gross 1988: 191). Conversely, the revelatory and possibly inspirational nature of photographic appearances might, if properly constituted, create a positive agenda for inherent ambiguities. As Berger and Mohr suggest, 'Everything depends on the quality of the quotation chosen' (1982: 119): this applies equally to ethnographic 'documentary' and to photographic expressive.

Experimentation around the idea of the postcard, not merely as an image format but as a material *object* in its own right, is central to the workings of the currency of the image. As material culture objects, postcards collapse iconographic form, content and material form into certain cultural expectations of the function of the object. Thus the 'appropriateness' of the image is vested as much in the image-as-object as the image-as-meaning. Elizabeth Williams's photographs explore this idea of the relationship between image and object in a series of highly formalised fragments of material culture: in this instance, articles of clothing in the collection of the North Sinai Heritage Centre. The modernist appearance of the clothing fragments is immediately fractured by the addition of cowrie shells, mother-of-pearl buttons or press-studs sewn over the image of the same item on the surface of the photograph itself

These applied three-dimensional items fracture the flat plane of the photograph as material object and launch it on another trajectory, a sort of transpace between image and object. Thus the communicative and revelatory possibilities of these images and others from the same body of photographic work are based not only in ambiguity of content but in the way in which they fracture the cultural expectations of the object itself. This can be extended to posit fundamental questions about how images are received, for much theory of meaning in photographic discourse has overlooked the very plasticity of the image/object. To what extent can the image itself, as object, interrupt or challenge the discursive environment?

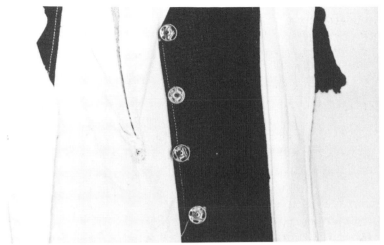

Figure 3.5a Elizabeth Williams, 'Strange Territory: Objects – Poppers', 1993.

Figure 3.5b Elizabeth Williams, 'Strange Territory: Objects – Shells and Buttons', 1993.

Certainly such photographs are not easy to comprehend. They do not slip easily into preconceived notions of reading culture, depending, as they do, on response to culture where subjectivities of both production and consumption are clearly articulated. The metaphors are those of the creator/viewer, not the culture itself – how could they be otherwise? The intersection of this subjectivity with the nature of photography itself perhaps raises questions that linger. They may not necessarily be answered – this we have to accept if we are to admit alternatives beyond the realist – but I would argue that the questioning in itself makes the viewer acutely conscious of lived experience and the ambiguous nature of its representation precisely through the agency of lyrical photographic expression, embodying narrative depth, through association and a multiplicity of closures. Such images make no claim to be primary documents in the conventional sense of the 'knowability' of culture. They draw instead on those ambiguities which have come to characterise the postmodern photographic aesthetic. In many ways these characteristics reflect moves in anthropological writing in which anthropological authority is decentred to stress the imperfect control of the ethnographer, an inconclusive narrative being used to open up a closed authority (Clifford 1988: 43). As I argued above, through the 'new documentary' movement the rationale of the photographer is made explicit, and this might reflect his/her own uncertainty. As such photographs might create a interpretative space for reflexive reading, an 'openness' of the active co-construction of knowledge in a way similar to that argued for film by Martinez which involves the viewer in the need to look more actively:[23]

The positivist notion that the more 'objective' and distant accounts of culture are more 'truthful' and 'neutral' and therefore better entrées into 'authentic' instruction, may prove false and naïve because it overlooks the mediating role of interpretation before, during and after the construction of 'factual' knowledge and thus also conceals the ideological impact of visual media. (1992:53)

The strategies suggested here actually clear a subjective space where the subjectivity of both the creator and viewer are brought to the fore.

Repositionings

I want to turn finally to another movement over The Boundary and consider briefly a sample of work by photographers working within contemporary visual arts who are using the visual documents of anthropology's history to counter the traditional anthropological categorisation of peoples and experience, and in some cases to confront and reinscribe the artists' own cultural identity and history. As such these works constitute an expression of faith and strength in a new order, and a positive renegotiation with the old. They represent part of a political struggle to assert the unique value of different cultural voices and claims to shared access to resources and institutions. Further, they represent not merely individual talent and creative urges but constitute a response to collective norms of judgement, for instance archiving and classificatory control. The generalising frames of anthropology are demolished in these works to be reconstituted as localised histories or contested histories and a re-articulation of that experience. Access to photography has allowed new perspectives on the kind of imagery which was commonplace in anthropology's history (Onus 1993: 293–4). Thus opening up the apparently fixed meanings of images has been fundamental to much black and indigenous image-making both in the documentary tradition and in visual arts practice. This applies not only to voices constructed within the visual arts but to readings of film, photographs and other 'traditionalist' anthropological texts outside the disciplinary mainstream (Martinez 1992: 149; Bailey and Hall 1992: 18). Clifford has argued (1988: 115) that the most problematic and politically charged aspect of the 'pastoral' allegories of 'other' is its relentless placing of the 'others'' present in the past, a process we saw with the postcard images discussed earlier. He poses the question of how ethnographies might be conceived if diverse cultures were represented as associated with the future. This would require a refiguring of the ethnographic text.

The kind of work under consideration here, the repositioning of anthropology's archival images into contemporary practice, represents precisely such a fracture, for it concerns itself with cultural identity, self-determination and future (Young Man 1992), a confrontation with cultural loss, and with re-engaging the temporally dislocated photograph within active histories. There is a danger that this kind of exercise can only be achieved by *recognising* the dominant codes and engaging in discourse with them. Because of the nature of photography – its stillness, apparent voicelessness and lack of obvious narrative – mere inversion of conventional codes does not necessarily decentre their hold, merely exchanging one fixity of identity for another, rather than instituting a fluidity which allows a full and sometimes contradictory photographic expression. For decentring means a move away from essentialism, in allowing 'identity' to signify a range of experiences which cannot be articulated in one form, one photography or one voice. This pluralism of representational practice in photography breaks up the realist relationship between image and spectator on which so much ethnographic work has depended (Tabrizian 1987: 35; Mulvey 1989: 184; Bailey and Hall 1992: 21). This is a similar frame of argument that applied to the ambiguity inherent in Elizabeth Williams's work discussed above.[24]

A number of artists working today are exploring these issues using photography as one of a range of available media.[25] I am concerned here with specifically photographic practice incorporating or alluding to historical anthropological images. However, it must be stressed that while a broad thematic link is presented in my particular argument, the individual work is responding to distinct and historically specific cultural experiences. Perhaps some of the photographs most widely disseminated and evocative using 'anthropological documents' reworked into positive expressions are those of Leah King-Smith from Melbourne, Australia. Using ethnographic images from the State Library of Victoria, she has extended their more recent readings as strong documents of colonial encounter. King-Smith uses the emotional power of these images as expressive documents and as a point of departure for new and discrete works of art, using contemporary manipulative photographic techniques to 're-place' the Koori people captured within historical images in an Australian landscape of her own making, drawing on her own Aboriginal experience. The images thus work towards deconstructing definitions of Aboriginality, as constructed through colonial photography, to develop their own changing and different articulations of Aboriginality (Williamson 1994). As such 'this photo-composition series is essentially about renewing white people's perceptions of aboriginal peoples . . .' (King-Smith 1992: 8). In the resulting images, hugely printed in Cibachrome, the people appear as spectral figures, emerging from an imposed obscurity, reasserting power over the land, gaining power from the land, a land of the Koori's own making, symbolically remade by the photograph (Sloan 1992: 10). Their meaning is unmistakable, exemplifying the mutual compatibility of expression and closure.

In a similar vein some photographer-artists have used installation work to examine the intersection of histories in which anthropology is implicated. The work of Finnish photographer Jorma Puranen has used archival images of Sami people taken for Prince Roland Bonaparte in 1884 from the archives of the Musée de l'Homme in Paris. These have been rephotographed and enlarged on plexiglass panels and reinserted in the landscape thus constituting an imaginary metaphorical homecoming (Puranen 1993: 96) (Figure 3.6). In some cases the placing of light within the installation gives the impression of the images being rephotographed back into the land (Edwards 1995: 320). This return is saved from mere romanticism not only by the reference to modern land use, but more importantly, by the way in which the viewer is confronted with their own history and the nature of photographic appropriation.

Figures 3.6a and b
Jorma Puranen, from
the series 'Imaginary
Homecoming',
1990–91.

As the viewer looks through the images into landscape beyond they are confronted by faces of the past in the earth, on trees, staring straight into the camera. Yet at the same time the viewer is acutely aware of the historical nature of their action, re-viewing is placed inescapably in the continuing discourse. The temporal intersection which photography allows comes together in a spatial intersection, rearranging and reconstituting the spatial dimension of historical experience (Ripatti 1993: 14; Edwards 1995: 319–20). Further, these representations move from image to object and back to image, reflecting the materiality of the photograph as object and the people it represents. The representations move in different spaces, from the landscape of northern Norway and Sweden to the 1992 Rotterdam Photography Biennale where the material was shown as installation and where the photographs themselves actually enclosed space, an inversion of photography's usual spatial relationship.

There is also contemporary work which refers back to the postcard imagery discussed earlier, either directly or historically, through use of framing and colour. In this context, the postcard becomes the archetypal static objectifying image, commoditising bodies, transformed through image to exchangeable objects. Such consumptions of postcards render the voices of their subjects mute, they become literally a voiceless commodity. This issue has been tackled in Britain, for instance, by Ingrid Pollard who has used the idea of the postcard in a number of her photographic works. In *Pastoral Interludes* (1986) the rural English idyll, the Lake District landscape, combines with personal photographs. The prints are hand-coloured which emphasises the lushness of the landscape and the black people who populate it, conflating ideas of 'natural beauty' (Jones 1992: 100), yet there is a tension because the ideas of the past inherent in the reading of such idylls refer on one hand to the metaphor of freedom and transcendence which natural beauty suggests but at the same time to the unease of black people in a rural landscape. 'It's as if the Black experience is only lived within an urban environment . . . I walked as lonely as a black face in a sea of white . . .' (Pollard quoted in Jones 1992: 100). A 1993 exhibition *Message Carriers*[26] included a series of allegorical photographs by Carm Little Turtle. These works refer obliquely to postcards in their ambiguous framing and sepia toning, but are violently punctuated with vivid colour, reminiscent of the crude use of colour in 1930s postcards of 'Indians' of the American southwest (Carm Little Turtle 1995). Through metaphor of content, frame, colour and texture these articulate the suggestion of a spirituality of the whole beyond fractured appearance, a bridge between the visible and invisible that, as I have argued, is the function of photographic expression of culture. Taking a different perspective on the same issue, photographer and installation artist Shaheen Merali has used precisely the kinds of modern postcard images I discussed earlier to confront the packaging of the global village as a commodity in which consumers represent their own constructed worlds to themselves, marginalising the subject matter on which those would focus.[27]

In a similar conceptual vein to Ingrid Pollard's work, but integrating historical anthropological documents, Claudette Holmes used a page entitled 'The Lucknow Immigrant' from an album in the British Museum[28] as a base-motif for a series of photographic montages (Figure 3.7). Historical photographs, including one from Torday's 1906 expedition to the Congo (of Torday's servant, Sam, smoking a cigar) are torn and presented emerging from beneath semi-transparent gauze.

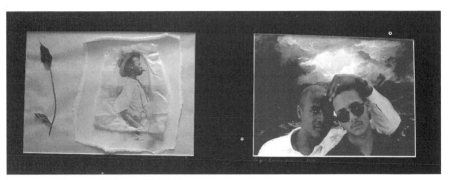

Figure 3.7 Claudette Holmes, 'Untitled', 1993.

Their fractured physicality stresses the crucial materiality of the photograph. Juxtaposed are strong positive images of black people's experience in 1990s Britain montaged into 'classic' English landscapes by very 'English' artists such as Constable and Turner. The contemporary figures, who are not metaphors but individualised and named, literally emerge from out of the landscape to express both the desire and right of black people to full unqualified belonging in Britain.[29] It becomes a fusion of personal and collective history.

All the work to which I have referred highlights questions of identity and expression, confrontation and absolution, which are deeply relevant to lived experience, an experience of reality which is always changing. The juxtaposition of images and realities in openly contradictory ways, as exemplified in Holmes's work, opens the debate and admits the possibility of creating another visual language, one which is rooted in both the reality of lived experience and incisive articulation of that experience (Hall 1983: 17). As authentic late twentieth-century expressions of identity, of cultural being, these photographs comply more fully with the classic notion of the anthropological document and thus should be of primary interest to anthropologists interested in such issues. However, if the project of contemporary anthropology itself is not necessarily fully

understood outside the discipline, there is a possibility that anthropological interest might be resisted, rather than seen as opening a space for mutual renegotiation.[30]

These problems of communication notwithstanding, photographic work of this nature becomes an important expressive body of material of which anthropologists should be aware for it challenges the whole institutional structure of the Western academy and the meanings of the photographs locked within this system (Young Man 1992). The aesthetic/artistic merits of works such as those discussed here are neither here nor there for this argument.[31] What is important is that it happens – it is an expression, a comment which sometimes operates beyond words or text. It is purely visual, exploitative of the photographic medium itself with all its special characteristics which have been perceived as so problematic. Again, like *Strange Territory*, discussed earlier, it creates a space for subjectivities which might permit constructed domains of truth as 'serious fictions'. These strategies, as Clifford has argued (1988: 10), once recognised allow the emergence of 'diverse inventive possibilities for representation'. Perhaps the expressive, subjective, serious fiction is precisely the 'counter-rule' which will suggest a role for still photography as an expression of culture. Just as the decentring of the authorial ethnographic voice has opened up and differently constituted ethnographic writing, so identity and representation cannot be articulated in one form, one photography or one voice (Bailey and Hall 1992: 21). Much of the work discussed here is concerned with making visible, in precisely the same way as other voices are being admitted and articulated in ethnographic texts.

All the material I have discussed is created and largely consumed outside visual anthropology. All of it relies on concepts and practices which have crossed The Boundary into other discourses. While I would not argue that such material constitutes a primary anthropological document, anthropologists should be aware of other ways of articulating their traditional territory – one which is fast fragmenting. They should be responsive to resonances of representations of their own making beyond The Boundary which flow from the practice of ethnographic photography within the broader currency of photography that recognises 'expressive' and 'realist' as two not incompatible rhetorics within this currency. Conversely, in delineating a 'counter-rule' the realist paradigm in still photography can itself be decentred. In that ambiguous yet revelatory space created by cogent photographic expressive, photography can yield to 'the desirability of not comprehending everything' (Pinney 1992a: 26). If one accepts, as I have argued, that the characteristics of still photography – its fragmentation, dislocation, non-narrative line – might be presented as positives, then the realist imperative which demands that all is revealed, laid out for our consumption, is indeed fractured by the *inevitability* of not comprehending everything. Yet photographs contain so much *more* that they continually reappear, make their presence felt, as they come back into different circulations. In crossing The Boundary the initiate must learn new knowledge to enable him/her to cope with the unfamiliar which will ultimately be absorbed and enrich. This chapter is a little push in that direction.

Notes

1. I am very grateful to Marcus Banks, Howard Morphy and the two anonymous readers for their many constructive comments and to Alison Devine Nordström, Joanna Sassoon and Joan Schwartz for feeding me so much material impossible to track down in Britain and their comments on various parts of the manuscript. Finally I am indebted to Claudette Holmes, Jorma Puranen and Elizabeth Williams for discussing their work with me at length and for allowing me to reproduce their photographs here; they are generous colleagues.

2. This might appear at first glance a somewhat fruitless, indeed Luddite, exercise in the face of the electronic imaging revolution which completely obliterates the assumed relation between physical reality and photographic image. I would turn this around and argue that it is precisely because analogical privileges of photography are fast disappearing, with dangerous consequences for the purely realist, notebook mentality of much anthropological photography, that if still photography is to maintain an active and meaningful voice, a total reassessment of its possibilities must be addressed. This paper is merely one of those steps in the realignment.

3. The poor quality of both photography and reproduction in many anthropological works suggests a systematic marginalisation of the visual in anthropological analysis.

4. For much more than film or video, the photograph is an object/image which one can hold in one's hands, inscribe, cut with kitchen scissors, paste into albums, send to one's friends.

5. By implication one cannot totally exclude photographic communication over cultural boundaries, but this is beyond the main focus of this paper.

6. In writing of The Boundary I am consciously reifying the space of encounter between anthropology as it perceives its disciplinary identity and that which it excludes. But this is a necessary rhetorical device to establish what photography has been categorised as 'ethnographic' and what has not. Anthropology as a discipline is, of course, far from static, its boundaries are indeed fluid, but little of this fluidity has related to its perception and use of still photography.

7. I am not concerned here with the many projects which have used photography in, for example, health projects, family therapy and other branches of psychiatric counselling (see for instance Berman 1993; Ruby 1995:180–82), for despite their structure and potency, their starting point has been based on social realist premises rather than expressive in the terms in which I am discussing it here.

8. The problems of this area are exemplified by the passionate arguments concerning the 'anthropological merits' of Robert Gardner's film on Banares, *Forest of Bliss* (Parry 1988; Moore 1988; Chopra 1989; Ostor 1989; Ruby 1989, etc.). The debate has been perceptively discussed by Loizos (1993) who parallels the expressive response found in Gardner's films to symbolist reaction against the realist position in art at the beginning of the twentieth century. I would argue a similar position for still photography in the late twentieth century.

9. That perfect value-free representation for instance?

10. This after all has been the guiding tenet of anthropology's enthusiasm for 'indigenous media' (see Turner 1992 and for critiques of that position: Moore 1992 and Faris 1993).

11. In her feminist critique of Clifford and Marcus' *Writing Culture* and introduction to the essays which constitute this special issue of *Critique of Anthropology*, Behar includes a series of photo-collages by Lisa Pope as the first essay. However, the visual is then marginalised in precisely the way Behar argues Clifford and others marginalise women's contribution to anthropology. The photo-collages are described as 'beautiful' and 'accompanying' with no comment on how they might communicate on different but equal terms with textual essays. The three lines given to them collapse into a comment on the accompanying *text.*

12. I am purposely avoiding the word 'aesthetic'. I find its suggestion of an 'absolute value' derived from Western connoisseurship, with the same claims to value and standards as painting or drawing, unhelpful. Within photographic writing and practice this has largely meant a classic, fine art-derived Western aesthetic which suggests a universalist judgemental position on photography which I find untenable in the contexts of much of the material I am discussing here.

13. For instance those involved in the Mass Observation unit in Britain in the 1930s attended Malinowski's seminars at the London School of Economics where the discussion was on anthropological method (rather than photography) which later moved across The Boundary to influence the work of that group (Firth 1957: 7).

14. For a much extended consideration of modern tourist postcards and traditional culture as a tourist commodity, see Edwards 1996.

15. For the purposes of this argument I am using the terms photograph and postcard interchangeably. The point is that a postcard is the means of transmission of a commercially produced and thus commercially targeted form of travel photography.

16. I am grateful to Nu-color-vue Productions for their co-operation in allowing me to reproduce this postcard and for the information that it was first produced about thirty years ago. My postcard was bought in about 1990, and thus illustrates the long shelf-life of images in this context.

17. Elizabeth Williams was a Leverhulme Fellow and working as British Council photographer-in-residence at the North Sinai Heritage Centre in Egypt.

18. A joint exhibition of this exploration, *Strange Territory*, ran simultaneously at the Pitt Rivers Museum, Oxford, and the Museum of Modern Art, Oxford, in September and October 1994. Another version was shown at the Derby Fotofest, October 1995.

19. Taking their object form from those sets of concertina fold-out postcards, 'Greetings from Brighton', and so forth.

20. Elizabeth Williams first trained as a painter before turning to photography.

21. Williams told me later that the tourists were trying to buy the women's actual clothing, extending notions of authenticity to almost photographic precision, the item literally 'taken off' the object of desire.

22. One should add that such a position must arise from expressive intent rather than incidental visual correspondences which ignore the historical circumscriptions of the image's production. For instance, the abstract forms of Roger Fenton's 'Royal Rifle Competition at Wimbledon' of 1860 have been greeted with delight by modernist critics, hailing Fenton as a proto-modernist! Jasper Johns' 'Target' series bears an uncanny resemblance to Fenton's photograph. (I am grateful to Dr. Bodo von Dewitz for drawing this particularly apposite example to my attention during conversation.)

23. It is significant in the context of this argument that Martinez prefaces his paper with a work of photographic expressive, a photo-montage by Stacey Rowe (after Martinez's own design) which articulates the ambiguous relationship between African women by a river and viewers/spectators of ethnographic film.

24. Beyond the scope of this paper are works which extend these ideas beyond the influences of anthropology; however, they should not be overlooked. A fine instance is *Zabat*, an electrifying series of nine photographic portraits by Maud Sulter. The portraits extend the ideas I have been discussing here using the rhetorical device of presenting black women's power in terms of the imagery of classical

Western portrait painting and with reference to the Greek Muses who themselves represented memory and later the arts and sciences. The implication is that these women are not merely to be looked at but heard (Richon 1990).

25. For instance the work of Jane Ash Poitras in Canada, Luis Benedit in Argentina, Tracy Moffatt in Australia and José Bedia in Cuba.
26. Photographic Resource Center, Boston, 1993 and US tour.
27. Some of Shaheen Merali's work, including the postcard installation, was shown in an exhibition entitled *Confrontations* at Walsall Museum and Art Gallery in October 1993.
28. The album page was used as the basis of a discussion of indexicality by Pinney (1992b) in whose text Holmes found it (personal communication). A transparency of the page was also used as a metaphor of anthropological inscription in the exhibition *The Impossible Science of Being*, Photographers' Gallery, London, October 1995–January 1996.
29. This series was commissioned by Birmingham City Libraries and was shown at an exhibition *Negative Stereotype to Positive Image*, September–November 1993, curated by Peter James. A reworked version of the exhibition was shown at The Watershed, Bristol, January–March 1995.
30. This is a personal view born of many conversations with artists and photographers over the years.
31. I shall leave this to the contemporary art curators.

References

Anderson, R and K. Anderson (1989) 'Art for Anthropology's Sake', *Visual Anthropology* 2 (1): 99–101.

Asad, T. (1986) 'Comment on "On Ethnographic Allegory"', in J. Clifford and G. Marcus (eds) *Writing Culture*, 19–122, Berkeley: University of California Press.

Badger, G. (1992) 'The Spider Who Spins the Sky', in D. Parker (ed) *Broken Images: The figured Landscape of Nazca*, Manchester: Cornerhouse.

Bailey, D.A. and S. Hall (1992) 'The Vertigo of Displacement', in *The Critical Decade Ten–8* 2 (3): 15–23.

Barthes, R. (1984) *Camera Lucida*, trans. R. Howard, London: Fontana.

Baudrillard, J. (1988) *Selected Writings*, ed. M. Poster, Cambridge: Polity Press.

Behar, R. (1993) 'Introduction: Women Writing Culture: Another Telling on the Story of American Anthropology', *Critique of Anthropology* 13 (4): 307–25.

Berger, J. and J. Mohr (1982 [1989]) *Another Way of Telling*, Cambridge: Granta.

Berman, L. (1993) *Beyond the Smile: The Therapeutic Use of the Photograph*, London: Routledge.

Brunner, E. (1991) 'The Transformation of Self in Tourism', *Annals of Tourism Research*, 18: 238–50.

Burgin, V. (1982) *Thinking Photography*, London: Macmillan.

Carm Little Turtle (1995) 'Work from "She Wished for a Husband, Two Horses, and Many Cows"', in *Strong Hearts: Native American Visions and Voices*, Aperture: Special Publication.

Chopra, R. (1989) 'Robert Gardner's *Forest of Bliss*: A Review', *Society for Visual Anthropology Newsletter*, 5 (1): 2–3.

Clifford, J. (1988) *The Predicament of Culture*, Harvard: Harvard University Press.

Clifford, J. and G. Marcus (1986) *Writing Culture*, Berkeley: University of California Press.

Cohen, E. (1989) '"Primitive and Remote": Hill Tribe Trekking in Thailand', *Annals of Tourism Research*, 16: 30–61.

Collier, J. and M. Collier (1986) *Visual Anthropology*, rev. edn, Albuquerque: University of New Mexico Press.

Corbey, R. (1989) *Wildheid en beschaving*, Baarn: Ambo.

Davis, M. and D. Wallbridge (1983) *Boundary and Space: An Introduction to the Work of D.W. Winnicott*, rev. edn, Harmondsworth: Penguin.

Edwards, E. (ed.) (1992) *Anthropology and Photography 1860–1920*, New Haven/London: Yale University Press.

— (1995) 'Jorma Puranen – Imaginary Homecoming', *Social Identities* 1 (2): 317–22.

— (1996) 'Postcards – Greetings from Another World', in T. Selwyn (ed.), *The Tourist Image*, London: John Wiley.

Faris, J. (1993) 'A Response to Terence Turner', *Anthropology Today* 9 (1): 12–13.

Feyerabend, P. (1993) *Against Method*, 3rd edn, London: Verso.

Firth, R. (1957) *Man and Culture: An Evaluation of the Work of Bronslaw Malinowski*, London: Routledge & Kegan Paul.

— (1992) 'Art and Anthropology', in J. Coote and A. Sheldon (eds) *Anthropology, Art and Aesthetics*, 15–39, Oxford: Oxford University Press.

Geary, C. (1988) *Images of Bamum*, Washington: Smithsonian Institution Press.

Graburn, N. (1978) 'Tourism: The Sacred Journey', in V. Smith (ed.) *Hosts and Guests*, 17–32, Oxford: Basil Blackwell.

Gross, L. (1988) 'The Ethics of [Mis]representation', in L. Gross, J. Katz and J. Ruby (eds) *Image Ethics*, 188–202, New York: Oxford University Press.

Grunberg, A. (1990) *The Crisis of the Real: Writings on Photography (1974–1979)*, New York: Aperture.

Hall, S. (1980) 'Encoding/Decoding', in S. Hall et al. (eds) *Culture Media and Language*, 128–38, London: Hutchinson.

— (1983) 'Interview with Stuart Hall', *Camera Work* 29: 17–19.

Jameson, F. (1990) *Signatures of the Visible*, London: Routledge.

Jeffrey, I. (1992a) 'Fragment and Totality in Photography', *History of Photography*, 16 (4): 351–7.

Jones, K. (1992) 'Re-Creation', *The Critical Decade Ten–8* 2 (3): 96–105.

King-Smith, L. (1992) *Patterns of Connection*, Exhibition catalogue, D. Eely and A. Devine–Nordström (eds), Daytona Beach: Southeast Museum of Photography.

Kracauer, S. (1960) *Theory of Film*, Oxford: Oxford University Press.

Loizos, P. (1993) *Innovation in Ethnographic Film*, Manchester: Manchester University Press.

MacCannell, D. (1976) *The Tourist: A New Theory of the Leisure Class*, New York: Macmillan.

Martinez, W. (1992) 'Who Constructs Anthropological Knowledge? Toward a Theory of Ethnographic Film Spectatorship', in P. Crawford and D. Turton (eds) *Film as Ethnography*, pp. 131–61, Manchester: Manchester University Press.

Mead, M. (1975) 'Visual Anthropology in a Discipline of Words', in P. Hockings (ed.) *Principles of Visual Anthropology*, 3–10, The Hague: Mouton.

Metz, C. (1990) 'Photography and Fetish', in C. Squiers (ed.) *The Critical Image*, 155–64, London: Lawrence & Wishart.

Moore, A. (1988) 'The Limitations of Imagist Documentary', *Society for Visual Anthropology Newsletter*, 4 (2): 1–3.

Moore, R. (1981) 'Raymond Moore Talking: An interview with Ian Jeffrey', *Creative Camera* March/April: 195–6.

Moore, R. (1992) 'Marketing Alterity', *Visual Anthropology Review* 8 (2): 16–26.

Mulvey, L. (1989) *Visual and Other Pleasures*, London: Macmillan.

Nichols, B. (1981) *Ideology and the Image*, Bloomington: Indiana University Press.

Onus, L. (1993) 'Southwest, Southeast Australia and Tasmania', in *Aratjara: Art of the First Australians*, 289–96, Cologne: DuMont Verlag.

Ostor, A. (1989) 'Is that what *Forest of Bliss* is all about? A response', *Society for Visual Anthropology Newsletter* 5 (1): 4–8.

Parry, J. (1988) 'Comment on Robert Gardner's *Forest of Bliss*', *Society for Visual Anthropology Newsletter*, 4 (2): 4–7.

Pinney, C. (1992a) 'The Lexical Spaces of Eye-Spy', in P. Crawford and D. Turton (eds)

Beyond the Boundary

79

Film as Ethnography, 26–49, Manchester: Manchester University Press.

— (1992b) 'Parallel Histories of Anthropology and Photography', in E. Edwards (ed.) *Anthropology and Photography 1860–1920*, 74–95, New Haven/London: Yale University Press.

Puranen, J. (1993) 'Imaginary Homecoming', in S. Gupta (ed.) *Disrupted Borders*, 96–103, London: Rivers Oram Press.

Richon, O. (1990) 'Zabat: A Photographic Work by Maud Sulter', *Portfolio Magazine* 8: 8–14.

Ripatti (1993) 'The Stations of the Gaze: Crossroads of Absolution,' *Index* (1): 10–15.

Ruby, J. (1989) 'The Emperor and His Clothes: A Comment', *Society for Visual Anthropology Newsletter* 5 (1): 9–11.

— (1995) *Secure the Shadow: Death and Photography in America*, Cambridge: MIT Press.

Sloan, H. (1992) 'Terra Australis Incognita? Perspectives on Cultural Identity', in *Southern Crossings/Empty Land: In the Australian Image*, London: Camerawork.

Sontag, S. (1978) *On Photography*, Harmondsworth: Penguin.

Tabrizian, M. (1987) 'The Blues: Interview with Mitra Tabrizian', *The Critical Decade Ten–8* 25: 33–6.

Theye, T. (ed.) (1989) *Der geraubte Schatten*, Munich: Staatsmuseum.

Turner, T. (1992) 'Defiant Images: The Kayapo Appropriation of Video', *Anthropology Today* 8 (6): 5–16.

Weston, E. (1980) 'Seeing Photographically', repr. in A. Trachtenberg (ed.) *Classic Essays on Photography*, 169–175, New Haven: Leete's Island Books.

Williamson, C. (1994) 'Patterns of Connection', *Photofile* 41: 28–31.

Wollen, P. (1982) 'Photography and Aesthetics', in P. Wollen (ed.) *Readings and Writings: Semiotic Counter-Strategies*, London: Verso.

Worswick, C. (1979) *Imperial China: Photographs 1850–1912*, London: Scolar Press.

Young Man, A. (1992) 'The Metaphysics of North American Indian Art', in G. McMaster and L.A. Martin (eds) *Indigena: Contemporary Native Perspectives*, 81–99, Hull, Quebec: Canadian Museum of Civilisation.

4

First exits from observational realism: narrative experiments in recent ethnographic films

Peter Loizos

Realism in trouble?

Auguste Comte died in 1857. One of the things he stood for in philosophy was a rejection of theology and metaphysics as ways of understanding the social world. The year before Comte died, a French painter called Duranty started a short-lived publication called *Le Realisme* which argued for an engagement with the life of ordinary people free from romantic trappings.

Duranty continued to think on these lines, and to influence such better-known painters as Degas. Duranty wrote in 1876:

> Let us take leave of the stylized human body, which is treated like a vase. What we need is the characteristic modern person – in his clothes, in the midst of his social surroundings, at home or out in the street . . . The observation of his home life and such peculiarities as his profession creates in him . . . a person with a back . . . which shows us a temperament, an age, a social condition . . . people and things as they present themselves in a million ways and involuntarily in real life.[1]

With appropriate changes, this could have stood as the manifesto for the observational realism movement which strongly influenced documentary films and ethnographic documentaries in the early 1960s, and for some time afterwards.

Issues of realism preoccupied painters and writers in the mid-nineteenth century, particularly in France. Much later, while painters were worrying about Cubism, Surrealism, and all kinds of non-realist modernist issues, documentarists started to argue about realism in films. When, for example, Flaherty was a dominant influence, his concern was to show his human protagonists with a certain nobility of spirit in their struggles with the natural or commercial world. This made Flaherty more of a Romantic than a Realist. He gave his protagonists a certain heroic dignity (as did Basil Wright in *Song of Ceylon*) but he was heavily criticised by Rotha, an influential critic and filmmaker (1952: 105-8), for failing to face the contemporary conditions of the peoples he filmed. The full title of Rotha's book makes abundantly clear where he stood: *Documentary Film: the use of the film medium to interpret creatively and in social terms the life of the people as it exists in reality*. In fact, Rotha admired Flaherty's films on one level – it was their political implications which worried him. But even if Flaherty had got the politics right in Rotha's terms his films would still have been difficult for social-realist critics because they were in most cases reconstructions, rather than direct observations of contemporary lifeways.

Nor were these difficulties confined to documentary: the Neo-Realism of postwar Italian commercial cinema was partly a reaction against the frivolity of so-called 'white-telephone' frothy bourgeois boudoir romps, which had dominated under Mussolini (Alpert 1986) and partly a reaction to the turmoil and privations of war and its aftermath. As is well known, the Neo-Realists – who sometimes used non-actors and actual locations rather than studios – elevated their subjects with a tragic dignity. The films were about situations which were recognisably contemporary and they took themes from the lives of labouring men and women, the jobless and desperately poor, old pensioners squeezed by inflation, struggling to survive without loss of self-respect. The forces against which they struggled were not nature, but unemployment, dislocation, predatory crime, and the insensitivity of their fellows. Thus, it could be argued that the fictions of De Sica, Rossellini and the Fellini of *Il Bidone* were at least as close to real lives as a Flaherty documentary, and Rotha, for one, might have argued that they were a good deal closer in spirit. Documentary as such had no guarantee of fidelity to real life, and the commercial cinema of fiction could accurately and persuasively convey real-world problems. Given these precedents, it is remarkable that in the early 1960s the observationalists succeeded in monopolising (however briefly) the virtues of authenticity in ethnographic film.[2]

Observational style in one form or another was strongly influential in ethnographic film between 1960 and 1980. Its naturalism, populism, its attempts to capture events-in-process, the flux of social relations, meant certain limitations upon what were acceptable narrative frameworks. These included a narrowing of narrative scope, a grounding of the imagination in empirical, immediately visible actualities. The aim of editing was to select peaks of ritual climax, crises, revelatory moments of arrival, departure, and of significant conversational disclosure. But sensitive to the conventions of Hollywood fiction, the filmmakers avoided giving to the episodic flow of daily life the heightened dramatisations of soap operas and serials. Inevitably, and particularly because of the high shooting ratios of typical observational films, editors discarded far more material than was offered in finished films. This fact alone should have worried those who argued for the inherent superiority of observational realism to other modes and genres. What was the character of the huge amounts of material which had been discarded in the cutting room? Those many thousand feet of raw, unedited actuality – what were their defects that they had lost their right to appear in a sixty-minute film? If nineteen rolls of film out of every twenty were consigned to obscurity, the observation of reality contained implicit selection assumptions which were hard for the ordinary viewer to assess.[3]

From the late 1980s under both external commercial pressures, and the inevitable reaction against a stylistic orthodoxy, new editing methods have been influencing television documentaries, such as faster cutting speeds, more flamboyant use of music, altering the colour of backgrounds during interviews, readiness to employ reconstruction, and enactment, and more flexible, playful, interpretive and experimental narrative frameworks. Ethnographic filmmakers have inevitably been affected by the mainstream documentary environment, and have turned away from an automatic adherence to the austerities of naturalistic, observational 'plain style' (Stoller 1992: 203). That kind of observational realism looks as if it might be, for the moment at least, In Trouble.

Experiments with form

Science is much concerned with predictability and repetition. One characteristic scientific procedure involves the use of experiments, and their procedures must be clear enough for other investigators to get the same outcomes. The procedures depend upon precision in defining questions and methods, identifying materials, describing the experiments employed.

But the arts are rarely concerned with being predictable. Artists aim to surprise us. Diaghilev asked Nijinsky to amaze him. Artists experiment, but with variation in form. And instead of predictability, they prefer allusion, resonance, metaphor, representational devices of a fuzzy nature. Much art delights in ambiguity and irony. There is little place for irony in science, except when criticising a colleague's work. Science may be imaginative, creative, exploratory and experimental, but nearly always, at the end of the day, 'under discipline', the discipline of a last-word fidelity to real-world processes.

When it comes to craft experiments with form, we should distinguish two (among several) levels of activity. There are contemporary movements, in which numbers of individuals experiment with a particular formal device at the same time: thus, when lightweight synchronous sound filming first became available to documentarists, films were made simultaneously in New York, Montreal and Paris which sought to find out what the new recording approach could do. Young filmmakers who had never made a film felt that there was only one kind of film worth making – they had seen the future, and 'it worked'.

A rather different kind of activity is experiment by a single artist: painters repeat a particular basic composition dozens of times for months or years, until they have grown tired of its possibilities, and are ready to move on. Filmmakers, too, can be understood to experiment with a particular way of making films, and to make several films in one way before seeking something different, more or less for the sake of the formal insights they obtain from working with the approaches.

Observational realism is an approach which is probably with us to stay, in the sense that it is likely to be rediscovered afresh by each generation of documentarists, and worked with, in the spirit of 'It would be an interesting discipline to make a film *in that way*'. After doing that, however, a particular filmmaker is likely to move on to other forms. At the moment, there are signs of restlessness, and experiment with frameworks of all kinds. These signs can be seen in the graduation films made by students of ethnographic film, and in British television documentaries. I would propose that what we are seeing is a reaction on several levels (young filmmakers, commissioning editors, youthful audiences) against both the predictability of observationalism, naturalism, and 'plain style' realism, and also the rather flat-footed truth-claims made on behalf of these approaches. I wish to explore a single strand of this reaction, by examining some films involving ideas of journeys.

Journeys

The Odyssey was an epic journey, and *Don Quixote* another. The picaresque novel turned the physical journey into an analogous spiritual journey: Stendahl's *Lucien Leuwen* has this type of development, as does Algren's *A Walk on the Wild Side*. Joseph Conrad, a much-travelled man who worked as a master mariner, made journeys, particular sea and river voyages, the framework for numerous novels, particularly *Heart of Darkness*. In Conrad, the physical and temporal journey always implies moral change for a central character.

Documentary film has also made continuous use of journeys. *Grass* is an early example (Crawford 1992) as is Buñuel's excursion into a poverty-stricken region of Spain, Las Hurdes, in *Land Without Bread*. *Night Mail*, by Basil Wright and Harry Watt, was another early example, using a poem by W.H. Auden to complement its images. Like Flaherty, Wright got a drubbing for the inadequacies of his political analysis (Winston 1988: 36–43), and recently the journey is almost a narrative cliché employed by such television ethnographic films as the *Disappearing World* series.[4]

The journey through space needs to be distinguished from another familiar framework, the structured unfolding of time; the format combines well with the idea of seasonal succession, as in Rouquier's

Farrebique, Geddes' *Meo Year*, Yorke's more selective *The Ho*. The MacDougalls' *A Wife Among Wives* did not use an annual cycle, but a playful, freely developing 'pages from a diary' format, which helped the film move through weeks and months easily, and David MacDougall returned to this approach in *Link-Up Diary*, in which the time taken is a single week with its particular 'case-load'. Melissa Llewelyn-Davies's *Diary of a Maasai Village* involved us with a group of people who dwell in a particular place, following their fortunes during many weeks of excursions, always returning to the laibon's homestead, the centre of their world. Here the diary and the journey combined easily. Patrice Faba's *Un Ethnologue en Chine* used a 'pages from a notebook' framework which allowed travels in an exploratory manner through contrasting Chinese contexts. Each new place and each new dateline introduced a different understanding of the principle of Tao.

The layering one upon another of compatible narrative frameworks is important – a journey may have a diary added on to it. It may have an identified person's spiritual development existing as a third layer. A striking recent example of a television documentary which uses a journey, as well as departing in many respects from observational realism, is Alan Ereira's film *From the Heart of the World: the Elder Brother's Warning* (1990). This film takes the viewers on a mysterious journey into the territory of a people who we are told have cut themselves off from contact with the modern, capitalist world.

Figure 4.1 Frame fom *The Elder Brother's Warning*: Kogi men guarding the access into their society.

These people, the Kogi, of the Colombian Sierra Nevada give the film-makers a 'warning' about the ecological destructiveness of capitalist life-ways, and the film team are sent back with it, as messengers. The film becomes the warning. That, at least, is the film's narrative framework. This is assisted by a variety of musical devices, long-drawn out, 'rising'   *85* and portentous chords, to signify the gravity of the Kogi, their isolation, and their warning; and arresting drum beats. The commentary voice has an authoritative tone, and the words are arresting, but risk overstatement: 'Almost every animal and every plant from anywhere in the world can find a home somewhere in the Sierra. . .' – a thought which would not have impressed Darwin greatly. There are puzzling, arresting images, such as beautiful but enigmatic pools of water, and reflecting surfaces on gold ritual objects, photographed in isolation from context to enhance their separation impact; there is the use of fragments of Kogi myths, in the commentary. There is a running theme of tomb-robbery, as a metaphor for the destructiveness of modern aquisitive lowlanders; there is the dramatisation of the Kogi themselves, by the use of several actors (Donald Pleasence is one) to give voice to Kogi speech in a way which invokes character, particularly the stern, intense and admonitory 'elder brother', more persuasively than subtitles could do. There is much more, particularly details of Kogi culture and the extraordinary training of the children who will become priestly rulers, to make the film memorable as a revelatory, puzzling journey.

Figure 4.2 Frame from *The Elder Brother's Warning*: a labour task being performed by commoners under the direction of the priest-leaders.

On first viewing it was unclear to me, as a viewer, how far the organising concept of a formal warning was something which the Kogi had decided to do for themselves, and how far it was a compelling but producer-driven way of buttonholing the audience to put across ideas which are implicit rather than explicit in the Kogi's perceptions of the outside world. I am not suggesting that most films, even observational realist films, make their own constructional conventions any clearer. However, a subsequent book by director Alan Ereira (1990), a review of the film (Tayler 1993: 219–21) and a Comment by one of the anthropologists closely involved (Townsley 1993: 223–26) confirmed that the warning, the resistance to intrusion by outsiders, and much else in the film, were what the Kogi wanted to convey. They had of course had the benefit of many patient discussions with Townsley, Felicity Knock and Ereira, who had gone to some trouble to explain the power of television to them. Townsley gently noted places in the film where elements of media hype had suggested the Kogi were in some kind of Lost World, and that contacts with the film crew were the first contacts in a very long period (Tayler lists three other film sources on the Kogi, and their neighbours have been filmed by at least three other teams). But his overall judgement is strongly positive. He supports the political advocacy of the film, and its extraordinary outreach impact. He suggests that observational realism was in danger of losing any serious audience impact and turning ethnographic film into an orthodoxy for the discriminating and epistemologically fastidious few. He regards the Kogi as fortunate in having been filmed by Ereira – a director outside the observational tradition.[5]

Figure 4.3 Frame from *The Elder Brother's Warning*: a Kogi sacrament.

Kracauer (1960) noted that film has particular affinities with movement through space, with the surprises which are revealed in the exploration of settings, whether landscapes, as in the classic Western, urban settings, as in the routine cop-chase, exploring the dark, frightening house of mystery, and, more recently, the road-movie. In documentary, journeys usually have a political or spiritual point. We set out in one state of mind, and by the end of the film-journey we should be in a different one. A journey which did not change us, if only by informing us, would be pointless and boring – we might as well have stayed at home. That, perhaps, is why Robert Gardner has suggested that one of his aims as a filmmaker is to *transport* his audience 'but not anywhere' (personal communication).

Journeys in ethnographic documentary are likely to be three-fold movements – through spaces and places, through time, and through states of consciousness. They will exploit an element of surprise. I shall now consider several recent films because of the inherent interest in how they use the journey framework, and in how far they depart from observational realism. The academically fastidious reader is warned that while some of these films are conventionally ethnographic, others would not score high marks by the Heider–Ruby criteria as formulated in the mid-1970s – there is not always a qualified anthropologist at the helm; there may not be an explicit theory as intellectual framework; we may not see whole bodies, full contexts, completed actions; close-ups are common, and the soundtrack may not have been recorded wholly and exclusively at the time the images were captured!

Journey 1: 'Cannibal Tours'

Dennis O'Rourke is a Sydney-based filmmaker who has made a number of documentaries about people and situations in Australia, the Pacific and Papua New Guinea (Cohen: 1988). His film 'Cannibal Tours' gives us insights into the phenomenon of tourism by Europeans and Americans to coastal Papua, and offers us a series of ironic episodic encounters between tourists and locals. The film is very definitely not an observational record of a single time-bound visit to a single identifiable place. It is quite difficult to form a sense of particular places (although a small number are mentioned [MacCannell 1990]) and there are no clues as to time. Although the film appears to start with an arrival and ends with a departure, almost everything that happens in between has an arbitrary, unlocated, unspecific character to it. The only constant is that locals comment on the visitors, alternating with visitors commenting upon the locals. And there is a sense that the visitors' perceptions are usually countered with a specific anti-perception by a local. That is clearly a very deliberate construction, even if it is made to look spontaneous, and balanced in a tit-for-tat exchange process.

Perhaps the opening of the film is intended to playfully evoke Conrad's *Heart of Darkness*, but it could equally well be a spoof on a Tarzan film. The film starts out in a boat, a little bit out from a coast. We hear bulletins of news from different radio stations around the world. We approach slowly by water through shots of enigmatic palm trees, a young boy who stares and drops his eyes and stares again. A local man is carving a ritual object. There is an atmosphere of Mystery.

Then a white man aims a camera at the landscape – is this to make us think of Conrad's description of the gun firing into a Continent? A white tourist is shown a place where he is told by a local that 'human sacrifices' took place. He wishes to photograph it. He is clearly enthusiastic about the idea of human sacrifice. He is a plump middle-aged man, German, Swiss, or Austrian(?) who reappears throughout the film. He is weighed down with cameras. He turns out to be much travelled, articulate, and aware of the arguments against the very form of tourism he is enjoying. Is he Mr Kurtz? (MacCannell [1990] seeks to link him to National Socialism, even though he could scarcely have been born by 1945. Would National Socialists have chosen to spend their holidays on the Sepik?).

Figure 4.4(a) (*above*) *'Cannibal Tours'*: some of the protogonists; Figure 4.4(b) Dennis O'Rourke.

One theme of the film is mutual incomprehension – but with a difference. The tourists are 'informed' superficially about Sepik culture. They know there is no longer cannibalism of any sort. They know the people have been changed, and that they once lived in some sense closer to their local environment. But they are stuffed with preconceptions, such as that with the locals you have to bargain for what you buy. Or that the locals are happy as they are, still living a life in which they can easily satisfy their wants without money.

But the locals tell us that they feel poor, and are not happy as they are, and that if they were paid more for the things they sell they too could be tourists and travel. And they tell us that they really do not understand the whites – particularly, why they take photographs, but more profoundly, who they are and where they come from.

The incomprehension is partly because of the differences of power, and also, we can see, because of the lack of common languages. The visitors cannot speak the local trade language, Tok Pisin, and few of the locals we meet can speak good German or American English. We come to appreciate the sense in which the contacts are inevitably superficial, and lead to little real insight.

One comment on the film deserves to be disputed. MacCannell has written, 'The tourists are most unattractive, emotional, self-interested, awkward and intrusive. It is difficult to imagine a group of real people [i.e. non-actors] simply caught in the eye of the camera appearing less attractive. This is not because of any obvious filmic trick' (1990, 1994: 106). This is in contrast to the locals, who are 'attractive . . . lightly ironic . . . clear-sighted and pragmatic . . .' I wonder how MacCannell would react to a documentary about the Khmer Rouge, or the Kray twins, if these tourists are the most unattractive people he can imagine? Surely, as documentarists are fully aware, the *casting* of central characters is crucial here, and, as I hinted above in comments on shooting-ratios, the selection and *discarding* of material, equally so. Whether we call them 'filmic tricks' is a matter of taste, but there is no reason to suppose that these tourists are thoroughly typical of all visitors to the Sepik. They have been carefully framed, in several senses.

There is one crucial difference in the attitudes of visitors and locals. The locals are clear about what they do not know or understand, but the visitors are complacently sure that they know a good deal about whom and what they are seeing. They appear, then, to make an anti-journey which takes them nowhere and teaches them nothing. Such reflection as there is, is done by the locals, and, through further layers of irony, by the audience.[6]

Journey 2: Polka

90 The subtitle of this film is *The Roots of Mexican Accordion Music in S.*

Texas and N. Mexico. It was made by Robert Boonzajer Flaes and Maarten Rens (Boonzajer Flaes 1989). The film involves journeys of various kinds, but the master narrative frame is that of a detective story, a journey in the mind, the unravelling of a problem by following up clues. The problem is superficially one of identification, but it is more profoundly one of understanding cultural meanings. This is not so much the discovery of a corpse, as the commissioning of the detective to track down a missing person. We might think of the detective-ethnomusicologist as having been commissioned – buttonholed – by history. A type of music has come to his attention, but its antecedents are unclear.

Figure 4.5 Frame from *Polka*: Flaco Jimenez, on accordion and two sidesmen, playing Texas-Mexican polka.

The film starts with a close shot of a guitar and piano which are playing a lively melody. After a few bars, we cut to a series of one-line characterisations of the music and its possible origins. These also act as clues: a Chicano activist suggests that the music is an original music which symbolises the Chicano identity, part Mexican, part Spanish, part American. (The film cuts to an accordion which plays polka.) A Chicano musician declares that the Americans don't like the music because it's Spanish, and the Mexicans don't accept it because it isn't Spanish. (The accordion plays on.) Another Chicano musician says that maybe it came from Germany, but 'not all of it' because 'we have original music in Mexico and in Texas, also.' (Accordion plays on.) An Austrian says 'No one in Austria would play like that', adding that it reminds him of gypsy music. (The accordion plays on.) A Texas German says that the Texas Mexicans keep to themselves and would not allow him into their music-making. (The accordion plays on.) Another Chicano musician says the accordion is going strong and the more you play it the more people like it. (The accordion plays on.) Finally, the original activist and the film's maker agree to call the music 'Metro Polka'. (The accordion music climaxes, and ends, and the main title appears.)

These, then, are the 'clues' which point to the problem the film will pursue through the gumshoe work of the ethnomusicologist Boonzajer Flaes. He pursues each of them more or less singlemindedly until he runs up against new paradoxes – answers that don't add up, as the gumshoe would say.

It is a film that could only have been made after Rouch and Morin's *Chronique d'un Été* (1960), probably the first film to have shifted from an external filming of a passive world, to what Rouch calls provocation, which means, making things happen so that when filmed, they provide a record of an inquiry (Eaton 1979; Feld 1989; Stoller 1992). The 'reality' is the one created by the very process of enquiry itself, and by the act of film-making.

So, in the course of his investigation, the *Polka* filmmaker plays different bits of music to different people, and checks their reactions. Whereas the Chicano musicians seem happy to pick things up from other ethnic groups, to incorporate them, and *play* with them to make them work, other groups, notably some of the Austrian folk musicians, see themselves as having a high-cultural mission. They apparently see melody, instrument and performance style as the *corporate property* of specific ethnic groups, and expressive of their inner core, in a way we would now call essentialist.

Figure 4.6 Frame from *Polka*: accordionist Leit'n Tony and his son play proper Austrian polka.

The film intellectually explores several interpretative possibilities. First, that this kind of polka is Chicano music but entirely derived from German originals, which have somehow had chilli stirred in. It is clear that forty years ago young Chicanos were eager to see what the Germans could do with the accordion, and imitated them. But they experienced social exclusion, came up against a hard cultural boundary. Then, it is established that some kind of accordion tradition existed in Northern Mexico in the last century, and that it is not a derivative of German models. The issue of class now enters the film and we come to see that there is a strand in the Chicano tradition which is associated with the cantina – the bar, heavy drinking, and a non-bourgeois life-style. It is suggested that middle-class Chicanos may not be comfortable with the music because of its association with the lower-class milieu.

Some Chicanos stress the cultural politics in the music – how its use of occasional English lyrics, or American jazz trills, makes it *Chicano* rather than simply Hispanic. Others are willing to admit this, but stress that for them the music is more importantly about love, and usually unhappy love at that.

Figure 4.7 Frame from *Polka*: an elderly Mexican recalls how he got his first accordion.

Gradually the film travels towards an ending, and the favoured solution seems to be that the music is indeed distinctively Chicano. By the end of the film-journey into the roots of the music, we have been transported to a number of interesting places, have heard from a number of lively and musically gifted people, and been made to think quite hard about diffusion, cultural boundaries, and subcultural values. The detective has cracked the puzzle, and the spectator's guided tour is at an end.

Journey 3: Over the Threshold

There has been much discussion of reflexivity in recent years, somewhat earlier in relation to ethnographic film (e.g. Ruby 1980) than in relation to ethnographic writing, implying a contextualising reflection upon the research process and its uncertainties, as a matter written into or filmed into the ethnographic account.

The three main ways in which filmmakers have addressed the issues have been, first, to identify themselves, usually visually, early in the film, as the filmmakers, so that a film is seen to be made by persons, and not by impersonal, godlike forces. A second means has been to leave various bits of material in the film which indicate the nuts-and-bolts of filming: clapper-boards with shot and take numbers, mike-taps, Academy leaders, are now commonplace, even being used to give spurious authenticity – pseudo-realism – to TV soap-powder commercials. Thirdly, and most significantly, films often contain comments by the subjects about the filming process, and what they think about it, and indeed, discussions with the filmmakers about their intentions, or the disruptiveness of filming.

Sometimes these devices and approaches are used in the service of a heightened realism. That is, the very dialogue about filming stands to add greater authenticity to the otherwise natural and spontaneous surfaces of the film's action. It is as if both filmmakers and subjects were saying 'This film is not the result of some sort of specially constructed situation to illustrate a point. It is rather a real record of the self-conscious interactions between filmmakers and film subjects. Here, see for yourself.'

But at this point the easy categories of realism and contrasting modes begin to blur. On the one hand, first-generation realism of a Flaherty made it appear that the documentarist filmed an ongoing real world as faithfully, naturalistically and unintrusively as possible, even though most filmmakers knew better (Brody 1977). But modern reflexive realism, following up on Rouch-Morin's notion of provoking reality into becoming by asking questions, runs the risk of playing God in a new way, by creating worlds which have not previously existed. Does this matter less, perhaps, if the filmmakers do it with their own families?

Over the Threshold was made by Christine Lloyd-Fitt and Yoshi Tezuka (1989), while students at the British National Film and Television School. It is a radical exercise in self-reference, because the two filmmakers, having recently married each other in Britain, decided to go to Japan so that Lloyd-Fitt could get to know that country and her husband's family. And, she explains early in the film, to see if she would

Figure 4.8 Frame from *Over the Threshold*: Christine Lloyd-Fitt trying on Japanese clothes.

enjoy the idea of living in Japan. Because they are filmmakers, she tells us, making a film is their way of finding out about things.

A good deal of the film's action is inside Tezuka's parents' home. Both parents are divorce lawyers. There are two unmarried children, a boy and a girl, and the girl's boyfriend, about whom the mother has reservations. And because the mother is an outgoing, expansive talker, a good deal of the action involves her talking back to her son's eliciting questions, which are coming at her from behind the camera. Christine is sometimes in picture, acting as a normal family member, and is sometimes working as sound recordist – a fact which is established even before the film's main title, when we see her making a microphone tap to synchronise the picture with the sound.

Figure 4.9 Frame from *Over the Threshold*: Mrs Tezuka and two colleagues with their law graduation scrolls.

In order for Christine to find out how foreigners find life in Japan, the couple shoot some vox pops on busy streets, and visit several other couples in contexts where a European girl has settled down with a Japanese boy. These informal conversational interviews reveal minor problems. One Japanese boy's male friends tend to stare at the girl (she is Swiss) but don't really talk to her. An English woman with three children by a Japanese husband is clearly anxious that her children are considerably more Japanese than they are English. She feels a vague threat.

So that Christine, and the viewers, can appreciate the complex position of working wives in modern Japan, we learn about Yoshi's mother and grandmother. Grandmother was wronged by her first husband, did better with the second, and came to appreciate that education was an important security guarantee for women. So Yoshi's mother was encouraged to go to university. She stopped work to have her three children, but started again when they had grown up.

Figure 4.10 Frame from
Over the Threshold: an
Englishwoman married to a
Japanese speaks of her
feeling that her children are
rather more Japanese than
English.

In an amusing incident, Mrs Tezuka at work in the kitchen asks her husband's opinion about whether the husbands of working wives should help more in the home – in the film he is normally seen dozing and relaxing while at home. But the camera, and her son, reveal that while she has been asking the question, he has gone off somewhere without replying!

Further insights into Japanese marriages are produced by another ironic episode in which the filmmakers accompany Mrs Tezuka and a neighbour on a walk. Mrs Tezuka tells the young filming couple that the neighbour is a model Japanese housewife, who cares for her husband's every need with true devotion. But the neighbour demurs. 'If devotion means doing things willingly, then we cannot say I am devoted,' she insists. Mrs Tezuka looks discomfited, but adds that nevertheless, to the external eye, everything the neighbour does is really well done. But the audience may draw different conclusions.

The film achieves many of its effects through the tensions produced by its gentle but insistent interrogation of the parents. The high point is when they are asked about their attitudes to divorce. Why do people get divorced? Have the parents ever considered divorce? The father smiles, and says from his experiences with his clients, most divorces come about because of 'selfishness'. But he does not discuss his personal situation. His wife is more forthright. She says that when she hears the reasons many of her clients produce for wanting divorces she feels that with grounds like these, she would have obtained a divorce long ago – had she wanted one. She adds the last thought with a firmness of tone which suggests she is a woman of strong character, who if she thought herself seriously wronged, would act decisively.

The film moves towards an inconclusive conclusion. Christine does not tell us if she will wish to settle in Japan. We have come to appreciate the tensions in modern Japanese marriages, and the resolution and tolerance of Mrs Tezuka. We have also come to understand that everything a foreigner does in Japan is seen as different, and attributed to the person's foreign origins, even if it is sometimes something that some Japanese do too. Mrs Tezuka, for instance, comments in some detail on the differences between the way she herself removes wet laundry from the washing machine and hangs it up, and the different way in which her English daughter-in-law does these things. Christine, meanwhile, has been seen resolutely trying to fit in, from cutting up octopus, early on, to participating in memorial rituals for dead Tezuka grandparents.

If it is all right with you it is all right with me

Figure 4.11 Frame from *Over the Threshold*: Mrs Tezuka and her neighbour Mrs Meisawa discuss the feelings of parents towards a child's choice of partner.

In a coda sequence, Mrs Tezuka and her neighbour puff up a hill pushing their bikes, and discuss how one should react to one's children's choices of marriage partners. They agree that whether a child is marrying a foreigner or a Japanese, there is always a strong parental interest, and one has to know when to keep quiet, and accept a child's choice. There are several layers of irony and ambiguity here. The film suggests that something inherently difficult – a mixed marriage – has passed off well, so far.

Figure 4.12 Frame from *Over the Threshold*: the Tezuka family and Christine bid the viewers goodbye.

97

The last words are from Mrs Tezuka and are wholly positive, if also clearly constraining. She says she thinks Christine will produce beautiful grandchildren, and adds, anachronistically, 'I love your children.' We have reached a point of farewell on the journey into the Tezuka extended family and the position of women in changing Japanese culture. The last image shows all the Tezukas, including the filmmakers with their equipment, smiling, in a line. The reflexivity of the opening sequence has been consistently maintained, and the circle is now closing for us as spectators, in the film's narrative space, but not, we may suppose, for the people who revealed themselves to us on film.

Journey 4: Nice Coloured Girls

This film was made in 1987 by Tracy Moffatt, an Australian Aboriginal director, who has now completed a feature film. Of the films discussed here it is the one furthest from any kind of realist style, although we might use the term 'magical realism' to describe it. It stretches the conventional meaning of the term 'ethnographic' to the limits, but is very much the sort of film which Faye Ginsburg (1994) uses to illustrate her argument that while in the past, Euro-Americans made ethnographic films in the spirit of the Scientific Observer filming a Native People, while nowadays, with the diffusion of video cameras, Aboriginal citizens produce films about their lives and cultures which are under their own creative intellectual control, and that these 'challenge a long-outdated paradigm of ethnographic film built on notions of culture as a stable and bounded object . . .' (ibid.: 14). This is not the place to discuss a complex of questions about how far the classic notion of bounded cultures which 'contained' customs, rituals and culturally specific practices was valid in the past (but see Kuper 1992); nor how far a revision of such a notion dissolves the problem of how to approach a film like this one. Is it a product of a contemporary Aboriginal culture, or of a single person? Or is it better understood as part of Australian 'national' culture? Neither? Both? Where you end up on this kind of question is likely to depend on where you have started out from. My only certainty is that an approach to 'ethnographic film' which fails to consider this film and others like it is narrow to the point of blindness.[7]

Nice Coloured Girls in the brief compass of seventeen minutes attempts to make us think about relationships between white men and Aboriginal women over a period of 200 years. For it combines readings from early travellers' 'first contact' accounts with native Australian peoples, with stylised enactments (not documentary observations) of contemporary encounters. There are three individual white male voices, and a chorus of black women speaking and laughing together.

Figure 4.13 Frame from
Nice Coloured Girls: three
young women in a bar.

The film opens with night-time aerial vistas of Sydney, and a neon-lit strip. Over this we hear a man talk about the social and sexual character of Aboriginal women in 1788. His voice is distanced, authoritative. In contrast, captions appear on the screen over shots of drunken white men and detached young black women explaining that the women will try to get money out of the men by various means. Another more gentle and reflective white male voice starts to recount an episode concerning a girl called Gordiana, whom he found attractive, and for whom he felt compassion. By playing on his sympathy, and claiming that her husband beat her, she aroused his chivalrous charity to the point that he gave her a major share of his provisions. She subsequently eluded him. A third male 'voice' reads out another written contribution, implying that native women are both self-possessed and highly manipulative.

These voices intertwine, producing contrasting impressions. Meanwhile, two kinds of 'action' unfold visually. A trio of modern young black

Figure 4.14 Frame from
Nice Coloured Girls:
evocation of an historical
encounter.

99

women lead a drunken 'Captain' further into inebriation, until they can filch his wallet, and are watched over by the image of an ancestral woman from 'first contact' times. There are also stylised evocations of girls climbing aboard a sailing ship, and various symbolic plays are made with shattering images, and with impressions made on white bodies by black hands and vice versa. Various songs add texture to the soundtrack, in particular 'Do you think I'm a nasty girl?' and 'I'm an evil woman'.

The overall effect of this film is to hint at the complexity, and the repetitive nature of certain themes in sexual encounters across cultural divides. White men appear in several guises – as cold and predatory observers, but also as wondering, credulous and compassionate, or patronising, depending on your point of view. Aboriginal women are presented as spirited, defiant, calculating, and a match for the men. There are hints (but no more) of violence, and suggestions of poignant misunderstandings, as in the case of an Aboriginal mother of a pale child who tried to smoke it to a more acceptable colour.

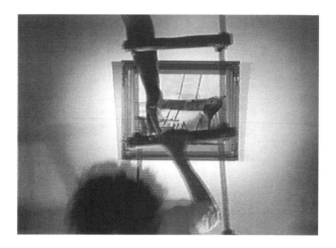

Figure 4.15 Frame from *Nice Coloured Girls*: evocation of Aboriginal women coming aboard a ship during the early 'contact' period.

It is clear that while this film could have been attempted in realist, documentary styles, it would have run into formidable problems. First, there is the probable non-cooperation of contemporary good-time girls and their victims. Secondly, there is the absence of any historical visual material to illustrate the written sources. Because such sexual encounters were frowned upon by the moral guardians of both Aboriginal and white societies, visual records which could be evoked in a realist documentary do not exist to be exploited. Nor were the sexual fantasies of the period available as visuals. So, non-realist modes of representation proved a way out of that particular problem.

But there are other reasons as well for the narrative style of the film: the picture of black–white relations which emerges has a good deal more wit and humour in it than has been the case in some earlier films made by black or white radical activists. One result is that Aboriginal women come through less as victims, and more as members of a kind of spontaneous resistance movement. So far, no mainstream ethnographic filmmaker has done anything so short, sharp or with such light and easy brush-strokes. Nor is this an isolated case: Lucy Panteli, a young London filmmaker of Greek Cypriot origin, has made a powerful short film about memories of her mother also in a non-realist vein. I am particularly intrigued by this film because in the course of making it she took images from an ethnographic film of mine and worked them into her own film text. This re-appropriation of an anthropologist's materials by an individual artist working with the complexities of her own personal and cultural identities seems to suggest possibilities which go some way to bridge the earlier gaps between colonial 'observers' and native 'subjects'.

Conclusion

Marcus and Fisher recently identified an experimental moment in the human sciences, but they found time for only a couple of thin paragraphs on ethnographic film (1986: 75). It seems that to them, written experiments are the ones that really matter.[8] In discussing here a few examples of a turning away from observational realism, and from presentational 'plain style', I am making no programmatic proposals, or assertions that the way forward is through following these expeditionary forces. I am more interested in exploration than prescription.

We are said to be living in postmodern times, although it is doubtful if many people are thinking of Chaplin's powerful satire on industrialism and authoritarianism when they use a modification of that phrase. It might more aptly be described as a post-Marxist phase, since so many former Marxists are now adopting postmodernism as their theoretical compass-point. One gain from the change is a decline in the amount of programmatic prescriptive writing about ethnographic film. There is a greater tendency to get down to a discussion of actual existing films, rather than how films ought to be made. Perhaps we are turning away from the linearity of 'models of succession' in theory – the assumption that new theories render previous ones invalid, and that progress involves a succession of ever more appropriate frameworks. Perhaps now we are entering a period where we see ourselves as involved in 'models of addition', that is, that we are adding to a stock of ever more sophisticated ways of thinking. That is why I argued at the start of this chapter that although we are now apparently in the midst of a rejection of observational realism, it will surely come round again in the near future, albeit in an enhanced, more self-conscious form. So, we are more in the position of the Flying Dutchman – condemned to perpetual intellectual motion – than we might wish to think. In that sense, journeys in the mind not only describes certain films, but in part our whole enterprise.

Notes

1. The quotation is from Eduard Huttinger's *Degas*, Milan: The Uffici Press.
2. On realism in cinema, see Andrew 1976, and Williams 1980. Williams includes Flaherty within the realist tradition, but he has to make many concessions to do so.
3. We must await with interest an analysis of unused footage for some observational classic. At the moment we get glimpses of the selection criteria in some master-classes.
4. For a critical review of television films with anthropological components, see Banks (1994).
5. In so far as one ever knows why one starts thinking along particular lines, it was Townsley's presentation at the Manchester R.A.I. Film Conference which started me thinking about the retreat from observational realism. This article was in late draft when I read his 1993 'Comment'.
6. MacCannell finds a great deal more postmodern irony and many more implications than I do. While some of his insights are impressive, the article is oddly confusing in its use of tenses. The 'Sambia' for example are written about as if they are currently taking heads, in the present tense.
7. Tracey Moffatt, in a personal communication, writes: 'I hate Anthropologists writing about my work. The thought of being an "essay subject" for Anthropology students for the rest of my born days makes me puke . . . I just wish your article was going into some groovy art magazine or film journal. Instead it will be filed away with the rest of the "old bones" at the Institute of Anthropology, Oxford. . . .'
8. Marcus has however continued to make use of filmic representation to advance his arguments. See his paper in Devereaux and Hillman's recent book (Marcus 1995).

References

Alpert, H. (1986) *Fellini: A Life*, London: W.H. Allen.

Andrew, J. Dudley (1976) *The Major Film Theories: An Introduction*, Oxford and New York: Oxford University Press.

Banks, M. (1994) 'Television and Anthropology: An Unhappy Marriage?', *Visual Anthropology* 7 (1): 21–45.

Boonzajer Flaes, R. (1989) 'Video and Anthropology: The *Polka* Project', in P. Chiozzi (ed.) *Teaching Visual Anthropology*, 145–51, Florence: Editrice il Sedicesimo.

Brody, H. (1977) 'Seeming to be Real: *Disappearing World* and the Film in Pond Inlet', *Cambridge Anthropology*, Special Issue on ethnographic film: 22–31.

Cohen, H. (1988) 'Expeditions, Exoticism and Ethnography: Film and the Pacific', *Photofile*, Spring: 34–40.

Crawford, P. (1992) '*Grass*, the Visual Narrativity of Pastoral Nomadism', in Crawford, P. and J.K. Simonsen (eds) *Ethnographic Film Aesthetics and Narrative Traditions*, Arhus: Intervention Press.

Eaton, M. (1979) *Anthropology – Reality – Cinema: The Films of Jean Rouch*, London: British Film Institute.

Ereira, A. (1990) *The Heart of the World*, London: Cape.

Feld, S. (1989) 'Themes in the Cinema of Jean Rouch', *Visual Anthropology* 2 (3–4): 223–47.

Huttinger, E. (no date) *Degas*, Milan: Uffici Press.

Ginsburg, F. (1994) 'Culture/Media: A (Mild) Polemic, *Anthropology Today* 10 (2) April: 5–15.

Kracauer, S. (1960) *Theory of Film: The Redemption of Physical Reality*, Oxford and New York: Oxford University Press.

Kuper, A. (1992) *Conceptualizing Society*, London and New York: Routledge.

MacCannell, D. (1990, 1994) 'Cannibal Tours', first published in *Visual Anthropology Review* 6 (Fall 1990), repr. in Taylor, L. (ed.) *Visualizing Theory: Selected Essays from V.A.R. 1990–94*: 99–114. New York and London: Routledge.

Marcus, G. (1995) 'The Modernist Sensibility in Recent Ethnographic Writing and the Cinematic Metaphor of Montage', in L. Devereaux and R. Hillman (eds) *Fields of Vision: Essays in Film Studies, Visual Anthropology and Photography*, Berkeley: University of California Press.

Marcus, G. and Fisher, M.M.J. (1986) *Anthropology as Cultural Critique: An Experimental Moment in the Human Sciences*, Chicago: Chicago University Press.

Rotha, P. (1952) *Documentary Film: the use of the film medium to interpret creatively and in social terms the life of the people as it exists in reality*, London: Faber and Faber.

Ruby, J. (1980) 'Exposing Yourself: Reflexivity, Film and Anthropology', *Semiotica* 3: 153–79.

Stoller, P. (1992) *The Cinematic Griot: The Ethnography of Jean Rouch*, Chicago: Chicago University Press.

Tayler, D. (1993) 'From the Heart of the World' (film and book review), *Visual Anthropology* 6: 219–21.

Townsley, G. (1993) 'Comment – Lost Worlds Found: Advocacy and Film Rhetoric', *Visual Anthropology* 6: 223–6.

Williams, C. (1980) *Realism and the Cinema: A Reader*, London: Routledge & Kegan Paul, in association with the British Film Institute.

Winston, B. (1988) 'The Tradition of the Victim in Griersonian Documentary', 34–57, in L. Gross, J.S. Katz and J. Ruby (eds) *Image Ethics: The Moral Rights of Subjects in Photographs, Film and Television*, 38–57, Oxford and New York: Oxford University Press.

Films analysed in the text

'*Cannibal Tours*' 1987 (70 minutes) colour and black and white. Produced, Photographed, Directed by Dennis O'Rourke. Associate Producers: J. Henderson, C. Owen. Sound Recordists: Tim Litchfield, Chris Owen. Film Editor: Tim Litchfield. *Distributors:* Dennis O'Rourke, GPO Box 199, Canberra 2601, Australia; fax: 61 6247 7233. USA and Canada: Direct Cinema Limited, PO Box 10003, Santa Monica, CA 90410–10003, USA; fax: 310 396 3233.

From the Heart of the World – The Elder Brother's Warning, 1990 (87 minutes) colour. Director: Alan Ereira. Camera: Bill Broomfield. Sound: John Wills. Editor: Horacio Queiro. English narration and subtitles. *Distributors:* UK: BBC Enterprises, 80 Wood Lane, London W12 0TT. USA: Mystic Fire Video, 225 Lafayette St, Suite 1206, New York, NY 10012. Sale, only: £12; or $29.95.

Nice Coloured Girls, 1987 (17 minutes) colour and black and white. Director: Tracey Moffatt. *Distributors*. UK: Australian Film Commission, Victory House, 99–101 Regent St, London W1R 7HB. Australia: AFI Distributors Ltd, Little Latrobe St, Melbourne, Victoria 3000.

Over the Threshold, 1989 (58 minutes) colour; Filmmakers: Christine Lloyd-Fitt and Yoshi Tezuka. Producer (and UK Distributor): The National Film and Television School, Station Road, Beaconsfield, Bucks, HP9 1LG.

Polka: the Roots of Mexican Accordion Music in S. Texas and N. Mexico, 1986 (52 minutes) colour; Filmmakers: Robert Boonzajer Flaes and Maarten Rens. Editors: Marja Sonneveld and Carla Van Den Berg. Producer and Distributor: University of Amsterdam Audio Visual Centre, Oude Zijds, Achterburgwal 185, Amsterdam. (This video may be copied free by Chicanos of San Antonio, Texas.)

5

Burlesquing knowledge: Japanese quiz shows and models of knowledge[1]

D.P. Martinez

> When the tyrant of Syracuse asked how he could discover what Athenians were like, Plato advised him to read the comedies of Aristophanes.
>
> (Hadas 1962: 2)

Introduction

This chapter is not just about Japanese forms of visual representation and models of knowledge, but also about British forms of visual representation – particularly the representation of Japanese knowledge. In a sense, then, and to use an image which I hope is in the reader's visual knowledge, the situation that will be described is a bit like that of Escher's well-known drawing of two hands on a piece of paper each holding a pencil and drawing the other. Thus, the viewers are watching two amputated objects creating each other. In the case of Escher's picture, we know that it is not possible and that it is just a clever drawing. His inclusion of the edges of the paper and the table in the drawing is a sign of the fact that the representation is unreal, perhaps surreal: it is definitely not a representation of reality. However, in the cases of British television documentaries on Japan and Japanese quiz shows, the very medium of representation requires us to suspend our *disbelief.*

That is, television as a medium of representation is one which relies on our perceptions of the process of filming: unless the viewer is presented with animated sequences, the images on television are seen to be based on reality. The threat of virtual reality notwithstanding, even fictional television programmes can be said to be a form of realism.[2] The definition of television as a form of realism, rather than real, implies certain problems with the way it may represent the world. So, despite the awareness among theorists that film can be a fun-house mirror of reality, and despite the awareness most audiences have these days that there are such things as special effects, the producers of most documentaries and, in this case, of certain Japanese quiz shows, are relying on many people's perception that if a camera has captured it, it is quite likely true. In short, the audience is rarely meant to question the images they consume in these programmes:[3] the viewer can say 'I know it is like that, because I *saw* it on television.' And this is not a reference to hypothetical situations, for, in years of research on Japan, and when working with a British production company, I frequently have been told that x knew y about Japan or Britain,[4] because they had seen it on television.

It may appear that I want to travel the by now well-worn path towards asking: how is it that we acquire knowledge? One standard Western answer, somewhat simply put, is that we know about many things because we have seen them – they have, as the ancient Greeks might have put it, *presented* themselves to us and thus we have *experienced* them. In this century questions have been raised about the propensity to believe that we have knowledge about things we have only seen represented, that is duplicated: do we not live in a time of simulacra which have subsumed representations, as Baudrillard (1983) would put it? MacCannell, who writes on tourism, argues that it is an awareness that only authentic experiences constitute knowledge which fuels modern travellers, for the Western traveller feels that in her/his own society such authenticity is no longer available. Cut off from reality in postmodern society, we try to find it in other places. In his article, 'Cannibalism Today' (1992), MacCannell argues that both tourism to and documentaries on other societies fail in their quest for the authentic, the real, because the very nature of touring or filming makes it impossible to cross the boundary between the staged and the real. Knowledge, then, cannot be gained through representations.

The very ethnocentricity of such arguments is picked up by scholars such as Ivy (1989) who has asked: what do we make of a culture in which knowledge has long been acquired through representations of representations or deconstruction rather than as we in the West would have it, through experiencing? If Japan has long been borrowing its images, knowledge and forms of representation from other cultures, what can we say about its consumption of knowledge?

While all of this is interesting and forms a subtext to the issues of this chapter, it will take another road: I want to describe how the images viewers see presented on television are, for the most part, unquestioned as true representations. And this is one important link between these two very different types of programmes – serious documentaries and quiz shows – their unquestioned realism. After briefly outlining the cases for Britain and Japan, the chapter will return to the problem of representation and knowledge.

Defining the borderlines

In the introduction, it was noted that Escher includes the paper and the frame in the drawing which should be taken as a template for both the structure of this paper and for the analysis of the programmes within the paper. It is necessary, then, to give the reader some sense of the frames which form the boundary of this study. The first aspect to be noted is that of the time frame. The British programmes to which this chapter refers in a very general way span the years 1987–92.

In 1987 I became briefly involved with the world of television; it was also the year in which one television producer felt that Japan was it: his decision to specialise in programmes from or about the country was based on his feeling that it was an untapped market. 'Why', he once asked me, rather rhetorically, 'do we watch so much US-produced television and not that of other societies? Why not Japanese programmes? They are an up-and-coming superpower, are they not?' His vision of importing Japanese programmes for regular British viewing has not yet materialised, but I think his interest in the region (one about which he knew little, if anything, at the time) spoke of a growing awareness of Japan in this country.[5] Indeed, the number of documentaries on Japan as a whole grew and culminated with the Japan Festival in 1992, when a recession hit this successful Other and a definite waning of interest has been apparent. The years of interest, however, coincide not only with the epoch of Japan's number one status in economic terms, but also with the more local intrusion of the Japanese into British economic life: they became major employers and investors in this country.

The Japanese quiz shows briefly described here also grew up in the 1980s.[6] There were a few around in 1984–85 when I first did my field-work; by a 1991 return visit to Japan, not a day of the week went without at least one quiz show being broadcast. As late as 1993, when this paper was given at the ASA conference, Japanese friends were able to add to a growing list of types of quiz programmes in Japan.

This time-frame (1987–92) is itself framed by economic concerns and a particular set of relationships: Britain found itself wooing Japanese businesses, perhaps this was felt as yet another marker of its long economic decline; and Japan was allowing itself to be wooed, signifying its somewhat reluctant determination to act out some sort of role on the economic global scene. Britain was no longer a great imperial power, Japan was now having to 'internationalise': both societies, as we shall see, were not entirely happy with their new roles. Their responses to this situation were varied, but it is rather telling that one part of the British response was to shower the viewing public with prime-time documentaries on Japan, while the Japanese response included documentaries at odd hours of the day, and an increase of quiz shows which incorporated material from abroad on prime-time. Thus another important link between these two types of programmes is the fact that they were both broadcast when it was assumed that most people would be watching: between seven and ten in the evening.

My own interest in the subject of popular culture forms another frame: this interest was fuelled by the experience of working on one such documentary for a two-week period in Japan in 1987. But, I must note here that I have done little in terms of assessing how these programmes are consumed by their audiences. On the one hand, for the British programmes, I am relying on the sort of examples which friends and students have used over the years to justify their opinion on the Japanese education system as proof of the validity of my reading of these documentaries. And on the other, I am claiming that having been involved in the process of filming also informs my analysis. I cannot, however, make such claims for my Japanese material: my examples of how these programmes are read relies on much more general viewing: sometimes done with Japanese, sometimes alone. It is in this area, then, that readers might be able to fault my representation of this particular situation.

Representing the other: British documentaries on Japanese education

The point of departure for this section is from a fact which researchers on popular culture already know: documentaries are not spontaneous recordings of reality, but are composed of images which have been carefully selected. In the case of films on Japan and Japanese education, a specialist might be consulted for the background research on the subject, but the selection of images used has more to do with what the filmmakers already think they know about Japan, than the reality of what it is to acquire knowledge in Japan. These truncated images when presented on television are rarely questioned, for they only reaffirm what the general public already thinks it knows about Japanese education and the acquisition of knowledge. Thus, the popular press's emphasis on Japan's examination hell, learning by memorisation, the importance of the group and the very 'otherness' of Japan gets translated into images which reinforce this 'knowledge' of Japanese society. Important to note as well is that any mention of Japanese education in programmes not specifically on education in Japan or on Japan itself often means that a producer will go to film archives and re-use a series of images which have been already broadcast.

What sort of images are these? They are not false images, that should be noted straight away – nor are any interviews conducted with worried Japanese educators or tired teenagers false either – but they *are* decontextualised images. Not only is the context missing which would give the viewer a sense of where examination hell comes in a person's overall experience of education, but the images appear to be selected to meet our expectations of how the 'group-oriented', 'insect-like' Japanese experience education as a sort of 'conditioning' (these phrases are taken from documentaries on Japan).

Let us consider the most recent hour-long documentary on Japanese education shown as part of the Nippon Series broadcast on BBC2 in 1990 ('The Learning Machine'). The theme of the programme was that despite the fact that the Japanese education system produces a high percentage (98 per cent) of numerate, literate people, there is a price to pay; for the system produces uncreative, unhappy people, who are prone to suicide when under stress. This is an old theme and one which many people in the West cite as a reason for feeling somehow worried about Japan – what they know of the education system seems wrong to them; it goes against their liberal expectations of what acquiring knowledge should be.

What is of interest, however, is how these ideas are represented in the documentary. Lots of images of schoolchildren are used, but generally only shots of middle-school adolescents (both male and female) who wear a dark blue uniform modelled on the uniforms worn by German schoolchildren at the turn of the century and these children, we are told, go to state schools. Already narration and image have worked hand-in-hand to ring a few bells of apprehension: uniforms for state schools and *German* uniforms at that! Then, there are the shots of the students lining up to enter the classroom, often harangued by male teachers who appear violent, followed by a shot or two of the children in the schoolroom. These are often filmed from above, so the room appears to be vast and there seem to be endless rows of dark-suited children, heads bent over their books: it is not difficult to compare these images to those used in programmes on the military.

No programme on Japanese education is complete without explaining the *juku* or cramming school system. And this offers the opportunity for interviews with anxious students (usually male), still in uniform, but perhaps now wearing a headband with slogans on it. They look exhausted and somewhat hysterical, the strain on their faces close to the images often shown of the Japanese novelist Mishima in the moments before his suicide (for which he wore a uniform and headband).

Of all the facts which might be narrated over such images, we are rarely given the most interesting ones: that only about 50 per cent of students set out to take the examinations which will get them into middle schools that will prepare them for university. Of these, it is 30 per cent of all schoolchildren who finally succeed in the examinations and get into university. Of this 30 per cent, another 30 per cent go to junior colleges or technical schools. Also, we are rarely told how, for most Japanese, *juku* and examination hell are associated with Tokyo; so the audience is unaware of how location-specific these images are.

Nor is it revealed that most Japanese children, until they are confronted with the competition for university, are actually very happy at school. Rarely do we get represented what is a common sight in Japan, that is, primary schoolchildren who, if they look uniformly anything, look content. We are not told that their experience of school is one

where it is impossible to fail or to lose (at sports days for example); in general everyone is treated as equal; and that as they grow older school clubs for sports or arts become important to children because they are fun.[7]

The images we are given of the sort of extra-curricular activities in which university students get involved also remain unexplained. Here, I am referring to Clive James's and Chris Tarrant's use of clips from the programme *Gaman* (Endurance), which are presented on English television to show us how strange the Japanese are. No mention is ever made of *who* these masochistic Japanese are exactly. We are not told that of all the images of what Japanese students do, especially what university students do for fun, it is purely the clips from these programmes which give us our idea of what all that examination hell is about: to get one into a university where, with some exceptions, student life is a series of parties, sports and club activities and fraternity-like dares. Knowledge is far down on the lists of these university students' priorities. Appearing on *Gaman* makes a student a typical member of Japanese university life, but not of Japanese society.

The fragmented images presented to us on British television tell us little about knowledge and education in Japan. What they do tell us is what we already think we know about what life is like for children in Japan and, thus, what it is like to be Japanese. Regimentation, cruelty, suffering and knowledge acquired by rote are the points most often made. The most common image used is that of rows and rows of children all doing the same thing – bowing, playing the violin, reciting English phrases, etc. Nowhere in our representations of Japan does there seem to exist room for something which the Japanese themselves are very good at: burlesquing knowledge. It is this which will be considered in the next section.

Figure 5.1 (*facing page*) Autumn Sports Day. All the children of Kuzaki Primary School stretch before the day's events. The photograph is typical of the kinds of scenes documentaries on Japanese education prefer to show Western viewers.

Figure 5.2 The last day of school in Kuzaki village. The children gather for a day of fun and games. The relaxed attitude of the children was typical of almost all the events I attended at the primary school.

The sensei *and the* talento: *representing knowledge on Japanese television*

In the introduction above, it was argued that one standard Western model, perhaps the most dominant, of how knowledge is acquired is that we learn by seeing or experiencing. There is also a model of knowledge which is gathered by memorisation, although this is somewhat out of fashion at the moment since it is deemed to be inferior to knowledge acquired by creative reasoning. Representations of Japanese knowledge acquisition emphasise schoolchildren's learning by rote, indirectly contrasting it with the more creative approach of the modern British system. What is interesting for us, is that when the Japanese (and some scholars of Japan)[8] look at Western models of knowledge they emphasise how coldly rational the West is compared to the warm, intuitive Japanese. For the Japanese, knowledge arrived at by reasoning is an arduous process, for it takes years of rote learning before one can begin to reason creatively with new ideas.[9] There is room, of course, for 'indirect or intuitive reasoning', or 'understanding from the belly' (*haragei*), explained in terms akin to those used for the process of enlightenment in Zen. Japan has had a place for individuals who reason in this way (cf. Dore 1965; Miyanaga 1991), but despite being seen as necessary, they are often marginalised.

Japanese models of knowledge thus differ somewhat from ours if we think in terms of the process of knowledge acquisition, but resemble ours enough that translations of the terms *wakaru, shiru* and *chishiki* as 'understanding', 'to know' and 'knowledge' respectively are not wholly   *111* inaccurate. In contrast to English however it is rare (but not unknown) in Japanese to say 'I see' when something has been understood. But what might be the greatest difference in models of knowledge is, as already mentioned above, that there has long been a propensity in Japan to acquire knowledge from representations alone: the question of authenticity, so central to our consumption of knowledge and to a Western definition of postmodernism, seems not to be so important for the Japanese. One clear and relevant example of this can be found in the Japanese visual arts which could be described more as attempts to evoke the experience of some reality than as attempts to accurately reproduce that reality. Visual representation, then, is not meant to be accurate nor even to attempt accuracy – reproduced realism is not the central point. Thus, visual knowledge of the 'I know it because I saw it' sort might be deemed to be the domain of traditional Western art or modern Western technologies such as the camera.

To assume, however, that the Japanese use film, particularly television, in order to represent reality more accurately than the British, for example, would be foolhardy indeed. As any viewer of Japanese television can relate, even advertisements in Japan aim more at creating a mood, an ambience, than at hard selling a product: they are meant to evoke what life would be like if the product were used. Thus, we must step carefully when looking at television representations of the holders of knowledge, for the learned *sensei* (master, teacher) is often filmed in terms we might label as realistic, while the wild *talento* (literally, talents) who are also filmed in a realistic manner, represent a sort of intuitive, even surrealistic, approach to knowledge.

There are seven public television channels in Japan and two of these, NHK1 and NHK2, are like the BBC, in that they are government-funded and the latter is educational. Even channels which do not emphasise education follow the NHK format when it comes to passing on information. If the topic is one upon which an expert can be found, the learned *sensei* will be brought before the cameras. For some topics there are well-known experts who appear regularly, but a few general points can be made about most of these individuals. The first is that they are invariably middle-aged men. They will be dressed in suits, mostly dark, but grey is permissible, and they will use visual aids to make their points. The television station will supply these: developing photographs, accompanying the expert on location trips, and, most commonly, printing up important points on large sheets of cardboard. The *sensei*'s manner is dry, he generally speaks polite Japanese, the interviewer (often female and very deferential) will ask for clear explanations on technical points, but will generally not interrupt. The feeling is one of the classroom where the *sensei* pours his knowledge into the students who passively take it in.[10] The set for these discursions into sometimes quite detailed knowledge (for example, biographical background with Mozart's scatological puns laboriously translated from the German when discussing the symphony just broadcast) is simple: a coloured background and a chair for the *sensei* to sit in. Sometimes there is a table, to remind the viewer of the classroom, but this is not necessary.

Contrast this with the standard British Open University approach which often combines anonymous voice-overs with lots of examples of the subjects (for example, of arches if architecture, of babies if child development); while interviewed casually dressed experts are frequently shot in their labs or offices which are crowded, often messy places. The Japanese *sensei* is not brought before the camera to confirm a point made in the narration, but is the central figure, the font, as it were, of knowledge on this subject. Documentaries on foreign societies, to compare like with like, generally (but not always) have a visible interviewer who leads the viewer through the programme. These presenters are not necessarily *sensei*, but dress similarly to signal the fact that they are also experts, often in foreign languages or on the subject (American politics to cite a recent NHK/BBC2 co-production). All of this is a wild contrast to the way *talento* are presented on quiz shows, especially on quiz shows which use visual information from foreign countries to pose the question.

From the 1980s quiz shows (*kuizu*) in Japan have increased in numbers.[11] There are shows on the lines of 'The Generation Game', documentary-style quiz shows (i.e. where a serious documentary alternates with shots of a panel who have to guess what happens next), programmes on things Japanese, quiz shows on foreign places, and even shows on foreign documentaries! The sociologist Kato Hidetoshi once explained this propensity for quiz programmes in Japan as the cheapest sort of programme that could be produced (private communication). This may be true for the majority of shows, but not for programmes which send presenters out into the field, as it were, to gather the quiz material. That is, several quiz shows in Japan will send a camera crew abroad to collect interesting and unusual material to show to the panellists who must then guess what it is all about. Thus, Japanese quiz shows are not about ordinary people who have gathered extraordinary knowledge and are being challenged as in 'Mastermind' or 'Fifteen to One'; they are about wild guesses made by panellists who are anything but ordinary: the *talento*.

Talento are famous for being famous: they often have no other talent. The very fact of being a foreigner who can speak fluent Japanese (the sight of which appears to be somewhat equivalent to seeing a chimp talk) is enough to qualify a person to be a *talento*. Japanese *talento*, on the other hand, must embody the anarchic qualities of the foreigner in some other way: they dress outrageously, talk affectedly (in 1991 there was a female *talento* who sounded exactly like Shirley Temple speaking Japanese and who dressed like Orphan Annie), crack good or poor jokes (a comic will be added occasionally to provide humour on a panel), and can make dirty puns. The last thing they should be able to do is to speak knowledgeably on any subject: making outrageous guesses is not only permitted but encouraged. On programmes which include clips from abroad as the questions, the presenter of these clips – in contrast to the presenter of documentaries – is often female, young and bursting with enthusiasm. Knowledge of foreign customs and/or languages is not a requirement. Between the short clips and the jokes of the panellists, the world outside Japan is made to seem bizarre, incomprehensible and, yet, somehow funny.

Figure 5.3 May 1991. Part of the panel from *Sakaimaru Mie* (Looking Round the World) quiz show, known in English as *World Great TV. From left to right:* a ubiquitous female presenter, Kamida N., the comedian Tokoru George and the comedian, actor and director, Beat Takashi (dressed as a Mifune Toshiro clone).

It could be argued then that if the audience feels somewhat foolish and lost in this global mishmash, at least the *talento* are there to defuse any terror through their jokes. The anthropologist Ohnuki-Tierney (1987) might very well ask us to consider the *talento* in the same way as she has analysed her monkey performers: both could be said to be 'an expression of a new and changing aspect of contemporary Japan. Or more appropriately, they are an index of the fact that a profound change is going on at the moment' (Ohnuki-Tierney 1987: 199). Because Japan is going through such profound changes, she argues, there is a need to develop full-blown clowning acts, 'playfully challenging the basic assumptions of Japanese society' (ibid.). Yet, it might also be argued, that like trickster figures who try to have their cake and eat it too, such performances are also reassuring: the laughing at strange foreign customs makes them somehow acceptable.

It is tempting to pose the *sensei* and *talento* as two strongly opposed categories, but given Japanese models of knowledge, I would argue that the emphasis is more on their complementarity. At first glance, the *talento* is a caricature of the student, wildly guessing on a comic version of the multiple choice quizzes which form part of examination hell. Yet the *talento* and the female presenter of clips in some of these programmes

Figure 5.4 January 1995. Two of the contestants on *Naruhodo za Worudo!* (Of Course, the World!). The two unidentified *talento* are dressed to look like young university students. Behind them stands one of the show's presenters, Trump Man – a magician specialising in card tricks who was brought into the show to shore up ratings.

are also clear parodies of the *sensei*: both are asked to provide explanations of the seemingly bizarre. In the end, the female presenter may reveal all, but the fun lies in the very strange and funny explanations which the *talento* make up along the way.[12] All of this relies on the fact that in Japan, the purpose of acquiring knowledge is to attain wisdom: the former can be acquired by repetition and/or fact-gathering, the latter is often intuitive, indirect, almost irrational. For the rare few wisdom can be attained suddenly, without hard work, but for most individuals it takes years of effort.

Furthermore, I would argue that visual knowledge as well is a category of knowledge which the Japanese do not regard as easily attainable. New images can be difficult to comprehend without a guide. On Japanese television the outside world (which can include remote rural areas of the country itself) is not accessible through images and narration only, it is a labyrinth which requires a guide. The guide may be a very serious, learned, professor who displays all his knowledge on the screen or it may be a bizarrely dressed *talento* who acts just as ignorantly as the viewer may feel, but who is not afraid to make leaping assertions. Either way, these two figures provide a key towards understanding the representations flickering on the screen, thus allowing them to become part of the audience's visual knowledge: 'I know it is so, because I saw it on television' is something heard in Japan as well as Britain. The difference is that the 'guides' in Britain traditionally have been concealed within the structure of the programme, pointing us towards an understanding with selections of images and narration while feigning objectivity. In Japan, there is little attempt to be objective or subtle about the process, perhaps because – compared to traditional forms of visual representation – film representations of reality seem fairly brutal and unsubtle anyway; it is only its subjectivity which makes filmic realism palatable.

Conclusion

This chapter began with an illustration of how one-sided British visual representations of Japanese knowledge can be; it has ended with an example of how equally incomplete are Japanese visual representations of foreign countries. There are differences in the way each represents the other, but despite these differences the programmes described have similar aims: to add to our knowledge about the Other. The question, to return to the Introduction, is whether the Japanese or British succeed in this task.

It could be said that it is possible to learn something about Britain from its representations of Japan and something about Japan from its representations of Britain. The most obvious point to be made is one that Said has already made: representations, of one form or another, are political in nature. Armstrong and Tennenhouse (1989) elaborate on this when they write about the violence of representation; the choice of what to represent involves assuming a position on the subject – whatever is being represented is distorted by the very fact of being chosen. If a criticism needs to be made of Said's position, it is the assumption that only people in power create representations with political meanings and repercussions for the Other being represented. Armstrong and Tennenhouse prefer a model closer to that of Foucault: power can be inverted by the Other and it is often done so through representation.

A second point to be made is that representations of the Other often reflect only our own concerns, fears and weaknesses. If the British education system appears to be in a mess, as is the economy, and Japan appears to succeed, 'let us look at why' is the starting point of most education in Japan programmes. What results is a 'mirror image' story about loss of individualism, about education as coercion and a platform for dominant ideologies – what might be if Britain went back to 'old-fashioned' methods of teaching knowledge. In the fragmented and fractured images of the outside world we get in Japan are reflected concerns about understanding and engaging with alien societies: 'is it even possible, do we even want to, and if we do will we be made fools of?' are some of these programmes' implied queries. In both cases, the representations serve to reaffirm the very otherness of these societies, and, as Lacan (1968) might argue, to reinforce a sense of identity on the part of the producers. Representing the Other then is not a purely Western or imperialistic prerogative, but a basic part of any identity formation. Thus, it is not just that Japanese quiz shows burlesque their own process of serious knowledge acquisition, but that they also openly burlesque other societies, which is important, for these acts of clowning help assert the viewers' identities as Japanese. British programmes on the Japanese education system could be read also as a burlesquing of the Japanese through the implicit comparison with the 'creative' and 'individualistic' West.

The term burlesquing has been used here with complete awareness that it implies caricature and parody for the purpose of deriding (cf. the *Shorter Oxford English Dictionary*) – but what is being imitated, for that is what parody also involves? If the answer given to this question were 'reality', we might well find ourselves in the realm where the meaning of postmodernism is debated. In fact in a recent article, Aoyama (1994) offers us parody as the form of knowledge consumption in postmodern Japan. Thus in the postmodern world, knowledge acquisition seems only possible through the fragmentary process of burlesque – the issues of authenticity and experience fall by the wayside and we are left with no critical way of assessing these programmes, and, perhaps we do not need to.

While I am not sure that I want to follow Aoyama in tying parody so firmly to the experience of the postmodern, for burlesquing others is an ancient art, I must make a third and final point. That is, to note (following de Lauretis [1989] and Lindisfarne [n.d.]) that making theories about representation is a political and violent fact in its own terms – yet another type of representation. One could say that there is no end to the process. This is, perhaps, what Derrida (1990) means when he cautions us to think about the very term representation and its sudden prominence in this century. We need to be somewhat wary of the entire subject, to be aware, as Escher makes us aware in his print of two hands drawing each other, of the borders and the frame. We also need to be aware of the ways in which the perceived subjects turn others into subjects. Only when all of this gets included in the picture can we begin to try and understand what it is that we are seeing.

Notes

1. The fieldwork, if I may call it such, for this paper was done over several periods. I watched a great deal of television with my host families in Japan in 1984–86, as well as with fellow foreign students, when I was a research student at Tokyo University. Watching as various documentaries were filmed in the village in which I lived was also an important experience (see Martinez 1992). A return trip in 1987 with Clark Productions proved fascinating as was the more purposeful television watching and very brief interviews I conducted while on Familiarisation leave from SOAS in 1991. Many thanks to the various people who helped in formulating this paper: D.N. Gellner, Kit Davis, John Breen, Tim Screech and K. Tanaka. N. Lindisfarne provided a useful framework, albeit without knowing it, with her paper for EASA 1992. Any misrepresentations are my own.
2. I am following Fiske (1987: 24) who adapts Barthes' definition of realism for television: 'realism is typically narrative in form'. Thus it can be said that all television, whether documentary, drama or comedy, falls into the category of realism which does not 'just reproduce reality, it makes sense of it' (Fiske 1987: 24).
3. I use the adjective rarely here because I am aware that some documentaries may very well want to challenge our perceptions of what is true or false. In general, I would argue that we are expected to accept the information gained from documentaries as fundamentally true.

4.   I will use the terms 'British' and 'Britain' throughout this paper in acknowledge-
     ment of the fact that the producers and consumers of these programmes can be
     from anywhere in the UK. This, of course, may seem naïve as issues of class, status
     and region may crosscut through both the categories of those who produce and
     consume, but this issue will not be discussed in this paper. A similar argument
     might be made about my use of the term Japan and Japanese.

5.   It would be tempting to argue that the efforts of this producer have had a profound
     effect on British television, perhaps even helping to change the nature of some
     British quiz shows (see note 12 below), but I have no real evidence for this rela-
     tionship between the local and global (cf. Miller 1995).

6.   *Naruhodo za Worudo!* (Of Course, the World!) was among the first and initially
     broadcast in 1981.

7.   For several years now, Joy Hendry has been approached by various producers
     interested in filming Japanese kindergarten children, but the proposed pro-
     grammes have never been made, since the notion of happy children did not fit the
     expectations of these filmmakers. Only now has someone with a specifically 'let's
     get new images of Japanese education' agenda managed to do any filming (Hendry,
     personal communication). This is a common experience amongst those of us who
     are frequently asked for advice by television producers. The questions usually begin
     with 'Isn't it true that . . .?' and any statements to the contrary get ignored.

8.   See, for example, the essays in Moore's *The Japanese Mind* (1967), especially
     Moore's own contribution which argues that the Japanese are enigmatic because
     both indirect and direct reasoning (irrational and rational) exist in Japan simulta-
     neously.

9.   Hendry (n.d.) discusses how the learning of both the arts and physical tasks in
     Japan – done by copying, repetition and constant correction – consists of long years
     of work on how to reproduce the object or movement correctly. Only after the
     external form has been properly absorbed can an individual try something new of
     their own and the inspiration for this is often described as coming from indirect or
     intuitive reasoning.

10. There may be an older source for this representation of *sensei*, that is the lectures
     (or *kôdan*) given by Buddhist priests to explain *sutra* which developed into the art
     of storytelling also known as *kôdan*. This form of narrative was popular from the
     fourteenth century until the early twentieth century. According to H. Morioka and
     M. Sasaki, *kôdan* recitations are called readings (*yomimono*) and '[t]he performer
     always sits behind a small desk. . . . As a rule, however, he does not use a manu-
     script. Most *kôdan* stories tend toward moralizing' (1990: 5).

11. According to the *Shorter Oxford English Dictionary*, one of the original meanings of
     quiz was 'to burlesque', but I do not know if the Japanese, having adopted the for-
     eign word, are aware of this double meaning.

12. British readers of a certain generation may well think of 'Call My Bluff' or even
     'Have I Got News for You' as the closest examples of this sort of show in the UK.

References

Aoyama, Tomoko (1994) 'The Love that Poisons: Japanese Parody and New Literacy',
     in *Japan Forum* 6, (1).

Armstrong, Nancy and Leonard Tennenhouse (1989) 'Introduction: Representing vio-
     lence, or "How the West Was Won" ', in their edited *The Violence of Representation,
     Literature and the History of Violence*, London: Routledge.

Baudrillard, Jean (1983) *Simulations,* trans. Paul Foos, Paul Patton and Philip
     Beitchman, New York: Semiotext(e), Inc.

de Lauretis, Teresa (1989) 'The Violence of Rhetoric: Considerations on Representation
     and Gender', in *The Violence of Representation*, ed. N. Armstrong and L.

Tennenhouse, London: Routledge.

Derrida, Jacques (1990) 'Sending: On representation', in *Transforming the Hermeneutic Context*, eds G.L. Ormiston and A.D. Schrift, New York: State University of New York Press.

Dore, Ronald (1965) *Education in Tokugawa Japan*, London: Routledge & Kegan Paul.

Fiske, John (1987) *Television Culture*, London: Methuen and Co., Ltd.

Hadas, Moses (1962) *The Complete Plays of Aristophanes*, New York: Bantam Publishers.

Hendry, Joy (n.d.) 'Forging for Excellence: A Japanese Approach to Discipline and Knowledge', a paper presented in the 1992 London Intercollegiate Seminar Series on Anthropology of/as Discipline.

Ivy, Marilyn (1989) 'Critical Texts, Mass Artifacts: The Consumption of Knowledge in postmodern Japan', in *Postmodernism and Japan*, ed. H. Harootunian and M. Miyoshi, Durham, North Carolina: Duke University Press.

Lacan, Jacques (1968) *Speech and Language in Psychoanalysis*, trans. Anthony Wilden, Baltimore, Maryland: The Johns Hopkins University Press.

Lindisfarne, Nancy (n.d.) 'Local Voices and Anthropological Responsibility: Finding a Place from which to Speak'. Paper presented at the EASA Workshop, 'The Ethics and Politics of Anthropological Research: Changing Paradigms', Barcelona, 1996.

MacCannell, Dean (1992) 'Cannibalism Today' in his *Empty Meeting Grounds, the Tourist Papers*, London: Routledge.

Martinez, D.P. (1992) 'NHK comes to Kuzaki: Ideology, Mythology and Documentary Film-making', in *Ideology and Practice in Japan*, eds R.J. Goodman and K. Refsing, London: Routledge.

Miller, Daniel (1995) 'Anthropology, Modernity and Consumption', Introduction to his edited *Worlds Apart, Modernity through the Prism of the Local*, London: Routledge.

Miyanaga, Kuniko (1991) *The Creative Edge: Emerging Individualism in Japan*, New Brunswick, New Jersey: Transaction Publishers.

Moore, Charles A. (ed.) (1967) *The Japanese Mind: Essentials of Japanese Philosophy and Culture*, Honolulu: East–West Center Press, University of Hawaii Press.

Morioka, Heinz and Miyoko Sasaki (1990) *Rakugo, the Popular Narrative Art of Japan*, Cambridge, Mass.: Harvard University Press.

Ohnuki-Tierney, Emiko (1987) *The Monkey as Mirror: Symbolic Transformations in Japanese History and Ritual*, Princeton: Princeton University Press.

6

Balinese on television: representation and response

Felicia Hughes-Freeland

This chapter addresses problems of procedure and constraint on the interpretation of representations from other cultures. The representations in question are produced by means of trans-indigenous technologies, in this case, television. Anthropologists who study visual data have recently become interested in how peoples from different cultures represent themselves (Ginsburg 1994; Hughes-Freeland 1995) but here I wish to move the discussion further, and to consider questions about how indigenous audiences respond to such representations and some of the implications for analytical attempts to evaluate the significance of television for a particular group (Gillespie 1995). I will first outline some general issues about audience response and then turn to the specific case of the responses of two Balinese men to particular representations of Balinese culture broadcast on the Balinese channel of Indonesian State Television in 1990 and 1991.[1]

The issue of response

During the 1970s there were a number of studies of the impact of television on social change in Indonesia. This research intensified when the Palapa satellite was launched, making TVRI accessible to most parts of the Republic. Until the late 1970s, television had been an urban phenomenon while radio was the most pervasive mass media in rural regions. The extended reach of television and its role as an information source for development did not, however, supplant existing systems: television alone does not have the power to persuade (Susanto 1978). Results of research into audience response to television in Indonesia suggested that television's power to accelerate and determine social change was limited. The 'two-step flow of communication theory' as developed by Paul Lazarsfeld in the late 1960s appeared to explain various Indonesian cases (Rauf 1979: 2). This theory asserted the crucial communicatory role of opinion leaders as the necessary link between television and audience understanding. It is local leaders such as these who are the actual broadcasters. Rather than altering communication flows, television technology supports traditional communication and information hierarchies (Rauf 1979). Indeed, Indonesian anthropologist Budhisantoso claimed that without supplementary sociocultural back-up, television could frustrate rather than encourage support for national development programmes (1979: 19). These findings suggest that there is a discrepancy between governmental assumptions about the power of the media and its social uses. As another Indonesian researcher states, 'television is important but not sufficient' (Alfian 1987: 13).

These findings indicate that initial assumptions about the power of television based on its ability to communicate practical development information have been exaggerated. They do not however automatically provide answers about changing standards and norms in performance, aesthetics and entertainment. Nor do they account for changes which result from any altered time budgeting consequent on the availability of television as an alternative source of entertainment or inactivity: what television viewing prevents you from doing is as important as what it may or may not persuade you to do. The Balinese case is only one example of the government of a developing country using television to develop national consciousness. Televisual media might indicate that globalisation is well and truly with us. If this is the case, then the nature of the television programme as text becomes problematic, and as my example will demonstrate, it is dangerous to assume that one's own sense of problem or contradiction is shared.

Studies of non-Western television production and apprehension offer invaluable and necessary opportunities to arrive at a broader theoretical perspective, and challenge the assumption that technology brings about the same relationships between power and practice everywhere. The Balinese example illustrates Friedman's point (1988) that although the technology may be global, there are many forms to its appropriation. Styles of use and styles of interpretation are culturally specific.

Likewise, it would be wrong to generalise responses *within* a culture. Ways of seeing are not only culturally specific, but specific to the individuals who look, and the experience which they bring to their looking. Practical experience informs the gaze and response of Balinese individuals, just as age, gender and status bear on their use of language tactics. Responses are mediated by language, so there is a double determination in the research process which goes against the grain of easily gained generalisations. If the process resists generalisation, we might be more circumspect about the routes we take to our conclusions about 'cultural' responses to television representations.

As the discussion will show, a television programme is not a closed text, and may be broadcast in a different version, with supplements and deletions. Such a revisioning not only indicates a more fluid relation between televisual text and reader, but assumes that the audience for such versions is constantly renewed, prepared both to consume and forget the latest version. Neither is the message of a narrative fixed in terms of the text. The act of watching television is not necessarily the fact of a text being inscribed on a viewer.

More importantly, the different messages which are represented cannot necessarily be correctly interpreted by the outsider. Viewings of these documentaries with Balinese demonstrated that the Balinese bring specific ideas of order and meaning to narrative sequences which present *apparently* incoherent and conflicting messages, as well as specifying precisely who the audience for such programmes would be. The importance of viewing recorded programmes with Balinese rather than assuming that their narrative and content are accessible is emphasised. The case will indicate that it is important to consider optionality, supplementarity and amnesia as important elements in how responses should be evaluated, in the Balinese case, for the generation of accounts of the past, and of versions of the present and its imagined futures.

The project has so far been based on close textual analyses which tend to support the view that television need not obliterate cultural specificity. But there is a problem in talking about cultural specificity of television, because it is unclear whether that specificity lies in the text or in the reading. Two problems arise with the textual approach. Methodologically, the researcher's own interest and sophistication may influence the way in which the data are interpreted *and* constituted. When I sat down to watch television with Balinese people, the focus of the research on the programme would influence the form of their responses and the nature of the attention they brought to the programme. The responses were not *the* Balinese response but the response of two particular Balinese trying to satisfy (and sometimes divert) the particular research agenda of a British anthropologist.

Secondly, there is a theoretical dimension: as one recent commentator on the current debate points out, there is a danger in the 'polysemic' approach, where the programme is seen as an open text and not a programmatic sign of domination (Morley 1992: 20ff). The exclusive concentration on the micro-analysis of text precludes the structural dimension which determines the production of the text: if researchers concentrate on creativity and pleasure-seeking as bases for audience response, they run the risk, inadvertently, of validating Hollywood's domination of the worldwide television market (Seiter *et al.* 1989, Introduction). Morley suggests that we cannot afford the luxury of a textual analysis without recognising the structural constraints both on the kind of texts which may be seen and the kind of interpretations which are possible and agrees with Murdock *et al.* that the crucial question is '. . . not simply "What kinds of pleasure do these technologies offer?" but "Who has the power to control the terms on which interaction takes place?" ' (cited in Morley 1992: 32).

Balinese culture on television

Indonesian State Television came into full operation in August 1962, but was not received in Bali until 1977, when every subdistrict (*kecamatan*) was given a television set. Indeed, when I made my first ever trip to Bali that year by night bus from East Java, my first glimpse, peering out of the bus window into the darkness, of what I took to be the famed ritual of this 'island of the gods' turned out, once we drove by, to be a group of men gathered around a television set.

By 1991, 800 television sets had been registered at the office of the head of *désa* Tengahpadang, the administrative village unit where the project is located.[2] Before the arrival of the grand Sony colour television set used for project recordings, the household had boasted a twenty-inch black and white set for some time. In Indonesia as a whole in 1990 there were about nine million registered television sets. The fact that people watch television at community centres or in the homes of friends or relatives means that of a population of nearly 200 million, over 140 million people are 'able to watch television' (*Indonesia Handbook* 1990: 214–17).

The Balinese television station of Indonesian State Television (TVRI) has a regular weekly slot for traditional performance. This forms part of programmes classified as education, art and culture which constitute 37 per cent of broadcasting. The cultural programmes are made up of broadcasts of 'traditional' Balinese performance and ritual which show a number of classical dramatic forms and new traditions which are emerging from the Balinese Academy of Performing Arts (STSI). These include two forms of dance drama: *sendratari* which developed in academies during the 1960s, and more recently, *derama tari*. The performances are sometimes studio productions, but more recently there has been a tendency to show 'live' performances from temple festivals or the annual Balinese Festival of the Arts (*Pesta kesenian*). A second type of cultural programme, the 'arts appreciation' variety, will also be discussed below.[3] But first, in order to avoid undue generalities about the Balinese responses to these broadcasts, I will briefly introduce my Balinese viewing companions to establish the interests they brought to their television viewing.

The Balinese audience of two

I Ktut Sutatemaja (henceforth Ktut) is the head of the household where the research project is situated, in a region known for its intensive dramatic productivity. Now in his mid-fifties, Ktut's professional role has been three-fold: driver of trucks and minibuses, theatrical impresario and anthropological informant. Like 90 per cent of Balinese he is of the *jaba* (commoner) caste, but belongs to the Pulosari descent line, which in former times was of the twice-born castes (*triwangsa*) (Hobart 1979). He is thus a special kind of commoner, proud of his descent line responsibilities as bodyguard to the court. He also served as the religious head of the village (*klian désa*) during the 1980s.

Ktut's theatrical enterprises took place mainly in the 1960s and 1970s when he ran a group which performed *jangèr*, a popular performance tradition in Bali (Zoete 1938: 211–17). He also acted in Western-influenced plays (*derama*), specialising in tear-jerking roles. Today he has ritual responsibilities in carrying the sacred *barong* Ratu Gedé during ceremonial peregrinations at the Galungan and Kuningan festival which takes place every 210 days to re-establish cosmic balance. In 1992 he participated in his community's attempt to set up a Ramayana Ballet, taking on the role of a priest, the demonic king Rawana in disguise. His response to television broadcasts about performance are thus informed by long-standing interest, but not by a monolithically professional commitment.

The second viewing companion, Anak Agung Pekak Oka (known as Gung Kak), is of *cokorda* rank from the lower echelons of the *satriya* caste. As there are no top level *brahmana* in the ward of Pisangkaja, the *satriya* are at the apex of the status system. Now in his mid-eighties, Gung Kak delights in sharing his extensive knowledge of Balinese culture with other Balinese and foreigners alike. Until 1962 he specialised as a performer and teacher of Arja, a form of danced opera.

The stocky, self-assured Ktut (Figure 6.1) and the elegantly fragile Gung Kak (Figure 6.2) make a good double act; despite their difference in rank, they have a close friendship based on shared thespian pasts and fostered by a sense of mutual obligation. In the evening they often sing songs Gung Kak knows from Arja performances (Figure 6.3), or recall

Figure 6.1 (*left*) Ktut Sutatemaja.
Figure 6.2 Anak Agung Pekak Oka (Gung Kak) demonstrates Arja.

Figure 6.3 Ktut and Gung
Kak sing Arja songs.

affecting or hilarious episodes from various plays. Ktut and Gung Kak
watched many cultural programmes with me, and it was Gung Kak's
interest in Arja which drew me to the way in which it had been represented on television.

Arja

Arja is a form of dance-drama which has been compared to 'our idea of
opera, or rather of musical comedy' (Zoete 1938: 196) and is made up of
singing, dancing and dialogue. Both men and women take part, but many
of the male roles are played by women. Its plots derive from legends of
Javanese kingdoms of the middle ages. In Bali, theatrical and musical performances are offerings to the gods, and are traditionally associated with
festivals held at different kinds of temples. Arja is usually performed as a
night-long entertainment outside a temple during a festival.

The Arja has recently been the object of a government revival scheme, having lost popularity in the 1960s due to the emergence of other kinds of
performance. Gung Kak's extensive practical knowledge of Arja made it
particularly fortunate that Arja has been the subject of several documentaries on the Balinese performing arts.

The first of these, 'Arja: heading for development and preservation' (5
December 1990, Project Video 10) was a narrative made up of different
reconstructions of Arja in the past. These examples did not make for the
kind of true 'art history' we might expect from the BBC. Rather, the different representations of Arja were used to give weight to the case for the
inevitability of Arja being developed. The programme seemed to be
motivated by interests in rationalising current cultural policy and
revealed features similar to those used to structure reality in certain
Balinese historical narrative texts during the eighteenth and nineteenth
centuries. These features suggest that the distinction between fiction and

125

non-fiction in both historical and documentary narratives needs to be considered carefully in the light of specific cultural practice (Hughes-Freeland 1992).

On a subsequent visit to Bali I was disconcerted to find among our recordings another 'art appreciation' programme entitled 'The art of Arja has nearly disappeared' (3 April 1991, Project Video 21). Although Ktut's eldest son who makes the recordings assured me that it was merely a repeat of the first programme, a cursory viewing proved that this was a different kind of narrative. This second programme uses sections of the first, but takes a different approach to how a tradition might be verified in terms of filmic narrative and imagery. It appeared to conform more closely to BBC standards of television documentary than the first programme, an impression which was due to the more overt causal connections made between narrative sequences and the inclusion of more factual ethnographic coverage. As it turned out, my own expectations and interpretations were not congruent with those expressed by Ktut and Gung Kak, as will become clear when we consider the sequence of the programme and their comments on particular scenes.

'The art of Arja has nearly disappeared': narrative sequence and responses

The 29-minute sequence may be summarised as follows: (1) music; (2) arena; (3) lighting; (4) performer in her village; (5) crowns; (6) costumes and language; (7) elderly woman; (8) Herders' Arja; (9) dance lesson in a glade; (10) Gambuh theatre; (11) A concluding speech. I will describe each sequence and give Ktut and Gung Kak's comments.

Scenes 1–2 The programme opens with a performance of Arja as a commentary addresses the current state of the art and then turns to an analysis of the music, the arena and the lighting.

In these scenes Ktut and Gung Kak identified various performers, noted that the context was the annual Arts Festival, and identified the song as coming from Sanghyang Dedari, a traditional trance performance.

Scenes 3-4 A transition backstage introduces one of the most celebrated older female Arja performers, 58-year-old Jero Made Pada Arsa (Figure 6.4), the focus of the fourth sequence. As the commentary praises her loyalty and devotion to the art, we are shown shots of Jero at home, tending pigs, chickens and fields. Verbal praise for her loyalty is represented emblematically in a shot of her certificate of commendation for contributions to the state. The sequence closes with a long shot of Jero walking towards camera, overdubbed with singing. This scene counterpoises the discourse and emblem of the loyal citizen with images of Jero's work

Figure 6.4 Jero Made Pada
Arsa dances the king in Arja.

in the household; her role as performer does not replace her role as a farmer and householder. She is framed not simply as performer but exemplary citizen: a performer who is also wife, mother, villager.

Ktut and Gung Kak referred to Jero as a 'true artist', who has been known as 'Galuh Grana' since the struggle for independence and famous for her stage presence or charm (*taksu*), popularly attributed to the fact that she has an extra finger on her right hand. The television commentary had alluded to Jero's desire to have this extra digit removed, and her husband's insistence that she keep it. My viewing companions had explained that Jero's husband had forbidden her to have the operation because it would bring bad luck and destroy her power to attract audiences and delight them. They discussed whether this power derived from magic (*guna*) or from a specific stage charm (*taksu*), and finally agreed that magic concerns daily life, and comes from one's own body, while charm is a gift from the gods.

Scenes 5–6 These sequences focus on Arja's costumes, in particular the distinctive crowns of carved gold leather, decorated with fresh flowers. The richness of the costumes is a sign of Arja's association with the old Balinese kingdoms, as are the characters, who represent kings, queens, ministers and attendants. The use of etiquette, language codes, and hierarchy are features described in the commentary as 'inseparable from Arja's courtly origins'.

These scene sequences elicited remarks about ritual offerings made to crowns which take place before the performance, after the make-up is done, and on set days; there was some disagreement about which days, and whether both forms take place. Gung Kak observed that Arja was royal, not because it was the prerogative of the king in an exclusive sense, but because it tended to be performed in the palace rather than being a required theatrical form (*pemuput wali*) for temple ritual. The costumes and manners are copied from kings of old. The stories mostly refer to   *127* kingdoms such as Jenggala, Kediri and Mataram mentioned in the *Babad Bali*, and the other 25 per cent come from Pañji stories, also used in Gambuh. There was some discussion about difficulties in resolving the sources for other kingdoms mentioned in masked plays (*topèng*), which are now in Arja and Gambuh as well. Ktut approved of the singing, and both said that the performances were good. There was some discussion about the sources of the plots.

Scene 7 An elderly, unidentified woman speaks briefly in a nationalist idiom about the importance of developing and preserving Arja.

Ktut observed that she was speaking Indonesian, not Balinese, and that she is a former Arja dancer. Ktut's son, a school-teacher, politely disagreed, observing that her language was a mixture of Indonesian and Balinese. Everyone agreed that this speech indicated that the programme was aimed at young Balinese to help them understand the significance of Arja for promoting national development in Bali.

The problem scenes

The next four scenes elicited more discussion, and are more complex. Scenes 8, 9 and 11 had been part of the first documentary, and were associated with rice culture. This seemed (to me) inconsistent with the emergent courtly theme in the new programme, which is developed in a new scene (10) about Gambuh. I will outline the subject of these last four scenes, identify my sense of confusion, and finally present the commentaries from Ktut and Gung Kak.

Scene 8 Moving back from courtly to agrarian associations, we see farmers, singing in their fields (Figure 6.5); this is an extended version of a sequence with a commentary in the first documentary and is referred to as Herders' Arja (Arja *pengangon*).

Figure 6.5 Rice harvesting scene.

Scene 9 Idyllic scene of an Arja class in a glade, again a repeat and without commentary. An unidentified teacher trains a group of female dancers in a glade to the accompaniment of a small orchestra (Figure 6.6).

Figure 6.6 Dance class in the glade.

Scene 10 Moving from the bucolic to the courtly, we are shown Gambuh, a dance drama alleged to have come to Bali from Java in the fifteenth century (Figure 6.7). Like Arja its plots derive from legends of Javanese kingdoms. We are told that Arja dancers were often trained in Gambuh, but while stories and movement names are common to both forms, movements in Arja are much simpler than those of Gambuh. The performance is from Batuan, where Gambuh itself is being 'preserved', a point emphasised by the fact that a researcher (or serious tourist) is shown videoing the performance.

Figure 6.7 Gambuh.

This scene struck me as significant: there had been no allusion to Gambuh in the first programme, and I was feeling more confident that this second programme aimed to represent Arja's courtly associations rather than making a simple identification with rice culture as had been the case in the first programme. I expected the courtly theme to be developed, and a different conclusion to be presented. I will reserve the concluding scene for later and will present the comments of Ktut and Gung Kak, who like you, were ignorant of the closing comments of the programme.

Responses to the last four scenes

Scene 8 The rice harvesting scene Neither Ktut nor Gung Kak (nor Ktut's son) had ever heard of Herders' Arja. As the singers are not farmers but lecturers from the Balinese Academy of Performing Arts, led by the famous narrator/puppeteer (*dalang*) I Ketut Kodi, it could be a recent creation from the Academy. But having said that, it is true that when Arja was performed as part of processions people would later sing its songs while they were working – for example when they were harvesting rice, working together in rows. Today the replacement of the rice knife by scythes for harvesting means people don't work closely in rows any more, so you no longer have the fun of the group atmosphere. Gung Kak explained that people in the rice fields want to preserve Arja so that it doesn't disappear, because it is connected with the Hindu religion. They interpreted this sequence as a lesson for the youngest generations, as an example for the future, as *projective*: that it expresses a wish for Arja to be learned by many, but that you can't make people learn Arja straight away, because it is technically complex. A first stage would be to encourage people to sing at work; the singing in this sequence was obviously this preliminary stage to studying Arja proper. They did not read the scene as a bucolic reconstruction of a past practice which is what I understood it to be, particularly in view of the historical framing of the first programme (Hughes-Freeland 1992). Whereas I had been thinking about origins, they were thinking about futures.

Scene 9 The dance class in the glade Both Ktut and Gung Kak recognised the teacher as Ni Candri, a famous Arja comedienne. Gung Kak was puzzled by the setting, and queried whether such an arboreal setting was an appropriate place to hold a dance class. Balinese cosmology associates woodlands with disruptive forces, and as such is not a fit place for training in action which will form part of offerings made to deities. Gung Kak also spoke as an apologist for the programme: 'Maybe they're beginners!' he hazarded, in the programme's defence. When I asked him if he used to teach beginners in a wood, he laughed: 'Not at all! we started at home at first, and then when people gained confidence, we moved to the community hall (*balé banjar*), or the palace courtyard. Those are the only appropriate places for studying dance.' Ktut demurred, proposing that this scene was intended to demonstrate the nature of artists' souls, freed from conventions and devoted to their art: they don't care where they practise, they'll even dance in an unclean (*nenten kedas*) place like a wood.

This sounded to me like a modernist stance on Ktut's part, but it was interesting to hear this rationale from someone who considers himself a traditionalist. Despite this caveat, the staging of the scene which to a Western eye might suggest an image of an unspoiled and harmonious relationship with nature does not fit Balinese ideas of human interactions with the natural environment. Dancing, as a holy act, should be done in a place appropriate to it, and not in some demon-infested woodland.

Scene 10 Gambuh Ktut and Gung Kak supported the association of Arja with Gambuh. This is indeed a recognised sign of Arja's courtly antecedents. Unlike myself, neither of them saw any contradiction between this and the previous agrarian images.

Scene 11 Concluding sequence The documentary does not enlarge on the relationship of this courtly antecedent to contemporary Arja. We are instead taken back to the rhetoric of rice culture by Dr I Made Bandem, 'cultural expert', although this programme does not subtitle him as such

Figure 6.8 Dr I Made Bandem sums up.

Figure 6.9 Bath-time in the river.

(Figure 6.8). This is the same clip as in the first programme, in which he speaks of the importance of Herders' Arja as one among a number of influences of contemporary Arja. His speech is intercut with images to illustrate how Arja is to do with rice, work and play: songs are sung at bath-time in the river (Figure 6.9), and at rest while visiting family and friends. The art of Herders' Arja is a single crucial influence on Arja today which has to be saved from imminent oblivion (see Appendix).

My Balinese companions were somewhat nonplussed by this conclusion, and reconsidered their comments about the harvesting scene (scene 8 above), which they had not interpreted as a depiction of past practices which were being lost. Having seen the conclusion, they re-interpreted the harvest scene as representing a past practice, and Herders' Arja as a prototypic form of Arja.

I then explained my theory that the programme gave a dual history of Arja, and kept a balance between courtly and agrarian visions of Bali, or between conflicting egalitarian and feudalist histories and ideologies (Schulte-Nordholt 1986; Vickers 1990). This interpretation impressed, but failed to convince: they would not have thought of explaining the programme in this way, and did not see it as representing contradictions. Despite having to rethink their interpretations of Herders' Arja in view of the conclusion's claim that this is the source of Arja, Ktut and Gung Kak nonetheless maintained their view that the programme was not about Arja's past history, but its role for the future. They did not perceive any contradiction in the programme between courtly and agrarian references, and therefore did not share my problem in how to interpret this programme. They agreed that the programme was trying to create a connection with the culture of the rice field, not the culture of the palace, and that as such it was linked to the natural world. However, there was a problem in how this link was represented, because it was not in terms of a Balinese cosmology, particularly in the dance-training scene in the wood. Rice culture in Bali is the result of natural resources being controlled and civilised by the work of humans (with the blessing of the gods), not the untamed nature of woods and forests. As already noted, they felt that the programme was aimed at young Balinese; this was suggested by the use of Indonesian, and the rather simple rhetoric of development.

Overall their comments aimed to justify or account for the individual scenes, rather than to make open criticisms. This conforms with other experiences of Balinese commentaries as being based on the style of incorporating versions into an acceptable view of the world, rather than discriminating against them. However, this politeness is not inevitable, as demonstrated by their response to another programme, 'Art appreciation: Sapi Gerumbungan (cow racing), Rengganis' (3 September 1991, Project Video 34), produced in North Bali by the Government Arts Department.

This programme also presented a number of Balinese performances introduced by the 'natural rice culture' analogy. The first part was structured by an alternation of rice growing technologies and cultures, such as bird-scarers and cow-racing (a speciality of North Bali) with dances referring to the activity in question choreographed by the Balinese Academy of Performing Arts and performed on their lavish stage: the 'Peasant dance' showed rice cultivation (Figure 6.10), 'Java finch dance' represented birds that eat the rice.

Figure 6.10 'Let us go to the paddy fields'.

Then followed a scene of Rengganis, male group singing, performed in a shelter in a rice field in which one man (not clearly identified by the camera) told a story while the others made vocal sounds. Next came a scene of a group of women pounding in a long wooden rice mortar, a form of music-making called Ngoncang. Then followed a scene where women made brightly coloured offerings from the rice-flour (*jajan sarad*), which can be built up into enormous statues. The programme ended with a staged choreography from the Academy based on a ritual temple dance called Rejang, performed against a back-projected slide image of Besakih, the 'mother' temple of Bali (Figure 6.11).

Figure 6.11 Rejang temple dance performed by STSI students in front of a slide of the Besakih temple.

Gung Kak and Ktut noted that this programme endorsed the origin of Balinese culture in rice cultivation. Ktut's son said that, unlike Herders' Arja, Rengganis is a regional tradition and not a 'creation' performed by staff of the Dance Academy. Ktut and Gung Kak agreed that Rengganis is part of 'a peasant gathering', but could not identify the story; the singing they recognised as *jejangèran* (in a *jangèr* style).

Their responses to this programme were in the form of a twofold complaint. Firstly, they felt that the programme misrepresented the region it depicted. Buleleng is famous for its dance drama (*wayang wong*) and chronicles (*babad*). These are part of the courtly inheritance of the region, an inheritance which was selectively ignored because of the agrarian identifications of the programme. Again, my two viewing companions did not wish to pursue my view of why this might be so.

Gung Kak and Ktut criticised the programme mostly for its confusion and lack of clarity: 'It's not clear what's going on in the work scenes, and the dancing isn't clear.' The programme misrepresented the proper context for the performances in question because the work sequences were not in the right order.[4] Also, they felt that the shift of location from Buleleng to a ceremony at Bersakih was inappropriate, given the kinds of offerings shown: to be consistent with the narrative line there should have been a harvest ritual, which is what *jajan sarad* are used for, instead of a big temple ceremony in another part of the island: 'It isn't clear what it's for; the sequence isn't clear, and it isn't right either. . . . Even if it is only giving illustrations, it isn't clear where they are from, in competitions, or what.'

Because of this, their concluding comment and overall response was that this programme was aimed at a non-Balinese audience living in Bali who have come from Java, Sumatra, etc. 'to show them what goes on in Bali', but the representation of Bali was inadequate. The Arja programme, by contrast, was aimed at Balinese people, especially children: its intention was to act as an inspiration to the Balinese to preserve Arja. This other programme did not inspire any such ambition to maintain cultural traditions.

Responses for what?

So, how collective are these representations, or rather, the responses to them? This is by implication a question about the extent to which things seen on the screen become instrumental in becoming part of cultural practice. The question therefore concerns the extent to which homogenisation arises from filmed representations; a long-term aim of the project is to analyse the perceived effect of these televised representations on performance practice in Bali. In spite of changing conditions and increased literacy and communications networks of all kinds in islands such as Bali, it is not clear whether what is presented on television influences, alters, or maintains behaviour and attitudes.

The responses to the ethnographic examples above demonstrate a respect for what is shown on television, as the justification of the Herders' Arja and the glade scene suggest. Their comments were made in a spirit of humility: even if they disagreed, they constantly corrected criticism by trying to justify what the television had shown. This was probably out of respect for the performers who had been involved in the programme. These productions have come from the powerful and form part of strategic cultural programmes, but as representations they need to be understood according to the criteria by which they are used, or responded to, in the context of Balinese practices, rather than being taken out of context and treated as texts which are susceptible to transcultural assumptions.

The typicality of responses has also been identified as a problem for analysis: an individual with a particular life history cannot simply be claimed to represent a general response. And what that viewer may or may not do with the impressions gained from televisual representations is also unpredictable: the fact of the act of forgetting the first Arja programme is a significant counter to the oversolidification of representations as durable cultural realities.

It remains to be seen, then, whether the intention to construct possible futures from imagined histories which lurks somewhere between the Ministry of Information in Jakarta and the production offices of TVRI Denpasar will take root and produce a transformed collective conscience in the anticipated audience, or whether new diversities and tactics will be catalysed. There have already been startling developments which testify to a local awareness of the diversity of television audiences. In 1993 TVRI Denpasar started to broadcast 'Balivision', an evening magazine programme in English, aimed not at Balinese and Indonesian viewers but international tourists. Broadcasters have already had to recognise that sources of television are becoming diversified with cable and satellite channels providing more choice. Today they have to respond to the fact that audiences are neither captive nor homogeneous, but heterogeneous, and in need of captivating. Audiences may respond by switching channels, representations are therefore having to compete for audiences, and control is being challenged by the possibility of consumer choice.

Meanwhile, the project has a rich source of texts which document six years of broadcasting, and it continues to generate a fertile supply of questions which require new projects and personnel to explore. The work of the Balinese Academy of Performing Arts is clearly a precondition for the televisation of many of the programmes which have an overt cultural educational agenda, providing rhetoric for shaping responses to traditional culture, rather than merely broadcasting particular versions of it. In January 1995 a recent Academy production of the new *derama tari* genre was broadcast. The story dealt with a new problem for the Balinese: AIDS. If Balinese dramatic representations are able to assimilate negative developments such as these, it seems that the response will be less to the *experience* of the illness, than to the mediated gossip about it.

It remains to be seen, then, whether responses to broadcast dramatisations will catalyse and deflect ongoing cultural transformations in the terms of reference which orientate Balinese people to a sense of their own identity, or whether the response to *witnessed televisual representations* of intrusions into Balinese experience will result in a firming up and fossilisation of the diversity of local response. The determinants of the forms of rejection or acceptance in themselves are also at issue here: will Balinese responses in the future be Balinese, or versions of Balineseness controlled by the Indonesian state?

Appendix

Translation of Dr I Made Bandem's closing speech on Arja:

> Arja is a Balinese performing art which derives from drama, song and dance. It grows out of the instinct for play. One form of Arja is Herders' Arja in which peasants and buffalo- or cow-herders entertain themselves in the rice fields when the harvest is over. They make instruments from rice stalks, called rice-stalk flutes, and they also use mattocks, rice knives and other tools as an accompaniment to their entertainment. In this way Herders' Arja grew.
>
> In addition to this, in Bali every evening young men and women go to the river to bathe, and sing *macapat* songs. These songs then became one of the main elements of the Arja we know today. The relationship with the work ethos is also expressed in the visits of the young to their parents' homes to chat, and to show their willingness to sing and play, until this also becomes a major source for the growth of contemporary Arja.
>
> Herders' Arja has a close connection with rice culture, which is now being developed with advanced technology, so that peasants and herders no longer drive cows and buffaloes, but instead use tractors. This puts pressure on their way of life with the result that Herders' Arja will soon have become extinct. Because of this it would appear to be an art which needs to be preserved as a source of inspiration for the development of the forms of Arja we can see today.
>
> (Translated by the author from the transcript in Indonesian, Project Diskfile Arja1.app.)

Notes

1. This material comes from the project 'Television and the transformation of Balinese

culture', a collaboration with the Balinese Academy of Performing Arts and its direc-tor Dr I Made Bandem. The project started in 1990, and is designed and coordinated by Dr M. Hobart (School of Oriental and African Studies, London University), and developed with my collaboration. The recordings and transcriptions are done by members of the household where Dr Hobart has been doing his research for over twenty years. As of the end of August 1995 our archive contained over 929 hours of television programmes on video tape. Of this, 506 hours are broadcasts of 'tradi-tional' Balinese theatre; there are another twelve hours of live Hi-8 video recording of temple performance made by F. Hughes-Freeland in August 1992. A longer ver-sion of this chapter appeared in *Indonesia Circle*, 69, June 1996, entitled 'Balinese Culture on Television'.

2. Of these, ninety-nine were in Pisangkaja, the *banjar* (ward) where research was car-ried out. These statistics should be taken with a pinch of salt. The total of five tape recorders listed for our *banjar* was fewer than the number in the project household.

3. Between August 1990 and September 1993 five of these had been broadcast and recorded. Educational or information material about the performing arts is more usually incorporated into the regular magazine programmes about village life, *Nusa Ning Nusa* and *Banjar Kita*, as well as being one aspect of regular weekly broadcasts on Hinduism and Buddhism, *Mimbar Agama Hindu* and *Mimbar Agama Budha*.

4. Similar criticisms had been made in comparing a live and televised version of the *derama gong* play *Ayu Ratih* (Hobart forthcoming). The extra scene shifts in the live play which were more dramatically effective were estimated by the Balinese to be confusing because the motivation for a cut to another location at that point was not clear.

References

Alfian (1987) 'The Impact of Television in Indonesian Villages', mimeograph, Inter-national Institute of Communications Annual Conference, Sydney.

Budhisantoso, S. (1979) 'Initial Reception of Television in Indonesian Villages', mimeo-graph, given at East–West Center Workshop on Evaluation and Planning for Satellite Communication Research 15–18 July, Honolulu: East–West Communication Institute.

Friedman, J. (1988) 'Cultural Logics of the Global System: A Sketch', *Theory, Culture and Society* V: 447–60.

Gillespie, M. (1995) *Television, Ethnicity and Cultural Change*, London: Routledge.

Ginsburg, F. (1994) 'Culture/Media: A (Mild) Polemic', *Anthropology Today* 10 (2): 5–15.

Hobart, M. (1979) 'A Balinese Village and its Field of Social Relations', PhD, London.

— (forthcoming) 'The Plight of the Beautiful Moon: A *Derama Gong* performance of Gusti Ayu Ratih as explained to the author by Balinese'.

Hughes-Freeland, F. (1992) 'Representation by the Other: Indonesian Cultural Documentation', in P. Crawford and D. Turton (eds), *Film as Ethnography*, Manchester: Manchester University Press.

— (1995) 'Making History: Cultural Documentation on Balinese TV', in *Review of Indonesian and Malaysian Affairs* 29 (1, 2): 95–106.

Indonesia Handbook (1990), London: Indonesian Embassy.

Morley, D. (1992) *Television Audiences and Cultural Studies*, London: Routledge.

Rauf, Maswadi (1979) 'Television and Opinion Leadership in Bali', mimeograph, in East–West Center Workshop on Evaluation and Planning for Satellite Communication Research 15–18 July, Honolulu: East–West Communication Institute.

Schulte-Nordholt, H. (1986) *Bali: Colonial Conceptions and Political Change 1700–1940*, Rotterdam: Erasmus University, CASP.

Seiter, E. *et al.* (1989) *Remote Control: Television, Audiences and Cultural Power*, London: Routledge.

Susanto, A. (1978) 'The Mass Communications System in Indonesia', in K.D. Jackson and L.W. Pye (eds), *Political Power and Communication in Indonesia*, Berkeley: California University Press.

Vickers, A. (1990) *Bali: A Paradise Created*, Singapore and Berkeley: Periplus.

Zoete, B. de with W. Spies (1938) *Dance and Drama in Bali*, London: Faber and Faber.

7

Computer software as a medium: textuality, orality and sociality in an artificial intelligence research culture

Georgina Born

The more technical and specialist a literature is, the more 'social' it becomes . . .

(Latour 1987: 62)

Introduction

When visual anthropology has engaged with contemporary electronic media, it has done so primarily through the lens of reflexive concerns surrounding the practices and textuality of ethnographic film and television (e.g. Crawford and Turton 1992). By contrast with this reflexive awareness, it is striking that new digital technologies, on the few occasions in which they have been addressed within visual anthropology, tend to be conceived instrumentally, as unproblematic means for new kinds of ethnographic research or for the enhanced analysis and presentation of anthropological materials. Howard (1988) and Seaman and Williams (1992), for example, in discussing the relevance of hypermedia for ethnography, describe it in purely instrumental terms – as enabling a highly flexible integration of digitalised visual, sonic and written materials, initially as an aid for ethnographers' collection and organisation of data, and later for retrieval by interested others (students, scholars, the public). The thrust of these papers thus sits uneasily with the greater reflexivity of recent debates around ethnographic film.[1]

In this chapter, I pursue the other main project characteristic of visual anthropology as a field: that of analysing the textuality and visuality of a cultural system. I do so in relation to a pervasive and infrastructural digital technology, computer software. Drawing on an ethnographic study of software research and development, I offer an account of computer software as a medium focusing on its modes of visual representation and coding and how these invoke both oral communication and particular kinds of sociality. Analysing how textuality, orality and sociality are mutually implicated in the practices around software generates, in turn, a critical awareness of the vulnerabilities and limits of this complex   *139* contemporary medium. The aim is, then, two-fold: to introduce into anthropological debate on digital technologies a concern with their complex materiality – especially, in this paper, their mediating visual and graphic representations; and to indicate the insights gained by adopting a more searching and reflexive approach to new technologies within visual anthropology.

I want to begin by framing my approach in relation to several extant anthropological and social scientific approaches to information technology (IT) and the rationalities, such as cognitive science and computer science, informing it.

The instrumental attitude towards new technologies in visual anthropology that I have described forms part of a modernist perspective that is more widespread within anthropology. In this perspective, IT and cognitive science are seen to offer neutral tools or models for anthropological research (e.g. Sperber 1975, 1985; Bloch 1991; Fischer 1994). This may be for the analysis of data (such as kinship patterns); or for providing models of the kinds of cognitive processes which, it is held, underlie cultural and symbolic forms. By giving a sense of the encultured character of these models and technologies, this paper problematises the a-cultural assumptions with which they are imbued in the modernist approach.

A contrasting approach can be found amongst those espousing a postmodern perspective. Influenced by the deconstructive turn in the sociology of scientific knowledge, these writers want to interrogate the social construction of science and technology, including the supposedly fixed boundaries between humans and machines, and the classificatory dualisms, such as those of agency versus automation, which depend on this fixity and which resonate with an idealised organicism (Haraway 1991; Downey 1992). Instead, they erect a speculative and idealised notion of IT encapsulated in the transgressive figure of the 'cyborg'.

Yet is it really necessary to portray the cyborg as politically progressive because of its challenge to naturalised boundaries,[2] or to argue that machines have similar capacities for agency to humans, in order to disturb the dubious ideological underpinnings of the major dualisms – culture/nature, human/machine, male/female and so on? This can become a surrealist politics which celebrates boundary transgression for provocative effect; but which, in a kind of wishful linguistic determinism, leaves unexamined the resilient differences (such as those between humans and machines) on which those dualisms rest. I can sympathise with Haraway's intentions – to engage critically with the social relations of science and technology, and to resist the demonisation of technology in organicist discourse – while finding her provocation unsatisfactory.

Finally, there are writers who have worked empirically on computer cultures, such as anthropologist Suchman (1985) and sociologists Turkle (1984) and Woolgar (1991). All have produced microsociological accounts of, variously, the research, design, and use of computer systems focusing on the human–machine interface. While each study generates important insights, they lack critical distance and sociological acuity. Suchman, for example, adopts an ethnomethodological stance which evades consideration of the wider industrial and economic forces converging on the arena of her observations – Xerox PARC (Palo Alto Research Centre), a major IT research outfit for the Xerox corporation. Woolgar, rather than attending to the specificity of IT, uses his ethnography of a personal computer design business to promote currently fashionable themes in the sociology of technology. (Thus, the machine is treated as a text; configuring the machine is at the same time envisioning and configuring the user; and, once again, the boundary of human/ machine is questioned by problematising the issue of intentionality.)

Within anthropology we have, then, the modernists – for whom cognitive science and information technology have been treated as 'found' tools for human emancipation, and for cross-disciplinary theoretical scavenging; and a certain kind of postmodernist, who wants to question modernist instrumentalism, but who in so doing risks producing a highly speculative idealisation of new technologies.

Speculative theory in relation to IT is not unique to anthropology. Debates over the 'information society' have for decades oscillated between utopian and dystopian perspectives overdetermined by the bearer's wider theoretical orientation, generally unburdened by much empirical research. It is a phenomenon that has caused Poster (1990) to call for vigilance in theorising the specificity of what he calls 'the mode of information', and for an attempt to escape the reduction of electronic and digital media to the terms of the earlier orality/literacy debates, as well as to the theoretical terms of post-structuralism, dominated as those are by the problematic of language. Instead, Poster proceeds to reconstruct post-structuralism by reading it, as it were, through the lens of IT and electronic media.

In summary, the approaches mentioned tend to grant the technologies an unproblematic effectivity. None interrogates the textuality or materiality of computer media, or (with the exception of Poster 1990: 146–9) the discursive qualities of their informing sciences. All conceive of the media at issue as *a-social* and bracket out empirical consideration of their social character. It is these absences which this chapter addresses, in attempting to outline the 'practices of rationality' (Rabinow 1988: 360) of computer software.

In what follows I draw on two approaches. The first is the Foucauldian tradition of critical studies of expertise, of the relation between power and knowledge as they are embodied in the dominant discourses of the present, including not only linguistic forms but technologies, practices, institutions. It is the empirical detail and the materiality of Foucault's discursive genealogies which are so stimulating, and which achieve his aim of an 'ascending analysis of power' (Foucault 1980: 99). The legacy of Foucault demands a reflexive relation to contemporary scientific and technological discourses, and one more empirically informed, and more critical, than those currently on offer. One feature of Foucault's approach is his rejection of both sociological and technological determinism. Rather, the development of an apparatus involves the simultaneous constitution of the technical object and the human subject.

The second approach I will invoke is that of Latour (Latour and Woolgar 1986; Latour 1987, 1993), who places the anthropology/sociology of science at the centre of his reconstruction of social theory. Latour charges anthropology with failing to produce a reflexive analysis of Western science that would undermine for once and for all the rhetorical flourish which poses non-Western practices against an idealised scientific rationality. Latour is neither postmodernist nor relativist. Whereas Foucault provides a structural account of scientific arguments and apparatuses in their fully formed state, Latour gives an analysis of science in practice and in process. He argues that the constitution of the social as a separate realm of existence is the end result of a painstaking process of scientific work. Natural scientific practice involves what Latour calls 'purification' which, if successful, defines the category 'nature' by constituting it as completely independent of the social context of its production. Similarly, the aim of a great deal of engineering is to produce technical objects which function in a wide variety of different locations and do not depend on their makers' constant supervision; that is to say, which successfully separate the technical from the social.

One key aspect of Latour's argument is particularly relevant to my concerns in this paper. He emphasises the centrality for scientific practice of *inscriptions*: any written or visual text, such as a figure, diagram, experimental record or explanatory document, which translates a scientific object or process into graphic-textual form, and acts thereby as a kind of irrefutable, visually objectified evidence, and as the basis for potential replication (Latour 1987: 64–70). Inscriptions are mechanisms which seek to establish the autonomy of the scientific or technical object from the immediate circumstances (including the social conditions) of its production, to enable its mobility beyond its original location (Latour calls this the capacity to 'act at a distance'), and which work to support its aspirations to 'universality'. Crucially then for Latour, the 'a-social' character of technology is the goal of the social process of production, and one variably achieved, rather than some inherent characteristic or basic ontological state. And inscriptions – visual/textual translations and extensions of scientific practice – play an essential role in separating the scientific from the social so as to establish the autonomy of the scientific object, as well as in legitimising these processes, and thus in the attempt to establish the universality and effectivity of any technology or scientific discourse.

The empirical basis of this chapter is an ethnographic study of a prestigious scientific and high-technology research institute. The institute in

Figure 7.1 IRCAM: external view, 1993.

question is IRCAM (*Institut de Recherche et de Coordination Acoustique/ Musique*), a computer music research centre generously funded by the French state.[3]

IRCAM is the music wing of the Pompidou Centre. It opened in 1977 and was founded, and until recently directed, by the composer and conductor Pierre Boulez. IRCAM's cleaving to computer technologies is the contemporary outcome of a long-term tendency within the modernist tradition of musical composition over the twentieth century towards an increasing concern with science and technology as sources from which to derive new musical sounds and new compositional structures and ideas. After the Second World War Boulez took a prominent role in this development, becoming the leading European proponent of an intensified high modernism. By the 1970s he was advocating a complete reconstruction of the musical language through an intimate dialogue with computer technologies and related sciences (Born 1995, chapters 2 and 3).

Within IRCAM scientists, computer programmers, engineers and composers are engaged in the research and development of computer software and hardware primarily as aids for musical composition, but which also find wider scientific and industrial applications. IRCAM's research subcultures have a certain autonomy, and form part of an international network of research groups working on similar problems based in universities, public research centres and commercial corporations. IRCAM research staff are largely drawn from this international network, which is dominated by several leading American centres. Thus while   *143*

IRCAM is funded nationally, it is international in its reputation, personnel, and in the scope of its research.

Computer music technologies at IRCAM and elsewhere are developed to perform one of three functions: acoustic and psychoacoustic research – the analysis of sound and musical materials, and of their perception; the production and processing of sound materials; and the structuring and control of musical materials – that is, higher-level conceptual ordering for composition. The three may be closely linked, as when acoustic analysis of a synthesised timbre (or sound colour) is used as the basis of structural ideas for a composition. All of these functions depend on a symbiosis between scientific analysis and the development of sophisticated software. In this paper I focus on the development and use of software at IRCAM, from the use of standard music programs by IRCAM students, to research engaged in applying the vanguard field of artificial intelligence (AI) to music. AI is, both at IRCAM and beyond, perhaps the most mystified and ambitious area of high-level computing. The design of AI programs (known as 'expert systems' or 'knowledge-based systems') depends on prior scientific analysis of particular areas of knowledge or expertise, in order then to model them in the software – so-called 'knowledge engineering'. AI research at IRCAM addresses both basic physiological and perceptual processes (aural perception), and very high-level cognitive and encultured processes (musical cognition and musical structure). AI posits itself as a kind of meta-theoretical, and applied, 'science of sciences' (or knowledges). An AI research culture such as that at IRCAM is therefore a particularly suitable object for interrogating hegemonic forms of scientific expertise and their technological embodiment. But it can stand also as a microcosm instanciating general features of software research.

The remainder of the paper falls into three parts. The first focuses on the place of visual notations, codes and texts in the use and development of IRCAM software, identifying a number of problems that arise. Following this, I discuss the forms of oral and social mediation engendered by the kinds of visuality and coding that are characteristic of the software, and the antinomic tension between them. In the last part of the paper I bring together my findings on the visuality and sociality of software, and consider their implications for the wider practice of high-level software research and, more generally, for critical analysis of the scientific status of software.

Codes, mediation, and texts

There are three fundamental properties of computer software that must be grasped at the outset. First, software is composed entirely of codes, themselves conceived and written in graphic notations designed specifically for the purpose, or in extant programming languages. Second, to call programming codes 'languages' at all is misleading. They are, rather, graphic and visual systems – notations – which can only metaphorically be equated with natural languages – an equation with interesting effects, as I discuss shortly. Third, software is inherently multitextual. The use and the development of software involve the writing of coded instructions within a programming language, or of a completely new language, within the context of a vertical *hierarchy* of such languages. At each level of the hierarchy, a translation occurs between any two adjacent languages or levels of code. Instructions from the code or language at a higher level must be translated into a form whereby they can be 'read' and executed by the lower level code or language without any (or with minimal) loss of 'meaning'. The system is thus composed of a vertical hierarchy of mediations (Figure 7.2).

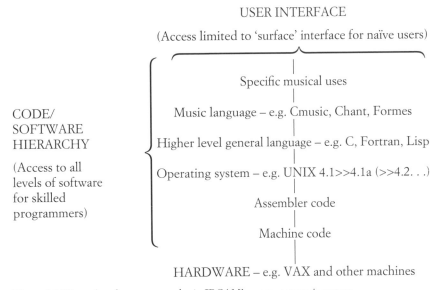

USER INTERFACE

(Access limited to 'surface' interface for naïve users)

CODE/
SOFTWARE
HIERARCHY

(Access to all
levels of software
for skilled
programmers)

Specific musical uses

Music language – e.g. Cmusic, Chant, Formes

Higher level general language – e.g. C, Fortran, Lisp

Operating system – e.g. UNIX 4.1>>4.1a (>>4.2. . .)

Assembler code

Machine code

HARDWARE – e.g. VAX and other machines

Figure 7.2 Hierarchy of computer codes in IRCAM's computer music system.

The lowest level of the hierarchy of codes normally operative in computer software is known as machine code – the instructions that drive the hardware, which are written in binary form. The next level of code up is assembler code, made of mnemonic abbreviations of machine code which themselves condense a number of lower-level operations. Above this in the hierarchy comes the general operating system (such as UNIX or MS-DOS), which is responsible for access to and management of the whole system, and which provides a framework for higher-level programming and a basic set of services. Above this comes any of the major computer languages, such as Fortran, Pascal, C, Prolog or Lisp. The point about the higher-level languages is that they provide condensed ways of expressing many thousands of lower-level operations in assembler or machine code. Thus extremely complex instructions can be encoded with economy. The rationale is also that they provide more meaningful forms of expression for particular uses. The history of software development, then, has apparently been a search for increasingly technologically and conceptually economical and powerful languages for different kinds of applications.

It is common to find yet further levels of mediating code above the major languages in the hierarchy: either higher-level languages with yet more specialist applications; or additional programs, or routines, written in an existing language. In computer music, for example, we find two further levels of mediation. First, music languages which are themselves based on one of the established general languages. Thus in the 1980s IRCAM used a music language called Cmusic, written in C; and IRCAM researchers had developed music programs called Chant, written in Fortran, and Formes, written in Lisp. And second, there are substantive one-off computer music programs written as the technological basis for particular compositions, based in turn on one of the IRCAM music programs or languages.

What is the character of the texts and codes involved in computer music and other software? Above all, one is struck by the condensed complexity and unintelligibility of programming notations, by their resistance to intuitive meaningfulness. This is exacerbated by the way that many programming codes and syntaxes are teasingly reminiscent of, and yet distort, natural language. Because of their reference to signifiers and terms drawn from natural language, programming notations create an illusion of closeness to natural language. This illusion seems to deceive some programmers, who find it difficult to perceive the intransigent opacity of the notations to the layman, or even to other researchers. Despite the claim mentioned earlier that high-level software employs expressions appropriate to its functions, it is hard to see how computer music languages can be seen as appropriate to musician users. Rather, they necessitate lengthy apprenticeship into complex technical knowledges and codes with only extremely mediated relations to music. Interestingly, one experienced IRCAM composer–researcher decided to program not in higher-level languages but in assembler code. He did this, he said, because his programs ran faster and he could control them more directly and easily in assembler than mediated through higher languages. Thus he found assembler just as 'appropriate' and amenable to encoding his musical needs.

Let us examine programming notations in greater detail (Figures 7.3 and 7.4). To use a program or language, the user must follow coding rules of great detail and precision. In the syntax, every letter, numeral, space, comma, semi-colon, bracket, change of line must be used cor-

Figure 7.3 (*above*) Programming notation from computer music: part of the programming in the realisation of York Höller's composition *Arcus*, Haynes 1984.

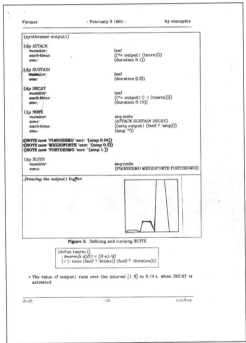

Figure 7.4 Programming notation from computer music: excerpt from a manual for the Formes music-structuring program. Internal IRCAM document, by Xavier Rodet and Pierre Cointe, February 1984.

rectly. The smallest mistake in code or syntax creates a bug – a logical error that prevents the program from running. When programming within an established high-level language there are certain protocols of expression to be followed, themselves arbitrary in nature but at least reinforced by conventional and commonplace usage, and thus open to meaningful variation and to an intuitive grasp of their logical foundations. However, in many substantive instances of programming there are

147

no intuitively strong, general rules underlying the detailed specifics of code and syntax. Thus to use and engage with such programming is to learn to follow by rote or imitation existing arbitrary procedures of coding, usually with little grasp of how these trigger underlying processes, or of their logical bases, while all the time being aware of the extremely limited and particular scope of the rules that have been learned.

Far from being open to different readings, then, these notations are barely open to decoding at all – except for those specialists initiated into the detailed specifics of the codes, who may in turn be unaware of how they produce their resultant effects. These are codes of such precision of expression, tied to such rigidity and specificity of function, that they are thin in meaning and have no polysemic density, just ranges of specified variables. There is a kind of tyranny in the demand that the user absorb so much trivial detail of expression in order to achieve the program's limited purpose. It is this nexus of profusion of detail, unintelligibility and unrelatedness to any other known or meaningful code, and limited purpose and application, that is so telling. In this sense programming codes form an endlessly expanding universe of particularistic inventions, a regime of signification untethered to powerful general principles, and even to the basic semiotic and classificatory principle of meaning being constructed through difference. That is to say, there is such an excess of difference in the world of programming – difference embodied in the particularities of different languages and their subcodes, in their specific enunciations and specialised applications, and in changes in all of these over time – that there remains, in fact, no sense of difference that can organise perception or that is conceptually valid. Instead this is a universe of absolute, fragmentary and fragile particularity.

When we look at the character of texts and communications designed to explain programs to users (Figures 7.5, 7.6 and 7.7), it is in implicit response to the absence of apparently meaningful general principles that many such texts have the tenor of constantly trying to establish general rules. In other words, to interest the user and teach how to use a program they try to reduce the incoherent complexity of the program to a series of basic meaningful parameters. Indeed explanatory texts often take the form of a stream of general statements of possibility, the purpose or relevance of which may be left hanging. The aim is presumably to reconstruct the logic underlying the production of the program in the first place. Nonetheless the judgement exercised in performing this reconstruction may be more or less convincing. In some cases it is as though the initial aims have become diffused or lost in the intervening process of technological implementation, and that program design has taken on an autonomous momentum of its own: programming without functionality.

The language of explanatory communication around software is itself characteristically unclear, as though infected by the intuitive opacity, and the distortions of natural language, of the program codes themselves.

MIX(1carl) UNIX Programmer's Manual MIX(1carl)

NAME

mix - stereo csound file mixing program

SYNOPSIS

mix [flags] < score > samples

flags:

- -v verbose, print a digested form of the score on stderr,
- -e en-tete, print the designation of the fields
- -bN make sound file buffer size = N (default 16K)
- -RN make sampling rate = N (default 16000)
- -s share open sound file descriptors if two notes play the same file
- -t show time

DESCRIPTION

mix is a stereophonic, score-driven *csound* file mixer. It reads its standard input for text lines of the form:

mix begin_time filename duration offset [chan] [step] gain1 gain2 [f1[f2]]

where:

mix is the literal string, mix,
begin_time is the time to start mixing, can be expressed in seconds (related to the sampling rate of the mixer) or in samples with the postoperator S,
filename is a (possibly partial) *csound* filename specification,
duration is the length of time to mix, can be expressed in seconds (related to the sampling rate of the mixer) or in samples with the postoperator S, durations less than 0 specify the end of the sound file (in this case the duration is calculated related to offset and step),
offset is an offset into the sound file of where to begin, can be expressed in seconds (related to the sampling rate of the file to mix) or in samples with the postoperator S,
chan is an optional field of the form: c#, where c is the letter c and # is a number (1 to 4), it designates the selected channel in the sound file to mix (default 1), the program detects itself the number of channels in the sound file,
step is an optional field of the form: s#, where s is the letter s and # is a real number, it is the increment to read the sound file to mix (default : sampling rate of the sound file to mix / sampling rate of the mixer's output, to enable mixing sound files with different sampling rates),
gain1 is the gain of the output1 (a real number or with the postoperator dB),
gain2 is the gain of the output2 (a real number or with the postoperator dB),
func1 is an integer number wich designates an envelope function to be applied to output1 (default 0), 0 is constant 1, 1 is a linear function from 0 to 1, 2 is a linear function from 1 to 0, other functions can be created with gen statements wich are like gen4 statements of cmusic.
func2 is an integer number wich designates an envelope function to be applied to output2 (default func1).

It ignores all lines that do not begin with *mix* or *gen* so you can include comments.

gen statements are of the form:

7th Edition CARL 1

Page 18

It is automatically checked and adjusted so as never to be longer than one-tenth the duration of the shortest of the two notes it functions between. The default value is .07 (seconds). Values lower then .02 produce an instrumental rather than a vocal transition; values as high as .18 can be used if the skips between successive pitches are larger than a fifth. The transition curve is a sine-wave section from 90 degrees to 270 degrees. The default value is .07 (seconds).

TVALA1 (TCLM)} | Times between selections of new random values for
TVALA2 (TDLM)} | variations of the vibrato Amplitude . The times between selections of new random values between +.5 and -.5, which are scaled by VALA1 and VALA2 and used in turn to change continuously the vibrato amplitude.

TVALF1 }| Times between selections of new random
TVALF2 }| values for variations of the vibrato Frequency

USER Flag for no-call (0) ,or call (-1) of the user's subroutines. For the computer-musician (!) who is curious to know better how this goes : The parameter user is only a flag for the first pass of chant (newcha) which allows him to call the standard second pass (calcul) or the own user's second pass (calcul[pro,nam]) that has been linked with his subroutines by the user.mic procedure .

VALA1 (QCLM) }| Stand for "Vibrato-ALeatoire-Amplitude" . Scalers
VALA2 (QDLM) }| controling the random variation of the vibrato amplitude value . They are linked respectively to TVALA1 and TVALA2 (TCLM, TDLM) (The times between selections of new random values). VALA1+VALA2 = the total desired excursion of the vibrato amplitude value ABOVE (or under) its mean value (VIBAMP) , i.e. 1/2 the TOTAL desired excursion. If VALA1+VALA2 =.015 the total excursion of the value (of the vibrato amplitude) will be .03 times the mean vibrato amplitude (from +1.5% to -1.5%) Each of them should be approximately 1/2 of the total desired excursion above or under the mean value .If VALA1+VALA2 =.01 and the vibrato amplitude (VIBAMP) = .04 (4%) ,the total excursion will be .02 times the mean vibrato amplitude : .02*.04 = .008 ,that is from .004 . above (.04+.008=.048) to .004 under (.04-.008=.032) .

VALF1 }| Stand for "Vibrato-ALeatoir-Frequence" . Scalers
VALF2 }| controling the random variation of the vibrato frequency value . They are linked respectively to TVALF1 and TVALF2 and function like VALA1 and VALA2 .

VIBAMP (CC) The amplitude of the vibrato. It is expressed as the ratio between 1/2 the vibrato excursion and the center frequency around which the vibrato is operating. For example, a value of .03 for VIBAMP results in a vibrato which moves from +.03 * the center frequency to -.03 * the center frequency.

VIBFREQ (DD) The frequency of the vibrato in hertz. In singers this value varies between roughly 4 and 7, and small changes within this range are quite noticeable. The default value is 5.5.

VUSER1,2,3,... Variables at the USER's disposal ,from VUSER1 to VUSER100 . See USER section 4 .

happening is very simple. The (invisible) indexes are being incremented internally and are varying from 1 to numdels. Generally speaking we need to do the following things with our invisible indexes:

. increment them: this is automatic.

. be able to state offsets: we do this with [+1] or [-1] etc.

. be able to reference the current value: we do this with [.] .

The idea here is to avoid having to explicitly declare, initialize, and increment special variables for this purpose. If in such a construct we do not want an index to change we simply give it a value and the copying mechanism will not override it. So we can say things like:

```
toto[]
toto[+1]
toto[-1]
toto[+5]
toto[.]
```

Lets go back to our mixer and make a complete definition in order to illustrate what we are talking about:

```
(outmix)=mixer( inputn/int acoeff/o inputs[]+ )
( { outputs[inputn]  inputs[inputn]   times/int }
  times = inputn - 1;
  COPY times
   { outputs[] = (inputs[] * acoeff) + outputs[i + 1]; }
  outputs[inputn] = inputs[inputn] * acoeff;
  outmix = outputs[0];
)
```

Here is another example which allows us to make 170 4A type oscillators.

```
(outclus[10])=4acluster(phaz[170] freq[170] ampl[170])
(
  COPY 10
  { (outosc[]) = osc(phaz[] freq[] ampl[] ZERO);
    COPY 16
     { (outosc[]) = osc(phaz[] freq[] ampl[] outosc[-1]); }
    outclus[] = outosc[.];
  }
)
```

Note that in this last example that we have nested COPY. The invisible index is the same in both cases.

-24-

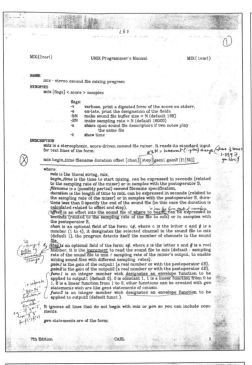

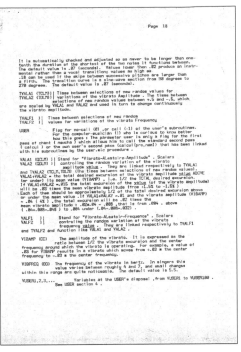

Figure 7.5 (*above left*) Text explaining the Mix music control program (excerpt). Internal IRCAM document, distributed for the IRCAM composers' course, January 1984 (author unknown).

Figure 7.6 (*above right*) Explanatory text: excerpt from a manual for the Chant sound synthesis program. Internal IRCAM document, by Xavier Rodet, early 1980s.

Figure 7.7 Explanatory text: excerpt from the documentation of the 4X Patch Language. Internal IRCAM document, by Andrew Gerzso, February 1984.

Looking at explanatory texts one is struck by the way the condensed mnemonics of programming sometimes spill over into them, revealing a carelessness with the language of explanation. There is commonly a disproportion between the amount of explanation and the code being explained: either a massive excess of exegesis, bewildering in what must be absorbed in order to understand, say, one short line of program code; or else an absence. In this case, because of the impossibility of imparting all the underlying programming knowledge necessary for the particular code at issue, a programming solution may simply be stated with little or no explanation. Potential users are posed with the task of first having to gain a background in relevant aspects of programming, and what is being assumed may be unstated and left for them to decipher. There may be wild swings between these two modes – the excessive and the absent – in the same explanatory communication.

To exemplify my points, I offer a reading of some teaching material for a computer music program, Cmusic, that was central to IRCAM's introductory course (*stage*) in computer music for composers in the mid-1980s – a course that I attended.[4] The language on which Cmusic was based, C, was closely linked with the UNIX operating system, then becoming a standard in combination with the well-known VAX minicomputers. Cmusic was therefore increasingly used both in Europe and the United States. It is a sound synthesis program that digitally simulates electronic techniques of sound production, and is known as a 'patch language' – one of a family of similar programs.

Let us look at what is involved in using this patch language. To produce sounds, the user must build up complete acoustic and psychoacoustic descriptions of the sounds desired from scratch, and then encode them into the language. The user writes a computer 'score' utilising a code with a very precise syntax in which, again, each tiny detail must be correct or a bug occurs which prevents synthesis from taking place. The 'score' file contains two kinds of information: an 'orchestra of instruments', that is, coded instructions that simulate analog electronic sound generators or transformers (oscillators, filters and so on); and a list of 'events', that is, code for a sequence of sound events to be produced by the generators. For each event, all basic parameters – starting time, duration, frequency, amplitude – must be specified, and each 'instrument' fully 'described'.

In the Cmusic teaching manual used on the IRCAM composers' course in the mid-1980s, there was an introductory section on how to write the simplest possible 'score' file which began with a disarming disclaimer: 'This example is so simple that it wouldn't even sound very good.' It then took more than two pages to explain the code protocols. The coding was dependent on a prior conceptualisation of the electronic instrument patch to be simulated, which in turn depended on a prior understanding of electronic music patching as well as a knowledge of acoustics. Overall, this introductory section was both extremely dense and unclear, exhibiting a great disproportion between exegesis and code. The 'sense' of the explanation was far from self-evident, and the meaning of terms wavered and multiplied. For example, late on it was mentioned that five terms – 'function', 'stored function', 'function table', 'wavetable' and 'lookup table' – all 'refer to the same thing', but this was simply asserted without explanation of the looseness of the definitions. Another part of the explanation contained an error.

Even this attempt at a careful and basic pedagogic exercise therefore contained a curious oscillation between extreme precision, looseness and imprecision in defining higher functions, absence of explanation, and even some faulty explanation. Faced with this kind of text, apprentices became bewildered by the combined excesses of trivial technical information and the highly mediated nature of the medium. Of a cohort of twelve on the composers' course, three dropped out within the first two weeks; while another confided, four weeks in, 'I haven't understood anything for days!' Few seemed able to make much use of the teaching. In private IRCAM researchers insisted that to begin to be truly 'at home' with IRCAM technologies took several years' full-time application.

Beneath computer music's surface textual complexity, then, lies a great density of vertical and lateral, technological and conceptual mediation. To use the patch languages and other computer music software for even the simplest exercise requires knowledge of several domains: acoustics and psychoacoustics; electronic music techniques; some basic general computing; and the dedicated area of computer music itself. These enter directly into the description of the sound desired, or into the manipulation of parameters which produce or control sounds. Moreover skilled use of the programs requires knowledge of the computer language underlying them. So in order to become adept at using the IRCAM programs Chant or Formes it is also necessary to be knowledgable in Fortran or Lisp. The problems this may cause are indicated by my diary note from a teaching session one month into the composers' course, in which we were learning to use the Chant program.

We're working with the Chant Manual on 'user subroutines' – sections of the program amenable to user manipulation. WOW writes up a new kind of syntax on the board, and before we've written it down he rubs it out! Everyone gasps, laughs, looks baffled. 'Leave it up till we've copied it down!' But WOW has moved on already. *Stagiaire* VT protests: 'But you've written it in Fortran! How can we learn how to use Fortran so quickly? It's impossible.' WOW explains that we need to know Fortran to use some Chant subroutines. This is the first we've heard. *Comment:* WOW baffles us by giving us too much to take in, a completely new language, and rubs it out before we've even taken it down, as though aware that it's impossible for us to learn this level of control.

151

Opacity and instability

I have been stressing the complex incoherence of software notations. For naïve or unskilled users, it is impossible to intuit the implicit logic of the codes, so that their use requires guidance and lengthy application. Even then, naïve users learn to control and interact with only the surface level of the hierarchy of codes. If there is a bug, they are powerless to enter lower levels of the system hierarchy to work out and correct what is wrong, just as they are powerless to alter or improve the system as a whole as they might wish. It is this kind of problem that has stimulated the AI aim to design what are called 'interactive' systems which would allow users to build 'customised' software environments for themselves. However, this cannot escape the material character of software: even with an interactive program, such as IRCAM's Chant, there are still layers of code underlying the program which naïve users have no skill to enter and modify.

More surprising is the fact that this problem of the *opacity* of program codes, and of the system as a whole, also seriously affects senior researchers and programmers. At IRCAM complete programs are usually written over a period of months or years by several collaborators: a gradual, collective bricolage. Software is, then, characteristically the result of multiple authorship. The process is far from being totally preconceived, and programming solutions to problems and aims that arise in the course of development are tried out, altered, and kept or discarded often without any record being kept of the why and how. One researcher described his fantasy of a program as a sort of monstrous baroque or rococo construction, made up of many fussy crustations added on to the main body, until the original body is obscured and becomes almost indecipherable. Skilled programmers complained that, looking back on programs they had written in collaboration with several others, the complexity of the codes made it extremely difficult for them to reconstruct afterwards from the codes themselves exactly what was done and how in the bits of code authored by colleagues, without asking them.

Thus due to its inherent social and temporal mediation, programming code – despite its image of transparent logic – is far from 'open', self-evident and transparent to decode even for highly skilled programmers, including its co-authors. However some IRCAM programmers delight in this intransigent opacity of programs since, despite the many difficulties that it causes, it makes programs appear artful and unstandardised expressions of collective imaginative labour. We will see that this forms part of a discursive struggle in which programming is aligned with artistic labour, rather than with the supposedly rational, replicable and routinised procedures of science.

The problem of software's opacity is linked to, and exacerbated by, the inherent instability of software as a medium. Several factors converge on this. First, the chronic instability of the wider technological environment, as driven by industrial and commercial interests. Computer technologies change constantly and rapidly. They do so as a result of both the need to absorb and respond to technical innovation, and the corporate desire for rapid obsolescence and so insatiable markets for new products. In the 1980s American-based multinationals led the market in large-scale computer hardware (such as the VAX's used by IRCAM which were manufactured by Digital Equipment Corporation). This was a highly monopolistic sector, compounded by the multinationals' control over the servicing of their own machines. American multinationals set the standards to which research outfits had to conform. Setting the standards, and constantly revising them upwards, gave these corporations the power internationally to force other national research outfits to upgrade and adopt their new standards. This was achieved by a pincer movement involving, on the one hand, financial leverage: the service charges for existing machines would rise sharply each year until it became uneconomic to continue using them and cheaper to upgrade to the new machine. On the other hand, the change to new technologies was induced by the desire to keep abreast of the latest, state-of-the-art research environment without which it was feared that research might become outdated. In these ways, the American corporations pressurised clients to take their new products. By setting the pace of standardisation in the high-technology sector, they imposed premature obsolescence on technologies which were still in many cases entirely functional.

IRCAM was, in the 1980s, fully caught within a trap of dependence on American technologies, in particular the VAX/UNIX combination which served as the basic institutional and research infrastructure. In 1983 the move to the VAX from the previous main computer, the PDP10, had been enforced by ever rising service charges. In 1984, IRCAM was induced to upgrade its UNIX software from the extant version 4.1 to the next generation, 4.1a. UNIX 4.1a was needed to allow IRCAM to link up to a major new, American-based international network facility, and to help create a local network of machines within IRCAM, necessary for the premiere later that year of Boulez's new masterwork. Each change of the technological infrastructure of this kind had enormous repercussions: with every significant change of hardware or software, all other levels of software had also to be adjusted. Thus the move from UNIX 4.1 to 4.1a required that all the programs in the house had to be rewritten or re-translated in terms of the coding of the new version. For this gigantic task, two American consultants were brought in for several months' work; and one expressed the view, even while bringing in 4.1a, that in order to keep abreast of wider developments IRCAM should really be investing in the next generation of UNIX, 4.2 – which was already being introduced in the United States.

The extreme instability and rapid obsolescence were embodied in the mid-1980s at IRCAM in the many bits of discarded computer technology, peripherals, and the racks of old software tapes strewn chaotically around the corridors. Some were just a couple of years old, yet they lay around as though suddenly useless.

The re-translation of programs into 4.1a – the rewriting of every bit of higher and lower code in the vertical hierarchy so as to interface correctly with the new operating system – caused severe problems. Each new translation caused bugs, and for some months, because of them, the computer system became extremely fragile, the VAX crashing many times a day. The instability caused by technological change is therefore exacerbated by the high degree of interconnectedness of the various hardware and software components of the system, and specifically by the vertical hierarchy of codes. We can see also how the opacity of the system is aggravated by this combination of interconnectedness and instability, in that if one element of the software changes, all else around it has to as well – yielding a state of constant flux which weighs against comprehensibility.

But re-translation, and the risk of bugs and need for debugging that it caused, were not simply enforced by the revision of external technological standards. This would be to ignore forces internal to the research culture: that is, the drive on the part of researchers to make voluntary experiments in bringing in new hardware and software, their surrender to the seductive temptations of new technological possibilities. For example, the IRCAM team responsible for the Chant and Formes programs, designed initially for the PDP10, rewrote them first for the VAX, then for IRCAM's own hardware, the 4X machine, and a couple of years later for the Apple Macintosh. Such processes were ubiquitous within the research culture. Typically, for each composer's visit researchers would create a new network of hard and software components, involving the writing of new linking programs. Once again, each change in a significant piece of software required all programs abutting it to be reworked accordingly. Thus researchers themselves courted the constant re-translation of programs for new contexts, each supposedly offering new advantages. Programmers were ambivalent about the phenomenon, yet they were also in some ways blind to the effects of their own actions. While they avowed that each such experiment provided useful knowledge, at the same time they railed against the chronic fragility and instability of the computer system – a fragility and instability exacerbated both by major changes in, and by their continuous toying with, the technological framework. The inherent vertical mediation of software, then, can induce a constant tinkering by skilled programmers, a play of re-translation between codes, of readjustment to challenging new circumstances – the longer-term productivity of which is questionable.

Another internal dynamic stoked the instability of the environment. IRCAM's software research contained discursive conflicts over two related oppositions: research versus production, and the relative merits of long-term, open-ended versus short-term research cycles. Management berated researchers for failing fully to stabilise their work so as to complete the research process, as it were in the short term, and create a fully operative 'tool' (software or hardware product) for musical production. Researchers, meanwhile, staunchly defended their right to engage in ongoing research for as long as they deemed necessary in order to achieve their more ambitious goals. This position was characteristic of IRCAM's internal intellectual vanguard, who articulated a utopian vision of long-term, collaborative, disinterested research powered by superindividual creativity. A member of the group conveyed the development of the Formes program as an evolutionary process of collective imagining and authorship, in these terms:

> Formes was developed a little by MC and JDK [scientists], who tried to put in certain musical capabilities. Then XU joined, who's a computer scientist, and he started developing these incredible ideas. It reached a first stage of development, and then the musicians came in: HY's used it, NR and HU have used it. They all found there were a great deal of problems, things they needed it couldn't do, which were *implied as possible.* And so they started firing all this stuff at XU, and it went into an incredible state of flux – because there was this very fast turnaround loop between a [musician's] suggestion and its implementation by XU. In a sense [the musicians] were serving as developers, by *imagining possibilities* that weren't yet implemented. It's the musicians – especially NR – who dove in there and understood at a very basic level 'what is this program doing', so they could then suggest concrete things to XU. So there's a constant movement between stability and instability, the fixed program and creative flux.

The same researcher responded as follows when asked about the issue of stabilisation, and of bringing long term software research to fruition.

> GB: Do things ever stabilise in research, so they can be used widely even within the house?
> HM: That's a real problem. For instance, in the early stages of Chant, it was always evolving so it was very hard to use it as a tool for production. There came a point when they decided they'd gone far enough, that any further things they would move into another project – and that became Formes. So after a few years Chant got sort of fixed; and at that point it really entered into production. But that took a number of years. And meanwhile [management] are saying, 'Well, it's been a year, you know, and we don't have any tools that are useful!' It doesn't work that way!

You have to get to a certain level before you make a version people can use. It's the same problem with Formes: it's been evolving constantly, and it's been a real frustration for people using it.

GB: So that's why there's been tension about Formes, with people saying it hasn't been stabilised enough to communicate?

HM: Exactly, it hasn't been stabilised yet because it's a bit too young. There's an agreement that they'll make a version in the next few months that'll be fixed and usable; and that should be documented. But first it has to get past a certain threshold. If you do it earlier, it wouldn't be as interesting as a tool because it wouldn't have the musical power that you want . . . I *could* make a tool that goes straight to immediate [musical] demands. [But then] it's good for nothing except that immediate demand. Whereas if I'm more careful about the path I take, and the possible spin-offs along the way, then this becomes a much richer domain and generates knowledge, in the sense of . . . [creating] a system as well as gaining an end goal.

Orality, sociality, and virtual sociality

The researcher refers in passing here to another major characteristic of IRCAM's research culture, linked to its instability: a chronic lack of documentation of research – in Latour's terms, a failure to create inscriptions. Both internal and external critics saw IRCAM programming as too much 'in flux'. They charged researchers with a lack of concern to develop and stabilise their experimental work so that it could be documented and thus diffused more widely. Some researchers, as in the second quote above, admitted that this was an issue while also defending it as a necessity. I return to discuss the documentation problem later. For now, it serves to introduce wider questions of orality and sociality in software research and use. That is, the instability and complexity of codes, and lack of documentation, call forth a culture of constant oral mediation: of exegesis of programs, transfer of knowledge, and translation of ideas into and out of programming terms, and between different programming modalities. This oral mediation is also, immanently, social mediation: given the problems of textuality and encoding, and in the absence of effective written documentation, the dynamics of technological knowledge sharing and withholding are structured by social relations. And in their local form within the research institute, the social dynamics of knowledge distribution are microcosmic of the wider social structuring of expertise.

I want now to examine the local forms of oral and social mediation, as exemplified by IRCAM. At IRCAM, orality was not simply a communicative strategy called forth by inherent qualities of software. It also formed part of a reflexive discourse on the nature of IRCAM as a research culture. Within the research and production sphere, as hinted in the earlier quotes, there was a strong ethos of collaboration, openness and knowledge-sharing which was closely linked by researchers to an image of IRCAM as an oral culture; and together these imbued the institute's intellectual sphere with a utopian and libertarian spirit.

The notion of IRCAM as an oral culture was initially decreed by an early IRCAM director, the composer Luciano Berio. Another director recalled it thus: 'Berio made the famous statement, which became law, that he would have *no documentation* in his studio, because "music is an oral culture." This was crazy; but it became the standard here, so that BU [the 4X Hardware designer, who then worked for Berio], for example, has never bothered to document his work.'

'Openness' and 'knowledge-sharing' were embodied architecturally and technologically. IRCAM's main underground building contained rows of glass-walled offices and open-plan laboratory spaces, so that work-in-progress and meetings were always on view to those passing by, and dropping in was encouraged. The institute had an interconnected loudspeaker system which enabled anyone to overhear the sounds being produced by whoever was working on the main computer system – an aural 'openness' akin to surveillance which provoked ambivalence in those whose sound experiments were thereby monitored. The VAX-based computer system composed an internal network which enabled users to make contact with, and even oversee, each others' work; and this internal network was linked up to various national and international computer networks through which researchers kept in touch and shared ideas with more remote colleagues.

Openness and knowledge-sharing were also enacted in the many formal and informal research meetings at which staff discussed ongoing projects and tried out new ideas. In these meetings intellectual workers acted as each others' first internal consumers or critics, so providing a first, experimental completion of the production–consumption cycle. Differences and conflicts were aired in the context of a collective speculation and projection encapsulated by the common use of the phrase '*imaginez que . . .*'.

Knowledge-sharing also occurred over time. Composers and researchers spoke of a 'pool' of accumulated IRCAM expertise embodied materially in both recorded tapes of sound experiments, and computer tapes of past programming, which were drawn from previous visits and projects, and which lay around the institute *ad hoc* and anonymously. Thus incoming composers could gain ideas from a collective pool of past ideas, unburdened by a sense of original authorial intent. No doubt such a process contributed to the gradual sedimentation of an IRCAM aesthetic. The means of producing these sound experiments were likely to be lost in the haze of past custom-built, undocumented technological configurations, if they were not stored in (human) memory by one of IRCAM's permanent staff.

But above all knowledge-sharing occurred in the longer-term collaborations between IRCAM researchers, or with composers; and in the constant informal consultations exchanged between workers trying to understand and use new bits of hardware and, especially, software. Over the working week, researchers visited one another to ask for help with problems which arose, or to enquire about possible resources. All of this informal consultation was by word of mouth. It was an oral culture of mutual help, largely unaided by documentation, as the technologies in question were usually still work in progress and so not yet stabilised, or they were custom-built one-off programming solutions. In either case, documenting the 'tools' was not deemed to be a priority or necessary to the researchers who were knowledgable about them.

The informal exchanges between researchers amounted also to the most pervasive form of direct, spontaneous sociality within the institute – one reserved primarily for intellectuals, who were less desk-bound than lower-status workers. In a sense this was the intellectuals' way of combatting the extreme social isolation and sensory deprivation of the long hours of computer terminal work. Researchers' collaborations thus functioned to 'socialise' the technology: several people would come together round a terminal, contradicting its implicit ergonomics, or round a piece of hardware, bringing complementary skills to bear on a problem. At other times workers maintained their actual terminal isolation while indulging in the computer's enjoyable substitute for direct human contact: computer mail. All researchers, when they first 'logged on' to the VAX, read the computer mail that came throughout the day from people at other institutions to which IRCAM was linked by national and international computer networks, and from individuals within the house. Having logged on, users deployed a command which listed all the people currently logged on to the system, and where they were located – at which IRCAM terminal. The listing also indicated what 'job' people were engaged on. Messages would fly between different terminals, sometimes for work and informative purposes, often for fun and light relief; they would interrupt work in progress by suddenly appearing on the VDU. The language was colloquial, the tone teasing and, between the sexes, flirtatious. These forms of computer-mediated sociality became substitutes for direct contact – a 'virtual' sociality. A worker could go in to the institute, log on to the system and work at his terminal all day; he could exchange computer mail with others in the house and know exactly who was there and approximately what they were doing, and yet never physically meet another person.

Most intellectual staff were amused by the epithet 'oral culture', with its egalitarian and collectivist overtones, for IRCAM. These aspects of IRCAM's technological culture, then, appeared to express a healthy disregard for individual authorship in favour of collective endeavour, as

well as a disdain for the fixing of research in textual form which would enable it to become realised as intellectual property. The oral, collaborative ethos appeared also as a counterbalance to the many rivalrous and ideological divisions within IRCAM's intellectual sphere.

However, things were not so simple. For one thing, visitors did not perceive IRCAM's research culture in this way. An American computer consultant who had worked for a major American rival, the commercial entertainments corporation Lucasfilm, questioned the collaborative ethos, commenting that 'The major contrast between Lucasfilm and IRCAM is that there's no co-operation here, no one works together!' Moreover, IRCAM's educational software licence legally enjoined the institute to maintain security on the commercial software, such as UNIX, that it received. This involved protecting the source code, the basic level of the software, from being spied on, copied or tampered with. Thus commercial interests and legal structures were supposed to prevent all levels of this technology from being openly accessible.

The Computer Systems team, in charge of managing and maintaining IRCAM's computing resources, said that it was as a condition of obtaining UNIX that they had been obliged to set up IRCAM's first computer security system: a system whereby access to working on the VAX was limited to those who had been allocated a secret individual password which they had to use when they first logged on. Before UNIX came, there had been no such security system limiting use of the main system, so that in principle anyone could log on. This had been a basic tenet of IRCAM's anarcho-libertarian computer subculture in the previous era, led by a few internal programmers and some computer science 'squatters' from the University of Vincennes including a Professor – a leading figure in French AI. The anarchists were proponents of a discourse widespread in international computer cultures, and supported by the technical difficulty of protecting computer data: the notion that computer technology is inherently democratic and an anathema to notions of private property in knowledge. Several of the Chant/Formes research group held this perspective, which related to their advocacy of software which evolves through a process of gradual input from users, of communal authorship. The Systems manager FA reported that when he had first introduced the password system, several of the computer anarchists refused to comply and would accept no password. They vowed to subvert the security, considering it to be ineffective window-dressing in any case. This set the scene for a half-serious, ongoing game of pseudo-guerrilla warfare around the issue of security between the anarchists and FA's Systems team, perceived as the system 'police'.

Ironically, the Systems team were sympathetic to the anarchist cause, and ambivalent towards security and their managerial role, so they oscillated between 'policing' and themselves subverting the security controls. Central to the password system were 'superusers': privileged users of the system who, for management purposes, knew a common 'superuser' password which allowed them access to all levels of the system, even its secret code. By contrast, users with ordinary passwords gained access to restricted areas of the system. Only Systems team members were supposed to be superusers and to know the superuser password. It became apparent to me, however, that knowledge of the superuser password was more widespread, and that the Systems team would let it be known to those with whom they were friendly or who were pragmatically useful. Thus, several of the senior scientific figures knew it, and a few senior programmers; once I had become intimate with the team I was let in on it; and a visiting computing consultant, BW, a close friend of Systems manager FA, also knew it. FA admitted that even his supposed ideological opponent, the squatter-Professor from Vincennes, knew the superuser password.

Rather than being a guarantor of security, the password was therefore a currency with restricted access structured by the exercise of patronage, and one which by virtue of its excessive diffusion had currently become debased. Indeed its content was a meaningful joke. In this period the superuser password was 'Men at Work', the name of a then highly successful Australian pop group. The Systems manager FA and his friend BW were Australian; and the password, invented by FA, was a poke in the eye for both IRCAM's high musical pretensions and those of the security system, since it vested the ultimate technological power of IRCAM in a fizzy 'Ozzie' pop group.

On the other hand, as I suggested earlier, the anarchic 'openness' of access to information at IRCAM also created ambivalence amongst IRCAM intellectuals since it seemed like constant surveillance and denied them privacy for their work in progress. So workers concocted various informal ways of protecting privacy and retaining secrecy: blocking the glass walls of their studies; working at night to prevent others knowing what they were doing, or even whether they were working at all. Two incidents gave me first-hand experience of the fear of surveillance and intrusion.

Some months into fieldwork I was writing an early paper about IRCAM on a wordprocessing editor on the VAX, working at nights and weekends to avoid informants' curiosity. One Sunday the following incident occurred, as recorded in my diary.

> I'm sitting typing, almost no one about, when RIG [Pedagogy director] comes in and stumbles about in the office, glancing at what I'm doing. He says, 'You're not still using "vi"? You should use the "emacs" editor. It's much better, I only use that nowadays.' I say, 'I don't know emacs, I only know vi because that's what I learnt on the *stage* [course]' – which he taught us! . . . He goes next door. About half an hour later he comes in and says, 'Excuse me for looking over your shoulder but . . .' and continues that I should learn some simple formatting rules which will

automatically lay out my text. *Comment*: this 'looking over my shoulder' means that RIG had been checking me out, spying on what I was working on at my terminal by getting into my directory and files from his terminal! I must be very careful of what I write, mustn't leave any confidential stuff in my files, because it seems that they can be examined any time . . . Later, I get scared that RIG will tell HM, HY and others about my article, that they'll all look and laugh at what I'm doing, turn against me.

My evident paranoia that anyone could look at my work stored on the VAX was less technologically than socially misguided.

Weeks later I asked visiting consultant BW, who had become a friend, for help with making my files more secure; and he wrote me a little program whereby I could cryptically encode my files – scramble them up and make them unreadable except by using a secret decoding device which only I (and he) knew. Later BW enlightened me about another area lacking privacy on the system: a file which stored all the past computer mail that I had sent. BW's telling me was ambiguous, because it indicated that he had probably been reading my past mail: another sensitive area, since I had thought my mail confidential. These discoveries gave me a sensation of others having access to my hidden inner thoughts. The ease of access to files and data, even 'protected' data, was confirmed by an IRCAM student, an iconoclast with a flair for programming, who confided to me a few weeks into the composers' course that he had found a way to see inside many confidential institute files on the VAX.

Individuals' desire to keep their work in progress private from rivals and critics relates also to tensions over differential access to research. The oral culture of research meant that to understand the technology one was dependent on the oral help of the informed, and, like the security system, this help was socially structured by patronage since it could be withdrawn or withheld as well as granted. IRCAM's two main technology research groups, one working on the 4X machine and the other on the Chant/Formes programs, were both notorious for the exercise of patronage; and this caused much ambivalence and frustration. For example, we saw above how the 4X designer took Berio at his word by resisting the documentation of his hardware designs and so retaining an oral research culture. A director described his encounter with this as follows:

I used to work on BU's machines – I did a piece on the 4A,[5] I wrote a lot of the 4A's software. But I gave up and moved over to the PDP10 because it was impossible to work on BU's stuff! You always had to go to him to ask what was wrong, how things worked. There was never any free information. BU has always been secretive and not let people in on his stuff. That makes it hell to work with.

This view of BU as withholding information was widely held, so that even a researcher working on software for the 4X complained: 'An oral culture! There's no documentation for the 4X, so one must go to BU or AJ [BU's assistant] for any knowledge about it.' BU was therefore known for bestowing information about his hardware orally on those he wanted to patronise, and withholding it from others.

Similar views of motivated inclusion and exclusion were held about the Chant/Formes group. For example, a founding member of the project who left and took another IRCAM post primarily to gain a salary rise, despite inhabiting the next-door office, found to his regret that the group would no longer confide in him. The Chant/Formes group also engaged in conflicts over secrecy and control with Systems manager FA. FA's job of 'disinterested policing' of the main system involved knowing the location and identity of each bit of programming going on in the VAX. But FA had ongoing tussles with the Chant/Formes group who hid parts of their work in the bowels of the computer, refusing to tell him. 'They hide their source code from me!', he complained. Such an atmosphere bred retaliation. There was an angry system message from Chant/Formes director MC one day, demanding to know who had 'stolen' some of their essential source code. Thus, despite its advocacy of the anarcho-libertarian, 'open' computer philosophy, Chant/Formes was a highly bounded group. Recruits to the project in the mid-1980s were limited to the director's own postgraduates.

In summary, IRCAM culture showed an oscillation or tension between its self-image as a collaborative and open oral culture, itself necessitated by the opacity and instability of software as a medium, and a combination of forces – the security imperative, informal rivalries, and researchers' desire to retain privacy for their developing work – which encouraged patronage in the structuring of access to information and which tended towards secrecy and closure. IRCAM's utopian principles of openness and collaboration did not simply flow from its technologies, from the supposed inherently democratising nature of the computer – a widely held notion that I have subjected here to material critique. They were equally discursive principles derived from currents widespread in the discourse of new technology,[6] as well as from aspects of Boulez's founding vision for IRCAM, in which he portrayed the Bauhaus as a model of collaborative cultural production. We have seen how, in addition to official security structures, subjects invented mischievous ways of restricting access to, and guarding the privacy of, their work. Ironically, IRCAM's oral culture and lack of documentation favoured secrecy and patronage; while the exercise of patronage was in itself both a strategy for accruing power and a source of social gratification.

I have identified the dynamics of patronage as a central force for the local social distribution of knowledge. These dynamics were a strategy of social positioning which affected only IRCAM's research sphere, and which in turn were imbued with, and enacted, various differences within this sphere: primarily discursive oppositions, but also disciplinary and other rivalries, and professional specialisation. The election of people to patronise, and debarring of others, was, then, a social differentiation within the unity of the intellectual cadre: a group evidencing the standard sociological profile for legitimate, institutionalised, vanguard intellectuals (overwhelmingly male, white, young, and highly educated – those in process of hoarding cultural capital). Meanwhile those servicing this cadre, the wider institutional workforce, were excluded entirely from the play of patronage. Of all factors, gender and level of education were, perhaps predictably, the most striking markers of exclusion from the game of access to technological expertise.

Resisting productivity: the labile materiality of software

The tensions I have outlined contribute to understanding IRCAM's problems of lack of stabilisation and documentation of research: problems which continue to threaten IRCAM's research reputation.[7] The discourse of IRCAM as an 'oral culture' was in part a utopian rationalisation of the chronic lack of documentation, and one that enabled patronage to flower in the realm of research. I want here to trace a nexus of additional forces working against stabilisation and documentation – concerning intellectual property, and the materiality of software.

Collaboration was not only a feature of IRCAM technological research, but also of composition projects. The production of a piece involved a visiting composer coming to work with IRCAM staff known as 'tutors', whose job was to assist the composer in translating her ideas into IRCAM's technological means, and then help to realise the ideas in practice. While composers were usually assigned one tutor, it was common for four or five tutoring staff to become caught up in a challenging music project, and to make considerable contributions. Tutors were supposed to be skilled both scientifically and musically, and often had programming skills. They intervened conceptually, practically and musically in the resulting musical work. Musical authorship at IRCAM therefore also had a collaborative dimension.

Both technological research and tutor-composer relationships were imbued with conflicts over intellectual property: over the principle of intellectual authorship, itself confused by ideological and moral tensions over the relative merits of individual or collaborative labour; and over 'real', material interests of ownership and copyright. In relation to software, then, as well as utopian leanings, the lack of stabilisation and documentation expressed subjects' insecurity as to whether their authorship would be respected, which generated ambivalence towards documenting their research. By neglecting documentation, researchers protected their work from others and appeared to retain control over it, both intellectual and material. They also failed fully to develop or communicate their work. Further, given IRCAM's difficulties with industrially and commercially developing its technologies,[8] and compared with the vanguard prestige and the social and intellectual stimulation of open-ended research and collaborative bricolage, researchers' incentives for completing a product and communicating their work were very unclear.

Three material factors compound this situation. First, we have seen that IRCAM's software research is extremely unstable due to its being embedded in a series of vertical mediations of hard and software, all of which are themselves unstable due to technological dependence and the enforced revision of standards and premature obsolescence which this entails. Since programs are continually being rewritten for new contexts, and also constantly written and then discarded, the task of documentation appears massive and, indeed, unproductive. Its value becomes debased, since a program documented this month is likely to be transcended or obsolete by next year, if not next month. In this strange symbolic hypereconomy, prestige is not so much gained by stabilised and working products as lost by not being linked in to fashionable wider developments. Hence the pressure on researchers to constantly revise their prototypes, and the seduction of responding to every new conceptual and technological trend that appears on the horizon.

Second, we have seen that programs are often developed over time through the collaborative imaginative labour of several authors. Because of this inherent temporal and social mediation, the resultant totality is extremely difficult to decode after the event, and thus opaque to the reconstruction of its total logic – the necessary prerequisite for documenting. This throws new light on the security 'battles' mentioned earlier; since according to a senior programmer, even with access to a program's full source code, this code is often so complex and resistant to intuitive decoding that programmers cannot reconstruct the program's higher meaning or functioning without the help of the author(s), or someone who already knows – that is, without the patronage of the knowledgable. Thus 'spying on' or 'stealing' the code of complex programs does not in itself allow one to decode or use the program. The hiding of source code was more a game simulating issues of control than the real locus of the issue.

The gradual collaborative construction of software, even more than the tutor–composer relation, renders authorship problematic, since it is hard to reconstruct afterwards who contributed what to the program. It becomes unclear both who is, in principle, the intellectual author, and so creatively responsible (as well as responsible for documentation); and who should gain which material rights in the product if it were to be documented and commercially developed – a powerful disincentive. Thus tensions of intellectual property are made particularly acute by the character of software as a medium and weigh against its full development.

A third factor concerns an aesthetics of programming bequeathed by the materiality of software. There was a conscious discursive polarity amongst IRCAM software researchers between those who conceived of the work in rationalist and mathematical terms, and those who saw it as an art, interpretative and inexact, its practice as aesthetically imbued. Whatever the discursive position adopted, in practice programming appeared to offer two implicit pleasures for researchers: on the one hand its *impermanence*, the pleasures of a bricolage that leaves few decipherable traces and so precisely lacks accumulation and consolidation; and on the other what this presentism necessitates – the constant recourse to social mediation and oral communicative exchange, themselves a site both of pleasure and struggle.

In relation to IRCAM's technologies and particularly advanced software, then, the combination of a discourse centred on the values of vanguard research and utopian collaboration, the lack of prestige, protection or material incentives for individual authors as well as for the completion of products, the existence of divisive ideological disputes, and all of these compounded by the material and aesthetic qualities described, worked to create a particularly self-absorbed research culture: one that was highly diffident about communicating research internally, and to the outside world.

This analysis has wider implications, since the key problems at issue are not unique to IRCAM and are found more generally in software research both in computer music and in AI. Roads (1990) describes the tendency for computer music research to result in a trickle of relatively trivial technological innovations, rather than deeper research which is systematically worked through and documented. He traces the problem to researchers' seduction by a series of external institutional and grant pressures – essentially, pressures for short-term legitimation by zappy results which do not so much delay as substitute for more productive and cumulative work. However, my aim has been to highlight factors internal to a research culture which have similar effects.

My observations also echo continuing debates within AI concerning the definition of the field and, specifically, the merits of 'experimental' programming (Engelmore 1980–85; Bundy 1991). This is a kind of improvisatory, pragmatic and 'empiricist' program-building in the search for software which can emulate intelligent behaviour, as advocated by pioneers of the field such as Marvin Minsky. Such an approach is criticised by AI 'formalists', who take AI research to focus on developing mathematical principles and models which may or may not be applied later in actual programs. In short, formalists chide experimental methodology for failing to extract and document general principles from what are often messy and over-complex programs with limited applications. AI music research is an area particularly associated with experimental programming and, as we have seen, aspects of IRCAM's research culture fit the description. Moreover, the formalist/experimental division is mirrored in the polarised positions taken by IRCAM programmers mentioned earlier. In the wider AI debates, both sides appear to take a voluntarist view – as though the question of whether AI should adopt a formalist or experimental method was simply one of competing principles (or competing aesthetics). Whereas I have indicated structural elements of the culture of advanced software research that resist voluntary change since they relate to the character of the medium and its technological, economic and social context; and which foster the lack of 'rational' progress in research.

The coexistence within IRCAM of an overproduction of technical codes and texts alongside the institute's oral culture of patronage and mutual help was therefore far from contradictory. Rather, the oral culture was necessitated by the hypercomplexity of those codes and texts given the lack or weakness of informative documentation, and by the chronic instability of the environment. As we have seen, some of these dynamics appear to be more generally characteristic of cultures of advanced software research. But they are also pervasive in situations of ordinary, unskilled software use. The material factors I have discussed weigh towards all cultures around software being primarily reliant on oral rather than graphic, notation-based communication.[9] Hence the contradictory status of textuality in these cultures: the sense simultaneously of both a vast proliferation of textuality (programming codes and notations; in advanced software and AI, texts representing the scientific analyses and expert knowledges which inform the programs); and an absence of coherent texts (of documentation and of explanation).

Barriers to 'perfect communication'

My conclusions disturb any assumption of the scientificity of advanced software research. We have seen that software is composed of representations – visual notations and programming codes – which, even for professionals and experts, are far from transparent to decode. They have a density and opacity which limit the capacity of both expert and naïve users to understand and engage with the internal processes of programs; and there is a marked absence of effective textual documentation in circulation to enable researchers and users to engage 'rationally' with the technologies. Oral and social mediation are thus essential to the circulation of programming knowledge. In short, the technologies tend to be very limited in their autonomy and generality.

The kinds of visualisation and coding described are at once materially immanent in the technologies, and the means of bringing about their instrumental ends. Yet paradoxically, that instrumentality is itself compromised and undermined by the incoherent textuality and labile materiality of software.

I suggested at the outset that both the modernist and postmodernist perspectives posit computer media as effective and a-social – as having an autonomy and integrity which places them apart from the social. Analysing the character of the visual representation and coding immanent in software development and use has shown that computer media never finally achieve the stable separation of the rational–technological from the social which their cosmology asserts – a 'purification' which, Latour argues, both signifies and actualises the generality and irrefutability to which sciences and technologies aspire, their capacity to 'stand alone'. Rather, the 'a-social' is always breaking down given the instability and complexity of the media, and so the sociality that they constantly invoke. There is, moreover, a lack of effective mobilisation of inscription devices – texts (documentation) that would reduce the complexity, establish the autonomy, and enable the comprehensive use and scrutiny of the technological object. Software is marked, then, by two striking 'failures' of scientific practice, both signalled by the *absence* of effective visualisation devices: the first at the point of conceptualisation and notation of program codes, the second at the point of their translation and exegesis.

In this context it is significant that computer hackers, on those occasions in which they overcome the barriers to 'perfect communication' with the computer, commonly express the fantasy that the computer offers a more stimulating and responsive partner than an actual human being – that it really does become a social actor. This is in fact the elation that accompanies technological *mastery*, the clearing away of the communicative chaos that surrounds computer media, yielding a state in which the hacker is finally 'liberated' from the uncertainties and dependencies of human exchange. Instead, humanity is projected into the computer. This is total instrumental control, aberrantly stripped of sociality, masquerading as human relations.

Notes

1. Macfarlane (1994), on the BBC Domesday videodisc project, indicates the potential for a different analytical relation to digital and information technologies by discussing the limits and problems, as well as great educational potential, of videodisc technology. Most interestingly, he describes the decision processes, the choices and conflicts, involved in constructing the classificatory systems on which the entire system was built (1994: 402–404).
2. For a non-idealising and wide-ranging discussion of the figure of the cyborg and how it is deployed in contemporary cinema, see Springer 1991.
3. Fieldwork was carried out throughout 1984 and in 1986, with further visits, the latest in 1992.
4. The IRCAM *stage* was aimed at composers and musicians with a range of skills – from no prior knowledge, to those who were experienced in electronic or computer music.
5. The 4A machine was an earlier version of the 4X machine.

6. For a critical overview of the neo-futurist discourse, in both its social theoretical and popular manifestations, which portrays new technologies as harbingers of decentralisation, democratisation and 'community', see Carey 1989, especially chapters 5 and 7.

7. A well-known American consultant was brought over for a year in 1992 specifically to attack IRCAM's continuing lack of documentation of its research. Having studied it, he felt that it was so deeply embedded in IRCAM's functioning that he would be powerless to change it – a message that he thought would be ill-received by IRCAM management.

8. During the 1980s, IRCAM was markedly unsuccessful at fostering a wider circulation of its research and technologies, both in terms of industrial and commercial links, and in terms of circulating them around the international research community.

9. I am deliberately leaving aside the complicating question of the role of electronic mail, introductory software packages and computer networking in the communication of software to users. It seems to me that these on-line forms of documentation and communication have some of the qualities of written documents. Like written texts, they are relatively autonomous from social mediation, thereby enabling a greater reflexivity than orally bestowed information; yet perhaps, in their interactive mode, they are more responsive than written texts to individual queries. However, functioning as software, they also partake of some of the characteristics that I have been analysing. Oral and social mediation continue to play a significant role in opening up the possibility of exploring and making use of these channels for ordinary users. Indeed the use of e-mail and networking for information is precisely dependent on the goodwill of the (institutional or individual) respondent – that is, they are a sort of digitally mediated orality, replete with social mediation. They also commonly have the same qualities of indecipherability as many software packages – only, in being software about software, the opacity is, as it were, 'squared'.

 It is a marvellous irony of my chapter that Fischer's (1994) summarising book on computer applications for anthropologists bears out so many themes of my analysis. His Appendix centres on an apology for neglecting to discuss specific software; but this was impossible because of 'the rapid rate of change in computer hardware and software . . . in earlier drafts . . . specific software was discussed only to drop out of existence or become so transformed as to be new'. He adds, with understatement, 'this is likely to be frustrating to many readers, since it is not always easy to locate software which meets your requirements' (p. 212). Fischer's only suggestion for how anthropologists reading his book can get hold of substantive practical information about software is to read one of the relevant journals, or to use Internet or e-mail to link up with information stored in his own University Centre's computer archive. There is a disproportion, then, between the very general principles and explanations given in the book, the expansive scope of Fischer's vision, and the very particular, local and personalised source of practical and up-to-the-minute guidance offered in the Appendix. It is almost as though, in order to make any real use of the book, it is necessary to make contact with the book's author – whether by e-mail or, less directly, through the archive. From a Latourian perspective, this reliance on the personal or mediated intervention of the 'engineer', and so the lack of autonomy of the textual object, reveals the weakness of its strategies of scientificity and the faults in the technology of explanation.

References

Bloch, Maurice (1991) 'Language, Anthropology and Cognitive Science', *Man* NS 26 (2): 183–98.

Born, Georgina (1995), *Rationalizing Culture: IRCAM, Boulez, and the Institutionalization of the Musical Avant-Garde*, Berkeley: University of California Press.

Bundy, Alan (1991) 'Clear Thinking on Artificial Intelligence', the *Guardian*, 5 December: 33.

Carey, James (1989) *Communication as Culture: Essays on Media and Society*, London: Unwin Hyman.

Crawford, Peter and Turton, David (eds) (1992) *Film as Ethnography*, Manchester: Manchester University Press.

Downey, Gary (1992) 'Human Agency in CAD/CAM Technology', *Anthropology Today* 8 (5): 2–6.

Engelmore, Robert (ed.) (1980–85) *Readings from the A.I. Magazine*, volumes 1–5, Menlo Park, CA.: American Association for Artificial Intelligence.

Fischer, Michael (1994) *Applications in Computing for Social Anthropologists*, London: Routledge.

Foucault, Michel (1980) *Power/Knowledge*, Brighton: Harvester.

Fyfe, Gordon and Law, John (eds) (1988) *Picturing Power: Visual Depictions and Social Relations*, London: Routledge.

Haraway, Donna (1991) 'A Cyborg Manifesto: Science, Technology, and Socialist-Feminism in the Late Twentieth Century', in Donna Haraway (ed.) *Simians, Cyborgs, and Women*, London: Free Association Books.

Haynes, Stanley (1984) 'Report on the Realization of York Höller's *Arcus*', *Contemporary Music Review* 1 (1): 60–61.

Howard, Alan (1988) 'Hypermedia and the Future of Ethnography', *Cultural Anthropology* 3 (3): 304–15.

Latour, Bruno (1987) *Science in Action*, Milton Keynes: Open University Press.

—— (1993) *We Have Never Been Modern*, London: Harvester Wheatsheaf.

Latour, Bruno and Woolgar, Steve (1986) *Laboratory Life: The Construction of Scientific Facts*, Princeton, NJ: Princeton University Press.

Macfarlane, Alan (1994) 'BBC Domesday: the Social Construction of Britain on Videodisc', in Lucien Taylor (ed.).

Poster, Mark (1990) *The Mode of Information: Poststructuralism and Social Context*, Cambridge: Polity.

Rabinow, Paul (1988) 'Beyond Ethnography: Anthropology as Nominalism', *Cultural Anthropology* 3 (4): 355–64.

Roads, Curtis (1990) 'La Recherche musicale: mythe et realité,' *Inharmonique* n. 6: 229–39.

Seaman, Gary and Williams, Homer (1992) 'Hypermedia in Ethnography', in Peter Crawford and David Turton (eds).

Sperber, Dan (1975) *Rethinking Symbolism*, Cambridge: Cambridge University Press.

—— (1985) *On Anthropological Knowledge*, Cambridge: Cambridge University Press.

Springer, Claudia (1991) 'The Pleasure of the Interface', *Screen* 32 (3): 303–23.

Suchman, Lucy (1985) *Plans and Situated Actions: the Problem of Human–Machine Communication*, California: Xerox Corporation.

Taylor, Lucien (1994) *Visualizing Theory: Selected Essays from V.A.R. 1990–1994*, New York: Routledge.

Turkle, Sherry (1984) *The Second Self: Computers and the Human Spirit*, New York: Simon and Schuster.

Woolgar, Steve (1991) 'Configuring the User: The Case of Usability Trials', CRICT Discussion Paper, Centre for Research into Innovation, Culture and Technology, Brunel University, UK.

8

To see or not to see: looking as an object of exchange in the New Guinea Highlands

Gillian Gillison

There are 'two modes of managing knowledge in social interaction' according to Barth (1990: 641), one typified by the Balinese guru, the other by the New Guinea initiator. 'More than merely transmitting knowledge to novices', Barth says, '[the initiator . . .] stage-manage[s] a spell-binding performance' (ibid.: 643). For novices in an initiation, 'it is knowing by seeing, being there, being acted upon. A Guru's . . . pupil does not need to have been there, or to have done it – he only needs to understand . . . and remember it' (ibid.: 644). A guru transmits knowledge that is internalised, 'available to the single person's memory', whereas an initiator provides a collective experience. Initiator and guru have opposite goals: while the first 'tries to *withhold* the essential truths from his audience', the latter tries 'to *lay bare* that essence' (ibid.: 642; original emphasis). The distinction Barth makes between systems of secrecy and revelation may also apply to the difference between visual and verbal knowledge and may operate not just between Bali and New Guinea but also within the sexually segregated societies of Highland New Guinea. Barth emphasises the role of secrecy in New Guinea but does not associate it either with conflict between the sexes or with the exclusionary nature of visual experience.

Among the Gimi of the Eastern Highlands of Papua New Guinea, both men and women conduct secret initiations yet, in more or less disguised ways, each sex can describe the other's secret rites, although only men can claim to speak from direct observation. Gimi women were once forbidden to look at men's sacred bamboo flutes on pain of death, while men participate in the climactic end of female initiation and, according to some men, watch in hiding the more esoteric female rites from which they are barred (see Gillison 1987). What each sex values and tries to hide from the other is not information or understanding of an abstract kind but a particular experience based upon looking, a 'knowing by seeing, being there, being acted upon'. 'To see' (*kagao*) is the Gimi word for to know, whereas 'to hear' (*feo*) often has the opposite connotation of misunderstanding, in the sense that words and sounds are multi-referential, ambiguous, and therefore inherently duplicitous, making speech itself suspect.[1]

Gimi women hear the flutes all their lives, are often expert at recognising and naming flute tunes and, as their separate myths vividly reveal, understand with the depth and subtlety of gurus the meaning of rituals they are supposed never to have seen. The whole machinery of male dominance was thus based upon a prohibition on looking at instruments whose sounds women were sometimes forced to hear and whose ritual meaning many women, especially older women, fully understood. Yet Gimi men, and men of other Eastern Highlands societies, threatened to kill any woman who laid eyes on men's flutes or who looked into a men's house where a group of initiates was secluded. What, then, was the meaning of the taboo on looking? Variations of this question have been asked since the last century, referring to other wind instruments like trumpets or bullroarers, and to other societies in Papua New Guinea, in Australia, and in Amazonia (e.g. Bamberger 1974; Dundes 1976; Gourlay 1975). Dundes suggests that the death, or threatened death, of the one woman who looked symbolised the death of them all. 'Initiation rites must be kept secret from women', he says, because whatever form they take, they always epitomise men's attempt 'to live without recourse to women' (Dundes 1976: 2). The violent prohibition on looking may thus have been a way to make women responsible for their own rejection and symbolic annihilation, a way to shift on to women the blame for men's desire to live entirely without them. Yet hostility to women, or to heterosexuality in general, does not itself explain the fixation on looking. What is the connection between the visual character of men's secret knowledge, acted out in male initiation ritual, and the traditional sanction for violence against women?

In 1973, during my first year of fieldwork among the Gimi, a group of women pushed me into a house to prevent me from seeing flutes being played in the midst of a passing procession of men on their way to initiate the boys of a neighbouring hamlet. But by 1983, flute-playing had become almost casual entertainment, and self-consciously secular. Young men deliberately showed flutes to children and even to me. What accounted for the radical shift in attitude? In the late 1950s and early 1960s, the flute cult had begun to fade in village after village as missionaries carried the flutes out of the men's house, showed them to women and children, and burned them as the prelude to a mass baptism (see Gillison 1993: 348). Missionaries showed women the flutes, Gimi men point out, but soon afterwards, Australian patrol officers, by virtue of the orders they issued and the medical personnel they sent in, showed childbirth to men, something they had never seen.

In the past, women gave birth in the menstrual hut [*kamidama*, literally *kamiba*/flute + *nama*/house, 'flute house'; see Gillison 1993: 176; 265-7] . . . but now the government has come to look after us and says, 'Don't send the women away . . . don't send the women to give birth in the *171* forest or another place. . . .' So they stopped us from following our tradition and women give birth in the compounds. Before, men never saw . . . But now, they've shown the flutes to women . . . and they know. . . . And men look at birth. The men who buy a woman, touch her.

A woman's father-in-law (never her own husband) may hold her in the early stages of labour but as the moment of birth approaches the woman retreats with her midwives to the bank of a river. Certain men, especially men of stature, may accompany her only to look or to lay on a hand if the labour is difficult. 'A man without a name (a reputation) would not go to watch. Men like K and R can go to the river and watch what happens when a woman gives birth.' They might touch her, but never the child, 'only doctors do that'. Gimi men nowadays dare to look at birth, and even briefly participate in it, they say, because women have seen the flutes.

Looking, birth and flutes are connected in the literal meaning of initiation: 'to initiate a boy', in the Gimi idiom, is 'to show him the flutes'; and once a boy has seen the flutes, men say, he is 'reborn'. Men give each flute the 'same name' as an initiate and say that the music is the 'cries' of the newborn. According to men's myth, the flute was invented by a woman who lived without a husband. One night her flute-playing woke her brother who was still a small boy asleep in the men's house. He crawled in the darkness to her house, laid in wait outside her door until morning, and then crept inside and stole her flute. He brought it back to the men's house and showed it to the other boys.[2] But he did not see his sister's pubic hair stuffed inside the blowing hole and when he tried to play it, his lips touched her hair and whiskers began to grow around his mouth, which is why men have beards. When he pulled out the plug of hair, his sister began to menstruate. As a consequence, she lost her independence and had to marry. But she told no one about the flute she had once had. Men keep this secret because, their myths says, if even one woman sees the flutes and lives to speak of it she would conspire with other women to take back what the first woman lost. Men would become utterly weak; gardens and pig herds would no longer yield; seasons would falter; birds and marsupials would disappear from clan forests (see Gillison 1993, chapter 9).

Women's myths retell the flute myth in other terms. In one, the heroine takes back the 'flute' a man steals from her and is not forced to marry. She lives alone in the forest like a marsupial, eating only wild fruits and berries. By specifying that the wild woman carries her child on her back inside a net bag, the way a bride 'unknowingly' transports flutes to her husband, the myth indicates that the child is also a flute (ibid.).

A wild man found the skins of fruits lying on the forest floor and realised a marsupial was above him eating in a tree. He went to get his bow and arrow and returned at twilight [to shoot it] but came upon a wild woman carrying her child on her back inside a net bag. The wild man just stood there and the wild woman mistook him for the base of the tree. She put her finger inside his nose and felt that it was not hot. She put her finger inside his mouth and felt that it was not hot. She put her finger inside his anus and felt that it was not hot. So she thought she was standing beside a tree and hung up her child on the wild man's shoulder [thinking his arm was a branch]!

Then the wild woman climbed the tree, broke off the fruit and began to eat it. While she was eating, the wild man took off with the child and brought it back to the men's house. The wild woman finished eating and came down the tree and saw that her child was gone. She followed the man ['s footsteps] . . . and realised that her child had been put inside one of the houses.

Meanwhile the wild man summoned all the men and women to the men's house and told them, 'I stole the wild woman's child!' Everyone gathered inside the men's house and he said to them, 'Don't speak. Don't make any sound!' . . . the wild woman arrived. She put her ear to one house after the other . . . but heard nothing. Then she came to the men's house and heard [the cries of her child]. . . . 'Hey, you people inside the men's house,' she cried. . . . 'Give me back my child and I'll give you all the delicious foods of the forest. . . .'

They gave her back her child and she brought them wild bananas, wild greens, and wild yams. 'I will bring you all the best foods and keep only poor fruits and berries for myself.' Saying this, she took her child and went back to her home [in the forest]. Where she lives now nobody knows.[3]

Like the boy in men's myth, the wild woman touches without looking. She 'climbs the tree', or has sex, after only feeling the man, probing his orifices and mistaking his identity.[4] She is hungry for fruit, a symbol of sperm, and does not see the man who sees her, who finds the discarded skins that are the signs of her careless appetite. The man stands still and she puts her finger inside him, into one orifice after another, and feels that he is 'not hot', not sexually aroused: while she still possesses the child, he remains passive and probed like a woman. She takes the man 'blindly', as it were, as the object of her desire and gives up her child unwittingly. She hangs it on his shoulder and he runs off with it to the men's house. Looking moves the sacred object in the direction of the looker, of the one who is 'not hot' while the other eats voraciously, the one who sees the other's desire while the other is unaware.

The same theme dominates another of women's myths which takes up the flute scenario at a different point in the cycle of theft and counter-theft. In this myth, the flute is symbolised not by a child in a net bag but by a pair of eyes in a bamboo tube, and the original thief is not a man but his wife. Unlike the wild woman, she willingly gives up what she stole, yet is horribly punished.

A man set a cassowary trap and went to inspect it. He saw that it held a cassowary and called out to the wild taro, 'O leaf of wild taro, here are my eyes!' He recited this and took out his eyes and laid them on a taro leaf. Then he disappeared up the anus of the cassowary into the belly and ate up the liver and all the insides. He came back out of the cassowary and cried, 'O leaf of wild taro, bring me my eyes!' and he put back his eyes. He hung the empty skin on the branch of a tree and went to inspect the other traps he had set.

He arrived at another trap and found that it, too, held a cassowary. 'O leaf of wild taro, here are my eyes!' he cried. Again he removed his eyes and went up the anus of the cassowary and ate and ate and ate until he had finished up her insides. 'O leaf of wild taro, bring me my eyes!' he cried and put back his eyes. He hung the empty skin on a branch of a tree and went on to the third trap. He saw that it was empty and went home.

He brought back the two empty skins for his wife and his mother-in-law and told them, 'I didn't check the traps in time and [marsupials] cats finished up everything!' He lied to the two of them and went back to his traps.

He kept lying so his wife decided to follow him and see for herself. She thought, 'You bring me empty skins. . . . I want to see what you do in the forest.' She hid behind a tree and heard, 'O leaf of wild taro, here are my eyes!' and saw her husband disappear into the cassowary. While he was eating, she stole his eyes and cleared out for home. She broke off a section of bamboo and put his eyes inside it. . . . She came home and went to sleep.

Her husband called, 'O leaf of wild taro, bring me my eyes!' and nothing happened. Again, 'O leaf of wild taro, bring me my eyes!' and again nothing. And again . . . and again. . . . He called out for his eyes but they were not there so he started for home, stumbling and falling. His eye sockets filled with mud and humus and worms. He arrived at the house and . . . [said to his wife] . . . 'Come here and clean out the mud and debris.' As she was cleaning the sockets, she put back his eyes one after the other. . . . He opened them and asked her, 'Wife, what kind of trick are you playing on me?'. . . . He was furious and said, 'Let us go together into the forest.' . . .

The husband made a pact with the python (literally: *kiri*). 'I am going with my wife into the forest. Follow us there!' he told the snake. . . . The two went off . . . and while they slept, the snake approached the side of their bush house, crying ki, ki, ki, ki, ki. . . . As the woman slept, the snake entered her vagina and came out her mouth. . . . Her husband awoke and lit the fire and looked at them. He watched the snake shaking its head inside her mouth and shaking its tail inside her vagina. He watched the woman die.

He left his wife and came home. His mother-in-law asked him, 'What happened to your wife?' And the man answered, 'I did not see her. I asked her to come into the forest with me but she did not listen and would not come. I went alone and came back alone.' The woman's mother and father went to sleep and waited for her to return [the next day] but she did not come. On the third day, they followed the husband's tracks into the forest and saw the python still shaking its head. The men [of the woman's lineage] said to the snake, 'Son-in-law! Your neck must be sore! Why don't you rest it on this piece of wood.' They cut a branch and slid it under the snake's head. Then the woman's father and brother cut the snake's neck with an axe.

They cut the snake and pulled it out of her mouth and out of her vagina. They carried the snake and the woman back to the settlement and made an enormous fire. They cut the snake to pieces and . . . killed a pig and cooked it with the snake. They laid in wait for the woman's husband [. . . and when he] came [they] shot him dead.

The storyteller immediately added that the head of the snake is a child. In another version, 'The snake . . . stuck its head out her mouth and called [to the husband], "Daddy! Daddy!" As the storyteller explained:

The wife bore a child. The snake was her child. They cut off the child's head and ate it [i.e. the pig as substitute for it]. That is how the huge snake was removed from her body.

'Eating the head of the child' is the Gimi expression for matrilateral payments (Gillison 1993: 54–8). Another woman commented that default in bride-price, which is the antecedent and equivalent of head payments, was the reason the man entered the cassowary in the first place:

Sometimes a woman gets pregnant before her brother has a chance to eat her pay. He may have died before her husband finished making payments. In that case, she may tell [the ghost of] her dead brother or her father, 'Go inside my vagina and into my womb and eat the child that is there.' . . . She speaks in anger because her husband did not make the payments. 'It won't do for me to bear the child and make my husband happy. You must kill it and eat it!'

The cassowary represents not only the man's sister or daughter, as the speaker suggests, but also his mother, because her anus is an orifice to which he *returns*. The anus of the cassowary is like a mother's vagina, Gimi explain, because it resembles a two-way passage: the droppings contain undigested fruits which look uneaten, so that what comes out of the cassowary seems ready to go back in. The man who enters the cassowary, said the same woman, 'goes back up the path down which he came into the world! Shame on him. His wife took his eyes and off she went. She stole his shame!' Removing his eyes, she added, was like taking off his foreskirt, getting rid of his sexual inhibition:

When a man puts a foreskirt over his penis, he hides his shame. When he takes out his eyes and lays them on [the taro leaf on] the ground, it's as if he takes off his foreskirt.

As symbol of the flute, the eyes-in-bamboo represent what the man did inside the cassowary without looking, without inhibition. They are encapsulations of his journey, condensations of a primal scene, as if the incest, or the wish for it, or the awareness of the wish, were a removable part of the body.

The man's taking out his eyes turns him first into a ravenous child and then into a vicious snake. But whereas he went into the cassowary's anus and came back out of it empty-handed, with an empty skin (explicit symbol of a flaccid penis), he went into his wife's vagina and came out her mouth quaking to produce a child. One of the myth-tellers had this to say:

> The woman died. The snake entered her and came out of her. The snake is her husband's penis going in and her dead child coming out her mouth. . . . She was pregnant and bore a child. That is the meaning of removing the snake. Then a pig is killed and cooked with the snake in an enormous fire. It's the same as making a feast for the newborn . . . but that child is dead! It's like *haro* (female initiation; see Gillison 1987) . . . It's the first-born child. It's as if the Moon killed her [i.e. as if she menstruated] and they are celebrating. They kill a pig and have the *haro* feast. . . . That is the meaning of this story.

Like all women's and men's myths, this one attributes menstruation to the loss of flutes, represented here by the snake losing its head, the child appearing 'head first' in the birth canal. A woman steals her husband's eyes-in-bamboo, his flute, and he, or men in general, take it back by cutting off the part of her which is part of him, the part she stole when he was not looking. By decapitating the snake, men remove an angry husband from her body and fill her 'mouth' with blood, just as the boy in men's myth pulls the plug of pubic hair out of his sister('s flute) and makes her menstruate. The dead 'head of the child', extracted from the mother, is a piece of her husband replaced by a pig and transformed into an edible commodity. It is the first gift and prototype of an object of exchange; indeed, the act of exchange is itself a means to empty and 'kill' the mother and revivify her child (Gillison 1993, chapter 1). But what men steal back from the woman while she is 'up a tree', gorging herself without looking, being filled by the snake in her sleep, etc., she gets back again later, the 'second time' she bears a child, when she is alive, awake and watching. Every living child is secondborn in the sense that menstrual blood is 'the same as the firstborn' and equated with the child whose head is 'not eaten' but discarded like the snake.

Gimi men attribute maternal closeness, and women's general talent for intimacy, to the fact that women automatically watch the births of their children. In the words of one Gimi man: 'Women have a great power on account of seeing us when we are born. Women give birth to us which is why – whatever we do in secret – they can see us. If a man makes love to a woman, another woman will say, "You made love to that woman and I saw you!" It's a power only woman have. It comes from giving birth to us' (Gillison 1993: 233; 341–2).

Showing the flutes to boys is, first of all, a rite of rebirth, a way to undo the original birth by disempowering the mother and transferring on to new objects the seamlessness and intensity of the relation to her. In the classic psychoanalytic interpretation of male puberty rites, it is the event of birth itself which binds a boy to his mother: 'attachment to the mother is due simply to the fact of being born of her, so that the only way to neutralise incest tendencies that stand in the way of friendly relationships with other men is to nullify the supposed cause of them (birth) by a symbolic rebirth' (Jones 1925: 121).

Initiation rites 'annul the original birth by the mother and substitute for it an imaginary homosexual birth' (ibid.). Ritual rebirth or 'the fiction of being born from the man is a nullification of birth from the woman . . . [and] . . . serves to detach the youths from [their mothers]' (Reik 1958 [1946]: 146, n.1; 146). But the question remains how looking, or not looking, achieves this radical alteration of history and shift in association.

In Northwest Amazonia, a Desana myth about the origin of flutes makes the connection explicit, showing how a mother's not looking at the birth robs her of her child (Umusin Panlon Kumu and Tolaman Kenhiri 1980: 115–19). Guelamun yé is the name both for flutes and for the first man born to a mother who never saw him:

The mother of Guelamun yé had no vagina, only a small hole for urinating. The first people made an opening so that Guelamun yé could be born. They pulled him out of his mother, who felt a terrible pain, and then put him inside a calabash. They closed the calabash and carried it to the sky. . . . The mother had no chance to see her son. . . . when the people were half way in their journey they opened the calabash to look and saw the most beautiful child imaginable! . . . the child cried [and] his cries were loud and wonderful like thunder.
(Cf. Harrison 1912: 56-66 cited in Dundes 1976; Tuzin 1984)

The men closed the calabash so that no one could hear the cries of Guelamun yé. But his mother heard them and said, 'You have not shown me my son.' 'One day he will return', the men replied. That is why Guelamun yé cannot be seen by women, because his own mother never saw him.

177

In Tatuyo and Tariana versions of this myth, the mother of the hero has a vagina but she closes it and refuses to copulate because she wants to make the child by herself. But the men trick her, infusing their sperm into fruits which they leave for her to find. She eats them and becomes pregnant but believes she has conceived the child alone. The men follow her and when the time comes, they open her vagina and pull out the hero without her laying eyes on him (Bidou, personal communication; cf. Biocca cited in Hugh-Jones 1979: 302–308).

Translated into rites of male initiation, the mythic taboo on looking at flutes becomes, in addition, a command to listen to them, a command that women be present while men show the flutes to initiates and play them out of sight on the other side of a wall or screen (Bidou, personal communication). Among the Tucano and Arawak of Northwest Amazonia, the command to listen highlights the 'not looking' as a central event in the initiation of adolescent boys inside communal long-houses called *malocas*:

The walls and roof of the *maloca* serve as a natural barrier to prevent women and children from seeing the Yurupari [the generic name for flutes in Northwest Amazonia, also called Guelamun yé by the Desana].

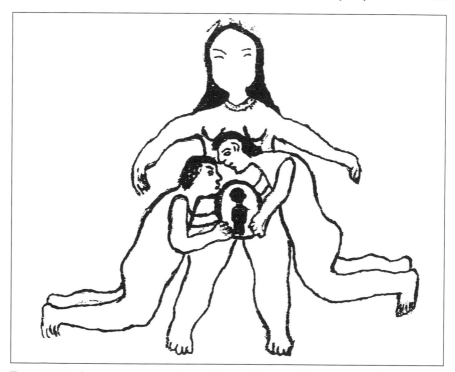

Figure 8.1: Guelamun yé, possessor of sacred flutes which can only be seen by men, because sacred flutes belong naturally and rightfully to men. At birth, men hide Guelamun yé inside a calabash to prevent his mother seeing him (drawing: Umusin Panlon Kumu and Tolaman Kenhiri 1980).

When the flutes are played outside, women and children are kept inside the *maloca*, and . . . when the flutes are played inside the *maloca*, women and children are made to leave. But . . . at the most important moment of the rite, when everyone is inside the house, a screen of palm leaves is erected at the back of the house to confine the women and children while, on the other side of the screen, the men play the musical instruments.

(Bidou 1996)

Boys are shown the flutes while their mothers are made to enact the 'not looking', as if the capacity to see flutes were being reassigned, transferred like the mythic flutes themselves from women to boys. Interpreted in these terms, turning boys into men – into those who can 'see' and attach new objects – requires infantilising their mothers, shifting onto the women their sons' newborn blindness. Like the mother of Guelamun yé, or the Gimi wild woman who did not look and gave up her child, women without flutes can only put their ears to the wall and listen.

In all these myths and rituals, Amazonian and New Guinean, there is a pervasive trade-off, an overriding rule of either/or: a boy can see the flutes and grow into a man only if his mother is forbidden to see flutes; he can be attached to his father, and to men in general, only if he is detached completely from his mother by being born again. One woman's glimpsing the flutes, even inadvertently, would effectively endow and empower all women, leaving men impotent and subservient; the initiates' being shown the flutes enacts the mythic theft, leaving entirely bereft a new generation of mothers, etc. Looking, giving birth, or making new attachments always implies a corresponding blindness or loss because, in the realm of sexual fantasy, these events refer to the central conflict between women and men. Disguised in images of stolen flutes, removable eyes, and decapitated snakes is the shared fantasy of sex as total transfer of an object: the penis, child, or self-awareness – everything that men represent in the flute, bullroarer, or other instrument – passes *in toto* from one sex to the other, radically diminishing the one and empowering the other. Anyone who is blind with desire and 'goes inside' another – the wild woman who put her finger into the wild man's orifices, the man who climbed into the cassowary's anus (his mother 'trapped' by his father, in the words of one informant), the child who 'sleeps' *in utero* – is robbed and 'loses his instrument'. The one who is unconscious and cannot see is depleted, his child, or inner self, made the appendage of the one who is 'not hot' and whose eyes are open. Looking is like being penetrated because the looker has less desire and can attach what he or she sees.

When a man 'goes inside' a woman for the first time, some Gimi men say, he is 'lost in the forest' of desire. He ejaculates, 'not thinking about making a child', yet the woman becomes pregnant (see Gillison 1993, chapter 9). Because the man was transported during sex, the ensuing

179

pregnancy is like a theft, the men point out, as if the woman took something the man was not intending to give up.[5] She steals the child while his eyes are closed and hides it until the moment of birth when, unlike a man ejaculating, she watches what comes out of her body and attaches it to herself. She watches the child 'pass between her thighs' and keeps it, just as she kept the man's semen in the first place. In women's cassowary myth, the child 'coming out' and the father 'going in' are still one and the same, like the snake who enters the woman's vagina and comes out her mouth, or like the man who enters and emerges from the cassowary's anus, 'retravelling the road of his birth'. In Gimi men's reckoning, outside the context of myth, father and child are identified in different terms. Coitus and its 'unintended' consequences are equally depleting for a man, they say. Pregnancy and mothering prolong a man's own 'unconscious' union with his wife in the sense that his child's attachment to her, both inside and outside the womb, extend, or hold in suspension, his own experience of detumescence and unwitting loss. As Kelly remarks of the Etoro, 'The state of a male parent after birth is comparable in nature to that of a man after copulation (although intensified in degree)' (Kelly 1976: 42).

A Gimi father remains in this postcopulatory, postpartum state until he initiates his son, shows him the flutes and opens his son's eyes. As his wife did after sex, he bides his time after the birth, waiting until adolescence to take back the child she took from him in a moment of ecstasy. Like the men who decapitate the snake in women's myth, the man who secludes his son in the men's house takes back the part of himself his wife stole and kept out of sight, bringing to an end his own long, debilitating 'presence' inside her. He restores himself to himself, so to speak, by taking back for his son what his wife took from him. Male initiation ritual alters the original birth by blinding the mother: her capacity for perfect attachment is transferred not to the father, who gave it up in the first place, but to the child/initiate. The initiate is the one who opens his eyes and attaches the first thing he sees, which is a whole community of men. The child escapes the mother the same way it escaped the father – while the father's eyes were closed (see Gillison 1993: 217) – but then, by opening his own eyes, watching his own birth (enacted in flute-playing), the child reattaches himself to the father as one of a group of men. Here, it seems to me, we have an explanation for why men did not traditionally watch real birth: by auto-prohibition they stopped themselves from creating the same guilty, seamless, dyadic attachments for which they reproach their wives, and which they work so hard to destroy in the interests of communal life.

The war between the sexes was waged over a child symbolised by the flute. But the flute stood not only for the 'crying' initiate 'pulled out' of his mother. In the imagery of women's myth, it also stands for his father's severed penis, the snake's severed head. And in men's exegeses, the flute stands for the mother's emptied body: the blowing hole, men say, is a 'vagina' etched with 'pubic hair' and stuffed with 'killed' meat to represent menstrual blood; and the flute's open end is a second 'vagina' where the child's cries emerge. The flute is thus far more than the direct equivalent of mythic persons or body parts. It is an arrested summary of the myth itself, as if the main characters and episodes, including those that are opposed or contradictory, were superimposed and condensed into the instrument and the music (cf. Freud 1976 [1900]). The flute is both a whole story, or combination of stories, and an object like a child, or a penis, or like the woman in whom it was once hidden and of whom it seemed to be physically a part. By stealing *this* flute, a man cuts out of his wife what she saw, understood, and felt when he climbed into the anus of his cassowary mother: he amputates her knowledge of his incestuous past together with her feelings of jealousy and exclusion so she cannot use them as pretext and model for seducing their son, for making herself irresistible meat in a trap.

Interpreted as part of a myth of incest, or an implicit sexual code, looking becomes theft, the acquisition of awareness by one sex at the expense of the other, as if awareness itself were a sacred object and magically creative like a flute. In questioning a 'purely phallic interpretation of the bullroarer [or flute]' Dundes asks: 'If the bullroarer [or flute] is phallic – as recent scholarship suggests it almost certainly is (cf. van Baal 1963), why would this need to be kept secret from women? Women are surely aware of the existence and nature of the male phallus. The phallic qualities of male initiates would therefore hardly need to be kept secret' (Dundes 1976: 223).

The classic phallic interpretation of the bullroarer or flute is easily sustained, it seems to me, if we add to it the idea that the instrument represents not simply a phallus, which Dundes rightly points out is inadequate to explain the need for secrecy, but a whole phallic scenario in which the penis circulates between the sexes and is repeatedly transformed by theft and countertheft. Seen in these terms, the flute represents a particular risky outcome, a penis converted not into menstrual blood or into a child seduced by the mother and attached exclusively to her – as it was in the first transactions between the sexes – but into a movable object that, once stolen back from women, circulates freely among men, creating a universe of male attachments. Men 'steal' the isolating, dead-end maternal bond and convert it into the instrument of male solidarity.

The flute-as-phallus in this expanded sense condenses the whole of men's myth and women's myth, too, since men's myth is also a response to women (Gillison 1993: 8). Considered as an arrested event, or series of events, the flute combines coitus with its various outcomes and treats them as an object that is unitary like a child, attached to the body like a penis, yet lost in ejaculation, menstruation, and at birth; an object that moves 'unconsciously' into and out of a woman. When men play these flutes, named for the initiates, they show them their own conception and birth, subverting the mother's power by altering the circumstance in which only she was able to see, in which she had 'a great power on account of seeing us when we are born'. The initiate is made fully present at his own birth: he is the one to see *instead* of his mother. He comes out of her blindly but goes back in with his eyes open, as the small boy first put his lips on the pubic hair plug, then pulled it out and blew into the flute; or, as the man first entered the cassowary's anus then, his eyes restored, headed for his wife's vagina. Looking at flutes may thus have the meaning of the initiate's achieving an Oedipal wish and possessing his mother. But looking also represents castrating her in revenge for her role, for her stealing him from his father in the first place, for her having had the awareness both he and his father lacked.

According to Gimi men's myth, the boy's stealing the flutes caused the first woman to menstruate, literally, to 'be killed by the Moon', which 'is the same as the death of the firstborn'. For the initiate, looking at flutes summarises his disastrous return to the mother in the midst of copulation, his moving toward her music in the night, a movement that ends their seamless attachment by causing his own death, his own violent removal from her 'mouth'. To become separate from his mother, the initiate goes back inside her with eyes open and 'dies' there like the firstborn. But at the same moment he sees his father's flute and, through the magic of looking, takes possession of it.[6] On the return journey into his mother, he becomes reattached to his father, as if he were his father's missing part, the snake's severed head, and is born again. Looking at flutes, and thus participating knowingly in the union of his parents, brings about the initiate's symbolic death (the onset of menstruation and separation from his mother) as the condition of his rebirth and reunion with his father.

According to these fantasies of phallic partition and recombination, the father's fluid/penis passes into the mother where it is converted into a child. But that child 'gets stuck' during menstruation, pregnancy and postnatal attachment, requiring that the father conspire with other men to steal it back from the mother who otherwise would not relinquish it. Menstrual blood is early proof of women's collective bad faith, of their intention to 'kill the firstborn' rather than give it up and keep it in circulation: only men have an organ of transfer between their thighs, a penis that automatically, blindly, 'places a child inside a woman'. Men reclaim the child at puberty and seal it inside a house or calabash or womb of their own making in order to change it *back* into a penis of a new order, one that women can never see, steal, divide, hide, bind utterly to themselves, or turn to blood again.[7]

In her 'Notes on the "Political Economy" of Sex', Rubin describes a similar fantasy to explain the organisation of small-scale, non-industrial economies. In traditional gift economies, Rubin asserts, the item of exchange represents the phallus as an object a woman can never fully possess: 'It passes through her, and in its passage is transformed into a child. When she "recognises her castration", she accedes to the place of a woman in a phallic exchange network. She can "get" the phallus – in intercourse, or as a child – but only as a gift from a man. She never gets to give it away' (Rubin 1975: 195). Why, though women 'get' the phallus, do they never 'get to give it away?' Why are women mainly producers rather than transactors (Strathern 1972)? What Rubin omits from the fantasy of exchange is that the first time a woman gets the phallus, it does *not* 'pass through' her and is not transformed into a child. The first sexual transaction produces menstrual blood: the child dies because the Moon or python, a symbol of the primordial father, blinds every woman with desire. The firstborn falls dead 'between her thighs'. But even afterwards, in a second exchange, when a woman opens her eyes and keeps the child a man gives her, she refuses to give it up! She keeps it entirely to herself, alive but lactating and helpless, and thus refuses to put it back in circulation. From men's point of view, the outcomes of the first transactions with women make them forever unsatisfactory partners in exchange.

'It has been increasingly recognised', Barth says in the article cited earlier, 'that Melanesian exchange transactions are themselves symbolically ordered, and embody a cultural construction of reality. . . . In their deeper and more collective aspect, Melanesians . . . are concerned with the enigmas of reproduction. . . . But a "theory" of reproduction is not articulated', he continues, 'only its application to material transactions' (Barth 1990: 649). If theories of reproduction order social arrangements, as Barth believes, then we need to do more than simply say so. We need to investigate those theories and make them explicit. What is 'not articulated', as Barth delicately puts it, what is unconscious in the theories that govern 'material transactions', is the mainly conflicting sexual fantasies of men and women that are disguised in their myths, rituals, and procreation beliefs. Unless we explore these fantasies, and expose their sexual content, we leave unanalysed the social systems we are supposed to try to understand and, according to a long tradition in anthropology, collude with those we study by using 'birth' or 'reproduction' as a harmless substitute for sex.

The unspoken theories of reproduction that Barth, Rubin and others concede are *the* models for traditional Melanesian economies also provide a key for understanding the general mistreatment and exclusion of women. The tendency to treat the invisible or intangible aspects of life, growth to adulthood, awareness of incest wishes, the capacity to understand, personal attachment, etc., as if they were material, indivisible and transferable like a flute – the association of every gain with loss, of every gift with theft – these characteristic features of Melanesian social systems stem from the rampant generalisation of a shared fantasy in which women's lack of a penis is a temporary and reparable condition. Sexual identity is negotiable: the flute/phallus is detached from one sex and reattached to the other during copulation or by a special kind of looking at birth. The phallus moves toward the looker, the one who sees the other's desire while the other succumbs to it and is unaware, and therefore experiences the looking retrospectively as theft of part of the self. Indeed, it is the looking or awareness itself – the objectification of the other's unconscious desire – that is transformed into phallus, child, flute, or wealth. These material things are thus as fleeting, or as fleetingly possessed, as is awareness or desire: they are always contested, stolen in a glance and regained, but never finally or legitimately owned, just as body boundaries and sexual identities are never fixed. Seen in these terms, menstruation, pregnancy and postnatal attachment symbolise women's attempts to end the vital circulation of the object, to keep the phallus forever, hidden like menstrual blood, or like a child in permanent gestation, and thus stop men from seeing it. Men attribute these ambitions to women and women, to an extent, and for reasons not explored here, accept the attribution, so that then men use it to justify a 'retaliatory' or 'pre-emptory' violence against women that stops them from looking at flutes.

Notes

1. The most powerful testimony a witness at a sorcery trial can offer is to say that he saw the guilty act – usually, the handing over of a sorcerer's fee – not in his waking life but in a dream. The visual nature of dreams, their seeming to pass before the dreamer autonomously, like images on a screen or stage, give them a kind of unimpeachable authority (Gillison 1993: 232–3). But the emphasis on visual communication, the privileging of dreams, ritual theatre, rites of divination, etc., as sources of truth has perhaps been cumbersome for the Gimi who were quick to adopt into their language the Melanesian pidgin word 'savi' which, like the English 'know', has no connotation of means.
2. Like most Gimi myths, this one deals with origins and describes the first woman, the first child, etc., and the first copulation and birth. Typically, however, it includes other characters who logically pre-exist or are contemporaries of the main players.
3. At the end of her tale, the storyteller chants a short refrain containing two intelligible words – the names of two sticks used to beat male initiates during their seclusion and instruction about flutes. For an uninitiated boy, one who has never seen the flutes, hearing women's myths during the daytime or outside a woman's house – that is, when he is no longer young enough to sleep with his mother and hear her stories at bedtime – would have the same effect on him as seeing the flutes. Like the little boy in men's myth who put his mouth on the blowing hole without looking and touched his sister's pubic hair, the uninitiated listener would sprout whiskers prematurely and permanently stunt his growth.
4. That the 'wild man' is actually the first man with a giant penis who will cause the woman to menstruate for the first time and lose her child is indicated right away by his mistaking her for a marsupial he wishes to shoot (see Gillison 1993: 112ff).
5. The logic of Gimi men, which treats pregnancy as theft, seems to contradict that of

the Amazonian myth in which the woman closes her body, or tries to conceive alone, and men trick her into accepting their sperm (above, p. 178). But the extreme opposites represent equally woman's desire to possess the child entirely, either by stealing it or refusing to give it up.

6. My reconstruction of the 'voyage' of an initiate back inside his mother condenses two separate rites of male initiation. Boys see the flutes, and hold them briefly in their laps, at adolescence, but do not play them until five or more years later when they participate in another cycle of initiation (see Gillison 1993: 264).

7. In the cassowary myth discussed above (p. 174ff.), it is not the woman but her fathers who decapitate the snake and provoke her menstruation. Unlike the flute myth and underlying logic of exchange relations, which I discuss here, that myth is invented by women and presents their side of the argument with men. For a fuller discussion of the 'debate' between Gimi men's and women's myths, see Gillison 1993.

References

Bamberger, Joan (1974) 'The Myth of Matriarchy: Why Men Rule in Primitive Society', in *Woman, Culture and Society*, ed. M.Z. Rosaldo and Louise Lamphere, Stanford: Stanford University Press.

Barth, Fredrik (1990) 'The Guru and the Conjurer: Transactions in Knowledge and the Shaping of Culture in Southeast Asia and Melanesia', *Man* 25: 640–53.

Bidou, Patrice (1996) 'Trois mythes de l'origine du Manioc (Nord-ouest de l'Amazonie)', *L'Homme* 140: 63–79.

Dundes, Alan (1976) 'A Psychoanalytic Study of the Bullroarer', *Man*, NS. 2 : 220–38.

Freud, Sigmund (1976 [1900]), *The Interpretation of Dreams*, trans. James Strachey (1958), Pelican Freud Library vol. 4, Harmondsworth, Middlesex: Pelican Books.

Gillison, Gillian (1987) 'Incest and the Atom of Kinship: The Role of the Mother's Brother in a New Guinea Highlands Society', *Ethos* 15: 166–202.

— (1993) *Between Culture and Fantasy: A New Guinea Highlands Mythology*, Chicago: University of Chicago Press.

Gourlay, K.A. (1975) *Sound-Producing Instruments in Traditional Society: A Study of Esoteric Instruments and their Role in Male-Female Relations*, New Guinea Research Bulletin no. 60, Port Moresby and Canberra: Australian National University Press.

Hugh-Jones, Stephen (1979) *The Palm and the Pleiades: Initiation and Cosmology in Northwest Amazonia*, Cambridge: Cambridge University Press.

Jones, Ernest (1925) 'Mother-Right and the Sexual Ignorance of Savages', *International Journal of Psycho-Analysis* 6: 109–30.

Kelly, Raymond C. (1976) 'Witchcraft and Sexual Relations: An Exploration in the Social and Semantic Implications of the Structure of Belief', in *Man and Woman in the New Guinea Highlands*, ed. Paula Brown and George Buchbinder, Special Publication no. 8, Washington, DC: American Anthropological Association.

Reik, T. (1958 [1946]) *Ritual: Psychoanalytic Studies*, New York: International Universities Press, Inc.

Rubin, Gayle (1975) 'The Traffic in Women: Notes on the "Political Economy" of Sex', in *Toward an Anthropology of Women*, ed. Rayna Reiter, New York: Monthly Review Press.

Strathern, Marilyn (1972) *Women in Between: Female Roles in a Male World, Mount Hagen, New Guinea*, London: Seminar Press.

Tuzin, Donald F. (1984) 'Miraculous Voices: The Auditory Experience of Numinous Objects', *Current Anthropology* 25: 579–96.

Umusin Panlon Kumu and Tolaman Kenhiri (1980) *Antes O Mundo Nao Existia*, Introduction by Berta G. Ribeiro, Sao Paulo: Livraria Cultura Editora.

van Baal, J. (1963) 'The Cult of the Bull-Roarer in Australia and Southern New Guinea', *Bijdr. Taal-, Land-Volkenk*, 119: 201–14.

185

9

A body painting in translation[1]

Françoise Dussart

The approach to art from the side of Western aesthetics . . . and indeed from any sort of prior formalism, blinds us to the very existence of the data upon which a comparative understanding of it could be built. And we are left, as we used to be in studies of totemism, caste, or bride-wealth – and still are in structuralist ones – with an externalized conception of the phenomenon supposedly under intense inspection but actually not even in our line of sight.

(Geertz 1983: 98)

Introduction

The commodification of visual representation produced by Fourth World people has increasingly gained the attention of anthropologists. Building on the pioneer works of Maquet (1986) and Graburn (1976), researchers have intensified their analysis of the effects of the consumption of non-Western art by the West. Such analyses among Australian Aborigines have proved particularly rich. Williams (1976), Megaw (1982), Morphy (1980, 1983, 1991), Taylor (1987), Michaels (1988), Sutton (1988), von Sturmer (1989) and Myers (1989, 1994a, 1994b) all explore the social and economic implications of Aboriginal art, both for Aborigines and society at large.

The Warlpiri residing at Yuendumu, an Aboriginal settlement located some 300 kilometres northwest of Alice Springs, expressing as they do a richly visual and dynamic ceremonial life, have long been the focus of such external attention. Their body designs, sand paintings, ritual performance, and acrylic representations of the cosmology known as the Dreaming increasingly attract the scrutiny of filmmakers, art critics, curators and anthropologists. In fact, art production now represents the principal non-governmental source of revenue for the settlement, dramatically modifying the role of iconographic representation in the construction of Warlpiri social identity.

In this chapter, I propose to analyse a single Aboriginal body painting design performed by women in three media: the traditional surface (i.e.

the torso), acrylic on canvas, and celluloid film. Understanding how the visual artistic system and the meanings associated with that system undertake translations from one medium to another offers insight into the Warlpiri ritual domain and forces the anthropologist to reassess the intercultural dynamic between the Aboriginal residents of Yuendumu and a public that stretches around the world.

From Dreamtime to torso: the first translation

The ritual life of the Warlpiri – a repertoire of Dreamtime stories sung, danced and painted – links the individual both to the land from which the Dreaming emerges, and to the kin group responsible for its maintenance. As such, the performance of ceremony serves as a kind of social, geographic and cosmological mastic, and provides an arena in which many non-ritual issues find expression. The act of drawing a circle or a set of lines on the torso of a woman – a procedure restricted to the ceremonial performance – reifies the nature of negotiation found at the core of Warlpiri notions of social exchange.

I would like to begin my analysis by describing what a body painting can say and how it can be said. I take as my model a single design recounting the Fire Dreaming at Ngarna. The traditional public version of this Dreamtime story involves two mythical brothers and their father, a blue tongue lizard. The story recounts the brothers' inadvertent transgression of a taboo, and the subsequent punishment by the father who 'sings' a magical fire to immolate them. The two brothers ultimately die in a secret cave south of Ngarna, a sacred site to the west of Yuendumu.

This Fire Dreaming evokes three of the many Ancestral Beings who emerged in the Dreamtime, a period during which the world was physically shaped and the social and moral orders were instituted. Warlpiri people believe that when their ancestors were asleep Ancestral Beings came to them to tell them how people should live. Much of the knowledge transmitted focused on rules of ceremonial performance, procedures by which marvellous acts performed by the Ancestral Beings could be re-enacted. The revelations are, following Ricœur's terminology, 'texts of narrated dreams' (1970: 5), and are translated by the Warlpiri people when they enact mythical events in their paintings, dances and songs. The nature of this translation varies most obviously along lines of gender, but is further informed by the variables as well of kinship, age and personal authority.

To understand the plurality of these variables one must first understand the complex nature of negotiations by which the painting is itself produced.

Body paintings, traditionally applied, can be placed on the upper torso of both men and women using a variety of natural pigments: red and yellow ochre, pipe clay and charcoal. A base of animal fat (baby oil in recent years) is applied to give the body a glistening look that the Warlpiri associate with health and beauty (*marrka*). The Warlpiri maintain that the shimmering effect of a painting evokes the qualities engendered by Ancestral Beings who first applied these designs on their own bodies in the Dreamtime.

There are a number of gender-specific techniques in the creation of traditional body designs. Women limit themselves to ochres and oil, while men often dot themselves with such additional materials as animal down and vegetable fibre. This distinction must be noted because, as I will show later, acrylic adaptations of the body designs combined the techniques of men and women, even though it is only women who actually produced acrylic paintings employing body motifs. For their acrylics, Warlpiri men mainly adapt designs taken from ritual object and ground paintings. Though some elements of the Fire Dreaming body painting of men differ from those of women, basic symbols remain invariant. The iconographic compositions of both employ circles, semicircles, lines, footprints, and meanders (see Munn 1973: 112). As is true of all body paintings, Fire Dreaming designs are all geospecific and associated with specific actions of the Ancestral Beings.

A body painting, traditionally performed, is only meant to last the duration of a ceremony, which never stretches more than half a day. In conjunction with songs and dances, body design enables the Warlpiri to call up the powers of the Ancestral Beings. When the ceremonies are

Figure 9.1 Judy Nampijinpa Granites and Dolly Nampijinpa Daniels, both *kirda*, dancing the final scene of the Fire Dreaming at Ngarna under the supervision of Ema Nungarrayi, a *kurdungurlu* for the Fire Dreaming at Ngarna.

over, the Warlpiri efface the design so that these powers do not remain. It is important to stress that the body painting derives its potency from this ritual context, and that an essential aspect of its execution is its temporary nature.

In its production, a traditional body painting represents a negotiation that connects the painted and the painter. The act also forms a connection between individual and other kin members, Ancestral Beings and the land inhabited by both. To bear the designs of the Ngarna Fire Dreaming, men and women must hold paternal rights (*kirda*) or maternal rights (*kurdungurlu*) to the Dreaming, or obtain permission from someone who holds rights as *kirda*.[2] Siblings, whether male or female, inherit these rights in the same way. *Kirda* have the rights and responsibilities to acquire knowledge, to pass it on and to perform ceremonies re-enacting the Dreamtime stories they inherited, and *kurdungurlu* must make sure that ceremonies are performed 'correctly'. Thus, for any given site and Dreamtime story there is an interconnected set of *kirda* and *kurdungurlu*. Some exceptions to this kin-based control of rights do exist. An extremely skilled painter – one capable of applying 'correct' (*junga*) designs 'from the Dreamtime' (*kuruwarri*) – will be granted the right to paint certain Dreamings even if the requisite kin ties to the associated site are lacking. The Warlpiri consider such 'correctness', and the accompanying fidelity to notions of the proper representation of the Dreaming, a means of enhancing the potency (*wiri*) of Ancestral Powers (see Munn 1973).

Negotiation extends beyond the rights to paint or be painted. Also at issue are the levels of meaning that individuals are allowed to possess for the painting that is produced. The Fire Dreaming at Ngarna contains a variety of interpretations, even when the pattern remains the same. Furthermore, the changed context for a ceremony may provide additional meanings known only to certain *kirda* and *kurdungurlu*.

The public story I sketched out earlier offers the most rudimentary and public elements of the Fire Dreaming story. Additional information is known to those ritual leaders who are active in maintaining the ceremonial life of the settlement. To give one example, the fate of the two brothers who are put to death by fire is modified in the story known to male initiates. This alternative version of the story is exchanged as a commodity in an environment which treats all such ritual knowledge as power. Certain elder women at Yuendumu may know this male secret version but are prohibited from revealing it or even admitting their knowledge. As such they cannot use it in ritual exchanges that are at the core of the Warlpiri ceremonial life (Dussart 1988, 1992).

All this suggests that traditionally applied body paintings reflect a complex system of collaboration involving kinship, gender, ritual exchange, and displays of technical skill, a system that has parallels outside Warlpiri culture. Similar issues of negotiation have been described among the Pintupi (Myers 1989), the Kunwinjku (Taylor 1987) and the Yolngu (Morphy 1991). As Morphy eloquently notes in his study of the Yolngu artistic system: 'Because art encodes meaning in the context of a system of revelatory knowledge, we must consider not only "what it means" but "to whom it means"'(1991: 216). There are, of course, many more nuances in the creation of the body painting, but for an analysis of a mediated visual system of representation, this schematic overview is sufficient.

From torso to canvas: the second translation

Morphy's quotation offers an apt transition to an analysis of the Fire Dreaming in its second translation, when it moves from torso to canvas for sale to non-Warlpiri buyers. This newly mediated artwork raises profound, sometimes troubling questions about the economic and ritual life of the Warlpiri. It also offers insights into the diversity of interpretations the visual representation can generate both within and beyond the settlement. This mediation between two cultures should come as no surprise since acrylic painting employs the materials of one culture and the visual system of another.

Though the Warlpiri at Yuendumu sporadically painted their designs for commercial purposes as early as circa 1960, they only began to paint acrylic canvases of their ritual designs in 1983, some ten years after the Pintupi, Pitjantjatjara and Warlpiri residing in the neighbouring settlement of Papunya pioneered the technique. The Yuendumu paintings sold well almost immediately and major exhibitions were organised quickly throughout Australia. In 1985, with the approval of the Warlpiri painters and the guidance of an adult educator, a company was set up called Warlukurlangu Artists Association. Aboriginal and state agencies provided grants to pay an art adviser and an art coordinator to organise and distribute supplies to painters, and to document 'the story' associated with the paintings. It was assumed, rightly, that such accompanying texts would stimulate sales to tourists, art galleries or museums worldwide.

From the beginning, the acrylic paintings served two purposes. There was, of course, the obvious financial compensation that came from sales of the work. Acrylic painting was, and still is, as a source of income second only to the social benefit checks provided by the Australian state. Concomitant with the economic incentives, acrylic representation of the Dreamtime affirmed the richness of Warlpiri culture. Though the nature of this affirmation has undergone change, the acrylics continue to be a means by which the Warlpiri undertake a form of social dialogue with the world outside the settlement. The Warlpiri expect that showing their paintings will make the world beyond Yuendumu 'care' and recognise the importance of their life and culture.[3]

Figure 9.2 (*left*) Close-up of Dolly Nampijinpa displaying a coolamon painted with the Fire Dreaming at Ngarna. In the background, Kumanjayi Nungarrayi, Lorna Napurrurla, Bessie Nakamarra, and Biddy Napanangka are painting wooden objects and canvases for sale, Yuendumu, 1983.

Figure 9.3 Women and young girls dancing with traditional objects and boards painted with acrylics during the visit of Minister of Aboriginal Affairs on 25 September 1984 to manifest their objections to potential legislation change for Aboriginal access to traditional Aboriginal land.

The first painters came exclusively from a pool of older initiates, both men and women, who actively maintained the ritual life of Yuendumu. The creation of acrylics adapted the collaborative nature of traditional ceremonial techniques to the new medium. In the first months of acrylic production, the painters, while painting in and for non-ritual contexts, rigorously maintained the patterns of ceremonial collaboration between *kirda* and *kurdungurlu*. This changed, however, as the number of painters increased. The collaboration between *kirda* and *kurdungurlu* was overwhelmed by new patterns of assistance that relied on spousal and kin associations. Co-residentiality reconfigured the methods by which the Fire Dreaming found representation.[4] There were rules, however, even as the medium changed.

An acrylic painting must begin with the selection of a background paint colour. The choices are generally limited to red, brown or black – colours that evoke the ground and the body. After the surface of the canvas is covered, the painters apply the main symbols associated with the segment of the Dreaming they wish (and are allowed) to evoke. Though the artists use brushes instead of their fingers, other elements of the procedure maintain a tie to traditional enactment. As with designs made during ritual ceremonies, precise and well-defined symbols are highly valued; the clarity of a design enhances its spiritual potency. Not surprisingly, the skilful artists who perform in the ritual milieu often find a prominent place in acrylic production as well. These painters can use an extremely large pallet of colours to dot areas of the canvas that are not taken up by the narrative symbols that tell the tale of the two brothers. The colours are generally chosen to display a vibrancy that the Warlpiri believe mirrors the shimmering qualities of their traditional surface. In fact, fluorescent paint is usually favoured by many painters.

Still, a number of crucial distinctions must be made between a corporeal painting and one that appears on canvas. There is, first of all, the matter of permanence. As I mentioned earlier, ritual body designs are not intended to survive more than a few hours, and never outlive the ceremony in which they are created. The acrylic works, devoid of ceremonial purpose, serve as a fixed register of the Warlpiri artistic system, but lack ritual power. On the practical level of production, another distinction must be made involving the patterned use of 'dots'. Though dots do not figure in the traditional body design of women, they do appear on the canvas adaptations. The reason for this modification offers an insight into the gender-based exchange among the Warlpiri that predates the acrylic movement. At the end of the 1970s, senior men gave senior women the right to use dotted backgrounds – an adaptation of the feathers and vegetable down traditionally restricted to male body paintings – for commercial, non-ceremonial purposes.

Nevertheless, certain patterns of exchange are rigorously maintained. Acrylic designs that recompose and combine significant segments of Warlpiri iconography from ritual objects and ground paintings involve extensive negotiation and require the approval of knowledgeable kin group elders before they can be painted. The artist who combines various Dreaming segments without approval of other *kirda* risks censure and punishment through acts of sorcery. When such unacceptable paintings are discovered, they are generally effaced or modified. Not to do so would threaten the balance of kinship relations.

To avoid potential conflict, many painters decided early on to restrict the acrylic repertoire to public designs. This had an unexpected impact on gender relations. Because women possess many more representations viewable by the uninitiated[5] they were far less restricted in the patterns they could paint for sale. Women found themselves with a measure of autonomy and power until men created public versions of their restricted designs.

It is important to note here that the Warlpiri acrylic movement has transformed the gender status of visual representation. When Nancy Munn conducted her fieldwork in the 1950s, prior to the development of the acrylic art market, she observed that the public body designs painted by women lacked the potency of men's secret designs. Secrecy was, during Munn's stay at Yuendumu, the principal criterion in the assessment of a design's ritual efficacy. This notion of potency has undergone change, however, with the creation of an acrylic art market. The public nature of the designs no longer suggests impotence. On the contrary, public display has become a way of reifying personal authority in the ritual domain. In addition to the issue of the public expression of ritual in the social interaction of the settlement, acrylic body designs have often provided a measure of personal autonomy for the female artists. Because body paintings require less negotiation than many other designs, it is possible to retain much of the economic proceeds generated through the sale of an acrylic, and thus mitigate many of the redistributive pressures common to contemporary egalitarian societies (Woodburn 1982, Myers 1986).

It is against this backdrop that Molly Nampijinpa Langdon painted her small canvas in 1984 (Fig. 9.4).

Figure 9.4 Fire Dreaming at Ngarna painted on canvas by Molly Nampijinpa Langdon, Yuendumu, 1984, 60.5 × 45.7 cm.

As I explained at the outset of this chapter, the acrylic design adapts a segment of the Fire Dreaming iconography applied to the body during a ceremony. The central motif on the acrylic replicates the patterns that Molly has had painted on her body and has painted on the bodies of her sisters, her brother's daughters, and her father's sisters in ritual context. However, the semi-circles and lines surrounding the central motifs do not serve as part of the traditional body design as such. These border symbols are adapted from publicly displayed ground paintings executed by male *kirda* for the Fire Dreaming. Molly was able to apply these supplemental motifs without negotiation because she previously obtained the knowledge required to reproduce them from one of her elder brothers.

Why did Molly paint the Fire Dreaming? Certainly, the possibility of selling the canvas for cash was a central factor in the decision. But this in no way explains why *that* Dreaming was chosen. According to numerous artists, including Molly, body painting designs were initially selected not only because of their public status, but for reasons of non-indigenous 'accessibility' as well. The artists believed that the patterns were so obviously allied to the shape of the human form that they would naturally appeal to non-Aboriginal buyers sensitive to a so-called 'figurative' tradition in the visual arts. (It should be noted that the modification of traditional iconography is not prompted solely by external commodification. The early record of the Central Desert dot-painting movement seems to suggest that the foreignness of the material itself – the acrylics and canvases – even when unconnected to intercultural transaction, stimulated 'figurative' experimentation in ritual design.[6])

This effort to engage the non-Aboriginal buyer with what the Aboriginal artists believe to be a more 'representational' work is not unique to Yuendumu. Bark painters from Western Arnhem land also decided to produce for sale forms of rock painting iconography that non-Aborigines would consider 'more figurative' (Taylor 1987). While this strategy proved successful for the Kunwinjku bark painters, it was ultimately rejected by the Yuendumu artists. Less than a year after Molly painted her small canvas, body designs no longer appeared in the repertoire of acrylic production. This decision was prompted by the artists' discovery that buyers of their work were unable to recognise the corporeal origins of the designs. It would be easy to assert that the artists were simply responding to market forces, but that is not completely true. Though body paintings sold well among non-Aborigines, the artists expressed a sense of frustration that their Dreamings and the stories associated with their Dreamings were not being 'recognised' by purchasers. As a result, the artists moved in one of two directions. They either intensified their efforts to make more 'representational' what had always been sufficiently representational to them. This was accomplished by substituting images of leaves where icons of leaves once appeared, placing trees previously filled with circles, and applying goannas in lieu of the symbolic representation of the desert reptile. The other tack taken when faced by non-indigenous incomprehension was to accept the impossibility of communicating the public Dreamtime stories, and to make paintings that contained symbolic significance acknowledged to be far beyond the scope of the uninitiated. The return of the body painting to its original design was emblematic of a deepened understanding by the Warlpiri of the limits of cross-cultural communication.

Now that body paintings are no longer produced on acrylic, the early autonomy of women painters has undergone noteworthy change. The newer designs, relying more heavily on iconography that require greater cross-gender consultation on matters of correctness has meant an increase in spousal assistance and collaboration, for the completion of the background motifs, which the artists have always considered a tedious part of the process. As such, acrylic production continues to serve as a dynamic arena of exchange between men and women, between various kin groups, and between the Warlpiri and the world at large.

In lieu of body designs, women now adapt the patterns found on other traditional surfaces (i.e. the earth,[7] wood) to their acrylic canvases. This diminution in the repertoire has meant that men's designs and women's designs display more iconographic similarity than they did in the early days of production. Furthermore, the increased collaboration between genders, wherein the brothers and husbands regularly allow their public designs to enter the repertoire of women's acrylics, has meant that designs that were once gender-specific now can share many visual elements. More important, the ways in which men and women think about, plan, narrate and execute designs increasingly overlaps.

I have, throughout this chapter, avoided the term audience when describing non-Aboriginal viewers. This is because while some sophisticated Westerners might *see* certain narrative elements in designs, almost none can sense the auditory, olfactory and sensory experience that attends the creation of designs in a ceremonial context. When Molly's body is painted with natural pigment, the creation is always accompanied by songs associated with the Dreaming design. This singing is obviously absent from the decontextualised painting that appears on acrylic, viewed under the artificial light of the gallery. Absent, too, is the painting's geospecific nature. Numerous efforts have been made to recontextualise the acrylic canvas in the setting of production. Nearly a dozen documentary films have attempted to 'explain' acrylics. Though the Warlpiri themselves have experimented with video cameras, they have not, to my knowledge, directed the camera lens at acrylic production. There is, however, a 28-minute promotional video by a non-Aboriginal Australian filmmaker that attempts to register the process. Produced between 1990 and 1991, the film was made at the request of a few Warlpiri painters and two non-Warlpiri art advisers. It was their hope that the film would generate international interest in acrylic painting. I do not, at this point, wish to analyse reactions of non-Aboriginal people to the film, or attempt to assess its economic impact. Rather, I am interested in the response of the Warlpiri themselves to a film. By exploring the Warlpiri assessment of the film, we can further understand how cultural identity is modified and lost in translation. Listening to the reactions of the Warlpiri forces us to reject the standard language of 'capturing' images on film. Far from being 'captured', meaning is dissipated in *Warlukurlangu: Artists of Yuendumu*. Worse than dissipated in fact. Another phrase may be more accurately used to explain what happens in the film: the body painting is disembodied, at least, this is the perspective of the subjects of the film.

From torso to film: the third translation

Warlukurlangu: Artists of Yuendumu was made by a filmmaker with long experience in filming the Aboriginal people of Central Australia. Intended as a marketing tool, the film was ultimately translated into a number of languages including French and German. Although the painters featured in this film gave approval for the filming, they had little control over the eventually distributed version.

In its uncut form, the film captures a great deal of unexploited, untranslated information, and offers insights into the dynamics of ceremonial performance. The filmmaker embraces certain anthropological techniques of fieldwork, and then edits them out of the film. Though he subjects the artists to a battery of questions, only their answers remain in the final print. The artists are placed in the role of informant, with the identity of the interviewer suppressed. For the potential art buyer it serves as a cryptic piece of promotion; for the anthropologist who speaks Warlpiri and knows the geography in which the film was shot, it is an opportunity to study conflicting intentions; but to the Warlpiri themselves, the film is a 'mistranslation' of a world they wish to share.[8]

The film shows a number of Yuendumu painters – both men and women – applying ritual designs to a variety of surfaces: their bodies, the ground and, of course, canvas. The camera zooms in and out between close-up shots of the symbols and wider views that register the methods of production. Interspersed among these images are shots of the land to which the designs are tied. The film does add a crucial quality in design production absent when viewing acrylics: the ceremonial context. Shown are portions of dances and songs that accompany the creation of designs, including the Fire Dreaming of Ngarna.

The film does not attempt to address the impact of acrylic painting on the settlement, its intention is to let the painters 'speak'. As such, there is no narration. The only voices heard are from the participants in the film. Though it is the artists who take up most of the footage, there are occasional observations from one of the settlement's non-Aboriginal art advisers offering a potted history of the 'movement', and comments from two enthusiastic museum curators from Germany, coincidentally present during the filming.

The manner in which the filmmaker chooses to represent the Fire Dreaming is worth describing in some detail. The very first image of the film, though not identified, is a close-up of a body painting of the Fire Dreaming. When the film shows the ceremonial activities required to perform the Fire Dreaming, one Warlpiri woman, Dolly Nampijinpa Daniels, offers a great deal of information about her relationship to the Dreamtime story she will enact. She is then seen painting and singing. While the camera moves from one painted torso to another, Dolly's words appear at the bottom of the screen: 'This is the Bush Fire Dreaming. We are dancing for this one. When we paint we don't do other people's paintings. We do our own, from our father's and grandfather's country.' She thus notes the pattern of inheritance through patrilineal descent that is more likely than not lost on the viewer. Dolly is later seen 'reading' her body painting for the filmmaker. She is also asked to itemise the symbols for an imagined non-Aboriginal viewer, a procedure to which she regularly submits, sought after as she is by linguists, anthropologists, curators and art advisers. She is cognizant that such 'readings' provide a superficial answer to the polyvalent question so often asked by non-Aborigines, 'What does it mean?' The first symbol she points to is a circle which represents the Blue Tongue Lizard who sings the Magical Fire. She explains while facing the camera: 'This one, this circle here, the Blue Tongue Lizard has been here. Then we have the Fire Stick here, these here are the bush fire and these two are the two Jangalas [the two sons].' As the camera pulls away from her body painting to an acrylic painting, Dolly states for the viewer the source of her learning and why she can learn to paint the Fire Dreaming:[9] 'My auntie Nangala [one of Dolly's father's sisters], she told me: "This is your country, you can have this painting, in the memory."' Later the camera gives the viewers a glimpse of two women performing segments of the Fire Dreaming. When the women stop suddenly and lie down on the ground, Dolly says, 'the two Jangalas are finished now'. By 'finished' Dolly means to evoke the immolation of the two Dreamtime sons, but this connection is never made explicit.

Highly edited and decontextualised, the substance of Dolly's statements remain, cryptic to those unfamiliar with Aboriginal culture. What Dolly states and what ultimately gets communicated are very different, and so the ethnographer and the uninformed viewer will have different responses to Dolly's account of the Fire Dreaming.

Crucial information contained in Dolly's account is often not offered in the film's subtitles. Let me give three examples. First, while the camera zooms in and out from women's painted bodies during the singing of a Dreaming, the link between the song and the design is never made explicit, thus losing the auditory nature of 'seeing' a body painting. Second, though the women make the point that they are the 'owners' of the Dreaming being sung, their proprietary control is never made clear by the filmmaker. The third unsubtitled comment comes from a performer who states that it is a hot day and that as a result the ground was very hot.[10] Such an assertion has totemic resonance for the participants. It implies a link to the pain felt by the two mythical brothers when walking on the ground inhabited by the heat of the Magical Fire sent after them by their father before they died by immolation. In fact at no point in the film is the story of the Fire Dreaming told to the viewers. These omissions say more about the filmmaker than they do about those filmed. To quote Banks: 'Ethnographicness is not a thing out there which is captured by the camera but a thing we construct for ourselves in our relation to film (as well as in relation to a variety of other things, such as fieldwork)' (1992: 127).

Though the filmmaker had been told versions of the story of the Fire Dreaming many times before and during the shooting, little attempt is made to help the viewer understand what is being viewed. I need to reiterate here that paintings do not tell a story. They are a *key* to a story. Therefore, Dolly's itemisation of some symbols of her body painting only hints at the multi-levelled and plural 'readings' a Dreamtime story can have. And while the filmmaker spent a great deal of energy shooting the sites associated with Dreamtime stories, he never clarified for the non-specialists the geospecificity of the body designs, the link between the sacred site of Ngarna and the Fire Dreaming. We only see two unidentified women performing a short dance in the desert. Why are they performing in the bush and not in their village? What are they dancing? Why do they lie down? Who are they representing? Why is Dolly's body painting the same as the two dancers? Are they all painted for the Fire Dreaming? Did they all inherit their rights to paint and be painted from their fathers and grandfathers as Dolly stated? None of these questions is addressed. As a result, the complexity of kinship rights, responsibilities and negotiations – issues central to Warlpiri cosmology – are buried or edited out, unstated or unexplained.

Because I had the opportunity to be present when certain Warlpiri women first viewed the edited film, I would like to touch upon the comments they made. All the women who watched the final version had previously seen the uncut version of the film. While the unedited footage respected the chronology of events, the final film undermined any notion of linearity, a temporal rupture that greatly surprised and confused the women. They wondered why the whole ceremony for the Fire Dreaming they had performed had been sliced into pieces and represented fragmentarily.

Dolly Nampijinpa Daniels and Uni Nampijinpa, two principal actors in the film (they are *kirda* for the Fire Dreaming) both speculated that viewers would be more impressed with the film if they had seen the dances for the Fire Dreaming in their entirety. Uni's initial reaction to the first image of the film – the completed body painting – was summarised in one word '*kuntangka*' which expressed surprise and shame at the same time. She wondered why the symbols on her body were taken so dramatically out of context, and why only parts of her torso were exposed. This created the troubling image of a decapitated body, a sense of disembodiment. Giddens reflects on this sense of disempowerment when he describes a culture and individuals being deprived of the right 'to make certain "accounts count" and to enact or resist sanctioning processes' (1979: 83). After they watched the edited film, gravely disappointed, the women returned their attentions to the unedited footage, which they considered a more accurate form of self-representation.[11] The edited film was ultimately approved for distribution beyond Yuendumu by the principal participants, members of two co-residential kin groups who not only dominated the filming but whose power extends to other contexts of intercultural exchange as well.[12] This prompted intra-Warlpiri conflict; two women unconnected to Ngarna argued that the film did not represent them or their Dreamings, they further accused the *kirda* and *kurdungurlu* of Ngarna of being insensitive to other ritual leaders, and of misrepresenting the diversity of the Dreaming repertoire. None of this internal conflict – a crucial component of how ritual is enacted – appeared in the film. The contested nature of kin group representation, so central to the Warlpiri at Yuendumu, disappears once the film leaves the settlement. This is reinforced by the sudden appearance of two German museum curators who offer non-indigenous testimony toward the end of the film. They linger on the 'spirituality' of the designs, and ignore completely the artists' concerns, many of which are in the film itself. The experts then advance a Eurocentric notion of aesthetics that side-steps the issue of translation by situating the acrylics in a universal visual language vaguely labelled 'contemporary'.[13]

Conclusion

As I hope this chapter has made clear, the translations of Dreamtime myth on to torso, on to canvas, and into film register more than the dynamic interaction between the Warlpiri and non-Aborigines. These adaptations register significant exchanges taking place among the Warlpiri themselves. The paintings clarify contemporary gender and kinship relations and serve as a locus of social exchanges. Molly's small canvas and the film's depiction of Dolly's body painting both reveal countless expressions of Warlpiri social identity. They evince ties to the land, to each other, to ancestors and to Dreamings that imbue their culture. To paint one's dreaming is to maintain one's rights and to profess one's knowledge.

When body paintings move beyond Yuendumu their meanings enter a discursive state shaped by the viewer and artist. Out of this intercultural flux emerge notions of 'Aboriginality' that undergo constant redefinition (see Ginsburg 1993). This process of redefinition is not restricted to non-Aboriginal people. As Marcia Langton has noted, '"Aboriginality" [is] a social *thing* in the Durkheimian sense. It arises from the experience of both Aboriginal and non-Aboriginal people who engage in any intercultural dialogue, whether in actual lived experience or through mediated experience such as a White person watching a program about Aboriginal people on television or reading a book' (1993: 81). To Langton's list we must add the representations of the Fire Dreaming at Ngarna.

Notes

1. I am grateful to those who commented on earlier versions of this paper presented at the ASA (Oxford) and at the AAA (Washington) in 1993, and I want to particularly thank Marcus Banks, Anne Marie Cantwell, Faye Ginsburg, Howard Morphy, Fred Myers, Janet Siskind, and Terry Turner for their insights. This paper has also greatly benefited from comments from Jim Faris, Nicolas Peterson, Allen Kurzweil and anonymous reviewers.

2. The Warlpiri system of acquisition of rights to the Dreaming and associated sites contains complexities that cannot be addressed in this paper. For a detailed exploration of kinship links at Yuendumu see Dussart 1988.

3. Attempts on the part of indigenous populations to establish ties to the non-Aboriginal world are not unique to the Yuendumu. Sutton (1978) working with Aboriginal residents of Cape Keerweer during a documentary film, and Myers (1986, 1989) in his study of acrylic production at Papunya and Kintore, make similar observations.

4. For more specific explanation of why traditional patterns of collaboration were transformed see Dussart 1989.

5. See Munn 1973: 36, 42.

6. See Megaw 1982: 206–208.

7. There are very few women's ground paintings performed today at Yuendumu. Those that generally are, are not done by the Warlpiri but by women who are *kirda* for countries associated with southern Aboriginal groups, such as the Anmatyerre.

8. The role of the viewer in film production, while outside the scope of this paper, presents a number of tangential issues worthy of study. See e.g. Worth and Adair 1972; Michaels 1986; Martinez 1992; Faris 1992; Asch 1992; Langton 1993; Ginsburg 1993.

9. The indigenous resistance to aesthetic explication has been noticed by many anthropologists such as Forge (1979) and Gell (1975). More recently, O'Hanlon convincingly demonstrates that an absence of *exegesis* is not the same as absence of verbalisation (1992). Here we may suggest that because so many anthropologists, art advisers, tourists, museum curators, etc. have asked Warlpiri people what their icons mean, painters understand that this kind of verbalisation is important, but return quickly to the way they 'talk' about their paintings. In other words, Dolly, like all Warlpiri people, is 'talking about' her painting when she verbalises her relationship to country, myth and other individuals, or when she sings the Dreamtime

story associated with her designs on the body, on canvas or in a film.

10. Women are always barefoot when they perform ceremonies.
11. It must be noted that it is not the fact of editing, but the nature of the truncation that alienated the Warlpiri women. The same audience is keenly appreciative of highly produced video and film intended specifically for the Warlpiri. The women regularly watch edited educational tapes such as *Manyu-wana*, and do not like looking at the uncut versions.
12. For a lengthier discussion see Dussart 1994.
13. See Megaw 1982; Morphy 1983; Michaels 1988; Sutton 1992. Myers provides some of the most extensive analyses of ethnographic material on how and why the West engages with acrylic desert paintings and the impact such engagement has on the production of 'Aboriginality' (Myers 1989, 1991, 1994a, 1994b and 1995).

References

Asch, Timothy (1992) 'The Ethics of Ethnographic Film-making', in *Film As Ethnography*, ed. P. Crawford and D. Turton, Manchester: Manchester University Press in association with the Granada Centre for Visual Anthropology.

Banks, Marcus (1992) 'Which Films are the Ethnographic Films?' in *Film As Ethnography*, ed. P. Crawford and D. Turton, Manchester: Manchester University Press in association with the Granada Centre for Visual Anthropology.

Dussart, Françoise (1988) 'Warlpiri Women's Yawulyu Ceremonies: A Forum for Socialization and Innovation', PhD Thesis, Canberra: Australian National University.

— (1989) 'Rêves à l'acrylique', in *Australie noire: les Aborigènes, un peuple d'intellectuels*, ed. C. Merleau-Ponty and A. Tardy, Autrement, hors série 37: 104–11.

— (1992) 'Création et innovation', *Journal de la société des océanistes* 94(1): 25–34.

— (1994) 'Exhibitions of Identity: Warlpiri Women and the Performance of Public Ritual', paper presented at the European Society for Oceanists, Basel, Switzerland.

Faris, James (1992) 'Anthropological transparency: Film, Representation and Politics', in *Film As Ethnography*, ed. P. Crawford and D. Turton, Manchester: Manchester University Press in association with the Granada Centre for Visual Anthropology.

Forge, Anthony (1979) 'The Problem of Meaning in Art', in *Exploring the Visual Art of Oceania*, ed. S.M. Mead, Honolulu: Hawaii Press.

Geertz, Clifford (1983) *Local Knowledge*, New York, Basic Books.

Gell, Alfred (1975) *Metamorphosis of the Cassowaries*, London: Athlone Press.

Giddens, Anthony (1979) *Central Problems in Social Theory*, Berkeley: University of California Press.

Ginsburg, Faye (1993) 'Aboriginal Media and the Australian Imaginary', *Public Culture* 5: 557–78.

Graburn, Nelson (ed.) (1976) *Ethnic and Tourist Arts*, Berkeley: University of California Press.

Langton, Marcia (1993) 'Well, I heard it on the radio and I saw it on the television. . .', Sydney: Australia Film Commission.

Maquet, Jacques (1986) (3rd edn) *The Aesthetic Experience: An Anthropologist Looks at the Visual Arts*, New Haven/London: Yale University Press.

Martinez, Wilton (1992) 'Who Constructs Anthropological Knowledge? Toward a Theory of Ethnographic Film Spectatorship', in *Film As Ethnography*, ed. P. Crawford and D. Turton, Manchester: Manchester University Press in association with the Granada Centre for Visual Anthropology.

Megaw, Vincent (1982) 'Western Desert Acrylic Painting – Artifact or Art?' *Art history* 5: 205–18.

Michaels, Eric (1986) *The Aboriginal Invention of Television, Central Australia 1982–86*, Canberra: Australian Institute of Aboriginal Studies Press.

— (1988) 'Bad Aboriginal Art', *Art and Text* 28: 59–72.

— (1989) 'For a Cultural Future: Francis Jupurrurla makes TV at Yuendumu', Sydney: Art and Criticism Monograph Series 3.

Morphy, Howard (1980) 'The Impact of the Commercial Development of Art on Traditional Culture', in *Preserving Indigenous Cultures: A New Role for Museums*, ed. R. Edwards and J. Stewart. Canberra: Australian Government Publishing Service.

— (1983) 'Aboriginal Fine Art, the Creation of Audiences and the Marketing of Art', in *Aboriginal Arts and Crafts and the Market*, ed. P. Loveday and P. Cook, Darwin: North Australian Research Unit.

— (1991) *Ancestral Connections: Art and an Aboriginal System of Knowledge*, Chicago: Chicago University Press.

Munn, Nancy (1973) *Walbiri Iconography: Graphic Representation and Cultural Symbolism in a Central Australian Society*, Ithaca: Cornell University Press.

Myers, Fred (1986) *Pintupi Country, Pintupi Self: Sentiment, Place, and Politics among Western Desert Aborigines*, Washington, Canberra: Smithsonian Institution Press and Australian Institute of Aboriginal Studies.

— (1989) 'Truth, Beauty, and Pintupi Painting', *Visual Anthropology*, 2: 163–95.

— (1991) 'Representing Culture: The Production of Discourse(s)', in *Meaning in the Visual Arts*, ed. E. Levin, Princeton: Princeton University Press.

— (1994a) 'Beyond the Intentional Fallacy: Art Criticism and the Ethnography of Aboriginal Acrylic Painting', *Cultural Anthropology* 6 (1): 26–62.

— (1994b) 'Culture-making: performing Aboriginality at the Asia Society', *American Ethnologist* 21(4): 679–99.

— (1995) 'Re/writing the Primitive: Art Criticism and the Circulation of Aboriginal Painting', in *Meaning in the Visual Arts: Views from the Outside: A Centennial Commemoration of Erwin Panofsky (1892–1968)*, ed. I. Lavin, Princeton: Institute for Advanced Study.

O'Hanlon, Michael (1992) 'Unstable Images and Second Skins: Artefact, Exegesis and Assessments in the New Guinea Highlands', *Man* 27 (3): 587–608

Ricœur, Paul (1970) *Freud and Philosophy: An Essay on Interpretation*, New Haven: Yale University Press.

Sutton, Peter (1978) 'Some Observations on Aboriginal Use of Filming at Cape Keerweer, 1977', paper presented at the Department of Anthropology and Sociology seminar, University of Queensland.

— (1992) 'Aboriginal Art, The Nation-State, Suburbia', *Artlink*, 12 (3): 6–9.

— (1988) (ed.) *Dreamings: Art from Aboriginal Australia*, New York: Braziller Publishers.

Taylor, Luke (1987) 'The Same But Different: Social Reproduction and Innovation in the Art of the Kunwinjku of Western Arnhem Land', PhD thesis, Canberra: Australian National University.

von Sturmer, John (1989) 'Aborigines, Representation, Necrophilia', *Art and Text* 32: 127–39.

Williams, Nancy (1976) 'Australian Aboriginal Art at Yirrkala', in *Ethnic and Tourist Arts*, ed. N. Graburn, Berkeley: University of California Press.

Woodburn, James (1982) 'Egalitarian Societies', *Man*, 17 (3): 431–51.

Worth Sol and John Adair (1972) *Through Navajo Eyes*, Bloomington: Indiana University Press.

10

Displacing the visual: of Trobriand axe-blades and ambiguity in cultural practice

Debbora Battaglia

My purpose in this chapter is to consider how the visual is problematised in cultural practice.[1] Specifically, I examine certain ethnographic situations in which the main subject of discourse is absent – that is, phenomenally invisible – and go on to explore the implications of this absence for a discourse-centred approach to culture. If culture is taken as 'localised in concrete, publicly accessible signs, *the most important of which are actually occurring instances of discourse*' (Urban's words [1991], emphasis mine), we must, I suggest, look again at situations in which such signs are not the main subject of discourse; situations in which they are rather displacements of a subject located – materially embodied – elsewhere and elsewhen.

The larger question emerging in this light is whether displaced subjects may actually subordinate those discursive sites and actions that a strictly empirical anthropology would judge 'the most important' sites of culture – whether acts of displacement may be more important to compare across cultures than is commonly recognised. This question becomes interesting, becomes consequential for theories of culture, only when displacement has a purpose for actors, that is, when it is an indigenous action of disjoining the material from the realm of sensorial perception – or as in the Trobriand ethnography that engages me here, when something is *made* invisible. When something is made invisible and hence problematised, it does not simply occupy the logical space or place of presupposition or product of discourse. Rather it makes apparent an attempt to assert that space or place – in a word, to control it. Thus the matter is a practical one, arising from the possibility that the practical relevance of 'actually occurring' phenomena may derive from their relation to other practices and objects they call attention to.

It follows that what otherwise might be construed as a purely abstract issue is perhaps better appreciated as an indigenous project of ambiguating relationships: by making an absence felt, by *concretising absence*, a presence, and the present, is asserted as ungraspable. It is this effect of ambiguity, in other words, which people are manipulating, politically and poetically, and which is the alternative subject of the discourse. If a discourse approach is to avoid precluding consideration of such deliberate (though note, not determinative) slippages of meaning – if it is to avoid getting in the way of understanding destabilisations of significance and how people problematise social experience – it must admit the realm of the unseen into its terms of reference.

Displacements of the visual: the urban Trobriand scene

The historical setting is Port Moresby in the harvest months of 1985. Trobriand residents are harvesting their competitive yam exchange gardens in and around the city. On the model of 'competitions' or *kayasa* in the Trobriand homeland, their yields will be measured and judged by a sponsoring headman or chief, who will then award prizes. Classically, the prizes include a stone axe-blade, or *beku* – ideally one 'with a name', that is, one of fine enough quality that a history of ownership attaches to it. In Port Moresby, it is announced that the prize for the largest yield is an axe-blade, a pig, and seven hundred *kina*.

The sponsor of the urban competition is John Noel, who is head of the National Planning and Budget Office for Papua New Guinea. He is calling his event the First Annual Trobriand Yam Festival, describing it as 'a new kind of thing', at once traditional and 'open' to national participation. But whereas Noel's initiative is widely acknowledged and admired by the men who are gardening, his sponsorship is problematic. For while he is recognised as a headman in his home village of Losuia, John Noel cannot claim (does not claim) headman status for Port Moresby. Nor is he a member of a chiefly subclan. In fact exactly to the contrary, John Noel is a Bau man: a member, by birth, of the lowest of the Trobriand ranked subclans or *dala* – what Malinowski described (speaking for his high-ranked consultants [1929: 385]) as the 'pariah' *dala* of the Trobriand system. In this regard, the urban *kayasa* presents a sharply focused – some believe a ludicrous – anomaly: the lowest of the low, structurally speaking, is representing Trobriand culture and the Trobriand élite on the national scene. One chiefly critic laughs when he hears of it: 'Never in my life has anyone followed a Bau man. You mark my words: from the beginning to the end [of the *kayasa*] nothing will go straight . . . A Bau man is never embarrassed. He never knows to be.' Another remarked: 'Bau can make mistakes. They're very lucky. They also swear a lot . . . John Noel is ruthless when he swears. We regard them as a bizarre group. No sense of direction. It's from their ancestors. It's understandable.' And then there are the 'Bau jokes', he continues: Bau men making fools of themselves, doing things 'upside down', building canoes out of stone, in general not 'getting it' – with sometimes disastrous consequences. I have discussed Bau jokes elsewhere in greater detail (Battaglia 1992). The point here is that nowhere in the manifest content of these jokes is there a reference to the common knowledge that motivates them – what Bau men (who are never the ones telling the jokes) refer to as 'the dark side' of Bau. This has to do with the connection of Bau to sorcery. Behind the elliptical Bau stereotype, the jokes' latent content in common, is the legend that Bau ancestors brought the most lethal forms of sorcery to the Trobriand Islands. 'Bau do stupid things', I was told, 'thinking their magic is strong enough to make everything straight . . . ' In Port Moresby, for example, they were conducting themselves as 'urban chiefs': painting their yams with the insignia of chiefly rank; talking of dressing their children in the emblems of rank at the yam competition awards ceremony; engaging men of chiefly subclans to garden for them.[2] In sum, Bau individuated (as opposed to endogamously replicating their given social position); they refused to contain themselves (took liberties with 'custom'); they wandered far from the geographic domain of their origins, and out of the reach of chiefly influence.

One result of the Bau anomaly was that the Bau sponsor's immaculate urban garden, his impressive yield (indicating, among other things, his possession of effective garden magic), his urban harvest competition, could mimic but never straightforwardly model or represent noble enterprise and legitimate productivity. The reputation for sorcery pre-cancelled any Bau activity as a model only of virtue; it qualified that activity's 'face value'. In short, the threat of destructive action was always *invisibly foregrounded* by the Bau presence on a scene representing constructive action – notwithstanding the level of Bau men's own self-experience, or of practical appreciation of a gardener's skills, and so forth.

Now, chiefs of the highest ranks, those who controlled the magic for the weather, who could thus bring about famine or abundance, feared and sought out Bau magic. They married into the Bau *dala* (cf. Malinowski, who described Bau as endogamous by default); were partners with Bau men in political exchange – as it were, supplementing each other's fear-potential. Thus, John Noel embodied a deeply felt ambivalence within his function of urban host. By his own description he was an 'urban cowboy'; an 'urban chief' and 'revolutionary' to supporters. Some persons of noble birth objected that he and his Bau relatives were conducting themselves improperly and inviting sorcery by their presumption of high status and leadership initiative along customary lines (see Battaglia 1995). One can appreciate how the cultural practices of the urban Bau man, which constituted a Janus-action of resistance to both the conventions of Port Moresby's late capitalist 'cash economy' (the Trobriand gloss) and to the prescribed relationality of the Trobriand system of rank, might at the very least represent the threat of a contagious, culture-bounding social disorder.

But I submit that more than a threat, the Bau man's 'joke' of (dis)empowerment held for urban Trobrianders a dangerous allure; that the Bau man was transformed by the postcolonial urban context from a figure of threat into an enticing figure of social slippage, embodying the temptation to play with and in other ways disrupt given orders of relationship. On the one hand, this licence derived its volition from the mimicry of colonial process and European identity which was a feature of urban Trobrianders' lived experience of Port Moresby – a mimesis which, as Homi Bhabha (1991) has pointed out,

> represents an ironic compromise . . . a desire for a reformed, recognizable Other, as a subject of a difference that is almost the same, but not quite. . . . [I]n order to be effective, mimicry must continually produce its slippage, its excess, its difference. The authority of that mode of colonial discourse that I have called mimicry is therefore stricken by an indeterminacy: mimicry emerges as the representation of a difference that is itself a process of disavowal. Mimicry is, thus, the sign of a double articulation; a complex strategy of reform, regulation, and discipline, which 'appropriates' the Other as it visualises power.

On the other hand, the slippage had a direct relationship to Port Moresby's violent social climate in the harvest months of 1985 – lawlessness having brought the city to a State of Emergency and earned perpetrating youth gangs the fear and regard of the nation (see Kulick 1993). In short, illicit empowerment was loose upon the land, at a close remove from most urban dwellers' personal experience, and its images likewise, in media reportage and editorials and interviews with gang members in the national press.

———

> I have been strongly advised not to give out *beku* because it represents life.
>
> (John Noel)

Having to some extent set the scene, it is now possible to delineate the matter of the stone axe-blade, the *beku*, which I have mentioned was one of the main prizes of the yam competition, and the site of a striking problematic of ownership for Trobrianders. The *beku* is described by an array of indigenous and other sources as the primary wealth object of Kiriwina, and by Weiner as the primary object of male wealth (Weiner 1976: 231).[3] And yet it has received astonishingly little attention in the ethnographic literature relative to *kula* valuables and women's wealth – items of less common use. One might actually speak of it as buried in the literature, as it is, figuratively, in Trobriand exchange within a myriad of small and large transactions oriented to birth, marriage and death. Weiner makes a point of noting that a *beku* 'may only be seen briefly during a transaction' (1983a: 158). The rare, named *beku* are often literally buried beneath their owners' houses, or hidden within them.[4]

In ethnography and for Trobrianders with whom I spoke, the *beku* is associated most often with 'life'. In the positive, it is linked to yams and sustenance; in the negative to sorcery and the threat of taking life: the ambivalence, the ambiguity in contexts of use, is set in stone. I might hear in the course of a single conversation, '*beku* is the source of food' and 'as *beku* moves, there are deaths involved'.

In its positive aspect, the *beku* is a feature of exchanges whose outcomes are anything but given from the point of view of urban Trobrianders – specifically, outcomes involving the expansion, supplementations and increases of yams and of relations through alliance. A *beku* is used in magical procedures to 'swell' the belly of the garden with developing yams (Weiner 1976: 196; Malinowski 1935); in *effecting* (not aiding) growth. It may be used to purchase such spells, or to purchase seed yams, or land (as *pokala*, land from maternal uncles [Weiner 1976: 70]). It is offered as an incentive to gardeners to plant larger yam exchange gardens – as Weiner states: 'When a man plants large quantities of seed yams, which the recipient of the yams has either accumulated or bought, he expects to receive a valuable [archetypically an axe-blade] for his labor . . . The valuable binds the relationship tighter' (1976: 147). It also 'binds' brothers-in-law as *takola*, a return on yams presented by a woman's brother to her husband. And in the mortuary exchange of *way-ala kaybila*, the increment of a *beku* obligates the kin of a widow or widower to contribute raw yams to a future mortuary feast, moving yams across clan boundaries (Weiner 1976: 70). Within the *dala*, a *beku* 'opens the yam house' of a major chief: as I was told, a woman of his subclan will present a chief with a *beku* to end the period of storage and open the main yam house to female *dala* mates for their use in organising and preparing public feasts.

More striking, however, and in Port Moresby more salient than the *beku* in its nurturant aspect, was the *beku* in context of the discourse of sorcery. Yams and sorcery are linked through envy. An envious person might respond to another's large yield of yams by enlisting a sorcerer to kill the gardener, 'compensating him for his risk' by giving him a high-grade axe-blade 'striped like clouds across the sky at night when it is still'. The axe-blade also 'pays for' his death if the sorcerer dies on the job. And I wish to linger over this next point: such a *beku* would be called 'to cut open the stomach of the sorcerer' [a reference to the binding contract between assassin and client – 'cutting through any barrier' (e.g. the stomach lining) between them]. 'Like a *beku*', I was told, the 'stomach is a round thing that encases food that becomes blood. It is like a sorcerer's stomach and the decisions within it. A sorcerer accepts an axe-blade and puts it close to his stomach, saying "Oh, it's like my food." It makes his stomach clench [get 'hard', *kasai*; inspires a visceral response]. "It's close to my heart." '[5] This *beku* then becomes the sorcerer's own.

I have called attention to this remarkable imagery (which was conveyed to me with great intensity) partly as a means of introducing the issues of ownership and 'replacement' of *beku*. In the only sustained discussions on the subject in Trobriand ethnography,[6] Weiner (1983a: 159) observes that:

> *Beku* either cause or reconstitute the loss of property and individuals via the actions of 'others' through time. Thus, the main value of *beku* is as object par excellence for securing replacement . . . of *dala* property, especially land, and . . . of individuals through compensation. In marriage and divorce, *beku* function [in exchange] to replace a child and to replace *dala*. In mortuary distribution, *beku* operate as final replacement for the original marriage transaction of valuables. But *beku* . . . do not reproduce new and continuing relationships through the basic process of embedding wealth and value in 'others'.

This is because *beku* are owned, not lent. '*Beku* provide protection against "others" and the protection is expressed idiomatically as "fear" rather than as "love" and "generosity".'[7] In sum, '*Beku* . . . are very important but very dangerous things for Kiriwina.' They 'are important in [the] beginning of new reproductive cycles – marriage, children, death . . . they are also used for compensation for "blood" (killing someone from another *dala* [subclan])' (Weiner 1983a: 158–59).

But what is it to 'own' a *beku*? The central 'paradox' (1976: 183) Weiner recognises here is that because *beku* are 'owned' rather than lent, their transfer constitutes a purchase and creates no continuing partnership between giver and receiver. Thus, they 'walk around' from owner to owner. However, a *beku* is only alienable at the level of the singular transaction. A man hopes eventually to 'walk after' his *beku* – following its path through the villages and hamlets of successive owners, seeking to buy it back – to reclaim it, one gathers, for his subclan. Leaving aside issues of emplacement which could figure more centrally than subclan here, a person's claims to 'original' ownership are only claims, which he supports by demonstrating a knowledge of the *beku*'s history greater than someone else's. 'Stone axe-blades should never become alienated from their original owners. A *beku* should return, but there is no guarantee' (Weiner 1976: 181). Now, what manner of inalienability is this which operates by means of its own potential for alienation? Might we just as easily say that the axe-blade is alienable in practice (being 'convertible into a wide variety of other valuables and services' [Weiner 1976: 180]), but engenders a *discourse of inalienability* which extends the potential for enacting social connection beyond the boundaries of lineage and birthplace? Which value is given – even culturally given? Is ownership in its economic consciousness more 'real' in this context than the object's capacity to extend, supplement, connect and to sever relations along its trajectory? And if it is not so in the 'now' of recent history, was it perhaps so in different historical circumstances – say, when warfare was endemic; when axe-blades were essential items in ceremonial prestations to solicit another village's support in raiding or ritual warfare (Leach 1983: 137)? It would seem that ownership, while an important issue for users, is not the only – perhaps not even the primary – issue for Trobrianders everywhere and always. Property models are outdistanced by the way people operate the object, and by their quest for it along the path of remembered (or fabricated?) 'owners'. For Trobrianders, this is the common sense of the matter.

Let us return to Port Moresby, and a sudden announcement by the sponsor of the yam competition, John Noel, that he will not be offering a *beku* as a prize for the largest yield, as custom dictates. His explanation to me: it 'represents life'. On one level, one might wonder if in fact he had a *beku* to offer. But this was a non-issue for people I spoke with – not a possibility to be seriously entertained – as it was assumed that a man of John Noel's material resources and networks could obtain the thing if he wished to use it; that is, if he wished to activate its effect, and to give this effect official status. Or one might wonder if in Port Moresby cash might have been a preferred substitute (cash, clay pots, and even *kula* valuables may substitute for *beku* in their operation as generalised 'wealth' or *veguwa*). But when the prizes were first announced they included one *beku*, a pig, and seven hundred *kina*. The different forms of wealth clearly had a significance. Why did participants take it as significant that John Noel did not materialise a *beku*?

I shall turn to what John Noel said about his decision not to produce an axe-blade – namely, that Pulitala, an important chief in the Trobriands, had come to Port Moresby during the yam competition to visit his daughter and observe the goings-on. When he suddenly became ill on the trip home and died on the Losuia airstrip, sorcery was (naturally) the presumed cause, and John Noel instantly became a suspect. He continued: '*Beku* represents life. It looks as if I carefully planned [the *kayasa*] to rally supporters and struck [Pulitala] at the precise moment. It will be years before people believe I had nothing to do with it.'[8]

Was John Noel's concern about his perceived agency in ending a life to be understood in terms of the loss of something or someone and its 'replacement' by an axe-blade? Perhaps, partially – the indigenous terminology of exchange does suggest an economic consciousness along these lines, as Weiner has observed. Yet I propose that the material value of *beku* in Port Moresby in 1985 cannot be understood apart from the social fact of Bau authorship of the yam competition; cannot be taken apart from the 'joke *and* threat *and* assault' (from Cottom 1989: 20) that Bau men also embodied there. Nor can the significance of axe-blades be considered apart from the cultural imaginary of violence of Port Moresby in those days. As the sorcerer clutching the *beku* to his stomach 'owned' the response of other peoples' fear, as his ownership contained the threat of fear's disruptive force slipping the bounds of productive process, John Noel sought to contain fear by not producing an axe-blade – turning the effect of the 'dark side of Bau' to his purposes.

The circumstance of chief Pulitala's death falling in conjunction with the yam competition in violent times overwhelmed the lighter side of Bau sponsorship and the positive associations of the axe-blade, restricting their range of impact. Even to be seen to possess an axe-blade would have fixed in stone this negative cast. Thus, the enactment of this ironic outcome of the harvest competition was pre-empted by the non-appearance of the *beku* as a prize. In this context, the material absence of the *beku* safeguarded its ambiguity: its material *invisibility* was representational – here, of a relationship intentionally vanished or left unconfirmed. Because it remained invisibly foregrounded as an implement of illegitimate power, the *beku* could not be reduced – could not reduce John Noel – to a figure of illegitimate power.

In so far as one appreciates Bau as emblematically subversive of given power asymmetries, one comes closer to understanding also the practical dimension of the *beku* in urban cultural practice. The *beku* was, in 1985, for cutting through barriers which defined Otherness ('solidifying', as one of my Trobriand consultants put it, alliances; solidifying relations of enmity). It was for confronting the limits of self-possession – for sending someone 'walking after' a capacity of self through others, beyond his place, beyond his lineage or clan, beyond what his existing life, if held on to, allowed him to know and to experience. It was also for the freedom of acting as if not knowing the difference between right and wrong. It was for shamelessly individuating. And so axe-blades – too 'sacred' (as John Noel described them) or too polluted – were kept out of sight at times, though far from out of mind.

On ambiguation and disambiguation

To acknowledge different cultural economies of displacement is to acknowledge a cultural value for ambiguity – a value for objects which elicit a response of ambiguity, and for experiences of ambiguity. Conversely, to acknowledge such economies is to reveal as non-essential, as culturally and historically situated, the value of any project of disambiguating meaning. For the complex work of ambiguation occurs at the borders conjoining the domains of the stated and the unstated, as it were of 'official' and 'unofficial' discourse, where the substitutability and representation of forms, of symbol and metaphor, give way to ruptures and relocations of significance, as objects move across the boundaries of cultural categories, across geopolitical borders, across locations in time, and so forth. Indeed, in the ethnographic contexts I have considered, the absenting of persons and objects was important and interesting for users in precisely this way, as a cultural action of opening up discursive space for speculation and debate.

Yet as I indicated earlier, the ethnography demands that the point be taken further. For beyond the control of ambiguity – as it were, beyond the assertion and 'owning' of an open question – we must consider the intended effect of foregrounding the object and relationships that were rendered ambiguous. By means of 'invisible foregrounding' something present-in-absentia gains in rhetorical impact – has this enhancement as its purpose – and is consequently set in play in what Lacan and others have termed the 'cultural imaginary' (Lacan 1977). In fact if we consider some of the salient features of invisible foregrounding, we come to appreciate the importance of 'rhetorically aware'[9] readings of discursive situations, and the embeddedness of absent subjects within larger contexts and operations of power relations.

First, the cultural action of invisible foregrounding invites questions about authorisation and authority. That which is foregrounded is displaced, if not concealed, and problematised accordingly – made to appear contingent. By the simple fact that this action may be owned, *or it may be disowned*, displacement allows agentive anonymity. In effect, the detachability and deliberate slippage of authority from the face of social action gives expression to authority's hidden life of negotiation. Invisible foregrounding, as an operation of an economy of displacement, is a cultural entailment *par excellence* of the slippage of power in indirect relations.

It is relevant in this connection that recognition of an invisibly foregrounded object is always elective. There can be no material proof that some person or persons intended to gain by setting up the conditions of invisible foregrounding: strategies of displacement do not determine or guarantee a reception or outcome. They are incompatible with a sense of entitlement – resist accountability.

This last observation suggests in turn a broader hypothesis, namely, that strategies of displacement will tend to be culturally elaborated and most apparent in situations where power relations are markedly asymmetrical. For they inscribe a capacity to destabilise ideologically fixed facts and statuses as these are embodied in official displays of authority. Invisible foregrounding is literally destabilising of fixed positions and relations in space and time: a discursive vehicle of conjecture, surmise, speculation, and so indeterminately forth. Rendering something or somebody materially absent is a form of abandonment or evacuation of an official, dominant or prevailing social order.

For urban Trobrianders, for example, invisible foregrounding was a political strategy for designating some object or person in its capacity *not* to be counted. I have not discussed here the outcome of John Noel's *kayasa*, and how key participants threatened not to attend the culminating awards ceremony. However, this discourse of absence was arguably the most serious threat to John Noel's success. People were invoking their cultural option not to appear in person – to be counted among the conspicuously missing.[10]

The poetics and politics of displacement

The matter of how to relate the phenomenal realm of sensory perception and sensuous cognition, and the material realm of physical properties, occupies a distinguished place in Western aesthetic theory, coming in recent history to a fine-grain focus in Paul de Man's attack on the category of the aesthetic in modern critical thought.[11] Basically, de Man argues the need to resist the notion (inherited from a romantic/symbolist tradition) that an experience of aesthetic forms can transcend contingencies of quotidian space and time. He furthermore resists the notion that an aesthetic experience can override the ontological gulf between words or concepts and the sensuous intuitions of the realm of nature. Such reasoning, he argues, valorises symbol and metaphor as structuring elements towards an organic unity, in opposition to metonymy, disruption, random occurrences, heterogeneous receptions, and other frustrations of the visionary impulse to rise above difference. The insistence on transcendent experience (e.g. of Hegelian or Kantian paradigms) denies how quotidian realities undo truth claims.

Hence de Man insists upon resistance to totalising theories, resistance to the seduction of aesthetic synthesis, by the method of 'close readings' of texts: readings which are 'rhetorically aware' – committed to rigorously demystifying aesthetic rhetoric – as opposed to merely 'aesthetically responsive', that is (as Kant would have it), an experience entailing an act of imagination of the subject. Within these terms, the only authentic reading can be an *undeluded* reading which reveals a rhetoric located in the stubborn materiality of the inscription – in a formal materialism, within the world of practical discourse. In other words for de Man the slippages, the gappiness itself, has only the negative value of revealing a delusional system.

From the perspective of Trobriand visual rhetoric, the problem with this position lies not in the place of privilege it accords rhetorical content, but in the negative valuation of rhetorical intent and the negative valuation of mystification. To commit the ethnocentrism of construing mystification as everywhere and always delusional denies a Trobriand process, for example, the work designated for it by actors of *prospectively* reconfiguring power relations. In short, alongside projects which (from Aristotle) seek to disambiguate meaning, room must be made for projects which seek to problematise meaning.

212   Overall, I have sought here to disentangle indigenous operations of

visual rhetoric from the categorically negative value we tend to ascribe to mystification and ambiguation. Further, I have suggested that these operations may have a positive value for users in their destabilisations of dominant Western ideologies – destabilisations which do not seek assimilation or even necessarily hybridity. Any impulse to disambiguate deriving from Western traditions of knowledge may thus lead us to view as paradoxical what is not paradoxical for indigenous actors – e.g. that one can have an experience of palpable absence, or make one's absence felt, to poetical/political effect.

It is tempting to describe this process as unfolding within a 'dialectic of presence and absence' (Vance 1979: 383). Yet here we must be careful. The image of a dialectic summons up the Hegelian project of reconciling differences – holds out the hope of integration as a universal cultural goal, of internalising antimonies to the extent of transcending them, of creating a realm of unified thought and perception. Yet this project has no place in the process I describe here of maintaining ambivalence, of purposively rendering less apparent and less lucid certain objectifications of relationship, even of 'committing anachronism', to take a phrase from Jerome Christensen that is resonant of the Bau/axe-blade syndrome, wherein such a commitment 'exploits lack of accountability as unrecognised possibility' (1994: 455).

From the ethno-rhetorical evidence we must, then, at least entertain the possibility that if symbolic forms have the unifying power often attributed them – what Eagleton (in opposition to de Man) refers to as the power of aesthetic judgements to free people from as well as to mask struggles for political hegemony (1990: 3) – social actions of purposively denying this power a physical audience, of 'pulling' it from the frame of phenomenally present cultural action, are important for the way they liberate cultural process from material locations in the present, but also for the way they unmoor visual rhetoric from any possible effect of it in the realm of social action. To say this is not, as Eagleton has charged of de Man, to displace 'the dilemmas of life under late capitalism into an irony structural to discourse itself': after all, invisible foregrounding, for example, is a cultural strategy, which finds a place within the postmodern condition but not exclusively there. As such, however, it must be recognised as finding its purpose in productivity, rather than in products or goals, and its subversive potential in disowning outcomes.

Notes

1. Field research in Port Moresby was funded by the National Endowment for the Humanities, the Wenner-Gren Foundation for Anthropological Research, and Mount Holyoke College. Portions of this chapter were presented at the session 'Visual Representations and Systems of Visual Knowledge' at the 1993 ASA Decennial meetings, and have since been published in *Man* (1994). I am very grate-

ful to Howard Morphy for his intelligent reading of an earlier draft of the chapter as it was developed for this volume.

2. In fact this was a highly complex business, culminating a long history of claims to knowledge.

3. Axe-blades seem to have accumulated on Kilivila, the largest of the Trobriand Islands, and have a significance there which is not typical of the other islands. For example, Scoditti (1983: 268) notes that axe-blades have only 'heirloom value' on the neighbouring island of Kitava.

4. This fact was first noted ethnographically by Seligman (1910: 518, 520).

5. One might here wish to note Montague's statement that 'only men kill in the Trobriand world' [because] 'only men possess bodies that are sufficiently *kasai* (hard or solid) to have any chance of fending off serious attempts at vengeance' (1989: 29). Although this is not the place to pursue a contrast with Trobriand flying witches in terms of hardness and softness (or perhaps hardness and porosity), such a contrast could prove instructive in context of rethinking women's 'soft' wealth, which Weiner indicates is the complement of the axe-blade.

6. Discussions from fieldwork are found in Weiner 1976, 1983b, and from a review of published literature in Williams 1988.

7. Note that as *takola* (described above), *beku* would appear to reproduce relationships between brothers-in-law. However, from the perspective of their capacity to elicit fear, *beku* seem more like concrete reminders or veiled threats of the consequences of any lack of generosity toward sisters.

8. This statement would seem to contradict for Port Moresby Montague's assertion that 'the likelihood is greatest that any given death will be caused by a matrilineal consociate', this being more rational in view of the work of the 'ultimate cosmic cycling' that falls to the *dala*, and *dala*-mates being most likely to obstruct his control over the maximisation of *kanua*, or 'human body-building food' [archetypally, yams] (1989: 27). However, it is worth considering John Noel's self-positioning in light of the rhetorical identifications sorcery accusations assert by reference to the idiom of blood: 'hard' blood having replaced matrilineal continuity and flow in this context.

9. I take the phrase from Paul de Man's project of deconstruction of printed texts (1986), but apply it here more broadly to issues of ethnographic interpretation.

10. The larger issue here is emplacement as this relates to power, and the importance for us of separating place from any European concept of landscape. I would hope that this essay might lend ethnographic support to the exposure of the separability of place from either landscape or geography, in terms that suggest further questions about sensorial experiences beyond the visual (see especially J. Weiner 1991, and Battaglia 1990, 1994, 1995).

11. The following discussion owes much to Christopher Norris's (1988) brilliant discussion of Paul de Man's conceptual rhetoric.

References

Battaglia, Debbora (1990) *On the Bones of the Serpent: Person, Memory and Mortality in Sabarl Island Society*, Chicago: University of Chicago Press.

— (1992) 'Displacing Culture: A Joke of Significance in Urban Papua New Guinea', *New Literary History* 23(4): 1003–17.

— (1994) 'Retaining Reality: Some Practical Problems with Objects as Property', *Man* (n.s.) 29(3): 631–44.

— (1995) 'On Active Nostalgia: Self-prospecting among Urban Trobrianders', in D. Battaglia (ed.) *Rhetorics of Self-Making*, Berkeley: University of California Press.

Bhabha, Homi (1991) 'Of Mimicry and Man: The Ambivalence of Colonial Discourse', *October* 28: 125–33.

Christensen, J. (1994) 'The Romantic Movement at the End of History', *Critical Inquiry* 20 (3): 452–76.

Cottom, Daniel (1989) *Text and Culture: The Politics of Interpretation*, Minneapolis: University of Minnesota Press.

de Man, Paul (1986) *The Resistance to Theory*, Minneapolis: University of Minnesota Press.

Eagleton, T. (1990) *The Ideology of the Aesthetic*, Oxford: Oxford University Press.

Kulick, Don (1993) 'Heroes from Hell: Representations of "Rascals" in a Papua New Guinean Village', in *Anthropology Today*, 9 (3): 9–14.

Lacan, Jacques (1977) *Ecrits: A Selection*, trans. Alan Sheridan, New York: W.W. Norton & Co.

Leach, Jerry (1983) 'Trobriand Territorial Categories and the Problem of Who is Not in the Kula', in J.W. Leach and E. Leach (eds) *The Kula: New Perspectives on Massim Exchange*, pp. 121–46, Cambridge: Cambridge University Press.

Malinowski, Bronislaw (1929) *The Sexual Life of Savages in North-Western Melanesia*, London: Routledge & Kegan Paul; Boston: Beacon Press, 1987.

— (1935) *Coral Gardens and Their Magic: A Study of the Methods of Tilling the Soil and of Agricultural Rites in the Trobriand Islands*, vol 1, New York: American Book Co.; Bloomington: Indiana University Press, 1965.

Montague, Susan (1989) 'To Eat for the Dead: Kaduwagan Mortuary Events', in Frederick Damon and Roy Wagner (eds) *Death Rituals and Life in the Societies of the Kula Ring*, pp. 23–45, DeKalb: Northern Illinois University Press.

Norris, Christopher (1988) *Paul de Man: Deconstruction and the Critique of Aesthetic Ideology*, New York/London: Routledge.

Scoditti, Giancarlo, with Jerry W. Leach (1983) 'Kula on Kitava', in J.W. Leach and E. Leach (eds) *The Kula: New Perspectives on Massim Exchange*, pp. 249–73, Cambridge: Cambridge University Press.

Seligman, C.G. (1910) *The Melanesians of British New Guinea*, Cambridge: Cambridge University Press.

Urban, Greg (1991) *A Discourse-Centered Approach to Culture*: *Native South American Myths and Rituals*, Austin: University of Texas Press.

Vance, E. (1979) 'Roland and the Poetics of Memory', in J.V. Harari (ed.) *Textual Strategies: Perspectives in Post-Structuralist Criticism*, Ithaca: Cornell University Press.

Weiner, Annette (1976) *Women of Value, Men of Renown: New Perspectives in Trobriand Exchange*, Austin: University of Texas Press.

— (1983a) '"A World of Made is Not a World of Born": doing Kula on Kiriwina', in J. W. Leach and E. Leach (eds) *The Kula: New Perspectives on Massim Exchange*, pp. 147–70, Cambridge: Cambridge University Press.

— (1983b) 'From Words to Objects to Magic: Hard Words and the Boundaries of Social Interaction', in *Man* 18: 690–709.

Weiner, Annette (1986) *The Trobrianders of Papua New Guinea*, New York: Holt, Rinehard and Winston.

Weiner, James (1991) *The Empty Place: Poetry, Space and Being among the Foi of Papua New Guinea*, Bloomington: Indiana University Press.

Williams, Jason (1988) 'Sorcery and Power in the Trobriands: The Political Economy of Fear', MA thesis, New York University.

11

Representing the bodies of the Jains[1]

Marcus Banks

This chapter attempts to outline the Jain iconography of the human body. It closely parallels work done by James Laidlaw (1995, especially Part III) using much of the same material and coming to broadly similar conclusions.[2] My aim here, however, is to provide an overview of Jain bodily representation to complement the more ethnographically focused accounts that Laidlaw provides (1995: chapter 11). The data are presented as supplementary confirmation of an argument that has been advanced by P.S. Jaini (1980) to address an issue that has long preoccupied scholars of early Jainism and more particularly early Buddhism: why and how has Jainism survived relatively unchanged for two and a half millennia in India, while Buddhism – its close cousin – died out in India after less than a millennium? I have outlined this argument elsewhere (Banks 1992: 229–30); briefly, most arguments prior to Jaini's which discuss the decline of early Indian Buddhism cannot account for the simultaneous survival of Jainism, as all the causes suggested would be equally applicable to both. Jaini advances a sociological argument, pointing out that Jainism laid more stress on the ties between ordained ascetics and the laity than Buddhism, but supplements this with a doctrinal argument relating to the position of the *bodhisattva*[3] (or heavenly mediator) in early Buddhism. He identifies the *bodhisattva* as early Buddhism's weak point, allowing for doctrinal and hence ritual conflation with Hindu divinities. Jaini hints that 'iconographical shifts' were hence possible as *bodhisattva* images were appropriated by Hindus (1980: 86–7). It is the resilience of Jain imagery to such iconographical shifts that I wish to demonstrate in this chapter.

I have argued elsewhere (Banks n.d.) that Jain visual representation uses commonplace visual forms (paintings in particular) and draws upon a widespread popular visual aesthetic to display and encode a uniquely Jain system of knowledge. In this paper I wish to narrow the field to consider only the human body as a site of visual expression. Jain doctrine places particular emphasis on the human body, arguing that all other forms of embodiment are ultimately inferior; even the gods in the heavens, with their miraculous powers and their pleasure-laden environment, ultimately tire of their fortune and wish reincarnation in human form, from which they will be able to achieve final liberation and ultimate bliss.

The Jains, who have a world-wide population today of between three and four million, follow a religion at least as old as Buddhism, and yet almost unknown outside India. Although in the intervening centuries Jainism, Buddhism and what came to be known as Hinduism, have constantly borrowed and exchanged ideas and doctrines, Jain philosophy has clung tenaciously to the idea that the supernatural actions of gods and other heavenly beings are of limited help in the human quest for spiritual emancipation, and it denies the existence of any supreme being who created or oversees the universe. Thus while the Jains revere certain key figures, the *tirthankara*s, who preached the message of personal salvation and revealed the techniques by which it is to be achieved, all religious acts on the part of the believers are quite explicitly self-directed and concerned in large part with freeing the immortal soul from the series of bodies (or embodiments) in which it is constantly reincarnated. Thus the body and its visual representations form a key part of the Jain religious discourse.

Jain representations of the body, and uses of the body as a site of representation, fall within a very narrow range of representational forms. The represented and representing body seems peculiarly resistant to artistic and other elaboration, such as one finds in other South Asian religious systems, or indeed elsewhere within Jainism. That is not to say that the represented and representing body is entirely homogeneous; that would scarcely be possible across the broad sweep of Jain history, regional variation and sectarian division.

The representations I wish to consider are best seen as ranged along a continuum or spectrum, ranging from iconographic attempts to portray bodily absence at one end, through a middle band of concrete yet apparently anonymous representations, to a far point where lie highly individualised and all too obviously present bodies. The path along this continuum is not smooth. At the mid-point we encounter a crisis of gender representation, reflecting one of the most deep-seated divisions within ancient and modern Jainism. As I have hinted elsewhere (Banks 1992: 76) gender relations may be one of the few areas where one can today find a uniquely Jain social formation, and the roots of it lie in much older textual and iconographic forms. At the far end of the spectrum we encounter a paradox. The recent historical bodies I consider – one male, one female – simultaneously represent absolute presence and the desire for effacement (and thus a looping back to the beginning of the spectrum). For convenience, the remainder of the chapter – apart from the conclusions – is divided into three parts, discussing in turn the effaced bodies at one end of the spectrum, the idolised bodies in the middle of the spectrum, and the living bodies that desire effacement at the far end.

Effaced bodies

The distinction between and separability of the body and soul is a key lesson which all Jains must learn, and is the basic teaching of a popular late nineteenth-century Jain lay scholar and teacher, Raychandbhai Mehta. In a doctrinal letter to a friend he outlined six basic propositions:

> The soul exists
> The soul is eternal
> The soul is the agent
> The soul is the experiencer of its actions
> There is liberation
> There is means of liberation
>
> (after Dundas 1992: 225)

The lesson is reinforced in school-children's primers today. These primers, written in vernacular languages and increasingly also in English for the children of Jain migrants overseas or for Indian Jain children at English-medium schools, are used in after-school religious education classes to which some parents (but by no means all) send their children. In the sections devoted to the soul, one commonly finds two line drawings side by side – one represents a human being with readily identifiable features (either a smartly dressed child or a *tirthankara* seated in meditation), the other attempts to represent the invisible soul, through an outline the same as the form of the human body in the first illustration (see Figure 11.1). But separating the soul from the body, while the basic aim of all schools of Jain thought, is for that very reason, highly complex.

A particularly good example of this is the Jain conception of *karma*. Whilst in other South Asian religious systems *karma* is the name given to an operating principle, akin to Newton's third law of motion, Jain schol-

Figure 11.1
Illustration from a child's primer; printed in Gujarat, c. 1976.

ars (for a variety of complex theological reasons) understand it to be a physical substance which sticks to the soul, like dust to a damp cloth, or which pours into the soul like water seeping into a leaking ship (Dundas 1992: 82–3). The soul, freed of *karma*, has the form of the human body but no substance. Our material bodies are accretions of *karma* particles, but the soul is permeated with them, and simply shedding the body at death is not enough to liberate the soul, for it may still be smeared or infused with body-forming *karma*s that bring about a further incarnation. Representing such an idea has exercised the Jains' ingenuity over the ages. For example, contemporary popular Jainism places great stress on *punya* and *pap* – (religious) merit and demerit. Actions can be meritorious or not, as can attitudes and intentions. But so too can *karma*s, and a good or evil action or intention will cause such *karma*s to stick to the soul and weigh it down. Some years ago, in a Jain procession in the Rajasthani city of Jaipur held to commemorate the birthday of the founder of modern Jainism, Mahavira, I saw the balance of good and evil *karma*s sticking to the soul represented on a float as part of the parade. On the pans of a huge balance sat small children, those on one side representing *punya*, those on the other representing *pap*. The effect of the balance was to show how these *karma*s weigh on the soul, although by a related metaphor the *punya* side outweighed the *pap* side. Although this might be thought to represent that good outweighs evil, Jainism holds that all *karma*s adhering to the soul prevent liberation – good as well as bad. The visual message therefore would appear to be that it is heavier – i.e. harder – to rid the soul of the desires for the things we value and enjoy, yet which prevent us from fulfilling the ultimate desire of liberation.

Raychandbhai Mehta's injunction that the soul exists, as does the means of liberating it, is not only basic but ancient. While the children's float in the parade attempts to dramatise the relationship, and the children's primers attempt to demonstrate the separation, these are 'as if' visual scenarios, or visualised potentialities in the latter case. Jain truth rests on the foundation that the separation is not only possible, but has been achieved. Specifically, it has been achieved by the twenty-four *tirthankara*s or hero figures of Jainism, human beings of the ancient past who through rigorous asceticism and mental discipline liberated their souls, but whose release was delayed so that they might teach the path they had discovered. It has also been achieved by many others, known as *siddha*s, who were inspired to liberation (often by hearing a *tirthankara* preach) but who, apart from their example, left no inspiration to others. I will discuss idols of the embodied *tirthankara*s below, but the specific moment of the soul's release is iconographically encoded in para-indexical symbols.

Perhaps the most dramatic example of this is seen in the temples of one of Jainism's sectarian nodes, the Digambara, which emphasises the liberation of the soul above all else. In the central shrine of Digambara temples one sometimes finds a flat brass plate about 30 cm high, standing on a narrow base (see Figure 11.2). The plate is unadorned, but cut out from it is a stylised human form in outline, which represents a *siddha*, or enlightened and liberated soul. The empty space represents the soul, without substance yet retaining the shape of its last body (always human, and always male for the Digambaras, who reject the possibility of female spiritual emancipation). This 'negative' idol contrasts sharply with the three-dimensional and hence solid images of the *tirthankaras* and revered beings that one finds elsewhere in the temples. It is an absence, not a presence.

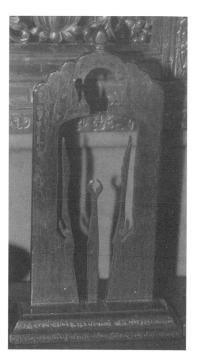

Figure 11.2 *Siddha* image in a Digambara temple, Jamnagar, 1983.

Less dramatically, in the temples of the Svetambaras (the other main sectarian node of modern Jainism) one finds footprint shrines. Here, one or more pairs of footprints are carved in low relief onto a slab of marble (see Figure 11.3). Like the cut-out figures of the Digambaras, the footprints represent those no longer with us. For the Svetambaras, however, who place as much emphasis on the transmission of doctrine through named teachers as on the liberation of the soul, lines of text in the shrine identify the (apparently identical) footprints as belonging to individual *tirthankaras* or more commonly to sub-sectarian teachers. These teachers are by no means all considered to have achieved liberation: indeed, after the death of Jambu, the disciple of the last *tirthankara*, Mahavira, no one is considered to have achieved liberation, nor will anyone do so for many millennia. The sectarian teachers have died, their bodies decayed or burned and their souls moved on to other incarnations, yet by linking them through the footprint shrines to the bodily absent *tirthankaras* and other *siddhas* a line of continuity is established.

१ श्री महावीर स्वामि पादुका
२ श्री गौतम स्वामि पादुका
३ श्री पुज्य श्री मेरुतुंग सुरीणां पादुका
४ श्री पुज्य श्री धर्ममूर्ति सुरीणां पादुका

Figure 11.3 *Paduka* (footprint) shrine, Jamnagar, 1983.

In the complex Jain world of visual representation – with its carved and adorned temples, their wall-paintings and idols, the magical symbols and diagrams that are printed in devotional booklets – the a-visual, a-material qualities of the pure soul are highlighted and thrown into relief by these two forms of representation. I shall return to this idea at the end of the chapter.

Idolised bodies

It is necessary here to digress slightly and discuss the classical (that is, textual) Jain understanding of the (human) body. There are two basic types to consider: the bodies of living human beings, and the bodies of the *tirthankaras* (still human, but perfected and transformed). Human bodies can be of three biological sex types: male, female and hermaphrodite (or, non-male). They can of course be young, old, whole, deformed, and so on. Jains recognise persons (as opposed to bodies) by external, visible signs or, as Jaini puts it (1991) 'inferential marks'. For example, ascetics of the Svetambara sectarian node are recognised by their white clothing, and are thus distinguished from Buddhist monks with their orange robes. They are also distinguished from Digambara ascetics, who eschew such material identifying signs, as they go naked and carry no essential possessions. That is, the inferential mark for the Digambara ascetic is an absence, not a presence, of such signs, a position which accords well with the Digambara *siddha* image discussed in the previous section.

However, as Zwilling and Sweet (1996) make clear, the gendered persons that the Jains recognise are revealed by Maussian habitus, the habits of their bodies, as much as by externally manifest signs (Mauss 1979). This is particularly the case when the possibility for ambiguity arises, as with the hermaphrodite sex body. An apparent biological male who wished to be accepted in the ascetic order was examined 'for marks of effeminacy in speech, deportment, and interests' to see if he fitted the profile of a third-sex person (Zwilling and Sweet 1996: 377). If these external and embodied signs reveal the person to be a hermaphrodite, then they could be barred from ordination, at least in the very early period of Jain history (c. 300 BCE). The Jains have long distinguished between biological sex and gender, understanding that the external signs of the body, and the internal orientation of the mind (and, for that matter, the libido) may not exhibit congruence (Zwilling and Sweet 1996: 366; Jaini 1991: 11 and passim). The body thus becomes the expressor and container of signs – some visible, some not – which reveal the true nature of the person. The external visibility of signs is particularly evident when we consider the body of the *tirthankara*.

Through meditation and austerities (that is, through transformative techniques of the mind and body) the *tirthankara*-to-be attains omniscience and becomes a *tirthankara*-proper. This is manifest in changes that occur on or just below the surface of the body. It is freed of all imperfections and impurities, the hair and nails cease to grow, the blood becomes milky, the body shines like crystal. Auspicious marks appear on the body, such as wheels on the soles of Mahavira's feet (Dundas 1992: 31–2). The body of the *tirthankara*, like the body of a woman, is a site of dispute for the Digambara and Svetambara sectarian nodes, the dispute centring in both cases on the biology and physiology of the body, rather than on any external signs. That is, the body is fully and permanently inscribed with representational force, which is either accepted or rejected. Thus the Digambaras reject the bodies of women, denying the embodied souls the chance of liberation, while the Svetambaras (conditionally) accept the same bodies. By contrast, each sectarian node describes the body of the *tirthankara* differently, and each rejects the other's description.[4]

Within Jain temples, human bodies are represented in a number of ways, most commonly in wall-paintings and as three-dimensional idols. I have discussed the wall-paintings elsewhere (Banks n.d.), and will here confine myself to a discussion of the idols.[5] Within Svetambara temples, carved idols of the *tirthankaras* are to be found in profusion, and perhaps less so in Digambara temples. Each temple contains one large idol in the central shrine, often flanked by two others, and a number of smaller idols (many hundreds in some cases) in subsidiary shrines (see Figure 11.4).

Figure 11.4 Subsidiary temple shrine, Jamnagar, 1983.

These idols are usually carved in white marble or alabaster (more rarely in brown, grey or black stone) and depict any one of the twenty-four *tirthankaras* of the present age. (The 'present age' – which stretches back many millennia – saw the birth of the twenty-four 'heroes' (*jinas*) who achieved enlightenment and preached the message of salvation, for which they are revered. Although their liberated souls now reside in bliss in the highest heaven, they are technically functionless and are revered for their example, rather than worshipped in the hope of their granting favours.)[6] Additionally, all temple shrines contain a number of smaller *tirthankara* images in cast metal. These small free-standing images are used in processions and in more complex temple rituals. The carved stone idols are almost all identical in style. Each depicts a naked seated figure, apparently male, his hands lying palm up in his lap. The shoulders tend to be wide, the waist narrow, and the ear-lobes elongated; the body is smooth and unadorned, save for small knots of hair on the head, a diamond-shaped knob in the centre of the chest and small knobs on the top of the head, forehead, throat, navel, shoulders, forearms, knees and feet: these are the nine points that Svetambaras anoint with sandalwood paste during worship (Digambaras do not actually touch their idols, though they make offerings to them).

Although each idol represents one of the twenty-four *tirthankara*s, with one exception and one apparent contradiction there is nothing about the carved body to indicate this. The idols are essentially identical and can only be told apart by a small cartouche carved into the base on which the figure sits. The cartouche contains not a name, but a symbol: Adinath (the first *tirthankara*) is represented by a bull, Mahavira (the twenty-fourth) by a lion, and so forth. The symbols are mostly of animals, but some are of inanimate objects (the moon, a conch shell) and some are simply symbols, which in turn stand for something else (a *svastika*, the four arms of which by one Jain interpretation represent the various 'destinations' of the reincarnated soul). Some symbols bear a link to an event in the life of the particular *tirthankara*, but they could be said to be arbitrary inasmuch as each life-story contains a number of significant events, any one of which might have provided the identifying symbol. For example, the identification of Neminath, the twenty-second *tirthankara*, with a conch shell derives from an account of Nemi entering the armoury of Krishna (his cousin, by most accounts) and seeing a conch shell trumpet. The keeper of the armoury tells him that none but Krishna can even lift the shell, let alone blow it, but Nemi does both with ease, causing those who hear it (including Krishna) to wonder what hero or mighty ruler moves among them.[7] However, Neminath is one of the few *tirthankara*s whose life-story is popularly known, and for many its most significant episode is not his rivalry with Krishna but his wedding. While on his way to his wedding he passed the animals that would provide the meat for his wedding feast being rounded up for slaughter; sickened by the senseless waste of life, he turned away and renounced the world, eventually attaining enlightenment. There is thus a contrast between the specificity of the identifying cartouche and the body form of the idol itself, which could be said to represent a more abstract ideal of *tirthankara*-hood.[8]

The exception to this comes with representations of the twenty-third *tirthankara*, Parshvanath. In a previous birth, the *tirthankara*-to-be saw a Brahman about to light a sacrificial fire. His already highly developed senses told him that a snake was sheltering in the wood, and he prevented the Brahman from setting light to it in order to save the snake. In his next incarnation, as he was meditating and on his way to achieving enlightenment, the Brahman, now reborn as an evil demon, attempted to distract him by raining fire and rocks on his head. However, the snake, now reborn as a minor deity, sheltered the *tirthankara* with a cobra's hood, allowing him to meditate and achieve enlightenment. Parshvanath is thus always represented with a cobra's hood arched over his head (see Figure 11.5).

Figure 11.5
Unfinished
Parshvanath idols
(on the left) in a
stonemason's
workshop, Jaipur,
1984.

Representing the bodies of the Jains

   There seems no clear reason why his images should be singled out this way, though the explanation could rest upon very specific historical circumstance, rather than a more satisfying (from my point of view) general cultural logic. The historical circumstance is this: of the twenty-four *tirthankara*s only Mahavira and Parshvanath hold any claim to be historical figures, Mahavira having lived in the sixth century BCE and Parshvanath some two and a half centuries before this. Some textual evidence suggests that Mahavira was initiated into a tradition influenced by Parshvanath's teachings, which he then slightly reformed. As a result, a distinction between Mahavira and Parshvanath at the iconographic level would seem to be warranted. In the early centuries of Jainism, as noted above, further differentiation between the other twenty-two *tirthankara*s was minimal or non-existent, and as after his death it was Mahavira's form of Jainism that was perpetuated, it seems reasonable to assume that his iconographic representation became the norm to which the other *tirthankara*s conformed, rather than Parshvanath's.

   The contradiction is in many ways more interesting. The nineteenth *tirthankara*, Malli, is understood by the Svetambaras (but not the Digambaras, who know 'him' as Mallinath) to have been a woman. As in most South Asian religious traditions (and probably most world religious traditions) the position of women is ambiguous and at times contradictory. Women by far outnumber men today as Jain initiates, and appear to have done so since the time of Mahavira. Jain women today also undertake far more ritual tasks and austerities than men, and again have probably always done so. Yet Jain women (initiates and lay) are barred from certain roles of leadership and authority, and as women are generally held (by men) to be weaker than men, more ritually impure, and as having flawed bodies. For the Digambaras these flaws are fundamental and irredeemably prevent salvation (the Svetambaras accept the flaws

225

too, but think they can be overcome in exceptional circumstances). Chief among them is that a woman is thought to harbour colonies of hundreds of thousands of minute life-forms under her arms, between her breasts and, crucially, in her vagina. All Jain sects and schools are highly alert to such tiny life-forms as their inadvertent destruction is so easy, and this violates the cardinal principle of *ahimsa* or 'non-violence'. The vaginal life-forms cause an itching sensation that can only be relieved by intercourse. Yet the act of intercourse is 'violent' and inevitably destroys these life-forms in massive numbers. Because 'violence' of this kind is inimical to the Jain path of salvation, and because women constantly desire the action that would bring about such 'violence', the Digambaras say they are unable to tread the path to its end (Jaini 1991: 13–14, 179).

Malli's final birth as a woman was in fact a form of 'punishment': in a previous incarnation (as a man) she cheated a set of companions by secretly performing more austerities than they had agreed, and as a result earned herself *karma*s that brought about her final reincarnation as a woman (Malli is not the only woman to have achieved enlightenment according to the Svetambaras, simply the only *tirthankara*). The surprising thing, once one has been told about Malli, is that none of the idols representing her portray her as a women. A single image said to be of Malli is known, dating from around the ninth century CE; it is a headless idol of a female ascetic with breasts and a long braid of hair.[9] Her idols are identical to those of all the other *tirthankara*s, Parshvanath excepted. Caroline Humphrey once told me that a Jain layman who pointed out an image of Malli to her in a temple tried to convince her (and, one suspects, himself) that there was a faint swelling of the image's breasts, a certain 'feminine' cast to the eyes and mouth. Humphrey was unconvinced and so am I, not least because *tirthankara* images today at least (and all other large temple carvings) are carved off-site by non-Jain masons and, with the exception of Parshvanath, are carved as 'blanks', their identity only being given when the cartouche is added to the base. Centuries earlier, the Digambaras had challenged the Svetambaras on this same iconographical point; they replied (weakly in my opinion) that she had become a *tirthankara* very early in life, before her breasts developed (Jaini 1991: 145, 181).

Apart from this biographical and bio-physical reason offered by the Svetambaras there are a number of possible explanations as to why Malli is almost never represented with a female body. The simplest and most straightforward for my purposes is that her gender identity is the least important thing about her. I have come across no one (Jain or scholar) who claims that women devotees have any special affinity for her, and I know of no special rituals that emphasise her gender. The soul, on liberation from the body, has no inherent sex or gender: if it is to be reincarnated then it carries the *karma*s that determine sex and gender (as well as those for other physical attributes), and if it is the final liberation then it remains genderless. In this light, Malli's gender is as important as her height or skin colour – known, but discounted for the purposes of iconographic representation. One story that is told by the Svetambaras about Malli, before she began her career as a *tirthankara*, acknowledges her sex and then goes on to repudiate it.

Malli was extraordinarily beautiful as a girl (her name means jasmine flower), and the rulers of neighbouring kingdoms (in fact, the reincarnations of the companions she had 'cheated' in their earlier lives) sought to marry her and fought over her (like all the *tirthankara*s Malli was born into a royal – Kshatriya – family). Malli had a hollow life-size image of herself cast in gold, with a lid that followed the hairline, and stuffed the image full with sweetmeats and delicious food. She then invited her suitors to a meeting at the palace. As they entered the reception room they saw the image and believed it to be Malli herself; as they were exclaiming upon her beauty, Malli entered the room and removed the lid of the hollow statue, filling the room with the putrid odour of the now rotting food. In this way, she proved to them that a woman's body, while beautiful on the outside, is full of blood and tissue which will soon rot. Thus, not only were the rivals convinced of the futility of chasing worldly goals, they were made aware that the exterior of the body – particularly the beautiful bodies of women – may conceal a hideous truth about mortality and worldly attachment (the story is told in Shah 1987: 159–60 and Jaini 1991: 15).

Laidlaw adds a further layer of explanation, claiming that even for the Svetambaras the *tirthankara* must crucially be male (1995: 256–7; Malli's birth as a woman and her status as a *tirthankara* is an event even the Svetambaras describe as a 'miracle', something that takes place only once on an 'infinite' time cycle [Jaini 1991: 27]). This is because male celibacy is an arduous task, resulting in the build-up of semen (thought to be formed from concentrated blood), which itself stokes the fires of austerity; women by contrast shed this blood untransformed during menstruation. The Svetambaras seem to imply that Malli was pre-pubescent at the time of achieving *tirthankara*-hood so the issue of menstruation, like the absent breasts on her idols, is dealt with. Hence Malli's biologically female body is effaced by her ascetically male body. But although Laidlaw claims that the bodies of all the *tirthankara* idols are 'unequivocally male' (Laidlaw 1995: 253), I don't think this is the case, at least for the Svetambaras. Secondary female sexual characteristics may be absent in the idols of Malli, but male primary sexual characteristics (that is, the external genitalia) are also absent or concealed, at least in Svetambara idols. While the broad shoulders and narrow waists of the idols could be seen as secondary male sexual characteristics, I note below that the broadness of the shoulders at least is interpreted without specific gender reference. I think it is therefore safer to assume genderlessness, rather than maleness, as the defining characteristic of the Svetambara *tirthankara* idol, while accepting Laidlaw's valuable points concerning Jain gender representation and significance in other arenas of iconography and discourse. For the Digambaras, the position is at once clearer and more complicated. Digambaras often represent the *tirthankaras* in a posture of standing meditation and always naked, so that the male genitalia are usually evident; but then the Digambaras are clear that all the *tirthankaras* as well as all other liberated souls were male so the concealment of the genitalia (by, for example, a conveniently placed creeper or branch of a tree) does not necessarily imply ambiguity about biological gender.[10] The Digambaras hold that nudity (indicating complete possessionlessness) is axiomatic for enlightenment, and that because women cannot go naked for reasons of modesty and fear of rape (Dundas 1992: 50) they cannot achieve enlightenment.

Idols, however, are not just passive representations of genderless human bodies, but rather act as processual representations of inner states in contemporary Jain practice. During individual acts of worship the temporally specific moment of the life-history of the worshipper intersects with the generalised life-history of *tirthankara*-hood. Svetambara *tirthankara* idols, seated in meditation and wearing the staring glass eyes that represent omniscience, represent the *tirthankara* during his (or her) career as a preceptor, the period between the attainment of omniscience and final liberation of the soul when the *tirthankara* preached the message of salvation. During the installation ceremonies of new idols, the entire life-history of the *tirthankara* is acted out during a series of rituals and staged tableaux, with particular emphasis being laid on the five crucial life-stages (conception, birth, renunciation, omniscience and liberation) (see Figure 11.6). The idol is thus infused with transcendent *tirthankara*-hood while physically representing the life-stage that is able to communicate that knowledge.

Figure 11.6
Concluding stages of a *pancakalyan* (five-stage) installation ceremony, Dhrangadhra, Gujarat, 1983.

Once consecrated and installed, a Svetambara idol must be bathed with milk and water, anointed with sandalwood paste and presented with a variety of offerings. In an analysis of the rituals of *tirthankara* idol worship Caroline Humphrey points out that the body parts of the idol represent qualities that the worshipper desires to emulate (Humphrey 1985). Sandalwood paste applied to the forehead of the idol, for example, reminds the worshipper of the mental effort by which the *tirthankara* achieved liberation.[11] Through concrete symbols (sandalwood paste, flowers, sweetmeats) and individual body parts (legs, shoulders, forearms), the relationship between the worshipper and abstract notions of the path to liberation is mediated.

Invoking again Mauss's notion of bodily habitus, we can see that the relationship between the body, the world, and liberation is thus engrained within the worshipper's own body. The surface of the idol's body is continuously transformed. Washed clean at least once each day, it is constantly decorated with pastes, oils and flowers. More rarely, thin sheets of gold or silver leaf are applied and at least once a year the major idols are decked out in jewelled head-dresses and breastplates. Yet such transformations are temporary and the idol's body constantly returns to a state of neutrality, a neutrality that reflects the necessary smoothing over of individual particularities of size, gender and colour in order to emphasise abstractions of *tirthankara*-hood. By contrast, the human worshippers of the idols have bodies that, because of the *karma*s they carry, necessarily reflect individual difference. For my third and final discussion, I wish to consider the ways in which the Jain layman or woman takes the raw material of his or her own birth body and transforms it to effect representations of belief and practice.

Living bodies

Jains, particularly Jain women, expend a large amount of cognitive effort and manual labour time over questions of ingestion.[12] This is for two reasons. First, the cardinal principle of *ahimsa*, usually glossed as 'non-violence', is manifested for the Jains in numerous and highly specific food prohibitions (on the whole items which directly involve the death of an animal are always avoided – thus meat and eggs – while some will also avoid root vegetables, leafy green vegetables in the rainy season, and flavourings such as garlic and chilli which inflame the senses). Secondly, and possibly as a result of the first, dietary restrictions play an important part in ritual practice, especially for women (see Figure 11.7).

The Jains are a predominantly urban, often wealthy group, and the common body form for women in their middle years is a Rubenesque plumpness. In common with a variety of non-Euro-American societies, the Indian middle classes view surplus adult body fat as a token of

Figure 11.7
Women perform-
ing the *ayambil*
dietary austerity,
Jamnagar, 1983.

prosperity and even health. For these women, who wear tight sari
blouses that restrain and clinch in the chest and upper torso, a 'cleavage'
between the shoulder blades and small folds of fat overhanging the
waist-band of their sari are to be expected, and – as far as I can ascertain
– desired. (Plumpness in babies and young children is most certainly
seen as a sign of health, and often commented on favourably.) Most
modern urban Jains would appear to share the same sentiments. Food is
abundant and rich on festivals and ceremonial occasions, guests are constantly chastised for not eating enough, and 'good wives' are those who
produce a constant stream of delicious meals and snacks.

However, the normally rich and highly calorific diet of Gujarati Jains
is eschewed by some women on occasions (and permanently by a few),
through fasting and highly restricted food intake. One of the most
severe of these dietary restrictions consists of taking one plain meal on
alternate days, with a total fast in between, for a year (or, in some cases,
two years). A woman would normally undertake this fast (known as
varsi-tap) only once in a lifetime, and then often only in middle-age
when her family and domestic duties have largely been discharged.
Many women never undertake the fast at all. The fast, like all such austerities, mortifies the body and burns off *karma*s from the soul. By the
end of the year, the woman's body-shape is dramatically altered. Her
flesh is stretched across her frame without being emaciated, her eyes
bulge slightly and seem large and liquid. But the body reveals more
than just nutritional status. On the one occasion I attended the post-
fast celebrations of a woman who had followed the *varsi-tap* regime,
several people asked me to note how clear her skin was, almost translu-
cent, and how it seemed to shine with an inner radiance. With so many
*karma*s burned away one could see the pure light of the soul beginning
to shine through.[13]

Such wilful transformation of the living body is of course by no means unique to the Jains, nor are their attempts to transform the body as extreme or as dramatic as those of many other cultures. The Jains do not tattoo or scarify their bodies and the women alone wear the earrings and nose-stud common to the vast majority of South Asian women. For the Jains the emphasis in most if not all religious contexts is on the interior of the body: the food ingested, the state of the soul, the presence or absence of particular *karmas*. Yet the external surface of the body is nonetheless an indexical sign of interior states and processes, and as with the *tirthankara* idols these are written upon the body for others to read (see also Parry 1989). This signification is dramatised when the body is not that of a women (for whom dietary austerity is commonplace and expected) but that of a man.

Although men do fast, and follow restricted diets, they do it less often than women and rarely if ever undertake the more severe fasts, usually claiming that the burden of being a breadwinner for their families allows them neither the time nor the energy. The most dramatic example of a male body transformed through fasting I know of is that of Raychandbhai Mehta who I mentioned at the start of the chapter, though he is more popularly known to the Jains as Srimad Rajchandra. Rajchandra (1868–1901) today is known for three things: his brief contact with Mohandas Gandhi (of which some Jains make more than is perhaps reasonable); his short verse composition *Atmasiddhi* ('Attainment of the soul') which expounds his view of Jainism; and the extraordinarily emaciated body he cultivated towards the end of his life. Rajchandra was a lay Jain, born in Gujarat into a family of jewellers. From an early age he began to explore Jain philosophy, which led him to reject current ritual practices and the lifestyles of the Jain monks and nuns. Instead, although he married and lived the life of a householder, he devoted himself to study, meditation and bodily austerity. He died young, perhaps worn out by continual fasting as Dundas suggests (1992: 226), and never established a sect in the conventional sense, although he remains well-known and revered throughout Gujarat and Rajasthan. In rejecting ritual and temple worship Rajchandra rejected the vast majority of visual representations available to the Jains. His body thus became the only medium for visual representation. Dundas notes, however, that later in life he became reconciled towards image-worship (ibid.: 225) and thus, in my terms, reconciled to representations of the bodies of others.

A number of photographs of Rajchandra exist, but one is perhaps more popular than any other (Figure 11.8). It shows him sitting cross-legged in a posture of meditation, his hands at the end of stick-like arms, cupped in his emaciated lap; his ribs and all his joints show clearly, his cheeks and eye-sockets are hollow and sunken.[14]

The photograph is prominently displayed in many Jain homes I have visited and I, like other visiting anthropologists, have often been told to

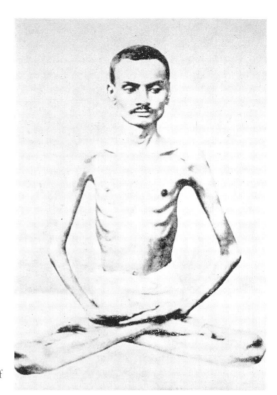

Figure 11.8 Srimad Rajchandra
(Raychandbhai Mehta); photograph of
unknown provenance, c. 1890s.

observe – through contemplation of the photograph – how the true Jain
disdains his or her body, its desires and cravings, in favour of the liberation of the soul. While in one sense this is true, in another the opposite
seems to hold. In cases like this, the Jains fetishise the body, making of it
a site for the visual representation of what they stand for or believe.
Indeed, a number of temples devoted to Rajchandra have been erected
since his death, and these contain not only the well-known photograph
but actual idols (*murtis*) depicting Rajchandra in his last emaciated years
(see Figure 11.9).

As noted above Jain idols (of all kinds) generally display a remarkably
limited range of iconographic conventions and attributes. The idols of
Rajchandra are unusual for attempting to portray the bodily form of a
known individual, and the only other example I have come across is that
of a recently deceased female Svetambara ascetic (Vichakshan Shri-ji
Maharasabh, 1912–80) at a temple in Jaipur, Rajasthan.[15] Although I
have seen this idol several times and was vaguely aware of Vichakshan's
story, I rely in what follows on James Laidlaw's excellent and full account
(1995: 262–7). Where the 'reason' for Rajchandra's popularity is evidently inscribed upon his body and thus upon images of his body,
Vichakshan's idol depicts an elderly, smilingly benevolent woman, seated

Figure 11.9 Srimad Rajchandra shrine image (background, right), Khambhat, Gujarat, 1983.

not in meditation but in a posture appropriate to preaching. Laidlaw notes that it is 'eerily lifelike' (ibid.: 263), the realism enhanced by the flesh tones of the skin and the pair of spectacles it is wearing (the only idol of Rajchandra I have seen was of plain white marble). Yet it would not, I think, be apparent why she of all nuns should be commemorated in this way. In part, this is because the key bodily event could not be depicted without a medical textbook illustration, but more importantly because the transformation she wrought upon her body was manifest in largely extra-bodily signs – in her preaching, and in the speech and actions of those who revered her in her lifetime and continue to do so.

Diagnosed as suffering from breast cancer, Vichakshan refused all medication and – according to Laidlaw's informants and his interpretation of their accounts – she transformed the passive, involuntary pain of her cancer into an active, voluntary ascetic practice. The passive pain of illness or misfortune is generally interpreted by the Jains to be the 'reward' (or punishment) of some past evil action; one must endure such misfortunes and thus burn off the *karma*s that gave rise to them; such endurance, however, brings no reward of its own, it merely settles an old debt. By contrast, the active and willed austerities of fasting and other bodily mortification (such as meditating in a place where one will

233

certainly be bitten by mosquitoes, as Rajchandra was said to have done) alters one's *karma* balance pro-actively. One either builds up a store of 'good' *karma*s which will bring future fortune (such as rebirth in a plea-sure-filled heaven, or examination success), or destroys 'good', 'bad' and 'neutral' *karma*s alike on the quest for freeing the soul of all *karma*.[16] Vichakshan became renowned during her lifetime (or at least, from the time her cancer was diagnosed) not merely for the fortitude with which she suffered her pain, but for her insistence on its beneficial properties. All world religions (and all major ideologies: Gellner 1979) make a virtue of standing the world on its head, of seeing fiery damnation in apparently innocent pleasures, of seeing heavenly blessings in worldly misfortune, and Jainism is no different to these. Vichakshan effected one of these headstands of secular moral logic, and it is easy to see how difficult it would be to represent this iconographically. In Euro-America, after decades of Cubism, Surrealism, Minimalism and a whole host of other artistic -isms, a variety of solutions might present themselves, but the Jain (and more generally South Asian) solution is realism (or 'almost hyper-realist' as Laidlaw puts it – 1995: 263), where the lifelike veracity of the image attests to the veracity of Vichakshan's experience.

The paradox that I mentioned in my introduction to this chapter is of course that while Rajchandra and – perhaps to a lesser extent – Vichakshan presumably desired bodily effacement once their work on their bodies had been completed to their satisfaction, the converse has happened and they have been (literally) idolised. I think there is an his-torical reason for this, just as I think a specifically historical (if highly conjectural) reason explains the differentiation of Parshvanath's repre-sentation from all other *tirthankara* representations, discussed above. Rajchandra has only just passed out of living memory, Vichakshan still remains there, and the presence of their bodies in the world of living Jains is still very recent. While forgetting the dead is an active and delib-erate cultural project in some societies, particularly those of Amazonia (Taylor 1993), this is far from true in South Asia, where Hindu (and Jain) society demands an incorporation of the dead (particularly a man's father) into the realm of the ancestors. Such tensions do not, however, appear to have broken the bounds of the narrow iconographic spectrum I have been describing, for there is nothing extraordinary about the idols and photo-graphs of Rajchandra and Vichakshan apart from their existence. The presence of such images, however, does prevent the spectrum turning back on itself, though perhaps this is only a temporary phenomenon.

Conclusions

Through this chapter I have tried to present a spectrum of Jain bodily
iconography, from the absent presences of the cut-out plates and the

footprint shrines, to the fleshy hyper-realist presences of recent histori-cal figures, by way of the medial forms of the *tirthankara* idols and the Rajchandra photographs where inner state and outer form exhibit con-gruence. In doing so I have drawn promiscuously from a wide range of Jain traditions, blurring sectarian, temporal and geographical barriers and boundaries. Such violence against tradition would be unacceptable to both the Jains and the scholars of their doctrines and practices: to the Jains, because each sectarian grouping or local community would feel that their forms of representation are the only acceptable ones; and to their scholars who rightly insist upon the historical and cultural particu-larities that provide the context and perhaps the causation for any par-ticular form. But the range of forms I have described exist under a broader umbrella of an atemporal, ahistorical Jainism that the Jains themselves at times insist upon (Dundas 1992: 2), and which at times make sense for the sociologist of the Jains and Jainism (Banks 1992: 227–31; Carrithers and Humphrey 1991). It is a vision of this atemporal and ahistorical Jainism that has survived for the last two and a half mil-lennia in India, while local communities of Jains have come and gone, and while doctrinal and organisational differences have caused rift after rift in the ascetic orders.

The iconographic traditions of South Asia are varied, but finite, no more so than when it comes to representing the human body. The Jain selections from this palette are even more restricted (for example, the Jains have never to my knowledge borrowed the Hindu tradition of showing revered beings in human form but with multiple limbs to express notions of puissance). While Jain representations of the universe and its non-human inhabitants can be highly ornate and at times extra-ordinarily abstract, even minimalist,[17] their approach to the human body has always been characterised by a remarkable restraint: colours are muted or absent, bodily form is either totally absent (the footprints) or quasi-naturalistic. The clinging fast to a little changing and colourless body form as a mode of representation mirrors the clinging fast to what Jaini calls an 'unexciting' but unique body of doctrine (1980: 88). Jaini's main argument over the survival of Jainism concerns the close ties between ascetics and laity in early Jainism; again, the restricted code of bodily representation, as outlined above, demonstrates fundamental linkages – as well as elements of difference – between all the main actors in the Jain drama: the absent *tirthankara*s, the long-dead founders of ascetic lineages, the living laity, and – crucially – the invisible souls of them all.

The Jain aesthetic we see at work in this spectrum of represented and representing bodies is very much an aesthetic of form, of surface and of externality. It revolves around contrast and opposition: absence and presence, fullness and emptiness, anonymity and identification, poly-chrome and monochrome; it also invokes the senses, primarily vision and touch, for these qualities of form are evident to the eye and hand during ritual. At times the contrasts are within the spectrum (such as between the representations of effacement, and the representations of solid if anonymous presence in temple imagery), while at other times the contrasts are between the spectrum and other areas of representation (such as between the polychromatism found generally within Gujarati Svetambara temples at least and the monochromatism of the idols' bodies within those temples). Certainly, there is no strict binary logic at work, but there are a set of nested conversations and dialogues between represented and representing bodies, and between them and the wider world.

Figure 11.10
Newly initiated
sadhvi (Jain 'nun')
meditating before
a small *tirthankara*
image, Jamnagar,
1983.

Following Morphy, it seems evident that these conversations are about value and the creation of value, as well as about meaning (Morphy 1994: 672–7). Value resides above all else in the body itself which, as I have demonstrated, is an iconographically marked and distinctive site. Within this category, value is accorded to work done on the body (fasting, discipline) over work done with the body (action, creation). At a still deeper or more focused level, value is accorded to absence and effacement, over presence and embodiment. Mauss's understanding of the habitus of the body (Mauss 1979) indicates how the Jains concretise and enliven this abstract process: living Jains through the centuries have experienced this process of value creation within their own bodies as they feast and fast, and as they meditate on the iconographically marked representation of bodies of others. An ideology of mind-body, or soul-body dualism is certainly implicit within Jainism, and occasionally made explicit, as with the illustrations in the children's primers I discussed early in the chapter. But it would be mistaken to see this dualism as dominant or exclusive, just as

it is mistaken to identify monism as the prime defining characteristic of the Hindu world (Parry 1989). The experience of living in a Jain body cannot be separated from the experience of being a soul on the Jain path. With the exception of the vexed issue of gender and the possibility of salvation for women, all Jain sectarian and local communities seem to have elected to portray and thus to experience the invisible soul on the canvas of the visible body within an obviously limited spectrum of stylistic choices, attesting through its narrow range to the simplicity and single-mindedness of the ultimate religious path.

Notes

1. This paper has benefited from the comments, suggestions, and advice of many people, but I would particularly like to thank Paul Dundas, James Laidlaw and Howard Morphy for the time they took to read it in draft and comment constructively.
2. In his recent book on the Jains of Jaipur (Rajasthan) James Laidlaw devotes a whole chapter to 'Embodied Ontologies' (1995: chapter 11). I read the book in manuscript some months before preparing the present article and realised that there were many similarities between Laidlaw's material and his interpretations of it, and my own. I have tried to write here from a slightly different standpoint, but I would certainly urge the reader to look at Laidlaw's excellent book, and in particular at the chapter mentioned here.
3. For ease of reading I have not included diacritic marks for the South Asian terms used in this essay, nor have I consistently followed the standard transliteration conventions. Full diacritics and more conventional transliteration for most of the terms used can be found in the Glossary appended to Banks 1992.
4. For a full examination of the Jain stance on women and their salvation see Jaini 1991. The dispute over the body of the *tirthankara*, which centres around the ingestion of food, is discussed by Dundas 1985.
5. 'Idol' of course, could be seen to be a contentious translation of the Hindi or Gujarati word *murti*. But 'three-dimensional religious image' seems too unwieldy, while the simple 'statue' does not connote enough of the religious overtones that *murti* can have. Although *murti* as a term also applies to apparently quite straightforwardly secular commemorative statues (of Dr Ambedkar, the Untouchable Independence leader for example), 'idol' implies a slippage between mere representation and sacred immanence that I will return to in the following section.
6. There have been previous series of *tirthankara*s and will be future series; there are also 'parallel' series in other parts of the universe.
7. The story is told in a twelfth-century CE text, the *Trisastisalakapurusacaritra* (commonly known in the West as 'The Universal History', with versions existing from the ninth century), and is cited by Jain and Fischer (1978: 16) who also reproduce a seventeenth-century manuscript illustration of the event (plate XLII).
8. Dundas points out that the association of *tirthankara*s with particular symbols (and indeed, the individualised biographies of the *tirthankara*s) is absent in the earliest texts and sculptures, and thus probably dates only from the early centuries of the Christian era (Dundas 1992: 35).
9. Figures 103 and 104 in Shah's volume on Jain iconography show the front and back views of the idol (Shah 1987). Jaini (1991: 191), while not disagreeing that this is a Jain image, now seems to doubt that it represents Malli, though previously he thought it 'probable' (1979: 72). See also Dundas 1992: 49–50.
10. Respectability and modern prudishness are different matters altogether. As a comment on modern Indian prudishness the following anecdote is, however, revealing. One of the most famous of all Jain images is the (Digambara) statue of Bahubali at Sravana Belgola in Karnataka, southern India. The statue, a thousand years old and

almost sixty feet tall, stands on the summit of a hill and is a major site of pilgrimage. It depicts the naked, standing figure of the son of the first *tirthankara*, Adinath, in meditation prior to achieving enlightenment. His genitalia are clearly visible. In the 1970s or 1980s a Jain hotel-owner in Bombay decided to adorn the exterior of his hotel with a marble replica of the famous statue, standing some twenty feet tall. The city council was not amused at the sight of the statue's genitalia on display on a major highway, but the owner refused to conceal them with a loincloth as this would make a mockery of Digambara doctrine which lays down nudity as an essential prerequisite to enlightenment. Eventually, he placed the hotel's sign board in front of rather than behind the image, where it conveniently concealed the idol's loins. Similarly, an issue of a popular children's comic book – *Amar Chitra Katha* – that I bought a few years ago tells the story of Bahubali. In the strip, Bahubali the man is shown naked in several frames as he undertakes his meditation, but his genitalia are always concealed or out of frame. His famous statue is also shown a number of times; while the genitalia are mostly concealed behind speech bubbles and convenient foreground objects, they are visible in some frames.

11. For a complete list of the nine nodal points of worship of the idol's body and their meaning, see Humphrey 1985: 15. Humphrey and Laidlaw (1994) examine Jain ritual acts in considerable detail.

12. As both Laidlaw (1995: 243) and more particularly Dundas (1985) note, the issue of ingestion has preoccupied the Jains from very early on with regard to the apparently trivial question of does the *tirthankara* – once he or she has achieved omniscience – eat? Briefly put, a long-running and often vitriolic debate between the Digambaras and the Svetambaras attempts to resolve a paradox: the *tirthankara* is a man like any other man (that is, not a supernatural being, a god or a magician) and thus must have a body like that of other men, one that feels hunger and must be sustained with food. Yet the *tirthankara* has achieved spiritual perfection, which should be mirrored in a perfect body that feels no hunger and requires no food. The Svetambaras support the idea of the ingesting *tirthankara*, while the Digambaras advocate the self-sustaining one.

13. Elsewhere I have described the consequences of a similar fast that went tragically wrong (Banks 1992: 87–8). Josephine Reynell provides highly detailed accounts of women's fasting behaviour in her work on the Jain women of Jaipur: see Reynell 1985a and 1985b.

14. In his own discussion of the Rajchandra photographs (1995: 242) James Laidlaw suggests they may have been fabricated, but points out that ultimately this does not matter as the fabrication proves a need on the part of Rajchandra's followers to see him like this. From what I have said above I find it very unlikely that the photographs have been fabricated or retouched, though I have not had a chance to trace one back to source. However, in his book Laidlaw reproduces a recent photograph (plate XI, p. 234) of a Rajasthani layman, Amarchand-ji Nahar, who died in the 1970s having modelled himself on Rajchandra. At least as emaciated as Rajchandra, Amarchand-ji is sitting in an identical meditation posture, and the crisp modern image – to my untutored eye – seems authentic. As Laidlaw notes: 'if the photographs of Rajchandra are artificial, then Amarchand-ji saw to it that life (or rather death) fairly exactly imitated art' (1995: 242 n. 13).

15. The temple is the Moti Doongri Dadabari; Laidlaw notes that there are at least three other temples in northern India that contain idols of Vichakshan (1995: 262 n. 50).

16. For an alternative and very different attempt to transform the effects of past *karma* see Banks 1992: 34–5. The question of which actions bring about what results in terms of *karma* is a difficult and vexed one, both for the Jains, and for the anthropologists and others who have sought to understand them; Laidlaw provides one interesting set of examples and a convincing analysis (Laidlaw 1985).

17. A good set of examples of early painted iconography can be found in Caillat and Kumar's *The Jain Cosmology* (1981); some of the seventeenth- and eighteenth-

century representations of sacred geography (for example, plates 38–9, 42–4) are so visually cryptic that I doubt that few lay Jains today could make much sense of them. For me they resemble the paintings of Joan Miró.

References

Banks, Marcus (1992) *Organizing Jainism in India and England*, Oxford: Clarendon Press.
— (n.d.) 'The Tirtha Pata: Contemporary Jain Art and Worship'.
Caillat, Colette and Ravi Kumar (1981) *The Jain Cosmology*, Basel: Ravi Kumar.
Carrithers, Michael and Caroline Humphrey (1991) 'Jains as a Community: A Position Paper', in *The Assembly of Listeners: Jains in Society*, ed. M. Carrithers and C. Humphrey, Cambridge: Cambridge University Press.
Dundas, Paul (1985) 'Food and Freedom: The Jaina Sectarian Debate on the Nature of the Kevalin', *Religion* 15: 161–98.
— (1992) *The Jains*, London: Routledge.
Gellner, Ernest (1979) 'Notes Towards a Theory of Ideology', in *Spectacles and Predicaments*, ed. E. Gellner, Cambridge: Cambridge University Press.
Humphrey, Caroline (1985) 'Some Aspects of the Jain Puja: the Idea of "God" and the Symbolism of Offerings', *Cambridge Anthropology* 9 (3): 1–19.
Humphrey, Caroline and James Laidlaw (1994) *The Archetypal Actions of Ritual: a Theory of Ritual Illustrated by the Jain Rite of Worship*, Oxford: Clarendon Press.
Jain, Jyotindra and Eberhard Fischer (1978) *Jaina Iconography, Part I: The Tirthankara in Jaina Scriptures, Art and Rituals*, Leiden: Brill.
Jaini, Padmanabh S. (1979) *The Jaina Path of Purification*, Berkeley: University of California Press.
— (1980) 'The Disappearance of Buddhism and the Survival of Jainism: A Study in Contrast', in *Studies in the History of Buddhism*, ed. A.K. Narain, Delhi: B.R. Publishing Corporation.
— (1991) *Gender and Salvation: Jaina Debates on the Spiritual Liberation of Women*, Berkeley: University of California Press.
Laidlaw, James (1985) 'Profit, Salvation and Profitable Saints', *Cambridge Anthropology* 9 (3): 50–70.
— (1995) *Riches and Renunciation: Religion, Economy and Society among the Jains*, Oxford: Clarendon Press.
Mauss, Marcel (1979 [1935]) 'Body Techniques', in *Sociology and Psychology*, ed. M. Mauss, London: Routledge and Kegan Paul.
Morphy, Howard (1994) 'The Anthropology of Art', in *Companion Encyclopedia of Anthropology: Humanity, Culture and Social Life*, ed. T. Ingold, London: Routledge.
Parry, Jonathan (1989) 'The End of the Body', in *Zone 4: Fragments for a History of the Human Body (Part Two)*, ed. M. Feher, New York: Urzone, Inc.
Reynell, Josephine (1985a) 'Honour, Nurture and Festivity: Aspects of Female Religiosity among Jain Women in Jaipur', unpublished PhD thesis, Cambridge University.
— (1985b) 'Renunciation and Ostentation: a Jain Paradox', *Cambridge Anthropology* 9 (3): 20–33.
Shah, Umakant P. (1987) *Jaina–Rupa–Mandana (Volume I)*, New Delhi: Abhinav Publications.
Taylor, Anne Christine (1993) 'Remembering to Forget: Identity, Mourning and Memory among the Jivaro', *Man* 28 (4): 653–78.
Zwilling, Leonard and Michael J. Sweet (1996) '"Like a City Ablaze": the Third Sex and the Creation of Sexuality in Jain Religious Literature', *Journal of the History of Sexuality* 6 (3): 359–84.

12

Pine, ponds and pebbles: gardens and visual culture

Joy Hendry

Introduction

The questions to be addressed in this chapter have largely arisen out of encounters between the author, an anthropologist, and lay people in Britain who share an interest in the country of Japan. Reactions to experience of the Japanese nation are very mixed, though a visit almost invariably sparks off enormous curiosity, and some business people can be quite vehemently negative about their Japanese counterparts, as well as baffled by their approach to the world. Others who have never ventured to visit Japan have read articles and watched television programmes, and, again, their attitudes are still sometimes very negative.

A stark contrast is expressed, however, in reference to Japanese gardens. These seem to be regarded almost universally in a highly positive way. Even those people who found their Japanese counterparts most difficult were enchanted by the temples and gardens in Kyoto, usually *de rigueur* as part of a visit to Japan, and splendid gardens within the grounds of the most famous hotels offer even the briefest visitor the experience of viewing a beautiful garden. Japanese gardens are also rather well-known amongst people who have never set foot in Japan, who have perhaps never had contact with Japanese people, and have no other interest in the country at all. What is it about this visual dimension of Japanese culture which entices beyond other forms of communication?

This chapter seeks to provide some answers to this question, and thereby to contribute to debates about the importance of visual anthropology. Is it possible to identify common features of visual communication independent of an understanding of other aspects of the language of the culture? Is this the nature of the appeal of gardens of one culture to members of another? And is it perhaps true that art created from the depth of one heart can communicate itself to the depths of another receptive heart, regardless of cultural differences, as advocates of Zen doctrine teach?

On the other hand, are gardens even placed in the same sort of category in different countries, specifically in Britain and Japan?[1] Is 'the

Figure 12.1 This temple garden, to be found at Nanzenji in Kyoto, is only one of hundreds waiting to delight the foreign visitor.

Figure 12.2 The garden at the New Otani Hotel in Tokyo is among the most splendid in the city.

Japanese garden' in Britain playing the role which gardens play in Japan, or has it been incorporated into British ideas of what a garden should be? Does it even perhaps command a category in its own right, which for some users may bear little relation to the modern, industrial nation with which it shares a name? Are British Japanese gardens Japanese at all, in fact, any more than Japanese British gardens are British, and, if not, what is it that seems to make them so universally pleasing and popular?

These questions will be considered in the pages which follow, in the context of wider ideas about gardens in Japan and Britain, and an attempt will be made to establish the extent to which levels of interest are comparable. In the next section, an ethnographic account of the first meeting of the Japanese Garden Society in Britain will provide an illustration of the British interest in Japanese gardens, and the section following will place this interest in an historical context. Then, some general ideas about Japanese gardens will be introduced, and the British material reassessed. Armed with this contextual information, we will be in a position to propose some tentative answers to our questions.

The founding of the Japanese Garden Society in Britain

In an effort to identify some of the features of Japanese gardens which seem to have such widespread appeal, I attended a conference on Japanese gardening held in the summer of 1993 at Tatton Park in Cheshire. Only a few members of the audience had been to Japan, and many had only very vague ideas about the country. The only Japanese people there were a young woman dressed in kimono, who said a few words about the tea ceremony and performed it for distant viewing in the tea house in the Japanese garden, and her husband, who recorded her endeavours with a video camera. Many people, however, seemed to think themselves rather knowledgeable on one or other aspect of Japanese gardening.

There were eight speakers, most of whom had spent time in Japan, although only two (apart from the Japanese woman herself) showed any great knowledge of the Japanese language, written, spoken or under-stood. Other members of the 101 delegates present displayed their knowledge as we walked around the garden – offering advice to the head gardener who was guiding us, or casually dropping details over lunch. The head gardener himself runs courses on Japanese gardening, and some of the people present were graduates of these three-day events. Several actually implied that Japanese gardens, even in Japan, would be totally neglected were it not for Westerners like themselves who were interested in preserving them.

Two of the speakers revealed a parallel interest in British gardens amongst the people of Japan. Each had been invited to Japan to create gardens there. The first had been shown a huge area of neglected park-land, which was to be developed to open to the public in the city of Mito, which already boasts one of the most famous gardens in Japan. He had been asked to design some English[2] touches which he explained would give the same 'cachet' in Japan as Japanese touches to gardens do here. The requests he had received were for a 'grotto', a 'secret garden', and an 'aromatic garden', to be incorporated at strategic points about the parkland. He had also been asked to identify suppliers of 'traditional English water mills', a snippet of information the British audience in Tatton Park found extremely amusing, although they were themselves most interested in 'traditional' Japanese artifacts they could acquire for their own gardens.

This speaker was actually rather apologetic about constructing an English garden in Japan, though the slides of his drawings and plans sug-gested that he possessed great skill and artistry. No such apology seemed required about the fact that speakers talking of Japanese garden design were also British. The second such speaker was a Scottish landscape artist who had also been invited to Japan to design gardens, this time surrounding pavilions and a bathing area at new golf courses recently constructed there. He made an interesting comparison between Japanese golf courses of today and British country houses of the last century, describing the former as the modern equivalent of the latter. It is to a golf course that company executives, the élite of Japanese society, take their guests to be entertained, he explained, and there they relax together, eating and bathing in pleasant surroundings after the game of golf is over.

Japanese gardens in Britain – an example of chinoiserie?

Japanese gardens are by no means new in Britain, of course, and one of the main aims of the Cheshire conference was to found a Japanese Garden Society to locate and restore an estimated 200 Japanese gardens which were built during a previous boom in interest in the Edwardian period (see, for example, Ottewill 1989). Many of the gardens have been neglected during the intervening years, and some have become extremely overgrown. Recent interest in restoring them could reflect an explosion of general interest in gardening since the 1980s and a parallel 1970s interest in Zen Buddhism and other mystical aspects of 'the Orient'.[3]

European garden historians usually discuss Japanese and Chinese gardens in relation to their spiritual qualities, and they tend to agree about the reasons for the initial nineteenth-century boom in interest in the case of Japan. They mention factors such as the mystery associated with the opening of a formerly closed country, the height of the British Empire, the 'apparent simplicity of design and material' (Hellyer 1980: 39), and the influence of a miniature Japanese village at the Vienna Exhibition of 1873, later reconstructed at Alexandra Palace (Elliott 1986: 200). In the 1890s, a book on Japanese gardening, published by Josiah Condor, an architect who spent several years working in Japan, was influential, and this now rather quaint tome is still in print. It is also still in great demand, according to the bookseller in Tatton Park.

Some writers are sceptical about the authenticity of the Japanese gardens even in the nineteenth century, however, and one even goes so far as to write that 'they bore no resemblance to the symbolic gardens of Japan' (Rohde 1932: 233). To another they were 'oversimplified' (Eckbo 1978: 67), and a third asserts that 'no physical imitation of a Japanese garden in the West succeeded until well into the present century' (Thacker 1979: 240). Even when Japanese gardeners were brought over to create them, the Japanese gardens ordered by British county families are said to have reproduced more of their own ideas than those of the inspiring people.[4]

A classic example cited is that of Tully House in County Kildare, during the residence of Colonel William Hall-Walker, who inherited the title of Lord Wavertree. Built during a period of four years' residence by a Japanese gardening expert and his family, who supervised the work of forty Irish gardeners, it is said to be 'yet one more example of mock Japanese garden-making' (Hellyer 1980: 40). However, it is also said that 'still, 70 years later, [it] so retains its power to beguile visitors that it is unquestioningly accepted as a genuine example of Japanese art' (ibid.).

Figure 12.3 The Japanese garden at Tully House in County Kildare.

In a book on 'The Creative Art of Garden Design', Percy Cane is in no doubt that, indeed, the Japanese influence *should* be kept quite literally in proportion. He writes, 'It is doubtful if a Japanese garden which conforms strictly to the Japanese tradition would find much favour in Great Britain.' He advocates trying to 'catch the spirit' of Japanese design which he sees displayed 'above all [in] the excellent feeling of balance that is obtained' (1966: 59). This must not be too Japanese, because '*we* like more spacious gardens as against the rather narrow walks and paths that are suitable for the Japanese whose physique is generally smaller than our own' (ibid.: 61). The human viewer must clearly be incorporated into Cane's equation.

The earlier interest in Japanese gardens in Britain may be placed in the context of interest in other Japanese, and indeed, Chinese art forms, but in the late twentieth century, when Japan has taken a leading role on the world stage, there seems to be a British category of 'Japanese garden' which is still held rather separately from other ideas about the industrialised nation in which it originates. It would seem, first, that the aesthetics of the garden are paramount. The slides shown at the conference which drew the most marked reaction from the British audience were those which made them sigh with pleasure, and words often heard during the day were 'beautiful', 'haunting', and that these gardens were evocative of 'emotion'. The photographs were generally of contemplative Japanese

Figure 12.4 Even this tiny garden at the entrance to a Kyoto temple contains the elements of the contemplative motif.

gardens, notably with arrangements of stones and pebbles, but preferably featuring some moss and a few trees and/or shrubs.

Another example of the British category of Japanese gardens, unrelated to the conference but demonstrating a commercial offshoot, is to be found on the supermarket shelf. This is an item known as 'Toilet Duck' cleaning fluid which comes in several varieties and fragrances, one of which, in a bottle of a delicate purple hue, is termed 'Japanese garden'. The label explains that this is 'a sophisticated new fragrance that fills your whole bathroom with the delicate aroma of the flowers and blossoms of an oriental garden'. This particular bouquet is obviously intended to be a big attraction for it has also been featured in a television commercial for the same product.

In fact, flowers are rather unusual items in gardens in Japan, although there is usually blossom in season, and a truer oriental fragrance might be closer to a longer-standing favourite on the supermarket shelf, namely pine. Nor is fragrance itself a marked characteristic of a Japanese garden, often more concerned with appealing to auditory senses, which is probably one of the reasons why an aromatic garden has been requested for the English park in Mito. The garden depicted on the label of this product, and in the television commercial, actually sports a Chinese pavilion and a combination of flowering plants which would be entirely impossible in the climates of Japan or Britain, *245* although it is true that ducks are sometimes a feature of gardens in both countries.

Many of the gardens constructed or recognised as Japanese gardens in Britain may still also be very different from the example described above. They range from a collection of plants of Japanese origin, included British-style in a shrubbery, or perhaps a maple grove, to a small plot consisting of raked stones and dwarf pines which is much more like a British rockery than a scene for Zen contemplation. One of the speakers at Tatton Park, Robert Ketchell, who had served a long apprenticeship in Japan and spoke most impressively about the history of Japanese gardens, has been for years designing 'Japanese gardens' in Britain. Privately, afterwards, he described the conflict he encounters between the principles of Japanese gardening he learnt in Japan and the demands of his clients. He noted, however, that a garden should have the ability to transform one's consciousness, 'to change one's frame of mind'.

Figure 12.5 A Robert Ketchell Japanese garden constructed, with the help of the Japanese Garden Society, at Warwick University.

Is there some primeval force being addressed here? Why should Japanese gardens, which are evidently *not* strictly authentic Japanese gardens, be so attractive to the British public? And why should a conference in Cheshire draw an audience from all over mainland Britain – for some of the visitors had travelled down from central Scotland, as well as up from Dorset. Do Britain and Japan share ideas about gardens, or ideas about the rest of the world, or is this mutual exchange of interest a characteristic of gardens in general? Is there some visual quality in Japanese gardens which can communicate beyond the strict parameters of their construction? In order to address these questions, let us now consider a Japanese view of Japanese gardens.

Japanese gardens in Japan – an anthropological interpretation

Gardens have been developed in Japan for well over a millennium, and some of the older ones have been preserved for several hundred years. First written mention of the word now used for garden in Japan was in a seventh-century chronicle where it stood for a cleared space, covered in moss or pebbles and bounded with a straw rope, a place where humans could communicate with the gods. Gods and spirits were held to reside in all kinds of natural phenomena, such as mountains, rivers and stones, and one writer surmises that a large stone would stand as a central feature of such an area (Hayakawa 1973: 27–9).

Another important early influence on Japanese gardens was a style developed in China. Typically a lake or pond would be constructed, with a rocky border laid out to represent and remind of the natural seashore, again a site where gods were held to descend (Ota 1972: 106–7). In the middle, there would be at least one hilly island, and the garden might well be built to recall a specific landscape. The Japanese (and Chinese) word for landscape is literally 'mountains and water' (*sansui*), so these

Figure 12.6 A pond with an island is a feature of Japanese gardens, which suggests a Chinese influence.

elements are very appropriate. In the Heian period (the ninth to the twelfth centuries) of flourishing courtly culture, courtiers would construct Chinese pavilions, and pole about on their lakes in Chinese swan-headed boats.

During this period, too, the first garden manual was written. The *Sakuteiki* (writings on garden construction) also makes a clear and explicit connection between observing the landscape and designing the garden 'recalling . . . memories of how nature presented itself' (Tachibana 1976: 1). There is much discussion and advice about the placing of stones (ibid.: 23–6), and procedure is also laid out for making waterfalls, with nine different types of falling, from 'facing falling' through 'running falling' and 'leaping falling' (ibid.: 11–16). Islands may be constructed to recall hills and fields, forests or clouds (ibid.: 9–11). Various recommendations are made about auspicious directions in which to plant trees (ibid.: 34–7), but there is no mention at all of flowers.

There was already a Buddhist influence in the design of gardens, and in the period which followed, people were concerned to create representations of the Buddhist Pure Land paradise, with a representation of Mount Sumeru, and the mythical isle, Hôrai. Some time later, in the sixteenth century, the stones were held to transmit more abstract messages. The famous Zen Buddhist garden at Daisen-in, in Kyoto, for example, which is on the one hand regarded as a work of art, like a three-dimensional version of an ink drawing, also carries messages about the course of life. A pamphlet which may be bought there explains that the white gravel represents water flowing around the large boulders, each standing for a stage in life: the impulsiveness of youth, the confrontation with the why of existence, and a broader stream of human understanding which leads on into the purifying ocean of eternity.

Figure 12.7 The garden at Daisen-in, in Kyoto, illustrates the three-dimensional ink-drawing technique, also carrying messages about the course of life.

Gardens of the Edo period, when the site of the present city of Tokyo became the capital, were constructed to represent specific sites in other parts of Japan, so that lords and their families who were forced to spend long periods there could be reminded of their homeland. The style chosen became known as the 'strolling garden', with a winding path which propelled the visitor from one viewing spot to the next, and descriptions of the arrangements draw on metaphors of 'layering' of space (Duff-Cooper 1991: 14) and 'unfolding' of scenery (Ota 1972: 122–3). In another Edo garden, views were designed to recall literary references.

A theme which runs through this brief historical survey of Japanese gardens is the way they are designed to *represent* something else. Even in the twentieth century, when European and American influences abound in public parks and open spaces,[5] the garden most often chosen for the private Japanese home is one which recalls a Japanese landscape. The tiniest space may be given over to a few rocks, or some raked pebbles and a carefully placed acacia tree, but there will be a mountain scene in the eye of the designer. Before a gardener will take on an apprentice, it is common practice to send him out to observe the work of past masters, and to visit and absorb famous parts of the landscape of Japan (Slawson 1987: 40–43).

This practice of representing nature in gardens has been discussed recently by the Norwegian anthropologist Arne Kalland who sees it as a means of controlling or taming the wild. He addresses the Japanese claim to love nature, which seems to be contradicted by some of their actions towards nature in the raw, as Kalland terms it, and he reconciles these apparently opposed views by arguing that this love is for an idealised form of nature in a cultivated or 'cooked' form such as that found in gardens, and also *bonsai* (Kalland 1992). Kalland discusses the spiritual or supernatural associations of Japanese perceptions of the 'natural' world, and he argues that nature is 'tamed' through the establishment of a mutual dependency with the spirit world (ibid.: 221–4).

In a Japanese folk view, spirits and deities are not always clearly separated from strangers, and many folk-tales recount advantages which accrue to those who help strangers, or strange creatures of one sort or another, who turn out to have supernatural powers. Yoshida Teigo (1981) has discussed this conceptual overlap in a paper entitled 'The Stranger as God', where he addresses the apparently ambiguous attitude of Japanese to foreigners. On the one hand they are extremely hospitable, he notes, but Japanese society is also said to be essentially closed to foreigners (ibid.: 1, cf. Hendry 1988). Yoshida argues that this attitude to strangers is not unusual, but in view of further Japanese associations between deities or spirits and conceptions of nature, I would like to argue that ideas about the control of nature and the spirit world may also be seen as attempts to control and tame the unknown, or outside.

The distinction between inside (*uchi*) and outside (*soto*) is particularly strong in Japanese social organisation (see, for example, Hendry 1984), but it operates in a series of concentric circles surrounding any one individual, and it is marked relative to a specific context. The family is perhaps the closest inside group, but others are neighbourhoods, villages, work groups, common-interest groups, teams and, ultimately, especially when travelling abroad, the Japanese people themselves. Kalland argued that the inside world (in any particular context) is predictable, 'one knows what to expect from one's relatives, neighbours and friends' (1992: 222), but the outside world is threatening – and, he goes on, 'this applies to one's social world as well as to nature' (ibid.).

Kalland stops short of the next connection, but I would argue that in the same way that gardens (and bonsai) may be seen as attempts to 'tame' (or 'wrap' – see Hendry 1993, 1994, 1996) nature, they may also be used to 'tame' or 'wrap' the exotic, outside elements of the wider world for domestic consumption. In the early days of contact with Europeans, when the Portuguese and Spanish arrived in Japan in the wake of the mission of Francis Xavier, these outsiders were referred to as *yabanjin*, barbarians or 'wild people', where the first character, *ya*, is also used to distinguish wild animals, plants and fruits from their domestic counterparts.

It then becomes quite appropriate that gardens and parks should 'tame' or 'wrap' foreign influences. Apart from the English (or Scottish) touches, mentioned above, there have recently been developments in Japanese parks representing whole villages from other parts of the world. Perhaps the most famous is Haus Ten Bosch, previously Hollanda-mura, or Holland Village, in Kyushu, which offers tuition to Dutch students of Japanese so that real live Dutch people may be seen in the streets. Canadian World and Glücks-Königreich are to be found in the northernmost island of Japan, Parque España on the Ise peninsula, and Tokyo Disneyland is a very convincing reproduction of the United States of America only ninety minutes from the heart of the capital.

Figure 12.8 A Spanish city plaza has been reproduced for Japanese enjoyment in Parque España, on the Ise peninsula, Japan.

Disneyland is itself a microcosm of the wider world, of course, with Swiss mountains, African rivers and Caribbean pirates, although Donald Richie has commented that the city of Tokyo is a superior version with its 'glorious architectural confusion' of 'something from every place on earth' (1987: 39). Richie has also noted that Japanese gardens long preceded Walt Disney in their propensity to reproduce microcosmic worlds to delight their visitors, and refers specifically to those which represented elements of the Buddhist paradise. He somewhat irreverently praises Japanese vision and technique for creating over a thousand years ago the first Space Mountain in a depiction of Mount Sumeru (ibid.: 42)!

The requests for English touches to the garden in Mito, described by the speaker at the Tatton Park conference, and possibly even the Scottish touches to the golf-course garden, may be interpreted in the same vein. They can be placed in the context of a 'taming' or 'wrapping' of the world beyond Japan's shores for local consumption, a practice which reflects the role of Japanese gardens throughout history to bring the wild and supernatural into the safe social world of human control. By recreating natural scenery in a bounded miniature form, humans express a kind of harmony with the natural world which is impossible in the unpredictable wild, and the same principles are used in bringing the unfamiliar into a manageable form.[6]

Japanese gardens in Britain revisited

British gardens are full of plants of foreign origin, indeed those which are most highly valued are almost all originally from distant parts of the world, but it would be difficult to make the same argument about contemporary Britain, even if there was in the past a parallel acquisition process. Nor are British gardens noted for their concern to 'represent', though they may be expected to have some spiritual qualities. However, in this last section it is possible to make some comparisons between the use and enjoyment of Japanese gardens in Britain and the general use and enjoyment of gardens in Japan.

First of all, let us return to the comparison made by the Scottish landscape designer of golf courses in Japan and country houses in nineteenth-century Britain. As he pointed out, both provide(d) places for the élite of a society to entertain their guests. At the same time, they allow these advantaged members of society to impress those same guests in a visual and artistic way with their level of international sophistication. The Japanese golf-course companies sought sophistication by choosing a designer from a part of the world which happens currently to give kudos to the golfing establishment, just as 'Colonel William Hall-Walker, later to become Lord Wavertree of Kildare', employed a 'reputedly expert Japanese garden-maker' (Hellyer 1980: 40) to create a garden in the medium which was thought to be impressive in late nineteenth-century Britain. The garden at Tully House may not look particularly Japanese, and Arthur Hellyer, who describes it, feels that a Japanese visitor would not even recognise it as Japanese (ibid.), but then the gardens surrounding the Japanese bathing area at the golf course did not look particularly British to me.

In each case, the ideas are placed within a local context, and in each case, it is more an expression of local engagement with the wider world than an attempt to bring parts of the wider world into the local scene. Actually, each is also a more sophisticated representation of the wider world to the local instigator than may be apparent to a casual native observer. The game of golf epitomises participation in a high-powered élite society for Japanese people, but they also know that the game originated in Scotland, along with whisky, and they want to extend what they see as a shared appreciation for these finer elements of life to the spatial wrapping of the club buildings. This is communicated in a visual and therefore quite subtle way.

Although Hellyer (1980) doesn't seem to appreciate the significance of the comparison, he describes the way the Japanese garden at Tully House in Kildare represents a pilgrimage through life, from birth to death, just as does the garden at the temple Daisen-in in Kyoto. Visitors are steered through the Gate of Oblivion, representing the soul seeking a body to inhabit, past a rocky cave of gestation, through a dark tunnel of ignorance and incomprehension, towards the Hill of Learning . . . and on past an Island of Joy and Wonder, associated with marriage, a steep and divisive Hill of Ambition, and a relatively inaccessible Well of Wisdom, which is only attainable just before the Garden of Peace and Contentment which precedes the final Gateway of Eternity. The fact that this kind of representation of life's journey is the theme of Japanese contemplative gardens would surely have been available to Lord Wavertree, through his Japanese gardener, even if Hellyer who 'soon gave up' (ibid.: 41) was apparently unaware of it.

In both cases – golf courses in Japan and country houses in nineteenth-century Britain – the benefits associated with experience of and access to the wider world are more directly concerned with prestige and status than with economic advantage, though the economic underpinning is of course vital. Very commonly, however, a headstart on knowledge of the wider world can be used to make a substantial living, particularly in a climate of internationalisation, such as Japan enjoys at present. The 'English parks' and 'Canada/Holland/Spanish villages' are undoubtedly commercial ventures, as well as providing an opportunity for coming to terms with the 'wild' outside world.

It was not just amateur aficionados of Japanese gardens who were present at the conference in Tatton Park. There was a well-stocked bookstall, and one of the speakers even set up a table to sell signed copies of his own book. There were also two suppliers of lanterns and other Japanese artifacts which seem appropriate to British Japanese-gardeners, and the Japanese Garden Society now has a separate commercial mailing list. The landscape gardeners, themselves, were obviously looking for contracts, large and small, and one man walked around with a supply of glossy brochures about his business as a specialist in supplying and preparing natural stone. Clearly the aesthetic interest was encouraged in at least some cases by serious economic concerns.

However, as mentioned above, the part of the conference which the British audience seemed most to enjoy was the slides which made them sigh with pleasure. They were also enthusiastic to acquire pruning and designing techniques so that they could go away and create a Japanese corner in their own gardens. The aesthetic and perhaps spiritual content of the 'beautiful', 'haunting' Japanese garden seemed to be their prime concern, just as Hellyer's impatience with the 'meaning' of the garden at Tully House is tempered by the fact that 'it retains its power to beguile visitors' so that 'it is unquestioningly accepted as a genuine example of Japanese art' (Hellyer 1980: 40, and above).

Gardens may certainly be considered as an art form – indeed, F.R. Cowell, the author of a book entitled 'The Garden as a Fine Art', refers on the first page to John Ruskin's distinction between craft, involving the head and hands, and fine art, which also involves the use of the heart (Cowell 1978: 8). Yet we run up against some interesting problems with gardens. There are few gardeners whose names reach the dizzy heights of fame accorded artists in other fields, and the substance of these works of art requires much more maintenance than most other art forms. Except in their components, these forms of art are also very difficult to transport and therefore particularly subject to alienation in their reincorporation.

In the case of Japanese gardens, certain components have been successfully commodified, notably in the originally Chinese form of *bonsai*, and in the ornamental fish found in many Japanese garden lakes, known here redundantly as '*koi* carp'. These are only aspects of the Japanese garden, however, and they have purposely been left on one side in this chapter, for my interest has been precisely in the attempts to transport something so literally embedded in its own cultural context. There is also the inevitable connection between gardens and the climate in which they are grown. Britain and Japan do both have the four seasons which are necessary to display different aspects of Japanese (and British) gardens, but I think there is something more in the Japanese garden which is being transported.

Cowell sums up this component in my view when he writes that Japanese gardens 'owe their effects less to what they show the spectator than to what he is able to read or project into them' (1978: 126; cf. King 1979: 51). Like Japanese poetry, painting and flower arranging, he goes on, gardens 'aim at stimulating an attitude of mind and awakening thought, rather than at merely imparting the ideas of the artist, writer or their patrons' (ibid.: cf. Condor 1964: 8). Is this mysterious quality of Japanese gardens truly a cultural artifact, then, which goes beyond the individual who creates them, and somehow transcends the local form wherever they are found?

If this is the case, then some of the British Japanese gardens may truly be Japanese gardens after all, inspiring thought and an attitude of mind in the viewer, rather than simply displaying the skills and views of the artist. Perhaps there *is* even a primeval force at work, inducing through the visual representation of natural (and cultural) phenomena a perception of harmony with nature, nature which in a Japanese view quite happily includes culture, but is in Britain appropriately scaled and selected to suit British ideals and expectations. The medium is also then entirely appropriate, for a visual form of communication which is independent of other forms of language can communicate beyond lexographic and syntactic limitations. In this respect, Japanese gardens may indeed be complying with Ketchell's demand, that a garden should have the ability to transform one's consciousness.

While driving through the Scottish hills some months ago, shortly after the winter snow had melted, I was suddenly struck with the idea of creating a Scottish landscape in my Oxford garden, using Japanese principles of representation. I was at first a little disappointed to find that another of the speakers at Tatton Park had had the same idea when he showed slides of views in Wales as possible inspiration, especially since his talk had not otherwise demonstrated a very deep knowledge of Japanese culture, but if the above thesis is correct perhaps the magic of Japanese gardens really does communicate itself more readily than other aspects of Japanese culture. It would explain the apparent appreciation of gardens demonstrated by such a large number of people with no special knowledge of or interest in Japan.

Notes

1. Malinowski (1935: 84–7) pointed out long ago in *Coral Gardens and their Magic* that the word translated as 'garden' in English may have various different meanings.
2. The speaker used the word 'English', rather than British, but the Japanese perception involved probably does not exclude other parts of the British Isles.
3. I am indebted to the editors for making these connections.
4. Other examples are described in Elliott 1986 and Ottewill 1989.
5. Laws about National Parks, for example, were only introduced in Japan in the 1930s (Kokuritsu 1981: 7), and these in my view exhibit some of the same classificatory principles as gardens (Hendry 1996).
6. In Zen gardens the same principles may be described as seeking to deepen an understanding of difficult abstract concepts, and in earlier gardens, as a means of communing with the spiritual.

References

Cane, Percy (1966) *The Creative Art of Garden Design*, London: Country Life.
Condor, Josiah (1964) *Landscape Gardening in Japan*, New York: Dover Publications.
Cowell, F.R. (1978) *The Garden as a Fine Art*, London: Weidenfeld & Nicolson.
Duff-Cooper, Andrew (1991) *Three Essays on Japanese Ideology*, Tokyo: Department of Humanities, Seitoku University Occasional Publication.
Eckbo, Garrett (1978) *Home Landscape*, New York: McGraw Hill.
Elliott, Brent (1986) *Victorian Gardens*, London: Batsford.
Hayakawa, Masao (1973) *The Garden Art of Japan*, New York: Weatherhill and Tokyo: Heibonsha.
Hellyer, Arthur (1980) *Gardens of Genius*, London: Hamlyn.
Hendry, Joy (1984) 'Shoes: The Early Learning of an Important Distinction in Japanese Society', in G. Daniels (ed.), *Europe Interprets Japan*, Tenterden, Kent: Paul Norbury Publications.

— (1988) 'Sutorenja toshite no minzokushi-gakusha – Nihon no tsutsumi bunka wo megutte', in Yoshida T. and H. Miyake (eds), *Kosumosu to Shakai*, Tokyo: Keio Tsushin.

— (1993) *Wrapping Culture: Politeness, Presentation and Power in Japan and Other Societies*, Oxford: Clarendon Press.

— (1994) 'Gardens and the Wrapping of Space in Japan: Some Benefits of a Balinese Insight', *Journal of the Anthropological Society of Oxford*, 14 (2).

— (1996) 'Gardens as a Microcosm of Japan's View of the World', in Pamela Asquith and Arne Kalland (eds), *Japanese Images of Nature: Cultural Perspectives*, London: Curzon.

Kalland, Arne (1992) 'Culture in Japanese Nature', in O. Bruun and A. Kalland (eds), *Asian Perceptions of Nature*, Nordic Proceedings in Asian Studies no. 3, Copenhagen: NIAS.

King, Ronald (1979) *The Quest for Paradise*, Weybridge: Whittet/Windward.

Kokuritsu Kôen Kyôkai (1981) *Nihon no Fukei (Shizen Kôen 50 shûnen kinen)*, Tokyo: Gyosei Ltd.

Malinowski, Bronislaw (1935) *Coral Gardens and their Magic*, London: Allen & Unwin.

Ota, Hirotaru (1972) *Traditional Japanese Architecture and Gardens*, Tokyo: Kokusai Bunka Shinkokai.

Ottewill, David (1989) *The Edwardian Garden*, New Haven and London: Yale University Press.

Richie, Donald (1987) *A Lateral View: Essays on Contemporary Japan*, Tokyo: Japan Times.

Rohde, Eleanour Sinclair (1932) *The Story of the Garden*, London: The Medici Society.

Slawson, David A. (1987) *Secret Teachings in the Art of Japanese Gardens*, Tokyo: Kodansha International.

Tachibana-no-Toshitsuna (1976) (trans. of eleventh-century ms), *Sakuteiki*, trans. Shigemaru Shimoyama, Tokyo: Toshikeikaku Kenkyûjo (Town & City Planners Inc.).

Thacker, Christopher (1979) *The History of Gardens*, London: Croom-Helm.

Yoshida, Teigo (1981) 'The Stranger as God: The Place of the Outsider in Japanese Folk Religion', *Ethnology* 20 (2): 87–99.

13

Collectivity and nationality in the anthropology of art

Nicholas Thomas

Introduction

The emerging anthropology of the 'visual' will incorporate the anthropology of art. This chapter is concerned with the ways in which studies of art within anthropology might be reformulated, if the field is explicitly understood as a wide-ranging enquiry rather than as one limited to 'non-Western' art and cross-cultural aesthetics. Those topics remain important, but research needs to be extended to art within 'Western' societies, not least because the Western/non-Western distinction has become confused by increasing cultural exchange. Art has been highly significant in the process of interaction, which suggests that much might be gained from the study of national and international art worlds, and of the movements and changing meanings of art works through these contexts.

If the anthropology of art is to be effectively redefined under these conditions, the subdiscipline might move beyond the strategy of much writing in the field to date. While the emphasis so far has been upon the cultural context and distinctiveness of indigenous art traditions, it may be useful to draw attention to the ways in which art may work in similar or analogous ways across cultures. The aim is not to develop highly generalised or universal propositions, but to create a common frame of analysis on the basis of loose affinities, while preserving the orientation toward contextualisation. This chapter is primarily concerned to sketch out how art works in diverse contexts can be understood to image 'collectivity' – social unity, nationality and ethnicity. Examples are drawn from Melanesian ritual practice and the work of both white and Polynesian migrant artists in Aotearoa New Zealand.

A contrast

Sociality has been understood increasingly as provisional accomplishment rather than functional reproduction (Bourdieu 1977; Giddens

1979, 1981). The once-axiomatic holism of the social sciences has been profoundly qualified by a shift from codes and systems to practical enactments and improvisations, that is manifest in fields as seemingly remote as colonial histories and the narration of myth (cf. Thomas 1994: 105–7; Weiner 1994: 592–3). Not only has society been detotalised, its status as a system, a universal and a unit of comparison have been questioned, most radically by Marilyn Strathern (1988). Her arguments proceed in a number of directions, emphasising that 'society' is only in tension with the 'individual' in the terms of a certain Western rhetoric, that it does not correspond either with 'groups' or 'social structures' in the New Guinea Highlands, and – the point I am concerned to take up – that Melanesian collectivities are not social aggregates but more typically images of unity. 'Images' may consist in artifacts, cult houses and groups of dancers – in other words the objects and performances that have provided subject-matter for the anthropology of art. 'Unity' is not solidarity but a 'oneness' that may mimic or animate the oneness of particular people: in other words, the relations between one collectivity and another, and between collectivities and 'individuals', are analogical and metaphoric rather than hierarchical and inclusive. So far from constituting 'society', collectivities may moreover be considered antisocial, or antithetical to other forms of sociality (1988: 12–15).

The present discussion sets aside the argument that these analogical relationships are peculiar to Melanesian as opposed to Western conceptions of collectivities. While that oppositional rhetoric was deliberately and effectively exploited in Strathern's *The Gender of the Gift*, one of the things that that book has enabled us to do is to explore how non-Melanesian socialities, and even 'Western' ones, have been obscured by 'Western' conceptions. If hierarchical rather than analogical relations indeed organise 'society' as it is typically conceived, the cultural form of the nation, on the other hand, has been constituted most crucially by a kind of isomorphism between the singular person and the totality, that Dumont has referred to as 'entivity' (1977). This one-to-one logic is often extended to art forms: a novel such as Patrick White's *Voss* or Malouf's *Remembering Babylon*, paintings such as those of Nolan or Drysdale, bear Australian-ness in the same sense that an individual Australian does. This is a statement both at the level of form and at that of contingent readings: the biographical and social inclusiveness of the novel, and the tendency for characters to be read as typifications, and for histories to be considered emblematic or constitutive, makes the form available to a national imagining, even though many novels cannot be fitted into the mould, and some of those that can, such as the works of White, appear as motivated by universal as by nationally particular themes. What may be important, then, is not the fact that art forms in fact unambiguously image nationality, but that they are taken to do so, at some if not all phases of their lives.

Strathern's category of 'collectivity' is relevant to contemporary nationhood precisely because nations are prejudiced by economic and cultural globalisation that undermines their sovereignty and ideological particularity. Collectivity is not the same as society; it is not a continuing field or container of relationships but rather an expression of a kind of unity or difference that may be belied by other expressions and affiliations. Particular forms of collectivity are therefore likely to be imaged episodically, even though they may exist implicitly, as memories, potentialities and sources of tension, at other times.

In Melanesia, making what is usually hidden or in the background explicit, can be surprising. The force of what is presented arises from the fact that collectivity is typically not presented through images that are simply created and left lying around; very often they are made visible, quite suddenly, under ceremonial circumstances in which objects and performances are, in effect, framed. To draw attention to this may be to run against the grain of anthropological writing on non-Western art forms: the emphasis has generally been on how these differ from Western art and aesthetics. However, elaborate ritual events such as stages in male initiation and major presentations in exchange cycles are taken by everyone concerned to be radically different to the usual flow of life. This differentiation or segregation from ordinary social life and ordinary practical domains surely invites comparison with the peculiar decontextualisation of aesethetically framed practices in Western societies. As Edward Said has suggested of Western musical performances, they are 'highly concentrated', 'even atavistic', 'and extreme occasions' (1991: 11). Strathern has recently written that 'People amaze themselves by their capacity for collective action, as the men of Mt Hagen are amazed when they decorate on exchange occasions. Their presentation evinces the power they hope to have encompassed, at once a divination of past success and an omen for the future' (1990: 30).

Accordingly, much activity around rituals and ceremonial presentations seems directed toward the creation of images of collectivity. In an early sequence in Ian Dunlop's remarkable film, *Baruya Muka Archive* (1979/1990), those already initiated are decorating the house central to the first stage of male initiation rites. We see a long line of men bringing bundles of banana leaves along a path, carrying them on their heads: what is striking about this is the fact of deindividuation. It would be easy for this task, and others connected with the production of the cult house, to be conducted in a more *ad hoc* way, but the co-ordination entails a kind of revelation, a bringing forth of collectivity. Of course, performances of this kind are not all directed toward the same effect: in the Hagen case the whole evinces the inner powers of the self, while among Waghi 'displays are regarded as revealing the state of intra-group relations' (O'Hanlon 1983: 331; cf. Strathern 1979). The key feature of these performances is remarkably similar to the 'simultaneity' that Benedict

Anderson has taken to be constitutive of national culture. In one of his most widely cited examples, that of the newspaper reader who observes 'exact replicas of his own paper being consumed by his subway, barber-shop, or residential neighbours' (1983: 39), the simultaneity is a quotidian and implicit fact, rather than a staged effort of deinviduation, or a display that elicits some sense of national subjectivity. I suggest that collectivities in most places are evoked at a variety of implicit and highly dramatised levels.

The discontinuity between collectivity and society, and the accomplished – or sometimes unaccomplished – character of the former is attested to by the fact that the major rites and ceremonies that anthropologists tend to render central in their ethnographic monographs, take place, in many cases, only very infrequently. It is sometimes suggested that Christianity, pacification and related forces have diminished the appeal or viability of such activities as Tambaran ceremonies and Baruya initiations (that may now be staged particularly because the people themselves or ethnographers want them documented), but it not always clear that they were ever conducted more frequently, and it is apparent that their staging is typically highly contentious (see e.g. Bowden 1983: 54–9). On this point, Tuzin has suggested that 'the Tambaran has always, as it were, had to fight for its life . . . the inertia of the system tends against undertaking anything so vast as a Tambaran initiation' (1980: 128). In another part of the Pacific, in rural Fiji, exchange events do take place often, but seem always to be preceded by a good deal of tension and uncertainty. Occasionally, people who are supposed to be either making or receiving a contribution – and imaging their own oneness in the process – simply do not turn up. The practices that elicit collectivity can, therefore, be elusive not only for anthropologists, but for people themselves.

The point of these examples, in relation to the anthropology of art, is that performances and certain artifacts can be seen as ways of imaging a collectivity that may not be otherwise evoked. They are not Durkheimian *expressions* or *reflections* of society, but *rhetorical efforts* that typically present unity in certain terms: these terms enable people to image themselves, but probably conflict with self-conceptions that emerge in other contexts. The effort to produce sociality is not provisional merely because all projects are improvised, as Giddens' rather general theorising might stipulate, but also because a oneness based on say patriclan membership eclipses others that may arise variously from maternal nurture, church affiliation, age grades, and so on. I am not putting this forward as a general theory of Melanesian art. The process is, however, of interest for the interpretative problems that it raises, and for what it makes visible in very different contexts. To these examples, I juxtapose the following.

Ian Scott is a significant figure in contemporary New Zealand art. Among his early works (from the mid-1960s) are landscapes, often of classic fiord and mountain scenery such as that of Milford Sound, into which icons of suburban and middle-class life such as weatherboard houses and sailing dinghys are introduced. He subsequently worked in a localised version of an American pop style, and then moved into abstraction; his best-known paintings constitute the 'Lattice' series, developed mainly between 1976 and 1982.

Figure 13.1 Ian Scott, *Small lattice no. 50* (1981), acrylic on canvas, 864 × 864 mm.

In the mid-1980s Scott moved definitively away from abstraction, into a series of appropriations, initially by superimposing artists' portraits over copies of their works, and subsequently through a kind of period signwriting over appropriated paintings. Although Scott began by reproducing the works of diverse European and American artists, including Turner and Hopper, the series turned toward the reproduction of major New Zealand paintings by artists such as Colin McCahon, Rita Angus and D.H. Binney. These painters were to varying degrees concerned with the distinctiveness of the New Zealand landscape or environment, and Scott drew attention to the regionalist or nationalist orientation of the art by overwriting the canvases with slogans such as NEW ZEALAND PAINTING, OIL PAINTING IN NEW ZEALAND, and AOTEAROA.

These strong billboard-like images raise provoking questions concerning the ways in which art has displayed and advertised New Zealand nationality and New Zealand culture. Subsequently, Scott has experimented with superimposing screenprints on to appropriated works,

Figure 13.2 Ian Scott, *N. Z. painting* (1987–89), acrylic and enamel on canvas, 1730 × 2590 mm.

Figure 13.3 Ian Scott, *God zone subjects* (1990), acrylic and silkscreen on canvas, 1480 × 1730 mm.

again primarily landscape paintings, to which stereotypic New Zealand icons are added – Maori *kowhaiwhai* painting, a portrait of Colin McCahon, the All Blacks rugby team, the kauri forest, the beach, and the parliament house.

Scott has, in other words, moved from early work that was preoccupied with location, into abstract painting that arguably could have been produced in New York, Paris or anywhere else, and then back to work that is very specifically concerned with nationality. This particular trajectory relates, in a somewhat ironic way, to long-running debates in the New Zealand art scene, concerning the value of modernist internationalism and nationalist landscape. The perception is that the latter belonged to a parochial and conservative tradition that has been effectively superseded by the accomplishments of senior abstractionists such

261

as Milan Mrkusich and Gordon Walters, and by a younger generation notably including Scott himself; on the cover of Francis Pound's *Forty Modern New Zealand Paintings* (1985), a Lattice painting is emblematic and almost authoritative, as a statement of where New Zealand art needed to go.

A decade ago, as feminist and postmodernist art were belatedly emerging in New Zealand, it seemed clear that nationalism was 'at last, an entirely dead issue' (Pound 1985: unpaginated). Now, however, nationality if not nationalism appears to have come back with a vengeance. While Scott has been concerned particularly to revalue the New Zealand artistic canon, other painters and documentary photographers have attempted to reappraise New Zealand's military and colonial history, and artists ranging from critical feminist photographers to those producing popular screenprints have been concerned with identity and New Zealandness. At the inoffensive end of the spectrum, landscapes and domestic interiors are being given a distinctive south Pacific accent in images widely reproduced on postcards and posters; at the more ironic and challenging end, an artist can frame and illuminate a text proclaiming that Art expresses New Zealand: 'New Zealand's distinctive atmospheres and skies, its forests of varied verdure . . . are finding worthy expression in the works of our artists' (Barr 1992: 14). What these endeavours have in common is telling precisely because they are otherwise diverse: it is not that they generally reject 'internationalism', but that they are positively concerned to reflect or critically reflect a sense of place and nationality (in some cases, most particularly a sense of history). It might be claimed that this is now mostly done in an overtly postmodernist and ironic way that has little in common with the older nationalist traditions; those traditions, however, have arguably been stereotyped, and may be characterised by much the same mix of uncritical affirmation and more searching negotiation of antipodean white identity that is apparent in contemporary art.

A set of questions that might arise from the recent history of New Zealand art, and from Scott's work in particular, concern explication and reflection. Why are people compelled at some times but not others to address the character of their own cultures or nationalities? Or, when are they compelled, not only to do this, but to acknowledge and reflect upon the fact that they do it? The issues are complex because there is an interplay of global determinations which appear to have encouraged a wave of ethnic affirmation and discourse about identity everywhere from Canada to Macedonia, and local factors. So far as the latter are concerned, it is clear that the Maori renaissance and the ascendancy of a new concept of New Zealand (or rather Aotearoa New Zealand) as a bicultural nation has prompted a new effort on the part of white New Zealanders to define their histories and identities. What may be formally akin to international postmodernism also expresses peculiarly local anxieties, and reinforces a sense that the redefinition of national culture is proceeding.

The differences between this and the Melanesian material with which I began may be too obvious to need underlining. The first set of examples belong of course to classic anthropological terrain; the art forms that I referred to in passing happened not to be material objects but performances, architectural forms and practices that were part and parcel of ritual activities. While anthropologists and others have had to argue for the inclusion of these cultural practices within the privileged category of art, my problem is almost the reverse: how can contemporary art, and specifically that of white people, become anthropological subject-matter? When I turned to the New Zealand case, I turned from an array of ethnographic examples to a chronology, from collectivities to an individual, and from performances to paintings. And while I began to subsume a puzzle that seemed to emerge from my narrative to an anthropological issue, the connection might have seemed insecure, because the transitions that I pointed to are easily reincorporated within a frame of art-historical interpretation. That is, Scott's shift is most readily seen in terms of the evolution of his own work. It is questionable whether it is emblematic of any wider development, and it appears contrived to take it as an ethnographic fact, akin say to the point that each of a pair of masked Melanesian dancers 'knows himself to be a man, but when he looks at his partner he can see a spirit' (Schwimmer cited in Strathern 1990: 31).

'Western' art and the anthropology of art

It is this very gap between the anthropology of art and contemporary art that this chapter is concerned to negotiate. In contrast with almost every other area of anthropological enquiry, research on art has persisted in focusing upon small-scale, tribal societies; virtually no work has been done on European or American art, either for a contemporary or any earlier body of work; while writing on Islamic, Asian, or Mesoamerican art has tended to be curatorial and art-historical rather than anthropological. In most areas of anthropology, of course, enquiries have ranged far more widely, and research 'at home', on kinship for example (Firth 1956; Schneider 1968), has long ceased to be unusual or at all unorthodox.

At one level, this limitation might be easily explained on the grounds that the anthropology of art has emerged directly from the study of 'primitive' art (Jopling 1971; Forge 1973a). Since both the word and the category have been discredited (Morphy 1994: 648), it has either been declared or presumed that the anthropology of art is the anthropology of non-Western art (Layton 1991; Coote and Shelton 1992). The fact, however, that the range of tribal case-studies is extended only through the inclusion of indigenous art for the market makes the category something of a euphemism: work continues to deal with Melanesia, parts of Africa, the northwest coast of America, and Aboriginal Australia, not with the whole range of 'non-Western' societies. In principle, of course, it might be argued that 'primitive' art really is distinctive, but given the diversity of both the primitive and non-primitive, and the general disfavour into which great-divide theories have sunk, this type of claim would seem peculiarly difficult to sustain (but cf. Gell 1992). This only makes it more curious that anthropologists generally find such social classifications objectionable, yet in this context honour them in practice.

I emphasise here that my intention is not to ascribe some kind of theoretical backwardness to studies of indigenous art. If the larger discipline's former focus on tribal cultures was a problem, it is not solved by abandoning those cases, but by complementing and recontextualising them; and, while anthropologists in most cases neither can nor would seek to speak for indigenous peoples, active engagement with them, however awkward or compromised, remains valuable, and – for scholars in settler colonial societies such as Australia, New Zealand and Canada – unavoidable. My interest is not therefore in 'moving beyond' the Melanesian, African and Australian ethnographies (e.g. Faris 1972; Forge 1966, 1973b; Strathern and Strathern 1971; Morphy 1991; Phillips 1993), but in drawing these into a common interpretative frame with the analysis of other European and non-European art forms.

The distinction between 'Western' and 'non-Western' needs to be rejected as an instrument of disciplinary framing because it has ceased to correspond with any real division of cultural domains or practices. Much indigenous art is now produced for a market; in some cases it is produced by people who have been trained at art schools, who work with 'Western' media and techniques, and who sell through dealer galleries rather than craft shops. Even those resident in remote communities and deeply grounded in traditional forms of knowledge may be well aware of the category of the artist and may be anxious to be recognised in those terms (with respect to Narritjin Maymuru see Morphy 1991: 33). In some cases work on new media is intimately connected with traditional iconography (as in the well-known Papunya dot paintings that transpose sand drawing to canvas), in other cases content and meaning are in some sense hybrid. Ian Abdulla's paintings for example are autobiographical in a fashion that is certainly discontinuous with any precontact Aboriginal art, but nevertheless expresses both particular Aboriginal experiences and arguably also a certain southern Australian Aboriginality.

Work of this kind makes the category of 'assimilated fine art' that Graburn in 1976 took to arise from circumstances of extreme cultural domination, no longer tenable. Posthumous reinterpretations have suggested that his prime example, Albert Namatjira, did not slavishly imitate conventional landscape but rather adapted it to his own concerns

(Megaw and Megaw 1992). More generally, the concept of assimilation has been discredited, and much contemporary work that 'looks' like Western or international contemporary art not only conveys a distinctive indigenous perspective upon colonial relationships (as Ian Abdulla does), but also conforms with the logic rather than the appearance of traditional art (see Thomas 1995a on Robert Janhke). There is a kind of symmetry between the neglect of patently 'assimilated' work on the part of anthropologists and the way in which non-anthropological critics privilege overtly hybrid and urbanised artists. While anthropologists have evidently not felt compelled to write about such Aboriginal artists as Abdulla, Robert Campbell, Fiona Foley, and Tracey Moffatt, Moffatt's work in particular has been singularly provoking for 'post-colonial' critics in cultural studies, who are correspondingly unable to interest themselves in artists such as Rover Thomas, David Downs, or Narritjin Maymuru. In other words, the larger division between the anthropology of art and art history, that formerly addressed primitive and Western art respectively, seems recapitulated in the current division of critical and scholarly writing on outback and urban indigenous art. This might indeed be appropriate if urban and 'traditionalist' arts really were fundamentally separated, but even in that case it would arguably be productive to sustain a dialogue between analytic discourses that would at least throw the untranslatable properties of the various frames into relief.

Of course, indigenous art traditions and aesthetic systems do differ from those elsewhere. Tracing those differences remains an important anthropological endeavour, but it is one that is always in the process of being short-circuited by the entry of the 'art' of 'other cultures' into markets and institutions. 'Mistranslation' is not just something that curators and anthropologists might run the risk of doing; it is something that indigenous artists (and their go-betweens) engage in themselves, necessarily: they define things that they have always done as 'art' and begin to do them differently. While this suggests that any effort to define art as a stable or general category must overlook reflexive processes that now frame most artistic projects, I do not suggest that this leads anthropologists into a postmodernist or simply relativist vision of art as a succession of redefinitions: that 'hall of mirrors' figure too easily homogenises the very different indigenous, colonial, metropolitan and postcolonial situations in which artists are working.

It may, however, be analytically productive to focus on the discrepancies that arise in processes of recontextualisation, that take place within as well as between cultures. Like Morphy, therefore, I find Goffman's notion of 'frames' useful: art works may move between frames, understood as defining sets of cultural practices, or exist simultaneously in two frames or more than two (1991: 21). While Morphy uses the notion to juxtapose Yolngu and art world meanings, I am here more concerned to trace projected framings and successive reframings within the 'cultures' of migrant Polynesians and of white New Zealanders. Art forms that were not made to image collectivities can be transposed into situations in which they are taken to do so.

The lacunae in present writing might suggest that while the art market and art museums can readily be analysed sociologically (e.g. Becker 1982; Bourdieu and Darbel 1990), the elaboration of anthropological interpretation has been hindered for a variety of reasons, such as ambiguity about which of a number of possible cultural and social contexts provides the appropriate frame of interpretation. These problems may be diminished by a strategic emphasis on processes of reframing. What is of interest is not the obvious fact that there is a plurality of interpretations, but the point that certain works may be drawn into national and ethnic frames, characterised by analogical relations between images, identities and persons. An artist who happens to be Niuean or Samoan is therefore a 'Niuean artist' or a 'Samoan artist', and his or her work is read for its expression of cultural identity and tradition. This is not the only process that is taking place in the present, but the much-noted proliferation of ethnic and nationalist conflict, and the associated, if broader elaboration of objectifications of ethnic and national identity, make it a peculiarly important one.

The growing importance of art in public expressions of national identity and official cultural diplomacy, moreover, makes it clear that ethnicisation is not merely a 'context' within which contemporary art might be, or should be, interpreted. Like Highland dances and Tambaran houses, art works and curatorial practices image forms of collectivity that are not reproduced smoothly and mechanically. As marginal ethnicities struggle to discover or redefine themselves within nation-states, as nation-states struggle to retain sovereignty and coherence in an epoch marked by radical economic internationalisation and by the growth of supra-national quasi-states such as the European Community, it is surely evident that national collectivities are increasingly tenuous and provisional: not only are their conditions of existence in general undergoing great change, but many individual ethnicities and nations are immediately threatened by secession, devolution, or incorporation. Even where these conditions do not actually prejudice the perpetuation of the nation-state, they are part of a climate in which national identities are subject to renewed explication and reformulation.

Earlier in this paper I referred to an artist whose choice of style and content suggested a process of reframing: some moments of Scott's work bear national signatures and others do not. I have elsewhere (1995b) discussed the case of the abstract painter Gordon Walters whose adaptations of the Maori *koru* motif were seen simply as rigorously formal 'internationalist' works in the 1960s; over the 1970s and 1980s they have been steadily 'nationalised'.

Figure 13.4 Gordon Walters, *Maheno* (1981), PVA and acrylic on paper, 1545 × 1145 mm.

The *koru* has been treated as a national sign and the question of whether the paintings engage in appropriation or not has been controversial (Panoho 1992; Pound 1993, 1994). Both Walters and Scott began their careers before the current wave of debate concerning biculturalism and identity (in the case of Walters, well before); their work has then been seen differently as the terms of debate changed, as has Namatjira's. In the remainder of this chapter I am concerned with a much younger artist whose work responds, to a much greater degree, to the preoccupations with national and ethnic identity that mark contemporary culture in Aotearoa New Zealand. It arguably incorporates a kind of internal reframing. I suggest that the paintings of the Niuean artist, John Pule, embody a primarily personal iconography, that nevertheless lends itself to translation into a collective image, and is projected in those terms. While the particular effect of these paintings is not easy to speculate about, they ideally elicit a sense of collective power and energy, and may in fact do so.

John Pule

John Pule, painter and writer, was born in 1962 in the village of Liku on   *267*

Niue, but has been resident in New Zealand since the age of two. His parents were among the many Polynesians who left the islands in search of jobs and opportunities in the decades immediately after the Second World War and who came to constitute substantial Pacific communities in south Auckland. If a lack of overweening attachment to place and tradition might be attested to merely by the fact of migration, a new degree of cultural pride and ethnic consciousness emerged among the Polynesians from the late 1980s that was stimulated and to some degree modelled upon the Maori cultural renaissance. The fact that ethnicity was less compelling even a decade ago is suggested by the lack of specifically Niuean content in Pule's early paintings: these were concerned with Christianity and nuclear testing in the Pacific.

Figure 13.5 John Pule, *Belauan Women* (1988), oil on canvas, 1000 × 1000 mm.

Although the issues are obviously of particular concern to Pacific islanders, the impact of missionaries and of contamination can be lamented more generally: although these early works express a good deal of personal pain, an uninformed viewer would not immediately attribute them to an indigenous artist rather than to an outsider with environmentalist or pacifist sympathies; certainly there was nothing to suggest that they were the work of a Niuean rather than a Samoan or Tongan.

Pule moved on to a series of works that, quite literally, wrote his nationality or cultural identity large.

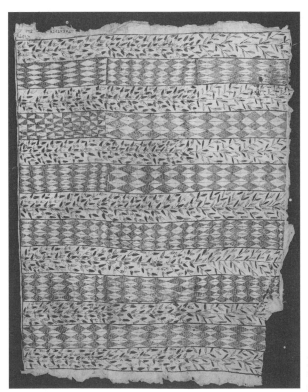

Figure 13.6 John Pule, *Liku* (1990), acrylic on canvas, 1850 × 2593 mm.

Figure 13.7 Niuean barkcloth, late nineteenth century, approx. 7200 × 9500 mm.

These paintings combined the texts of his paintings with strong fields of colour that suggested space and architecture. The intention was to confront viewers with the presence of the Niuean language; the effect was to draw attention to the asymmetries of the international cultural order. If they are to communicate, Niueans and other Polynesian migrants in New Zealand have to speak and write in English, while white New Zealanders and others are unlikely to learn Niuean, either to read these paintings or for any other purpose. Although the works (when unaccompanied by translations) mark rather than overcome the linguistic barrier, they can also be seen to be empowering: the very size of the canvas, and the transposition of writing on to a painted surface that is occupied by words, create a field of meaning and value that is distinguished by its Niuean-ness.

Pule's most recent paintings are inspired by Niuean barkcloth. Before contact, Niuean cloth appears to have been undecorated or decorated with freer, linear patterns, but the example of trade fabric seems to have stimulated a dense elaboration of motifs, that are usually geometric and abstract, and often organised within rectangular fields, though there are also figurative botanical forms.

Pule in no sense slavishly reproduces these designs, but draws more loosely on the structure of quadrilateral divisions, combining grids, triangles and flowing patterns with figurative imagery, sometimes in alternating bands, at other times in a less regular way. The stability of the geometric forms is complemented and unsettled by creatures such as open-mouthed fish and sharks, eels, birds, and by humans crucified, making love and shedding tears.

Figure 13.8 John Pule, *Moe (Sleeping)* (1993), oil on canvas, 2120 × 1820 mm.

Some of this iconography is loosely derived from traditional narratives: the shark for instance is a key symbol in many Polynesian cultures. Usually it counted as a prestige food to be divided between chiefs and common people, and according to kin obligations; sometimes it is a symbol of women's sexuality, and sometimes of rapacious and despotic chiefs. The predatory imagery is certainly present, and gives the paintings great vigour.

Other figures, such as the bird, derive from incidents in his own life that Pule takes as omens, and from his wide reading. His motivation for creating a personal iconography can, however, be linked to his understanding of the migrant predicament, that is typified by an incident in a screenplay he has written recently (currently in production, for New Zealand television) based on the life of a Tuvaluan–Tokelauan migrant. On the boy's first day at school, the teacher is unable to pronounce his name, and suggests that he may be Metusela at home but can be Matthew at school. The imposition of an unfamiliar name typifies the alienation created by the strange urban environment: an alienation that he feels for instance in his lack of recognition of the advertising images that he encounters. Pule takes the view that by creating his own symbols he creates images that he can live by: images that provide almost physical support and render him independent of the alien imagery one necessarily encounters over both short and long journeys.

Despite being personal, the iconography therefore negotiates a predicament that many migrants experience, and aims to redress a paradigmatic migrant condition of dislocation: as Puhia, the father-figure in Pule's novel, declares: 'And here I am, on another man's land' (1992: 65). Importantly, this redress is not accomplished through the acquisition of land, through anything like colonisation, that would make highly contentious claims to indigenous status within Aotearoa. It is arrived at, rather, through the display of imagery that I suggest is characterised by the kind of analogical 'oneness' that Strathern remarked upon in the Melanesian context. The paintings constitute a succession of images that happen to be personal and particular but are also recognisably Niuean and Polynesian. Icons such as the canoes refer to the Polynesian voyages of settlement, and the descent groups that were frequently named after canoes, while references to sea passages, tears, alienation and loss, relate to experiences that are not merely those of the artist but have simultaneously constituted a migrant predicament for a whole community. Like the actors in many ceremonial contexts, this artist deindividuates himself and eclipses an aspect of his own productivity and creativity as he images a collectivity (cf. Strathern 1988: 155).

Pule's paintings create an unusual hybrid pictorial space that is partly abstract, partly cartographic and partly narrative. The cartographic element emerges from his interest in representing Liku (the village in which he was born), and some paintings bear the names of particular tracts of land, imaging houses, paths and graves, and the sites where bones were formerly not buried but exposed. These places might of course have been represented in a more conventional way, but this approach precludes any understanding of the Pacific as a picturesque landscape of reef, coral and thatched houses. The place belongs not to the detached voyeurism of a tourist but to an imagining based on personal attachment to the land and its dead that merges mythology, genealogy, and autobiography. This stretched association with place, characterised by near-dissociation and yearning, is not an idiosyncratic problem of the painter's but a condition virtually constitutive of present migrant identity, most especially for those who were infant or second-generation migrants, whose connections are therefore peculiarly tenuous but who respond now to the discourses of roots and traditions that pervade discussions of identity in New Zealand. This response, in other words, is elicited by the Maori renaissance to the same degree as the new reflections upon Pakeha identity, though in each case the result is not simple mimicry of Maori affirmations but rather a transposition of a problematic of identity to a different location and relation with tradition. The mask-like faces, at once powerful and studded with tears, might be those of the gods that have been abandoned, or those of migrants who realise that they have lost their gods.

Although this loss is deepened by the movement away from land, garden, village and island to the urban space of Auckland, the scope for healing and creativity is not gone; the paintings are rhetorical efforts of the sort referred to earlier, in the sense that they provide material evidence for vitality. Despite their personal particularity they ideally image a kind of energy that is collectively available, that can be tapped by anyone in an analogous position to the painter – in fact any migrant who sees himself or herself as emerging from the experience of loss and dislocation. These unstretched canvases do not feel like remote museum property; they are close, alive and intimate; they make not only loss but survival and growth beyond loss very real. While it is difficult to speculate about precisely how these works affect their viewers, I suggest that Pule's success, and the presence of the paintings in art museums and public venues such as upmarket restaurants, are in fact sources of affirmation for other Polynesian artists, and those Polynesians trying to make their way as professionals (who number among his buyers), if not for the Polynesian community in general, who in general are not engaged in the contemporary art scene by virtue of class location as much as any other factor.

Conclusion

This chapter has been exploratory. The anthropology of art has generally emphasised the differences between 'non-Western' art and 'contemporary' art, but the separation has become less clear. It becomes increasingly important that a new discourse that is not organised by the art world's fetishisation of innovation and avant-gardism becomes available to discuss the range of artistic expressions that are no longer adequately compartmentalised by a Western/non-Western distinction. Rather than elaborate a theory of 'hybrid' art, that could only possess false generality, anthropology might create productive tensions by drawing attention to similarities as well as differences among a variety of artistic endeavours, including those in traditional or neotraditional contexts in New Guinea. The point of the exercise is not to return to universal categories but to use discrepant bodies of material to draw attention to properties and effects of art works that may not otherwise be remarked upon. I have suggested that efforts to image collectivity are conspicuous both in Melanesian art and performance, and in the international contemporary art scene, especially in societies undergoing national anxiety in what might or might not be seen as the colonial aftermath.

Under these conditions, contemporary art is closely engaged with the imaging of nationality and ethnicity. Whether artists are white people, members of indigenous minorities, or migrants, their work is frequently framed, captioned, distributed and sold in relation to their national and ethnic origins. While those who resist this parochialism might insist that good Australian art or American art is simply good art that happens to be produced in Australia or America, marketing and curatorial practices nevertheless frequently elicit collectivities that are no less endangered or provisional than those of Melanesia. Many art works, therefore, at certain phases of their lives are taken as images of a national or ethnic collectivity, and their recognition in these terms often elides other meanings. What might be identified in the recontextualisation of Walters' work – a shift from a personal project to one that is taken to be nationally emblematic – may be situated within Pule's own creativity. While Walters' earlier concerns may have been obscured, Pule empowers his work through images that have personal rather than collective associations, but proceeds to assimilate his biography and location to the generality of migrant experience. Framing in terms of collectivity is therefore in one case imposed upon the work subsequently, and from the outside, and in the other appears more intentional and internal. The new Polynesian migrant culture that Pule's work images and affirms is undergoing consolidation. What its revelation will in turn enable remains to be seen.

References

Anderson, Benedict (1983) *Imagined Communities*, London: Verso.
Barr, Mary (1992) *Headlands: Thinking Through New Zealand Art*, Sydney: Museum of Contemporary Art.
Becker, Howard (1982) *Art Worlds*, Berkeley: University of California Press.

Bourdieu, Pierre (1977) *Outline of a Theory of Practice*, Cambridge: Cambridge University Press.
— and Alain Darbel (1990) *The Love of Art: European Art Museums and Their Public*, Cambridge: Polity.
Bowden, Ross (1983) *Yena: Art and Ceremony in a Sepik Society*, Oxford: Pitt Rivers Museum.
Coote, Jeremy, and Anthony Shelton (eds) (1992) *Anthropology, Art and Aesthetics*, Oxford: Oxford University Press.
Dumont, Louis (1977) *Essays on Individualism*, Chicago: University of Chicago Press.
Dunlop, Ian (1979/1990) *Baruya Muka Archive* (film on video, with accompanying documentation), Sydney: Film Australia.
Faris, James C. (1972) *Nuba Personal Art*, London: Duckworth.
Firth, Raymond (ed.) (1956) *Two Studies of Kinship in London*, London: Athlone Press.
Forge, Anthony (1966) 'Art and Environment in the Sepik', *Proceedings of the Royal Anthropological Institute for 1965*: 23–51.
— (ed.) (1973a) *Art and Primitive Society*, New York: Oxford University Press.
— (1973b) 'Style and Meaning in Sepik Art', in *Art and Primitive Society*, ed. A. Forge, New York: Oxford University Press.
Gell, Alfred (1992) 'The Technology of Enchantment and the Enchantment of Technology', in *Anthropology, Art and Aesthetics*, ed. J. Coote and A. Shelton, Oxford: Oxford University Press.
Giddens, Anthony (1979) *Central Problems in Social Theory*, London: Macmillan.
— (1981) *A Contemporary Critique of Historical Materialism*, London: Macmillan.
Graburn, Nelson (1976) 'Introduction', in *Ethnic and Tourist Arts: Cultural Expressions from the Fourth World*, ed. N. Graburn, Berkeley: University of California Press.
Jopling, Carol (ed.) (1971) *Art and Aesthetics in Primitive Societies*, New York: Dutton.
Layton, Robert (1991) *The Anthropology of Art*, 2nd edn, Cambridge: Cambridge University Press.
Megaw, J.V.S. and Ruth M. Megaw (eds) (1992) *The Heritage of Namatjira: The Watercolourists of Central Australia*, Port Melbourne: Heinemann.
Morphy, Howard (1991) *Ancestral Connections: Art and an Aboriginal System of Knowledge*, Chicago: University of Chicago Press.
— (1994) 'The Anthropology of Art', in *Companion Encyclopaedia of Anthropology: Humanity, Culture and Social Life*, ed. T. Ingold, London: Routledge.
O'Hanlon, Michael (1983) 'Handsome is as Handsome Does: Display and Betrayal in the Waghi', *Oceania* 53: 317–33.
Panoho, Rangihiroa (1992) 'Maori: At the Center, on the Margins', in *Headlands: Thinking through New Zealand Art*, ed. Mary Barr, Sydney: Museum of Contemporary Art.
Phillips, Ruth B. (1993) *Representing Woman: The Sande Society Masks of the Mende*, Los Angeles: Fowler Museum of Cultural History.
Pound, Francis (1985) *Forty Modern New Zealand Paintings*, Auckland: Penguin.
— (1993) 'Walters as Translator', *Midwest* 3: 35–9.
— (1994) *The Space Between: Maori/Pakeha interactions in New Zealand art*, Auckland: Workshop Press.
Pule, John (1992) *The Shark that Ate the Sun*, Auckland: Penguin.
Said, Edward (1991) *Musical Elaborations*, New York: Columbia University Press.
Schneider, David (1968) *American Kinship: A Cultural Account*, New York: Prentice Hall.
Strathern, Andrew, and Marilyn Strathern (1971) *Self-decoration in Mount Hagen*, London: Duckworth.
Strathern, Marilyn (1979) 'The Self in Self-decoration', *Oceania* 49: 241–57.
— (1988) *The Gender of the Gift: Problems about Society and Problems about Women in Melanesia*, Berkeley: University of California Press.
— (1990) 'Artifacts of History: Events and the Interpretation of Images', in *Culture and History in the Pacific*, ed. Jukka Siikala, Helsinki: Finnish Anthropological Society.

Thomas, Nicholas (1994) *Colonialism's Culture: Anthropology, Travel and Government*, Cambridge: Polity Press and Princeton, NJ: Princeton University Press.

— (1995a) 'A Second Reflection: Presence and Opposition in Maori Art', *Journal of the Royal Anthropological Institute* (ns) 1: 23–46.

— (1995b) 'Kiss the Baby Goodbye: *Kowhaiwhai* and Aesthetics in Aotearoa New Zealand', *Critical Inquiry* 22: 90–121.

Tuzin, Donald F. (1980) *The Voice of the Tambaran: Truth and Illusion in Ilahita Arapesh Religion*, Berkeley: University of California Press.

Weiner, James F. (1994) 'Myth and Metaphor', in *Companion Encyclopaedia of Anthropology: Humanity, Culture and Social Life*, ed. T. Ingold, London: Routledge.

14

The visual in anthropology

David MacDougall

The visual as metaphor

Anthropology has had no lack of interest in the visual; its problem has always been what to do with it. This problem is historically related to another anthropological problem: what to do with the person – the sentient, thinking being who belongs to a culture but, from the anthropologist's point of view, can often reconstitute only a very small part of it. As anthropology developed from an armchair discipline to a study of actual communities, it seemed somehow strange that the person, the object of the anthropologist's attention, should remain largely invisible to the anthropological audience. An early remedy, as we know, was to bring exotic people to museums, lectures and such popular venues as world fairs and colonial expositions. In a sense this gave a gloss of scientific respectability to the existing practice of displaying indigenous people as curiosities at circuses and other entertainments (Corbey 1993; Davis 1993; Hinsley 1991; Poignant 1992; Street 1992). Ishi, the last of the Yahi, spent his final years at the University of California's Museum of Anthropology as Kroeber's informant and a kind of living exhibit. Franz Boas helped organise the Anthropological Hall at the World's Columbian Exposition of 1893 in Chicago, where fourteen Kwakiutl were displayed (Hinsley 1991: 348–50). Senegalese swam in the fountains of Paris during the Exposition Ethnographique de l'Afrique Occidentale of 1895 (Demeny 1896).

This provided visibility, but the anthropologist couldn't finally put a Wolof potter or Trobriand gardener into an ethnological monograph. A better alternative to importing people was to put photographs of them in the monograph and show films of them at lectures, as Sir Walter Baldwin Spencer did with his films of the Aranda at Melbourne Town Hall in 1902. 'What I would like to show would be the real native', he wrote to his friend Lorimer Fison (Cantrill and Cantrill 1982: 37), but by this time he meant only uncensored photographs of naked men and women. In any case, as anthropologists had discovered earlier, the body in question, removed from its usual surroundings, was often singularly

THE PYGMIES.

BORANE (CHIEF).
KUARKE (PRINCESS).   MONGONGA.   MAFUTIMINGA.   MATUKA.
ROTARY PHOTO. E.C.   AMURIAPE.
                                    COPYRIGHT
                                    W. & D. DOWNEY,
                                    LONDON, R.W.

Figure 14.1 Postcard sent on 26
October 1905 showing a group of
Batwa brought to London and
exhibited at the Hippodrome
Theatre. The handwritten message
on the reverse notes: 'These
creatures were here last week.'

uncommunicative about culture. The anthropological 'body' in fact
included much more, extending outwards from the person to include
the social group, the physical setting, the fields and pastures, the
dwellings, implements and other possessions. Photographs and artefacts helped fill this gap and took some of the pressure off the living person, who could now be assumed to exist at the fieldwork site.

If anything, the absence of the person strengthened the importance of
the visual, which through photographs, films and museum artefacts
began to replace it. But the problem remained that there was something
disquieting about visual images. They appeared to show everything, and
yet, like the physical body, remained annoyingly mute. The visual world
was like the husk you removed to get at the conceptual and verbal worlds
inside, but having done so you couldn't in good conscience throw it
away. Visible objects, having exerted great fascination as the products
and indicators of culture, but failing as expositors of it, began to acquire
a new function (in museums) as metaphors for anthropology. And as
metaphor, the visual flourished.

Figure 14.2 (*above*) Case of Fijian ivory ornaments, arranged by Baron Anatole von Hügel in *c.* 1910 at the Cambridge University Museum of Archaeology and Anthropology.

Figure 14.3 American Museum of Natural History: view of North Pacific Hall, looking north, 1910.

Victorian photographs of hunting expeditions often displayed tigers and antelopes in decorative heaps, the artifice enhancing the prestige of the hunter. Early museum exhibits displayed their artefacts in similarly symmetrical and intricate patterns of positive and negative space. This created an ornamental effect not unlike the bones of the dead stuck in the plaster of Neapolitan catacombs. At the Pitt Rivers Museum in Oxford some objects were organised solely by shape, although here a functional or evolutionary relationship was sometimes suggested. The aesthetic merits of individual artefacts, and their evidence of ingenuity and workmanship, became part of a larger aesthetic and spiritual design. The great halls of the Musée de l'Homme and the American Museum of Natural History communicated a religious aura of science celebrating mankind, much as palaeolithic caves once celebrated the animal world. Here the visual stood in for an absent humanity, as church architecture stood in for the invisibility of God.

278

For a general public imbued with ideas of social Darwinism, the visual appearance of exotic peoples was the most obvious way of placing them on a scale between civilised man and animal. Pictures became a substitute for more abstract or esoteric knowledge, which in any case was now beginning to contradict evolutionary theory ('primitive' languages, for example, were now recognised as highly complex). Features such as nakedness and the use of animal products (feathers, skin, hair and bones), communicated by means of photographs and visible artefacts in museums and magazine illustrations, became symbolic indicators of how close people were to nature.

These indicators were turned back upon anthropology in books (for example, H. Rider Haggard's *King Solomon's Mines* [1885]) and early films, as popular culture created its own literary and theatrical savages. In the first decade of the twentieth century the stereograph and picture postcard fads were reaching their peak. The Keystone *Stereoscopic Encyclopedia* of 1906, a guide to its first boxed set of 600 'views', contains 154 references to 'racial geography, peoples of all lands'. By 1907 the H.C. White company was capable of producing 15,000 stereo view cards per day (Darrah 1977: 50–51). In 1909–10 866 million picture postcards were posted in Great Britain alone (Peterson 1985: 166). A prominent postcard genre was photography of indigenous people in native dress (or nakedness), many, such as those produced by J. Audema in the French Congo, borrowing from the photographic systems of T.H. Huxley, John Lamprey and other scientists a self-consciously 'anthropometric' style. The dioramas of museums, usually showing animals but sometimes including models of 'primitives', imitated the framing of photographs and aspired to the *trompe-l'oeil* of stereoscopic views.

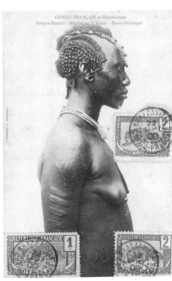

Figure 14.4 The 'anthropometric' style in postcards, French Congo, *c.* 1905.

(a) (*left*) 'Jeunes Diolas';
(b) 'Femme Banziri – Région de la Kotto – Haut-Oubangui'.

279

As anthropology developed in the colonial context, the visual had further primacy as a way of organising society by types. Like the collecting of artefacts and botanical samples, photography provided a new way of creating human models, against which further examples could be compared and classified (Edwards 1992: 7). For administrative purposes it was often more important to identify someone as a member of a group than to know much about the group itself. Visual clues, as Berreman (1972: 575–7) notes, help people identify members of other groups, but (at least in the Indian context) people 'are more knowledgeable about those superior to themselves in status and power than about those inferior' (p. 573). In the latter case, visible signs may be more important in defining people in relation to oneself than in relation to each other. The visible emphasises what one is not. For the colonisers as well as for the colonised, a concept of purity and impurity was an underlying principle of social segmentation. Manipulating human categories reinforced the colonisers' sense of difference as well as their sense of power. In India, the passion for anthropometry and photographic cataloguing of ethnic and occupational types – encouraged according to Pinney (1990a: 261) by India's extraordinary heterogeneity – was nevertheless no more than a subset of the larger anthropological and imperial project of typing the

Figure 14.5a (*left*) 'Kota Men. Neelgerry Hills.' Plate 435 from Watson and Kaye's *The People of India*, 1868–75.

Figure 14.5b Postcard sent 18 March 1910: 'Types malgaches – Guerrier Tanosy' (photograph: Richard, *c*. 1905).

whole world. Such forms of measurement may have paid meagre returns in terms of actual knowledge but they had the satisfying look of knowledge. Popular culture mimicked this knowledge: picture postcards from around the world bore such captions as 'Type indigène', 'Guerrier Tanosy' and 'A typical well-proportioned Zulu woman'.

Natural science, which used illustrations extensively in compiling its taxonomies, provided an early impetus for anthropology to study the visual aspects of culture. Anthropology was inspired by zoology, botany and geology to describe the world visually, and there was a corresponding emphasis upon those aspects of culture that could be drawn or photographed. Travellers, as well, considered it incumbent upon them to record ethnographic information. Nineteenth-century ethnographies and books of exploration are filled with line drawings of implements, body decorations, costumes, jewellery and architectural details.

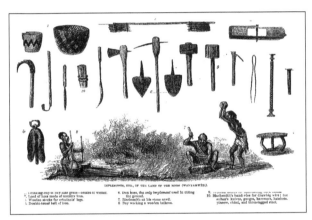

Figure 14.6 'Implements, etc., of the Land of the Moon (Wanyamwézi)'. Illustration from Speke's *Journal of the Discovery of the Source of the Nile,* 1864.

Photographs were a prominent feature of ethnographies until the 1930s but become progressively scarcer in later works. Hattersley's *The Baganda at Home* (1908), for example, contains eighty photographs. Junod's *The Life of a South African Tribe* (1912) contains 112 illustrations, most of them photographs. Rattray's *Ashanti* (1923) contains 143. But by 1965, an ethnography such as Spencer's *The Samburu* contained only four, and his *The Maasai of Matapato* of 1988 none at all. Some of the possible reasons for this decline have been summarised by Pinney (1992: 81–2), but the decline itself has perhaps masked the fact that visual anthropology – as an anthropology of the visual – appeared early and has a long heritage. If visual anthropology later became less focused on content than on method (ethnographic filmmaking and photography), as Morphy and Banks note in this volume (chapter 1), it is perhaps partly because such interests were soon hived off into studies of primitive art, technology and folklore.

But there were other reasons too. Grimshaw (chapter 2, this volume) argues that the end of the nineteenth century ushered in a shift in attitudes towards the visual in which the assumed coherence and superiority of European civilisation's vision of the world was finally shattered by the First World War. While this shift may have changed the role of the visual in anthropology, it did not immediately diminish it. The panoptic view of humanity was gradually replaced by a notion that the life of any people could be expressive *of itself* through images, as in the early films of Lumière and of the 1898 Cambridge Anthropological Expedition to the Torres Strait. These films emphasised simple 'showing' over 'telling' (Grimshaw: p. 41). Thus at this time seeing was apparently still construed as a way of knowing, as it had been earlier in the century. A demonstration of fire-making (such as that in the Cambridge Torres Strait footage) could act as a template for the process, allowing it to be reproduced, rather like following an instruction manual. Visual recording 'saved' the event in some reified sense, a view that was still being voiced by Margaret Mead (1975: 4) when she wrote of behaviour 'caught and preserved' by film 'for centuries'. Interpretation could be provided later; the crucial thing was to salvage the data.

Figure 14.7 Frame from A.C. Haddon's Torres Strait footage: 'Murray Island: fire-making'.

Visible culture and visual media

The early interest in visual anthropology, which began with such enthusiasm, gradually faded into perplexity. Félix-Louis Regnault's dream of an ethnographic film museum (Rouch 1975: 85) and A.C. Haddon's view of the film camera as 'an indispensable piece of anthropological apparatus' have been replaced in recent years by Kirsten Hastrup's view that, compared to anthropological writing, film is 'thin' description (1992: 15) and Maurice Bloch's belief that anthropologists who dedicate much time to film have 'lost confidence in their own ideas' (Houtman 1988: 20).

There are of course alternative views, but the history of visual anthropology suggests that most anthropologists have never known quite what to do with the visual. Vast archives of record footage remain unseen and unused. Sophisticated analysts of other societies profess ignorance and alarm when it comes to analysing the structure of an ethnographic film. To anthropology the visual often seems uncommunicative and yet somehow insatiable. Like the tar-baby, it never says anything, but there is always something more to be said about *it*. Words, on the other hand, have little more to say once you have written them.

Despite such sentiments, activities in visual anthropology are once again increasing, filling some of the roles once promised for it. But here we must make a key distinction, also made by Morphy and Banks in the introductory chapter to this volume. What activities are encompassed by visual anthropology? There is, on the one hand, the visual anthropology that studies visible cultural forms. On the other is the visual anthropology that uses the visual media to describe and analyse culture. In Sol Worth's terms, this is the difference between 'using a medium and studying how a medium is used' (1981: 190). The two will sometimes overlap – the study of visible systems sometimes demands visual communication – but the first form is essentially an extension of traditional anthropological concerns into new subject areas. The second proposes a much more radical break with anthropological modes of discourse.

As an anthropology of visible cultural forms, 'visual anthropology' is now broadening its scope in two ways. It is expanding to embrace indigenous media production as a parallel strand of cultural representation; and amongst academic anthropologists it is beginning to pay attention to a range of cultural forms that have received only patchy anthropological attention before: historical photographs, news photography, sports events, comic books, postcards, stereographs, body decoration, indigenous painting, 'tourist art', home movies, family snapshots, itinerant theatre, vernacular architecture, children's drawings, political regalia, court ceremony, gesture and facial expression (although these have a longer history of study), advertising, costume and personal adornment, industrial design, and so on – in short, any of the expressive systems of human society that communicate meanings partially or primarily by visual means. We may attribute part of this broadened view of culture to Barthes' exploration of 'mythologies' in the 1950s, which revealed a complex world of hidden sign-systems. Like those earlier anthropological findings in remote cultures that stimulated a cultural critique of our own, the discovery of new meaning systems in Western society has led to a re-examination of visual systems in what were once called 'traditional' societies, particularly in their historical engagement with the West.

Indigenous media production presents a more complex case, for it is perceived by anthropologists within two different frames of reference: first, as an evolving cultural form like many others (e.g. Australian

Aboriginal acrylic painting), and second, but more importantly, as a self-conscious expression of political and cultural identity, directed in part at countering representations by others. For indigenous people, the visual media can serve as an instrument of political action (as among the Kayapo), cultural reintegration and revival (as among the Inuit) or as a corrective to stereotyping, misrepresentation and denigration (as among many Native American groups).

Figure 14.8 Indigenous media production in Brazil.

The model of visual anthropology that indigenous media implicitly opposes is the canonical ethnographic film, framed in intercultural terms – a film made by one cultural group (usually Euro-American) attempting to describe another (usually of the Third or Fourth World). Such a definition increasingly applies to ethnographic films made *within* Western society, since the subjects are almost always from a class or subculture different from that of the filmmakers. However, Ginsburg has argued that much indigenous media production has a broader educative purpose, both within and outside an indigenous community. As a result there is a crossing of cultural boundaries between subjects and potential audiences as well as a project of mediating 'ruptures of time and history' in the communities themselves (Ginsburg 1991: 102–5). This provides some common ground between indigenous media and ethnographic filmmaking.

Further arguments have been put forward for considering indigenous media 'in relation to a broader range of media engaged in representing culture' (Ginsburg 1994: 6), in part because indigenous media production itself is rapidly changing. Its producers are increasingly addressing international audiences and situating themselves at the cultural crossroads, where there is a constant flux and interpenetration of cultural forces. Indigenous media is also entering the mass media, and vice versa. The indigenous person, along with the ethnic and diaspora person, is no longer contained within a social enclave, nor necessarily considers himself or herself a bonded representative of a cultural and political group.

All these factors place indigenous media producers and artists in an intercultural and intertextual position. Their work is both a product of, and commentary on, contesting cultural identities. Ginsburg further suggests that this expansion has implications both for what is represented and how it affects representation. It creates a 'parallax effect' which, by displacing the traditional view of ethnographic film, may in the end invigorate it (1994: 14). Nichols, writing in a similar vein, is perhaps not merely being ironical when he implies that as ethnographic filmmakers are becoming increasingly marginalised, they would do well to identify more closely with other marginalised peoples (1991).

As anthropologists discover new subjects – either in established visual cultural forms or in evolving uses of the visual media – they may well redefine the terrain of anthropology. As indigenous groups take greater control of the visual media they may well alter traditional anthropological representations of themselves. But in neither of these cases does visual anthropology pose a fundamental epistemological challenge to what has been called 'the anthropological project'. They merely make anthropology more sensitive to the politics and possibilities of visual representation. The more substantive challenge to anthropological thought comes not simply from broadening its purview but from its entering into communicative systems different from the 'anthropology of words'. In this, it revives the historical question of what to do with the visual.

The few steps that have been taken in this direction have tended to be isolated and idiosyncratic, and as is often the case in a developing discipline, the pioneers have often been outsiders (such as Flaherty and Marshall) or rebels (such as Bateson and Rouch). Jay Ruby's comment – 'if non-anthropologists can produce credible ethnographic films then why should anyone interested in producing films about culture bother being trained as an ethnographer?' (1994: 168) – reflects a widespread view that innovators must also satisfy the conservative mainstream. Even when new directions have been opened up by formally trained anthropologists, the results are often misconstrued. As Paul Stoller notes, 'Jean Rouch is well known for his technical innovations in film but not for the contributions his films make to theories of ethnographic representation' (1992: 204). For others, Rouch's films are acceptable only because their ethnographic content exists in addition to the different *kind* of anthropological understanding they make possible cinematically. This is perhaps to be expected, since most works of visual anthropology aim at far less. Nor is it likely that visual anthropology will be worthy of serious consideration *as anthropology* so long as it confines itself to illustrative uses of film, or tries to translate anthropological concepts into images, or grafts models of television journalism on to anthropological subjects. All

The visual in anthropology

285

of these forms remain wedded to earlier forms. None commits itself to different ways of speaking.

It seems clear that visual anthropology now urgently needs to consolidate itself within a theoretical framework that reassesses anthropological objectives. A fuller use of the properties of the visual media will entail significant additions to how anthropologists define their ways of knowing, which is to say that categories of anthropological knowledge will have to be seriously rethought, both in relation to science and to the representational systems of film, video and photography. The potential of ethnographic film can no longer be thought of simply as a form of filmic ethnography, as Ruby has sometimes defined it (1975; 1989: 9).

The visual media make use of principles of implication, visual resonance, identification and shifting perspective that differ radically from the principles of most anthropological writing. They involve the viewer in heuristic processes and meaning-creation quite different from verbal statement, linkage, theory-formation and speculation. As Gilbert Lewis has noted, they also have quite different ways of placing stress and contextualising detail. 'The painter can elaborate details without sacrificing the general effect. The picture may still retain its unity and simplicity in spite of the mass of details. You see it as a whole. But when a passion for details is displayed in literature the effect is quite different. After a long academic tradition of learning from the printed page, the ways in which we can represent the lives of others are changing' (1986: 414–15). Above all, the visual media allow us to construct knowledge not by 'description' (to borrow Bertrand Russell's terms) but by a form of 'acquaintance' (1912: 46–59).

Figure 14.9 Frame from *To Live with Herds*, filmed 1968.

Although there is a crucial difference between using and studying the use of the visual, there is an important link between them. The study of collective visual representations itself generates new questions about how anthropology can communicate about them. Do visual systems require certain forms of visual analysis and communication? Do they suggest distinctive patterns of understanding? A greater awareness of visual systems directs our attention towards a range of cultural domains that have long remained at the margins of anthropology, not least because they are linked to visual sign systems more familiar to other disciplines, such as art history. Visual anthropology may offer different ways of understanding, but also different things to understand.

Enlarging anthropology

In recent years there has been mounting anthropological interest in emotion, time, the body, the senses, gender and individual identity. Although the importance of many of these areas of study was recognised long ago, they have often been relegated to the disciplines of psychology, philosophy, medicine, linguistics and history. One of the difficulties of exploring and communicating understandings about them has been in finding a language metaphorically and experientially close to them. One of the reasons for the historical primacy of the visual has been its capacity for metaphor and synaesthesia. Much that can be 'said' about these matters may best be said in the visual media.

Use of the visual media for this purpose may not necessarily require the development of a specialised visual language ('a framework of anthropological visual symbolic forms which are conventionalised into a code or argot'), as Jay Ruby argued (1975: 104–11), but (as he also argued) it does require a shift away from making films *about* anthropology to making anthropological films (1975: 109). This, however, is likely to produce changes in what has been considered anthropological, as well as in how film (or photography, or video) is used. The subject matter may no longer lend itself to objectified scientific description, and visual anthropology may no longer fulfil conventional criteria for creating data,

Figure 14.10 From *Jaguar* (Jean Rouch), filmed 1954, released 1967.

articulating theory or describing methodology. But rather than rejecting existing documentary and fictional forms outright, visual anthropology is more likely to adapt them or use them in new combinations. Existing forms provide a common basis of cultural experience and points of reference between filmmaker and viewer, however much any given work may depart from them – just as written anthropology depends upon the conventions of expository and scientific writing developed over several centuries before anthropology emerged as a discipline. As Stoller comments, 'radically empirical' visual anthropologists such as Rouch will 'mix their genres, sometimes employing narrative style, sometimes employing plain style, sometimes blurring the lines between fact and fiction' (1992: 217).

Anthropological writing in recent years demonstrates a shift towards new cultural categories and concepts of knowledge. This is evident in the experimental ethnographies described by Marcus and Cushman (1982) and in the revision of anthropological assumptions about the meaning of fundamental institutions such as ritual (Bloch 1974; Lewis 1980; Jackson 1989; Piault 1989). It is also evident in theoretical writing, which has begun to make use of a lexicon newly charged with bodily experience. The language of postmodern anthropology is filled with such words as 'congeal', 'slippage' and 'rupture'. At the limit such writing suffers the consequences of its own innovation and self-absorption, leading its readers into obscurity. It may also demand of readers a more active and interpretive style of engagement. But essentially it reveals dissatisfaction with earlier models and a straining at the boundaries of anthropological understanding – a need to pass beyond received conceptions of representation to what Tyler (1987: 199–213) has called 'evocation' and Barthes has called 'figuration' (1975: 55–7). This is the experiential field that film and other visual media at least offer anthropology.

Here it is necessary to insist that visual anthropology is not about the visual *per se* but about a range of culturally inflected relationships enmeshed and encoded in the visual. Just as anthropology can read some of these in the visual, so too it can use the visual to construct works that give a richer sense of how culture permeates and patterns social experience. These works may bring into play familiar ways of engaging with visual media, such as realist strategies of narrative identification and description, or less familiar forms of juxtaposition and montage that address the viewer on multiple levels. They may make greater demands on hermeneutic processes than anthropological audiences are used to exercising, and ways of making cultural representations that are no longer simply declarative.

If we consider for a moment only the world of visual symbols, these new works may attempt to construct sets of relationships that resemble those of poetry in the verbal domain, since such cultural complexes must be grasped as totalities rather than piecemeal. If we consider the visual as offering pathways to the other senses and to social experience more generally, then what may be required of the viewer will often combine psychological or kinaesthetic responses with interpretive ones. For example, a work that invites us to enter into a visual narrative as a participant may also require us to place that experience within the context of how the experience has been created for us, and what indications there are of the visual anthropologist's own engagement with the situation at the time. The anthropologist may never be able to articulate this fully outside the matrix of the work itself.

Sometimes an anthropological understanding may be afforded chiefly through metaphor. Mimesis alone is rarely enough, because purely experiential responses across cultural boundaries can be profoundly misleading. It is unlikely, for example, that the viewer of a film will grasp the meaning of a ritual that has over the years been 'inscribed in [the] very bodies' of the participants, as Christina Toren puts it (1993: 464). Metaphor in film (as in life) can be the concretising of the self and experience in other things, not as simile or analogy, but as bodily extension. As Michael Jackson argues, 'To emphasise the psychological or social aspects of metaphor construction and use is unhelpful as long as it implies a dualistic conception of human behaviour. . . . My argument is that metaphor must be apprehended [as] . . . a true interdependency of mind and body, Self and World' (1989: 142). This collapsing of meaning is taken for granted in idioms of spoken language. It can be an even more powerful form of construction in visual media, as is clear in such 'documentary' films as Wright's *Song of Ceylon* or Franju's *Le Sang des bêtes* and the work of fiction filmmakers such as Antonioni. Indeed in film metaphor is almost always present, in the sense that environments and images of objects are persistently associated with feelings, actions and states of mind.

No doubt part of the attraction of the visual to early anthropology lay in its very contradictions – its promise of more than it delivered. In this respect, the visual (whether as museum exhibit, photograph or film) acted as it has in other contexts, promising commodities (as in advertising) or sexual fulfilment (as in pornography) but holding these in an unconsummated suspension. Pinney (following Christian Metz) has observed that the stillness and suspension of the photograph resemble 'the glance in childhood which fixes the fetish' (1990b: 43). What was paradoxical about visual imagery, as against written text, was its apparent plenitude, which flooded the observer with concreteness and detail, yet revealed little in the absence of a surrounding discourse. Just so, the advertised product speaks only within a cultural discourse of fashion and desire, the pornographic image within a narrative of improvised fantasy.

To the anthropologist who knew the cultural context, the visual image spoke volumes, but that power was also a source of danger. An uncaptioned photograph was full of undirected potential. Unlike written

289

descriptions, which always provided some sort of context, a photograph could be supplied with any sort of meaning by the viewer – from competing scientific discourses, or unwelcome popular ones such as racism. It all too easily escaped from professional control. Similar fears are heard today from anthropologists who deem certain films to be dangerous to the public (or their subjects) through what they omit to show or to say. There is a moral imperative against allowing viewers to jump to the wrong conclusions.

The declining use of photographs in monographs may well be put down to this cause, in concert with a shift away from evolutionary anthropology's omnivorous appetite for detail towards more holistic descriptions of cultures. The same threat of undisciplined interpretation may have been responsible for ethnographic films of the same period developing primarily into illustrated lectures, in which a text provided the supporting framework for the images. If anthropologists had felt confident enough to contextualise the contents of their films by any other means, they might well have done so, but this was often regarded with suspicion as 'art'. Thus we see the visual in anthropology kept in safe bounds, like a bomb with the detonator removed.

There are certain emblematic moments in the history of visual anthropology: the transition from chronophotography to cinema in 1895, the simultaneous appearance in 1922 of Flaherty's *Nanook of the North* and Malinowski's *Argonauts of the Western Pacific*, the day in the 1950s (perhaps apocryphal) when Jean Rouch lost his tripod in the Niger. Another such moment was the appearance in 1942 of Gregory Bateson and Margaret Mead's book *Balinese Character* – or rather, it might have been. It is interesting to speculate whether much that is happening now in visual anthropology might not have happened sooner if the famous Bateson–Mead project had taken a different turn. As it was, this innovative project, which had the potential to revolutionise visual anthropology, fell short of doing so. It neither legitimised visual research methods in anthropology nor turned film and photography into a channel of anthropological discourse and argumentation.

The reasons for this conclusion, and even its validity, deserve fuller examination than is possible here, but there are some provocative clues. The edited films that emerged from the project in the 1950s are unrelentingly didactic, with Mead's voice constantly guiding us and, at one point, telling us 'You will have to watch very carefully to follow any of this at all' (Bateson and Mead 1952). In part, this approach can be explained by American 'educational film' conventions of the time; but by asking viewers to find what they are told they will find, it may also indicate an intellectual predisposition of the research itself. In support of this is the account given by Bateson which suggests that the photographs were subordinated to, and seen very much in the context of Margaret Mead's prior written interpretations of the events (Bateson and Mead

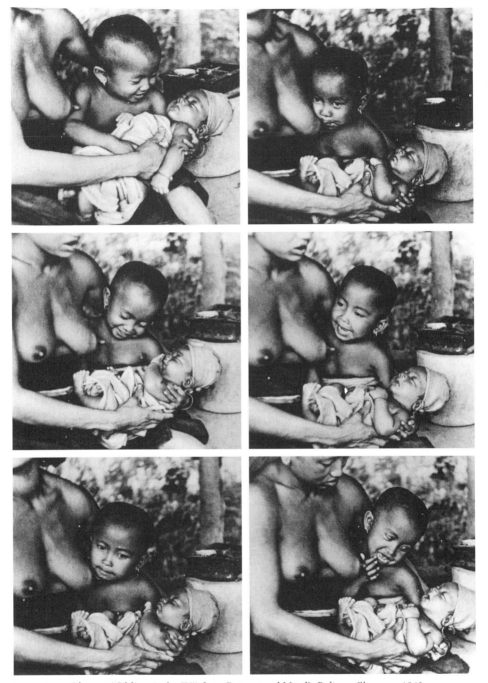

Figure 14.11 Plate 72 ('Sibling rivalry IV') from Bateson and Mead's *Balinese Character*, 1942.

1942: 49–50). A conversation between Bateson and Mead in the 1970s reveals a fundamental split in their objectives, indicating Bateson had wanted to conduct the enquiry by means of filming, but Mead had wanted to film first and analyse later (1977). One can imagine Bateson applying the exploratory approach of *Naven* (1936) to a film or photographic project, but not in this collaborative context. *Balinese Character* finally falls between two divergent conceptions of photography – one an extension of the mind, the other an extension of the eye.

> *Mead* [The] effort was to hold the camera steady enough long enough to get a sequence of behavior.
> *Bateson* To find out what's happening, yes.
> *Mead* When you're jumping around taking pictures . . .
> *Bateson* Nobody's talking about that, Margaret, for God's sake.
> *Mead* Well.
> *Bateson* I'm talking about having control of a camera. You're talking about putting a dead camera on top of a bloody tripod. It sees nothing.
> *Mead* Well, I think it sees a great deal. I've [tried to work] with these pictures taken by artists, and really good ones . . .
> *Bateson* I'm sorry I said artists; all I meant was artists. I mean, artists is not a term of abuse in my vocabulary.
> *Mead* It isn't in mine either, but I . . .
> *Bateson* Well, in this conversation, it's become one.
>
> (Bateson and Mead 1977: 79)

Many anthropologists still feel caught between the possibility of conceptual advances from visual anthropology and the more conservative paradigms of a positivist scientific tradition. There is continuing interest in studying such virtually untapped archival resources as the Bateson–Mead corpus and in using visual media for education. Both of these objectives are enhanced by world networking and the possibilities of multimedia. What remains unresolved is whether the visual can attain a more productive role in anthropology as a medium of enquiry and discourse.

The epistemological and methodological implications of such a shift are substantial. They involve putting in temporary suspension anthropology's dominant orientation as a discipline of words and rethinking certain categories of anthropological knowledge in the light of understandings that may be accessible only by non-verbal means. In exchange, visual anthropology offers the possibility of new pathways to anthropological knowledge, as in understanding the transmission of culture and in newly identified areas of cultural construction. Foremost is the need to build an intellectual foundation for visual anthropology by enabling a shift from word-and-sentence-based anthropological thought to image-and-sequence-based anthropological thought. Visual anthropology can never be either a copy of written anthropology or a substitute for it. For that very reason it must develop alternative objectives and methodologies that will benefit anthropology as a whole.

Visual anthropologists themselves have been notoriously reluctant to explain the anthropological value of their work, partly because they feel no need to justify it, but also because it is very difficult to justify it in the usual anthropological terms. Rouch's films fail miserably as demonstrations of 'scientific method', and if they theorise about their subjects, the theories cannot be reduced to a verbal précis. On the other hand, some anthropologists conceive of visual anthropology in such highly proscriptive and ideal terms as effectively to define it out of existence. Existing work is either tipped into the rubbish bin of naïve science (untheorised records) or naïve amateurism (untheorised impressions). Other visual works that might be considered as anthropology are said merely to resemble it, through a kind of mimicry.

But visual anthropology is not going to appear miraculously some day in the future. It is being created now, even if we do not always recognise it. There is already a substantial body of visual work that deserves to be examined more closely for what it has achieved. Ákos Östör made this point in 1990 when he wrote: 'It is time to lay aside the old debate about visual anthropology failing or succeeding in the quest for full-fledged disciplinary status, or about film finally becoming worthy of scientific anthropological inquiry. It is time to begin analysing and interpreting films' (1990: 722). Instead of campaigning for the creation of a mature visual anthropology, with its anthropological principles all in place, we would be wise to look at the principles that emerge when fieldworkers actually try to rethink anthropology through use of a visual medium. This may lead in directions we would never have predicted from the comparative safety of theory.

References

Barthes, Roland (1975) *The Pleasure of the Text*, trans. Richard Miller, New York: Hill & Wang.

Bateson, Gregory (1936) *Naven*, Cambridge: Cambridge University Press.

Bateson, Gregory and Margaret Mead (1942) *Balinese Character: a Photographic Analysis*, New York Academy of Sciences, Special Publications 2, New York: New York Academy of Sciences.

— (1952) *Childhood Rivalry in Bali and New Guinea*, (film) character formation in different cultures series, 17 mins.

— (1977) 'Margaret Mead and Gregory Bateson on the Use of the Camera in Anthropology', *Studies in the Anthropology of Visual Communication* 4(2): 78–80.

Berreman, Gerald D. (1972) 'Social Categories and Social Interaction in Urban India', *American Anthropologist* 74 (3): 567–86.

Bloch, Maurice (1974) 'Symbols, Song, Dance and Features of Articulation: Or is Religion an Extreme Form of Traditional Authority?' *Archives Européenes de sociologie* 15: 55–81.

Cantrill, Arthur and Corinne Cantrill (1982) 'The 1901 Cinematography of Walter Baldwin Spencer', *Cantrill's Filmnotes* 37/38: 27–42.

Corbey, Raymond (1993) 'Ethnographic Showcases, 1870–1930', *Cultural Anthropology* 8 (3): 338–69.

Darrah, William C. (1977) *The World of Stereographs*, Gettysburg: W.C. Darrah.

Davis, Janet (1993) 'Spectacles of South Asia at the American Circus, 1890–1940', *Visual Anthropology* 6 (2): 121–38.

Demeny, Georges (1896) *A Cinema Programme of 1896* (film), British Film Institute, 10 mins.

Edwards, Elizabeth (1992) 'Introduction', in *Anthropology and Photography* ed. Elizabeth Edwards 3–17, New Haven/London: Yale University Press.

Flaherty, Robert (1922) *Nanook of the North* (film), Revillon Frères, 70 mins.

Franju, Georges (1949) *Le Sang des bêtes* (film), Forces et Voix de la France, 22 mins.

Ginsburg, Faye (1991) 'Indigenous Media: Faustian Contract or Global Village?' *Cultural Anthropology* 6 (1): 92–112.

— (1994) 'Culture/Media: A (Mild) Polemic', *Anthropology Today* 10 (2): 5–15.

Hastrup, Kirsten (1992) 'Anthropological Visions: Some Notes on Visual and Textual Authority', in *Film as Ethnography*, ed. Peter Ian Crawford and David Turton 8–25, Manchester: Manchester University Press.

Hattersley, C.W. (1908) *The Baganda at Home*, London: The Religious Tract Society.

Hinsley, Curtis M. (1991) 'The World as Marketplace: Commodification of the Exotic at the World's Columbian Exposition, Chicago, 1893', in *Exhibiting Cultures*, ed. Ivan Karp and Steven D. Lavine 343–65, Washington: Smithsonian Institution Press.

Houtman, Gustaaf (1988) Interview with Maurice Bloch, *Anthropology Today* 4 (1): 18–21.

Jackson, Michael (1989) *Paths Towards a Clearing*, Bloomington: Indiana University Press.

Junod, Henri A. (1912) *The Life of a South African Tribe*, Neuchâtel: Imprimerie Attinger Frères.

Lewis, Gilbert (1980) *Day of Shining Red*, Cambridge: Cambridge University Press.

— (1986) 'The Look of Magic', *Man* (n.s.) 21 (3): 414–35.

MacDougall, David (1972) *To Live with Herds* (film), 70 min.

Malinowski, Bronislaw (1922) *Argonauts of the Western Pacific*, London: Routledge and Kegan Paul.

Marcus, George E. and Dick Cushman (1982) 'Ethnographies as Texts', *Annual Review of Anthropology* 11: 25–69.

Mead, Margaret (1975) 'Visual Anthropology in a Discipline of Words', in *Principles of Visual Anthropology*, ed. Paul Hockings 3–10, The Hague: Mouton.

Nichols, Bill (1991) 'The Ethnographer's Tale', *Visual Anthropology Review* 7 (2): 31–47.

Östör, Ákos (1990) 'Whither Ethnographic Film?' *American Anthropologist* 92 (3): 715–22.

Peterson, Nicolas (1985) 'The Popular Image', in *Seeing the First Australians*, ed. Ian Donaldson and Tamsin Donaldson 164–80, Sydney: George Allen & Unwin.

Piault, Marc (1989) 'Ritual: A Way Out of Eternity', paper presented at 'Film and Representations of Culture' Conference, Humanities Research Centre, Australian National University, Canberra.

Pinney, Christopher (1990a) 'Classification and Fantasy in the Photographic Construction of Caste and Tribe', *Visual Anthropology* 3 (2–3): 259–88.

— (1990b) 'The Quick and the Dead: Images, Time and Truth', *Visual Anthropology Review* 6 (2): 42–54.

— (1992) 'The Parallel Histories of Anthropology and Photography', in *Anthropology and Photography*, ed. Elizabeth Edwards 74–95, New Haven/London: Yale University Press.

Poignant, Roslyn (1992) 'Surveying the Field of View: The Making of the RAI Photographic Collection', in *Anthropology and Photography*, ed. Elizabeth Edwards

42–73, New Haven/London: Yale University Press.

Rattray, R.S. (1923) *Ashanti*, Oxford: Clarendon Press.

Rouch, Jean (1967) *Jaguar* (film), Musée de l'homme, 95 mins.

— (1975) 'The Camera and Man', in *Principles of Visual Anthropology*, ed. Paul Hockings 83–107, The Hague: Mouton.

Ruby, Jay (1975) 'Is an Ethnographic Film a Filmic Ethnography?' *Studies in the Anthropology of Visual Communication* 2 (2): 104–11.

— (1989) 'The Emperor and His Clothes', *Society for Visual Anthropology Newsletter* 5 (1): 9–11.

— (1994) Review of Peter Ian Crawford and David Turton (eds) *Film as Ethnography* and Peter Loizos, *Innovation in Ethnographic Film*, *Visual Anthropology Review* 10 (1): 165–9.

Russell, Bertrand (1912) *The Problems of Philosophy*, repr. edn, 1988, Buffalo: Prometheus Books.

Speke, John Hanning (1864) *Journal of the Discovery of the Source of the Nile*, New York: Harper & Bros.

Spencer, Paul (1965) *The Samburu*, London: Routledge & Kegan Paul.

— (1988) *The Maasai of Matapato*, Bloomington: Indiana University Press.

Stoller, Paul (1992) *The Cinematic Griot*, Chicago: University of Chicago Press.

Street, Brian (1992) 'British Popular Anthropology: Exhibiting and Photographing the other', in *Anthropology and Photography*, ed. Elizabeth Edwards 122–31, New Haven/London: Yale University Press.

Toren, Christina (1993) 'Making History: The Significance of Childhood Cognition for a Comparative Anthropology of the Mind', *Man* (NS.) 28 (3): 461–77.

Tyler, Stephen A. (1987) *The Unspeakable*, Madison: University of Wisconsin Press.

Watson, J. Forbes and J.W. Kaye (1868–75) *The People of India*, with letterpress by P.M. Taylor, eight vols, London: India Museum.

Worth, Sol (1981) *Studying Visual Communication*, Philadelphia: University of Pennsylvania Press.

Wright, Basil (1934) *Song of Ceylon* (film), Ceylon Tea Propaganda Board/GPO Film Unit, 40 mins.

Index

Aboriginality   200, 264; *see also*
   Australian Aborigines
absence   18, 203, 212, 211–13, 217,
   220, 222, 234–5, 278
Abstract Expressionism   65
acoustics (computer encoding of)
   150–1
aesthetic(s)
   of body form   229–30
   of computer programming
      165, 166
   of gardens   244, 252
   Jain   235–6
   judgements   213
   of museum displays   278
   in photography   58
   popular visual   216
   shimmering as an effect   188
   Western   186, 199, 212
Agee, James   45–6
AI (artificial intelligence)   139, 144,
   152, 165–6
AIDS   136
Amazonia   234; *see also* myth
ambiguity   203 ff., 210–12, 213, 228
American Museum of Natural
   History   278
The Andaman Islanders   9
Anderson, Benedict   259
anthropology   *see also* ethnographic
   film
   of aesthetics   22, 256
   American   10

of art   21, 256–73
   as discipline   1, 30, 37, 276, 285
   history of   39 ff., 70
   theory in   26, 140 ff.
   visual   276–93
      components of   21
      definition of   1–2, 5
      as method   13–15, 281; *see*
         also ethnographic film as
         method
      and redefinition of
         anthropology   285,
         292–3
      rethinking the place of   4
      scope of   283
      as theory   13–15, 26 ff.,
         286
   of visual cultural forms   283
anthropometry   279
Aotearoa   262
Aoyama, Tomoko   117
Apple Macintosh   154
Arab–Israeli War, the   65
Aranda   276
Argonauts of the Western Pacific   41,
   290
Arja (dance drama)   124–34
   costumes in   127
   courtly associations of   129–30
   etiquette in   127
   Herder's Arja   128, 130, 132,
      136
   and Hinduism   130

296